A-LEVEL AND AS-LEVEL COMPUTER SCIENCE

LONGMAN
REVISE
GUIDES

Titles available
Art and Design
Biology
Business Studies
Chemistry
Computer Science
Economics
English
French
Geography
Mathematics
Modern History
Physics
Sociology

LONGMAN A-LEVEL AND AS-LEVEL REVISE GUIDES

Series editors
Geoff Black and Stuart Wall

Titles available
Art and Design
Biology
Business Studies
Chemistry
Computer Science
Economics
English
French
Geography
Mathematics
Modern History
Physics
Sociology

A-LEVEL
AND AS-LEVEL

LONGMAN
REVISE
GUIDES

COMPUTER SCIENCE

David Bale

Longman

Longman Group UK Limited,
Longman House, Burnt Mill, Harlow,
Essex CM20 2JE, England
and Associated Companies throughout the world.

© Longman Group UK Limited 1990

First published 1990
Fourth impression 1993

British Library Cataloguing in Publication Data

Bale, David
   Computer Science. – (Longman A-Level revise
   guides).
   1. England. Secondary schools. Curriculum subjects:
   Computer sciences. Examinations
   I. Title
   004.076

ISBN 0-582-05782-5

Set in 10/12pt Century Old Style.

Produced by Longman Singapore Publishers Pte Ltd
Printed in Singapore

EDITORS' PREFACE

Longman A-Level Revise Guides, written by experienced examiners and teachers, aim to give you the best possible foundation for success in your course. Each book in the series encourages thorough study and a full understanding of the concepts involved, and is designed as a subject companion and study aid to be used throughout the course.

Many candidates at A-Level fail to achieve the grades which their ability deserves, owing to such problems as the lack of a structured revision strategy, or unsound examination technique. This series aims to remedy such deficiences, by encouraging a realistic and disciplined approach in preparing for and taking exams.

The largely self-contained nature of the chapters gives the book a flexibility which you can use to your advantage. After starting with the background to the A, AS-Level and Scottish Higher courses and details of the syllabus coverage, you can read all other chapters selectively, in any order appropriate to the stage you have reached in your course.

Geoff Black and Stuart Wall

ACKNOWLEDGEMENTS

I am grateful to Geoff Black and Stuart Wall for their help, advice and tolerance during the writing of the book, also to my family, Barbara, Belinda and Ashley for their support and for putting up with me during the same period.

I am grateful to the following for permission to use questions from past examination papers:

The Associated Examining Board, University of Cambridge Local Examinations Syndicate, Northern Examinations and Assessment Board, University of London Examinations and Assessment Council, Northern Ireland Schools Examinations and Assessment Council, University of Oxford Delegacy of Local Examinations, Welsh Joint Education Committee.

Any answers or hints on answers are the sole responsibility of the author and have neither been provided nor approved by the examination boards.

CONTENTS

NAMES AND ADDRESSES OF THE EXAM BOARDS

Associated Examining Board (AEB)
Stag Hill House
Guildford
Surrey GU2 5XJ

University of Cambridge Local Examinations Syndicate (UCLES)
Syndicate Buildings
1 Hills Road
Cambridge CB1 2EU

Northern Examinations and Assessment Board (NEAB)
Devas St
Manchester M15 6EX

University of London Examinations and Assessment Council (ULEAC)
Stewart House
32 Russell Square
London WC1B 5DN

Northern Ireland Schools Examination and Assessment Council (NISEAC)
Beechill House
42 Beechill Road
Belfast BT8 4RS

Oxford and Cambridge Schools Examination Board (OCSEB)
Purbeck House
Purbeck Road
Cambridge CB2 2PU

Oxford Delegacy of Local Examinations (ODLE)
Ewert Place
Summertown
Oxford OX2 7BZ

Scottish Examination Board (SEB)
Ironmills Road
Dalkeith
Midlothian EH22 1LE

Welsh Joint Education Committee (WJEC)
245 Western Avenue
Cardiff CF5 2YX

CHAPTER 1

STUDY AND EXAMINATION TECHNIQUES, AND SYLLABUS CONTENT

GETTING STARTED

All the examinations covered by this book include essay, or free response questions, and some include shorter questions requiring a concise reply in a couple of sentences. The aim of this chapter is to provide guidance on how to prepare for your own examination and to explain how to cope with the different types of examination question.

We also look at the major Advanced (A-level) and Advanced Supplementary (AS-level) syllabuses. These syllabuses are very wide and, and with the evolution of new technology, constantly changing. There is no attempt to cover the complete range of topics but rather to concentrate on the material which appears most frequently on the examination papers.

EXAM PREPARATION

TYPES OF EXAMINATION QUESTIONS

ESSAY WRITING TECHNIQUES

SHORT QUESTIONS

REVISION

IN THE EXAMINATION

SYLLABUS CONTENT

SOME USEFUL TERMS

ESSENTIAL PRINCIPLES

EXAM PREPARATION

The purpose of exams is to test your *knowledge and understanding* of a subject. If you do not know your subject well then you cannot expect to do well in an exam.

A constant effort throughout the course is important. Try not to miss lessons. If you do, catch up with the work quickly. Keep all the notes you write and the work you do. Do all your homework to your best standard. Learn your work as you progress. If you have any spare time, go back over the course and revise the work. Make sure you understand *all* the work you do. Use the library to look up topics you are unsure of. Reading another book about the same topic can often make things clearer. Improve your notes in the light of any new insights. If you have problems, ask your teacher.

> Summary notes are a useful aid

When you are preparing for the exams, this is the time to make sure you have learnt all that is required. A useful technique for learning a large volume of material is to repeatedly *revise, condense and learn*. Read through your notes and all the work you have done. As you revise your knowledge, make a *brief note* or *summary* of all the topics studied. These brief notes should cover all the important points in enough detail to refresh your memory of them at a later date. Try and learn these brief notes. If there is still too much material to learn, then condense these brief notes yet again. Your objective is to end up with condensed notes covering the major topics on your course. These can be learnt and revised frequently. You can carry them with you and revise on the bus, in the queue for the cinema, waiting for a friend or taking the dog for a walk!

There is therefore no short cut to success. Success is the result of consistent effort, thorough preparation, careful revision and good presentation of answers to the examination questions. Too many students only pay lip-service to these facts while experienced teachers will know that preparation for the final examination should not be left until the last few weeks or, even worse, days preceding the examination itself.

> Write outline answers to past questions

Rather than a last-minute panic, you should, *throughout the course*, check regularly your understanding of the basic concepts which have been covered. As a major part of this process of regular revision you should set down *outline answers* to past examination questions. The remaining chapters of this book contain a number of recent examination questions set by various examining bodies with specimen outline answers and a draft answer plan. In some chapters there are, as well, original questions of an equivalent standard and presentation. You should attempt *all* of the questions relevant to your own course at the appropriate stage in your course even though not all of the questions will have appeared in the particular examination for which you are preparing. The aim is to develop your understanding of each topic, and you should bear in mind that examiners often look at questions set by other similar bodies to gain inspiration for future questions.

Having completed an answer, or the outline of an answer, to the appropriate questions in each chapter, check your own approach against that given in the text. There is no suggestion here that the answers in the text are in any way definitive; indeed, in some cases it is possible to approach questions in a fundamentally different way. Nevertheless, by comparing your own answer with the one given in the text it will usually be possible to assess whether your approach is on the right lines, and to identify any mistakes you may have made. This is extremely important, and to improve your understanding of the subject it is essential to *learn* from your mistakes. If, after comparing your own answer with the one suggested in the text, you are still unsure about the validity of your own approach, check with your course tutor.

> Learn from any mistakes you have made

TYPES OF EXAMINATION QUESTION

There are a number of different types of **question** you may be required to answer in your examinations. Taking the question formats first we may consider:

- Short questions (definitions or explanations).
- Standard length questions.
- Problem-solving exercises.
- Extended problem-solving/case studies.

There is a similar variety in the types of **answer** you will be required to give in response to the questions:

- Concise explanations in a couple of sentences.
- Essays.
- Reports.
- Flowcharts and diagrams.
- System specifications (including block diagrams).
- Computer programs.

The most important examination technique lies in *identifying* the requirements of the question and *selecting* the correct form of answer required. We shall consider each of these aspects in turn.

Taking first the *identification* of requirements there are again two aspects, length of the required answer and of course understanding the question.

Regarding *length*, if a question or part question rates, say, two marks out of 100 in a three-hour paper, you should not spend more than 2 per cent of three hours (or about three minutes) on your answer since even if you write several pages of first-rate material you will still only get two marks for your efforts. Similarly if a question or a problem analysis carries 40 per cent of the marks on a three-hour paper, you would need to spend about seventy minutes on the answer in order to provide sufficient material to gain a good mark.

Regarding *understanding* or interpretation, this is the most crucial part of examination technique. Do *not* latch on to the first keyword you understand in the question and then reproduce pages of memorised notes; you must read the question in its *entirety* and endeavour to interpret *exactly* what the examiner intended to ask. If the question asks 'How are microcumputers used in hotels?', for example, you are required to explain the type of application and *not* to describe the principal features of a microcomputer.

It is equally important to identify the *form of the answer*, i.e. which of the six answer types listed above is required in the answer. For example:

- 'Discuss the social implications of microcomputers being used in the home' would clearly look for a *standard essay*.
- 'Describe the principal features of a typical home microcomputer' would require a more *formalised essay of the report type*, with sections and subheadings.
- 'Explain the meaning of the following terms . . . ' would look for a number of *short, snappy answers* of two or three sentences each.

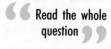

ESSAY WRITING TECHNIQUES

During your course you will almost certainly be required to produce essays or reports for marking by your course tutor. In some courses the marks for such essays count towards the final grade awarded. In most computer studies *examinations* you will be required to prepare a documented report on a program you have written or on a project you have prepared. The subject of program documentation will be covered in depth in Chapter 9, but more often the essays (and other assignments) are simply set as an aid to understanding and learning. In all cases you should ensure that when completed, each essay is written to the highest standard you are capable of achieving at that time.

Writing essays which are of a consistently high standard does not simply involve taking pride in your work, although this is obviously important. It also involves paying careful attention to many other points, and we shall consider these in some detail.

PREPARATION

For an essay set by your tutor, first note the topic covered by the title, then find the relevant parts in: a) your own notes; b) your textbooks; and c) articles in journals and periodicals. Read all the material through thoroughly, trying to understand everything, in order to do which you must *think* about the material you are reading. If, *after* having done all this, you are still struggling, consult your course tutor.

In considering the essay title you must think what it means and what it is asking you to do. If you are unsure, a useful tip is to try and write in your own words on a sheet of rough paper what you think the essay title means. For example, if the essay title is: 'What are the reasons for the widespread use of computers in local government?' it is asking you '*Why* are computers used in local government?' and to answer this it is necessary for you to *state* and *explain* these reasons. If the title had been 'Describe the principal applications of computers in local government?' it is asking '*How . . .* ' or 'In what ways do local authorities use . . . ': in this case it is *not* asking for a detailed list of the reasons why they are used, but you will be required to list the applications.

Once you have decided what the title means, you can *plan* what to put in your answer. Make a list of the following items:

- What to put in your introduction.
- What to put in the body of your essay.
- Whether a separate conclusion is needed.

a) What to put in your introduction

In general, this should be very brief and to the point; it is best to include a definition of the central topic of your essay where this is appropriate. For example, if an essay title asks you to 'Explain what is meant by . . . ' or 'Define . . . ' then it is best to start with a definition. Thus in answer to the question 'Explain, with the use of relevant examples, what is meant by the term "computer peripheral", you might begin by writing: 'A computer peripheral is a . . . '. Even where you are not specifically asked to define or describe something, it is good practice to do so: look out for this type of opportunity. For example, the title "Real time systems are used by airlines" – explain the meaning of this statement' does not *actually* ask you to *define* 'real time systems' but you must do so if you are to *explain* the meaning of the statement.

b) What to put in the body of your essay

Remember that essays sometimes involve drawing together knowledge from several parts of the course. The only way to be sure you are answering a question fully is to understand *all* of the topics that have been covered. To do this you must *revise regularly* those topics that have been covered in your studies. A good rule of thumb is to spend about half an hour each week revising and testing your understanding of earlier topics.

Note down the major items you will be dealing with. Consider how to divide these up into separate paragraphs. Remember each separate item, or subtopic, should be dealt with in a separate paragraph. At this stage you should note down examples or facts that you intend to use, diagrams that you will draw, and additional definitions that you will state.

c) Whether a separate conclusion is needed

In general, simply 'put one in'. In many cases it will be useful to summarise what you have said in the main body of your answer. For example, if you are asked to 'Explain what is meant by the basic elements of a computer', in your final paragraph you could write: 'Thus there are five basic elements of a computer, namely input, output, storage, arithmetic and control.' Sometimes the essay title will be a question and in your conclusion you must actually state what your answer is. However, there is little benefit in writing a conclusion which adds nothing to your answer or which does not make it any more obvious.

WRITING YOUR ESSAY

Try to write neatly and legibly. Follow your plan. Take care to express your ideas correctly and in a way that is understandable. Remember that all the sentences in one paragraph should be concerned with the same point and should follow logically from each other when you are outlining an argument.

In general try to avoid abbreviations but if you find it necessary to use terms such as CPU or EDS, give the interpretation in brackets the first time you use the abbreviation. Also, make sure you phrase your answer in a way that is appropriate to the title, so that it is clear that you are answering the question that was set. For example, the essay title might be: 'Describe how magnetic tape could be used to prevent loss of data in a seat reservation system', in which case you should not describe in detail the physical operation of a magnetic tape drive, however well you have revised it, but should concentrate on a structured development of the periodic back-up of the disc file to magnetic tape and also the retention of transactions.

As another example, if you are describing the applications of computers used by acountants, one sentence could begin: 'One application popular with accountants is . . . '. A second application might be described in a sentence that starts: 'Another application is . . . ' and then introduce a further application by 'A third application is . . . ', and so on.

Always try to write an essay to the best of your ability. If you do this, your essay technique will gradually improve. This is very important because if you do not *learn* to write clear, logical and well-reasoned essays in homework and classwork success will be more difficult to achieve in the examination.

CHECKING

> 66 Don't forget to check your answer 99

Once you have finished writing, do not think the essay is ready to be handed in, or the examination question completed: first it must be *checked* by you.

Look at your plan and check that you did include in your essay everything that you intended to. It is amazing how easy it is to overlook something when you are busy writing! Lastly, check that you have really written a full and complete answer to the question. Have you dealt with all parts of the question? Have you explained and described everything as fully as you could? It is a good idea to do this check some time after you have written the essay; coming to it afresh will allow you to consider it more carefully. In particular, in an examination, leave yourself some time at the end of the examination to read all your answers through before handing in the paper. Coming to an essay afresh after an interval of time will allow you to consider it more carefully.

READING MARKED ESSAYS

When the marked essay is returned to you, do not file it away and forget about it. You will find it difficult to improve your technique unless you *learn from your mistakes*. This means reading over your essay after it has been marked, taking note of the comments that have been added and thinking about how it could be improved. This will dramatically reduce the likelihood of your making the same mistake twice and, coupled with regular supervision, will markedly increase your chance of success in the examination.

> **SHORT QUESTIONS**

A number of examinations in computer studies employ the technique of asking short questions which require a definition, explanation or response in a couple of sentences. This type of question may occur as a sequence of, say, ten short questions, or as the type of question which starts:

> 66 Learn the skills needed to answer short questions 99

'Write brief notes on four of the following . . . '; or
'Explain the meaning of the following terminology . . . '.

The skills in answering this type of question are a little different from those required in a full-length essay and there are a number of guidelines to consider.

a) Budget your time

If a part question carries three marks out of 100 in a three-hour paper you cannot afford to devote more than five minutes to this answer. Thus if it asks 'Why is the binary number system widely used in computers', you must answer in five minutes using perhaps ten or a dozen lines. You may be well equipped to write a full-length answer for forty-five minutes and have a perfect recall of pages of course notes, but you will still only get three marks and have lost valuable time that should have been spent on other questions.

b) Identify the main point of the answer

Remember that the examiner is probably looking for a single sentence and for several keywords, and although your grammar should be good, this will not be marked as an essay. For example, if the question is 'What is meant by an algorithm?' an acceptable answer might be:

> 'An algorithm is a set of *unambiguous rules* for *solving* a problem in a *finite* number of steps.'

The examiner may well be looking to give a mark or half-mark for each of the keywords in italics. A three-page essay on problem-solving, computer programs and top-down design would gain no more marks than the sentence above.

Examples and applications are important

c) Try to include an example

It is not always possible, in the context of a question, but always try to include a brief statement describing either an example or an application. This serves two functions; firstly and pragmatically it is often looked for in the mark scheme, and secondly it helps to show your understanding of the topic or technique.

d) Re-read your short answers

In short questions, if you read through your answer and are *not* satisfied that you have performed well, using the points a) and b) above as measures, remember that as this is a *short* question you may well have time to cross out your first attempt and write the answer afresh. This may well be more productive than trying to edit or amend the original attempt.

e) Presentation

Take plenty of space; give a question reference and, where possible, a subheading to each short question or part question; leave space between questions. This will improve the appearance of your answers and, after all, you are not paying for the number of sheets you use!!!

Diagrams and charts can improve the presentation of your answer

■ Diagrams

Computer studies, in common with the science subjects, gives ample opportunity for the inclusion of *diagrams* and *charts* within the essays and reports required at each stage of the course. It is important that you exploit this technique as a means of improving the presentation of answers. Do not, however, go to the extreme of spending vast amounts of time producing high-quality diagrams and pictures which will not be rewarded by marks proportionate to the time spent. Nevertheless the diagrams need to be well drawn, using ruler, template and any other available aids, without seeking to produce a work of art more appropriate to a paper in art or technical drawing.

If a question asks 'Describe the basic elements of a computer . . . ' then a simple diagram showing their interconnection is almost essential. If a question asks for a description of ' . . . typical applications of disc storage . . . ' it is not necessary to produce a diagram of the disc surface with tracks sectors and head mechanism.

It is also important to avoid cramped diagrams; start on a new sheet of paper and give plenty of space between the text and the diagrams.

Finally, always give a title to the diagram. Always label the important features and, if you have several diagrams within an answer, give each a separate identity, e.g. Fig. 3.2 for the second diagram in question 3, and use these references within your answers. If diagrams are labelled in this way it is often a good idea to put all the diagrams on loose sheets at the end of your answer book, with each on a separate page, making sure that the examiner's attention is drawn to the existence of these diagrams at the start of each answer. This will make the reading of such answers much easier for the examiner.

■ Flowcharts

The topic of *flowcharting* is covered at several stages within this book and is well worth exploiting in an examination paper. Flowcharting is studied because it is one of the best ways of describing or specifying a sequence of operations, whether as part of a computer program, a complete system or even the clerical procedures in an information system.

There are a number of rules worth observing in the use of flowcharts:

1 Always start on a new sheet of paper to give yourself plenty of room, unless the chart is to be very small.
2 Always use a flowcharting template; it is very rare for an exam board to forbid the use of templates.
3 Always use standard shapes, ideally to the British Standard Specification (BSS) or the American Standard (ANSI).
4 Always try to be as neat as possible and to label the boxes legibly; also, where appropriate, include a brief narrative explanation of the major stages specified in the chart.

Useful rules when using flowcharts

5 Always prepare the charts in pencil, to allow alterations to be made without too much loss of neatness. Make sure you have some good quality 2B pencils and a pencil sharpener in the examination.

REVISION

There are no hard and fast rules about *when* to begin the final revision for the examination. This depends on the individual, the type of examination, the time available, and so on. All that can be said is that if you are to give yourself maximum chance of success, thorough revision of *all* the syllabus is required. Nothing can be left out, otherwise you might find compulsory questions you cannot answer, and your choice of essays or problem-solving exercises is very likely to be restricted. Therefore, you should begin revision at a fairly early stage, and indeed final revision should simply build on an already solid foundation established by regular revision during your course. It is probably best to begin final revision by making a detailed *plan* of when each topic is to be covered. You should make every effort to stick to this plan, but remember you are likely to find revision relatively easy at the start, but more difficult towards the end. Your plan should allow for this, and also for the fact that the more difficult topics will take longer to revise than others. You should take care, therefore, to ensure that your plan sets *realistic targets*. Sticking to the plan will lead to growing confidence as you progress from one topic to the next and as your understanding of the subject as a whole grows.

How to revise is very much a personal matter, but you might find the following practical hints useful:

1 Rewrite your course notes in a shortened form, using headings and making lists of points.
2 Learn these lists; it is useful to remember how many points there are in each list, e.g. learn there are four divisions in a COBOL program.
3 Make a separate list of clear and concise definitions.
4 Learn these definitions by rewriting from memory and then checking against your notes.
5 Practise examination questions and remember the three stages in producing an essay:

- Interpret the question
- Plan your answer
- Write you answer in the time allowed

> **Some practical hints for revision**

IN THE EXAMINATION

> **Follow the instructions**

The first thing you must do *before* attempting any examination question is to read carefully through the rubric on the front, or at the head, of the examination paper. You must follow these instructions to the letter; if the paper is subdivided, note carefully the total number of questions which must be attempted from each section.

You must also note the total time allowed for completing the paper and bear this in mind when allocating time between questions. This task can be prepared before the examination by studying the rubric on past papers since there is normally no change between successive examinations, unless centres have been notified.

Finally, in computing the time available for each question, or part question, do not forget to include time for reading the question paper at the start of the examination and for reading through your answers at the end.

Also allow a little extra time for 'over-runs'. In a three-hour paper you will have 180 minutes but it is a good plan to budget for a minute and a half for each potential mark, so that a twenty-mark question will take thirty minutes and a four mark part question six minutes. You will then have five minutes for the initial reading of the question, ten minutes at the end to read through your answers, and fifteen minutes spare to distribute for emergencies or to be used as extra time on those questions where there are a number of small parts, since these often take a few minutes longer.

> **Answer all parts of the question**

Examination essays

1 Choose essay questions carefully. First, read through all the questions, marking those that you think you may be able to answer. Next, for these questions, consider whether you can actually answer *all* the parts. There is usually little point in attempting a question if you cannot answer all of it. Finally, choose the appropriate number of questions (out of those you can answer) that you feel you can answer best. Remember that your aim is to show the examiner that you know and understand the subject of computing, and so this is what matters for the 'best answer'; do not think you can give a good answer just because it is easy to answer without using references to computing.

2 Plan what to put in your answer and write this down so that you can follow your plan. Think very carefully about actually answering the question. Notice how many marks are allocated for each part of the answer. This is a guide as to how important each part is; so it tells you relatively how long to spend on each part.

3 Write your answer carefully, expressing ideas correctly and in detail. Do not be vague and do give examples; computer studies is a practical subject so always take every opportunity to relate your answers to practical applications. Follow the rubric, i.e. set out your answer in the same way as the question; e.g. if the question is divided into two parts, a) and b), so must your answer be. Make a note of the time you begin each question and spend only the appropriate amount of time on it. This is important because you cannot afford to leave part of the paper unanswered.

> **Keep to the point of the question**

4 Keep referring back to the question and to your plan. It is easy under examination conditions to wander off the point and to include irrelevant material. Marks are not usually deducted for this, but the penalty in waste of time is high. Time spent in discussing irrelevant material is not then available to discuss relevant material, so that the penalty for this kind of error might be very serious. It only takes a short while to check that you are following your plan, and that what you have written is relevant to the question.

5 If you have any time left after completing your answers (and you should try to ensure there is time left) check your work for errors and omissions. Again, these easily slip in under examination conditions.

SYLLABUS CONTENT

Table 1.1 gives a broad outline of the topics and courses for which this book will be useful.

TOPIC/CHAPTER	A-LEVEL							AS-LEVEL					
	AEB	OXF	LON	CAM	NEAB	WJEC	NISEAC	AEB	CAM	OXF	LON	NEAB	WJEC
2 Information systems	✓	✓	✓	✓	✓	✓	✓	✓	✓	✓	✓	✓	✓
3 Memory systems	✓	✓	✓	✓	✓	✓	✓	✓	✓	✓	✓	✓	✓
4 Computer peripherals	✓	✓	✓	✓	✓	✓	✓	✓	✓	✓	✓	✓	✓
5 Data validation and error detection	✓	✓	✓	✓	✓	✓	✓	✓	✓	✓	✓	✓	✓
6 File storage	✓	✓	✓	✓	✓	✓	✓	✓	✓	✓	✓	✓	✓
7 Structured programming design	✓	✓	✓	✓	✓	✓	✓	✓	✓		✓	✓	✓
8 High-level programming languages	✓	✓	✓	✓	✓	✓	✓	✓	✓	✓	✓	✓	✓
9 Duties of data processing staff	✓	✓	✓	✓	✓	✓	✓	✓			✓		
10 The structure of languages	✓		✓	✓	✓	✓	✓						
11 Number systems and Boolean algebra	✓	✓	✓	✓	✓	✓	✓		✓	✓	✓	✓	
12 Low-level languages	✓	✓	✓		✓	✓	✓		✓				
13 The structure of data	✓	✓	✓	✓	✓	✓	✓	✓	✓	✓	✓		✓
14 Computer operating systems	✓	✓	✓	✓	✓	✓	✓	✓	✓	✓	✓	✓	✓
15 Computer applications and packaged software	✓	✓	✓	✓	✓	✓	✓	✓	✓	✓	✓	✓	✓
16 Systems analysis and design	✓	✓	✓	✓	✓	✓	✓	✓	✓	✓	✓	✓	✓

AEB	Associated Examining Board
CAM	Cambridge Local Examinations Syndicate
WJEC	Welsh Joint Education Committee
LON	University of London Examinations and Assessment Council
NEAB	Northern Examinations and Assessment Board.
NISEAC	Northern Ireland Examinations and Assessment Council
OXF	Oxford

AIMING AT SUCCESS

When you first start your course, set your sights on obtaining the highest grade. Stick to your aim and gear the level of your effort accordingly. Pay particular attention to those topics which you do not fully understand and *never* assume that an individual topic is unimportant. In a subject such as computer science, many topics interrelate and build on one another and fully understanding one topic is often impossible without a full understanding of what has gone before. Remember that if you find a topic difficult, others will also find it hard, which is why it is so important to persevere. Not everyone succeeds in the examination, but those who persevere with problems will have a clear advantage and at the end of the day, the highest grade is particularly important because so few people achieve it. This book cannot guarantee success, but, if used correctly, it should prove a valuable aid.

SOME USEFUL TERMS	Throughout the book we will define the important terms used in each chapter. However the following is a useful glossary, arranged alphabetically, for you to use as a first check if a term is unfamiliar to you.

Algorithm	A set of unambiguous rules to solve a problem in a finite number of steps.
Analogue to Digital Converter (ADC)	A hardware device to convert analogue voltage to binary digital numbers.
Ancestral or Generation system	The ancestral system for file backups consisting of the *son* (the latest version), the *father* (the previous version) and the *grandfather* (the version before the previous version).
Applications software	Software designed to do a specific job, e.g. payroll.
Arithmetic and Logic Unit (ALU)	The part of the CPU where arithmetic and logical operations are done.
ASCII	The American Standard Code for Information Interchange. This is used to uniquely represent characters in binary code in most computers.
Assembler	A program that converts a program written in *assembly language* (the source code) into *machine code* (the object code).
Assembly language	A low level computer language close to machine code.
Backing storage	A means of storing programs and data outside the memory, e.g. magnetic disc or tape.
Backup	A *backup* of a file is another copy of it. The ancestral system is often used for backups.
Bar code	A code represented by a series of vertical black and white lines, often used to encode an identity number.
Bar code reader	A hardware device used to read a bar code. This could be a light pen or a laser scanner.
Batch processing	A method of processing data where the data is collected into batches before being processed.
Binary	The base 2 number system. Allowable digits are 0 and 1.
BIT	A BInary DigiT. This takes the value 1 or 0.
Block	A block is a group of records on magnetic tape or disc that is read or written together.
Buffer	An area of memory used to accumulate data for transfer to or from a peripheral. A printer buffer is extra memory, usually in the printer itself, which is used to hold output while it is waiting to be printed.
Byte	A byte is a set of bits used to represent one character. There are normally eight bits to the byte.
Catalogue	A list of all the files on a disc.
Ceefax	The teletext service broadcast by the BBC.
Central Processing Unit (CPU)	The main part of the computer where all the processing takes place. It consists of the CU and the ALU.

Character	One of the symbols that can be represented by a computer. Characters include A to Z and 0 to 9 equivalent to a keystroke.
Character printer	A printer that prints one character at a time, e.g. a dot matrix printer.
Character set	All the characters that can be represented by a computer.
Check digit	An extra digit calculated from the original digits in a number, using a predetermined formula, and attached to the number. It can be re-calculated to check that none of the digits in the number have been altered.
Compiler	A program used to convert another program written in a high level language (source code) to machine code (object code). The whole of the *source code* is converted at the same time to produce the *object code* which can be saved on disc. The program is run from the object code. The compiler will report syntax errors in the source code.
Computer	A computer is a machine which inputs, processes and outputs data under the control of a stored program.
Computer Output on Microfilm (COM)	Output from a computer written directly onto microfilm. Output in this form is compact and does not deteriorate in storage as rapidly as printout.
Content free software	Software designed to do a range of similar jobs, e.g. a spreadsheet.
Control switch	A switch built of logic gates that is used to switch data lines on and off.
Control total	A meaningful total calculated from a batch of source documents that is used to check that the batch is complete.
Control Unit (CU)	The part of the CPU that controls the running of programs and the input and output of data.
Cursor	Usually a rectangular block one character in size that appears on a monitor screen at the point at which the next character entered through the keyboard will be displayed. The cursor usually flashes on and off to attract attention.
Daisy-wheel printer	A printer that has a daisy-wheel print mechanism, with characters at the ends of 'spokes'. They give high quality printout.
Data	Numbers or strings.
Data capture	Data capture is the collection of data prior to input. Data capture can be on-line, e.g. POS terminals for stock keeping, or off-line, e.g. questionnaires.
Data control clerks	The job of a data control clerk is to monitor the flow of data through a computer system.
Data preparation	This is the transfer of data from a source document to a computer readable medium, e.g. disc.
Data processing	Computers input, process and output data. In commerce this is known as data processing.
Database	A database is a collection of data structured to allow the data to be accessed easily.
DataBase Management System (DBMS)	The software needed to organise and access a database.
Delete	A file is deleted from a disc when it is erased from it by removal from the directory.
Denary	The base 10 number system. Available digits are 0 to 9.
Desk Top Publishing (DTP)	The combination of graphics and wordprocessing in a format typical of a newspaper with text in columns, varying character sizes, photographs, etc.

Direct access	A method of accessing a file where it is possible to store or retrieve data records without the need to read other data records first. Direct access is used with magnetic discs.
Direct data entry	Data entered direct to the computer but written to the backing store to await processing.
Directory	See Catalogue.
Disc	Magnetic discs are a backing storage medium. Microcomputers use floppy discs (5¼″ or 3½″) or hard discs.
Documentation	A written description of what a program does and how it is run, often containing details of program design, coding and testing.
Dot matrix printer	A printer that has a print head consisting of a matrix of steel pins. Character shapes are made up from a pattern of dots.
Electronic funds transfer (EFT)	A paperless method of transferring money between bank accounts using a communications network.
Electronic mail	A paperless method of sending mail, i.e. letters, etc., from one computer to another using a communications network.
Errors	*Logic* errors are mistakes in the logic of a program. *Syntax* errors are mistakes in the format of a programming language, e.g. PRONT instead of PRINT. *Execution* errors occur when a program is run, e.g. division by zero.
Execute	To run a program.
Expert system	Software that allows users to recognise particular situations and gives them advice on the appropriate action to take.
Feedback	Feedback occurs when a sensor detects a situation that causes the computer to initiate action that alters the data collected by the sensor.
Fibre optics	The use of very thin fibre glass strands to transmit data encoded as light pulses.
Field	A field is an item of data within a record.
File	A file is an organised collection of related records.
File librarian	The person responsible for the library of discs and tapes kept by a computer department.
File server	A computer attached to a network whose main function is to enable network stations to share facilities on the network.
Flowchart	A graphical representation of the flow of data through a computer.
Font	A set of consistently shaped characters.
Front end processor	A small computer used to control communications between a larger mainframe computer and the terminals and other peripherals connected to it.
Full adder	A logic circuit that inputs three bits and adds them together. *Input* is the two bits of the numbers being added and a carry bit from the addition of the two bits to the right. *Output* is a carry bit and a sum bit.
Graphics pad	A peripheral which allows the user to transfer drawings to the computer by drawing on paper resting on the graphics pad.
Graph plotter	An output peripheral that produces detailed pictures and diagrams on paper using a pen.
Graphic design package	A software package that allows the user to draw on the screen, providing a range of design tools, different colours and patterns.
Hacker	An unauthorised user of a computer system who has broken into the system either by guessing a user

identification (Id) and the associated password, or by bypassing them.

Half adder   A logic circuit that inputs two bits and adds them together without a carry bit. Two half adders are used to build a full adder.

Hard copy   Printout.

Hardware   The physical components of a computer system.

Hash total   A total calculated from a batch of source documents that is used to check that the batch is complete. The total has no meaning in itself.

Hexadecimal   The base 16 number system. Allowable digits are 0 to 9 and A to F.

High level language   A problem orientated programming language, e.g. COBOL, BASIC, Pascal.

Information   Information is data that is meaningful to us.

Information technology (IT)   IT is the use of computers and other technology used to process information.

Immediate Access Store (IAS)   The part of the CPU that is used to store programs while they are running and data while it is being processed.

Insert   To put into. 'To insert a record' means to put a new record into a file.

Integer   Positive and negative whole numbers, e.g. 1, −6, 0, 3, 7.

Inter block gap   A gap left between two data blocks on a magnetic tape.

Interactive processing   Interactive processing takes place when the user and the computer are in two-way communication.

Interface   The interconnection between two devices.

Interpreter   An interpreter is a program that executes a program written in a high level language. It converts one line at a time while the program is run. The program is run from the source code. Syntax errors are reported.

Key field   A field in a record used to identify the record. Used when searching for the record or when sorting the file.

Key-to-disc   A method of data preparation where data is entered at a keyboard and saved on disc.

Kilobyte (K)   1024 or 2^{10} bytes.

Kimball tag   A small punched card that is often used in clothes shops and identifies a garment and holds details of its size, colour, price, etc.

Laser printer   A page printer that works by etching a stencil of the page to be printed in an electrostatic drum.

Laser scanner   A hardware device that inputs bar codes by scanning the pattern of light reflected off a bar code by a laser beam.

Light pen   A hardware device that inputs bar codes by scanning the pattern of light reflected off a bar code. It is shaped like a pen.

Line printer   A printer that prints one line at a time.

Local Area Network (LAN)   A network with permanent links between all the hardware connected to the network. Probably located in one building.

Logic circuit   A circuit made up of individual logic gates.

Logic gate   A fundamental logic operation, e.g. AND, OR, NOT, etc.

Low level language   An assembly language or machine language.

Machine code   Program instructions in binary code that can be executed by a computer. All programming languages are converted to machine code before running.

Magnetic Ink Character Recognition (MICR)   A method of input where characters printed in magnetic ink are read directly into a computer.

Mainframe computer   A large, fast computer, probably having a variety of peripherals, including a high capacity backing store and many terminals.

Mark sensing	An input method where pencil marks on paper are detected. Their position on the paper determines their meaning.
Master file	A data file which is used to store most of the data for a particular application. It is updated by the transaction file.
Memory address	A number used to identify a storage location in memory.
Memory map	A plan of the computer's memory giving the addresses where programs and data are held.
Merge	To combine one or more files into a single file.
Microcomputer	A small computer based on a microprocessor. They are usually relatively cheap, slow and have limited backing storage.
Microfilm	An output medium similar to photographic film.
Microprocessor	A single microchip containing all the elements of the CPU.
Mnemonic	Assembly language operation codes are mnemonics, e.g. LDA represents 'load the accumulator'.
Modem	A MOdulator/DEModulator. Used to convert digital data output by a computer to analogue signals that can be transmitted along a telephone line and vice versa.
Monitor	A screen used to display the output from a computer.
Mouse	A hand-held input peripheral having buttons on top and a ball underneath. When the mouse is moved over a flat surface, a pointer on the screen moves in a corresponding direction.
Multiaccess	When many users are connected to a single computer using terminals.
Multiprogramming	When one computer is apparently running more than one program at the same time.
Multitasking	When one user is apparently running more than one program at the same time.
Network	A network is a system to connect computers.
Network station	A terminal connected to a network.
Non-volatile memory	Non-volatile memory does not lose its contents when the power is switched off. ROM memory is *non-volatile*.
Object code	A machine code program generated by a compiler or an assembler.
Octal	The base 8 number system. Allowable digits are 0 to 7.
Off-line	Not connected to the computer, or connected but not in communication with it.
On-line	Connected to the computer and in communication with it.
Operating system	The operating system is a program that makes the computer hardware more easily accessible to other programs. An operating system is always present when a computer is used.
Operator	An operator looks after the computer while it is running, changing discs, tapes and printer paper as required.
Optical Character Recognition (OCR)	An input method that can read printed characters. Special fonts are often used.
Page printer	A printer that prints a page at a time, e.g. a laser printer.
Parity	An automatic hardware check that data that has been transferred or stored has not been corrupted. An extra bit is added to make the number of bits set to 1 odd (odd parity) or even (even parity).
Password	A code that restricts access to a computer system. Usually associated with the User Identification.
Peripheral	A peripheral is a hardware device that is connected to a computer system but is not the part of the computer itself, e.g. a printer.

Pixel	The smallest area of a screen that can be used in building up a picture.
Point Of Sale (POS) Terminal	A terminal used to collect data at the point of sale. Often incorporates a laser scanner to read bar codes, and a dot matrix printer to print receipts. May be on-line to the supermarket's computer system.
Port	A connector used to link peripherals to a computer.
Portable	Portable programs can be run on a variety of different computers.
Prestel	The viewdata service run by British Telecom.
Printout	The output from a printer.
Program	A set of instructions used to control the operation of a computer.
Programmer	A computer programmer designs, codes, test and documents programs for a computer.
Pull-down menu	A feature of a WIMP user interface where a hidden menu can be revealed, i.e. pulled down, by pointing at it.
Random access	See direct access.
Random Access Memory (RAM)	Read/write memory within the memory. RAM is *volatile*.
Range check	A check that a data value is within realistic limits.
Read Only Memory (ROM)	Memory within the IAS that can only be read. ROM is *non-volatile*.
Real time processing	The processing of input data that takes place so fast that when more data is input the results of the processing are already available. Real time processing occurs in real time, i.e. as it happens.
Record	A record is a collection of related fields.
Relocatable	A relocatable program can be stored in any part of the computer's memory.
Remote access	Access to a computer using a terminal located a long way from the computer.
Sensor	A device used to sense environmental conditions.
Sequential access	Similar to serial access but the data records are stored in some order.
Serial access	A method of accessing data records. In order to access a data record in a serial access file, it is necessary to start at the beginning of the file and read all the preceding records. The records are not stored in any particular order.
Software	Computer programs.
Software package	A complete set of programs and documentation to enable a particular computer program to be used.
Sort	To put into order. Records in a file are often stored in key field order.
Source code	A program written in a high or low level programming language.
Source document	A document or questionnaire used for data capture. It is the source of the data input to the computer.
Speech recognition	A method of input to a computer by speaking to it.
Speech synthesis	Sounds generated by a computer that synthesise human speech.
Spooling	A method of queueing output directed to a device before output.
Spreadsheet	Spreadsheets are used to calculate and display financial and other numerical information in columns and rows.
Standalone	A computer that is not connected to any other computer is being used in standalone mode.

Systems analysis and design	The in-depth analysis of the software and hardware requirements of a computer based system and its detailed design.
Systems analyst	A systems analyst is responsible for the progress of a computer based system throughout the system's life cycle.
System's life cycle	Computer systems go through the cycle of systems investigation; feasibility study; systems analysis and design; program design, coding, testing and documentation; implementation; systems documentation; maintenance; evaluation.
Syntax	The set of rules which define the way an instruction in a programming language can be written.
Tapes	Magnetic tapes are a backing storage medium. Microcomputers use cassette tapes, tape streamers use tape cartridges and mainframes use reel-to-reel tape.
Teletext	A form of videotext accessible using a specially adapted television set, e.g. Oracle broadcast by ITV, or Ceefax by the BBC. It is non-interactive.
Terminal	A hardware device used to communicate with a computer from a remote site.
Time sharing	A method of meeting the demands of a multiaccess system where many programs are required to be run apparently at the same time. Each program is given access to the CPU for a very short period of time (a *time slice*) in rotation.
Track	A track is the path on a magnetic disc along which data is stored.
Transaction file	A file used to store recent data captured since the last master file update. The transaction file is used to update the master file.
Truth table	A table showing all the possible inputs to a logic circuit and the corresponding outputs.
Turnaround document	A printout which has data written on it and is then used as a source document.
Two's complement	A method of representing negative numbers in binary. The place value of the leftmost bit is negative.
Update	To bring a file up-to-date by amending, inserting or deleting data records.
User Id	The user identification number that enables a computer system to recognise a user.
Utility	A program that is used to do a task that is useful only in relation to the organisation of a computer system, e.g. a screen dump.
Validation	A check on input data before processing.
Verification	A check that what is written on a source document is accurately transferred to a computer-readable medium.
Videotext	A page-based information retrieval system, i.e. Teletext and Viewdata.
Viewdata	A form of videotext that is accessed interactively, e.g. Prestel run by British Telecom.
Visual Display Unit (VDU)	A keyboard and screen used as a terminal.
Volatile memory	Volatile memory loses its contents when the power is switched off. *Most RAM memory is volatile.*
Wide Area Network (WAN)	A network spread over a wide area, possibly international, making use of both permanent cable connections and temporary connections using the telephone network.

Windows, Icons, Mouse, Pointers (WIMP)

A user interface that avoids the need to remember complex operating system commands by providing *icons* that represent the commands. To select a command the user points at it and clicks a button on the mouse.

Wordprocessing

The preparation of letters and other documents using a computer in a manner similar to a typewriter but with additional features.

INFORMATION SYSTEMS

GETTING STARTED

It is easy to lose sight of the rapid growth in the history of computers since the end of World War II. Prior to that time there had been a number of mechanical and electro-mechanical computing devices, such as the seventeenth-century calculator of Blaise Pascal (after whom the language Pascal is named), and the Difference and Analytical Engines of Charles Babbage dating from 1822. This is acknowledged as the first *programmable* machine and, in connection with that computer, the first programmer was Ada Augusta, Countess of Lovelace, after whom the language ADA has been named. The first computers were the electromechanical Harvard Mark 1, dating from 1944, and the first fully electronic machine called ENIAC was completed in 1945. Up to 1951, all computers existed in the specialist laboratories of the universities and various companies which later became leading computer manufacturers, such as IBM and UNIVAC.

It was not possible to buy a computer of any type until the UNIVAC 1 of 1951, and it was not common to run a computer from an ordinary electrical mains socket until the 1970s or later. Indeed it was not until the introduction of the microcomputer in 1979 that it was possible to buy a computer in a shop. Prior to that time, even as late as 1977, to purchase a computer for use at home would have been thought of as a pipe dream by most people. Until the mid 1980s, few computer-users had direct access to the machine, but communicated with the machine by form filling and the subsequent receipt of tabulations.

ESSENTIAL PRINCIPLES

**CHANGE OF
EMPHASIS IN
THE USE OF
COMPUTERS**

The first computers were developed to solve advanced mathematical problems, specifically the solution of systems of differential equations. It was not until the late 1950s that computers were used for business data processing applications, and applications were even then, for many years, restricted to numerate tasks such as payroll, stock control and basic accounting functions. The introduction of on-line terminal systems led to the development of the use of large databases which could be interrogated by many different users, possibly at remote locations. One of the most significant developments was the first *spreadsheet* program 'Visicalc' which ran on the Apple II, the Commodore Pet and the TRS-80 Computers. It was significant in two respects, firstly it was implemented on *all* three top selling microcomputers, despite the fact that the TRS-80 used a different processor to the other two, and secondly it provided an environment where an accountant, with little or no knowledge of computers and no time or inclination to become a computer specialist, could design and implement sophisticated models and accounting systems. It meant that the systems could be designed without reference to specialist computer staff who would have to make themselves familiar with the application. Furthermore the package could be used in a small company or department with no access to computer specialists.

The 1980s saw a steady growth in the use of computers in businesses of all sizes, with perhaps the major surprise being the lack of growth of the home computer market after the boom around 1982 and 1983. It may have been that the massive oversell of cassette based computers (often with very little support and very little software) by supermarkets and chain stores had saturated the market and left many homes with computers which proved to be of little use. It is worth mentioning that many of the computers sold in this way were job lots of obsolete models, or even bankrupt stock from manufacturers who had ceased trading. This unfortunately put off many home users and has left the remaining manufacturers concentrating on the business market. It is quite significant that IBM, the largest computer manufacturer in the world, had initially opted out of designing an early 8-bit microcomputer, but when they produced their long awaited 16-bit PC they immediately dominated the market.

**COMPUTER
GENERATIONS**

All current computers are built to the basic design postulated by John Von Neumann and known as Von Neumann machines, the detailed design of which has now reached four or five generations.

The **first generation** of computers, dating from about 1945, was based on valve technology and used magnetic core memory. They were much faster than the earlier electromechanical machines, but were most unreliable, with the time between valve failures unacceptably short. These machines consumed vast amounts of electrical power, took up a huge amount of space, and needed engineers employed by the manufacturer to be resident on site. The memory was slow and cost a great deal since it had to be made by hand with wires threaded through a small magnetic core. There was no large scale file store, having to make use of drums and tape but not disc.

The **second generation** refers to the use of transistors. These were invented around 1949 and were used in computers in the 1950s. The basic design was fundamentally similar to the first generation computers but the replacement of valves by transistors greatly reduced the size and power requirements. This greatly increased the reliability, though the memory was still quite large and expensive. However for the first time, with the Univac I, it was possible to buy a computer.

The **third generation**, dating from about 1965, used integrated circuits. It is now referred to as SSI (small scale integration) and used the first silicon circuits, giving a further boost to size reduction. There was also a much reduced heat output as many components were now integrated on the same chip. The evolution of semi-conductor memory helped reduce the cost of 1K bytes of memory from £1,000 to £1. For the first time, computers no longer required special air-conditioned rooms and isolated power supplies and could now be transported by car or van. This led to the evolution of the minicomputer.

The **fourth generation**, dating from the mid 1970s, extended the use of integrated circuits to LSI (large scale integration) and VLSI (very large scale integration), although the distinction between them is not clearly defined. The number of chips per machine was greatly reduced, as was size, which introduced the possibility of 'computer on a chip' technology. This further miniaturisation brought about the development of the microcomputer and, for the first time, home computers became a possibility with the Commodore PET, the TRS–80 and the Apple II all dating from about 1979.

The 1980s saw systems designers looking forward to the **fifth generation**. This, it is hoped, will involve ultra fast and powerful computers, featuring parallel architecture and a data flow rather than instruction flow philosophy.

DATA AND INFORMATION

It is important to lay the foundations of information systems by covering some basic terminology and definitions, particularly the definitions of, and distinctions between, data and information. It is also important to define what is meant by a system.

The main thrust of this section is the idea of **data** being *processed* to provide **information**. Unfortunately, it is all too common for examination questions to be set which ask for a definition of these two terms; 'unfortunate' in the sense that, as we shall see for other terms covered in this chapter, precise definitions are difficult, if not impossible, without reference to a *specific* application or example. This is in marked contrast to other science subjects where unambiguous definitions are integral to the subject. Another factor which adds to the difficulty of this subject is that much of the jargon is ill-defined, being coined by the media and the salesmen rather than by those who understand the subject. This goes back to the 1960s when computers were normally referred to in the press as *electronic brains*, and is made worse by the many television programmes and magazine articles which tend to concentrate on the gimmickry connected with the subject.

> **Know the difference between data and information**

One important lesson from this introduction is that when answering examination questions, always take every opportunity to mention applications, to include examples and to provide illustrations.

Returning to the definition that *data is processed to provide information*, it is only within the context of this phrase that we can define the individual words. For example, take the process of purchasing goods at a modern computerised supermarket checkout; after the items have been processed, either by keying in or by reading the barcodes, the details can be printed out with the corresponding price. These *prices* can be regarded as **data**, processed by a simple operation of addition to provide a total amount to be charged to the customer. In the context of this example, the *total* is the **information**. A second interpretation or definition is that *information is data given some structure*, in which case the unit prices and quantities are the initial **data** which, by their position on the till receipt together with descriptions extracted from a file, eventually become **information**.

The example of the supermarket checkout now allows us to look at the definition of the individual terms. **Data** may be defined as *raw, unprocessed facts*, with **information** the *meaningful result of a process*. It is worth remembering that these definitions are very difficult, if not impossible, to explain in an examination without direct reference to one or more examples.

Take another example, more typical of computer applications: that of stock control. Each issue of stock and each receipt from suppliers will have been recorded. Files will have been created to hold, for each stock item, its product name, reference number, price, re-order level, order quantity, etc. All this data is then processed to provide the total inventory value, re-order lists, and stock movements, which, in this context, constitute information.

Notice that in each of these examples the identification of the information has been described as 'in the context of this process', and it is this proviso which indicates the problems of the definitions. Returning to the example of the supermarket checkout, we defined the total amount to be paid by the customer as the **information**. If we were to process this by adding up all the sales for the day, then the *customer total* would now be **data** in the context of computing the *overall total* for that till, which is in turn the **information** from this process. The overall total may itself be used as data when it is eventually processed to give, as information, a comparison with the previous week or year. We can develop this example over many stages and indeed can carry out a similar extrapolation for most examples.

ELEMENTS OF A SYSTEM

" Three key elements in a system "

The concepts of data and information being linked by a process can be used to introduce a further concept, that of a **system**. In fact, the concept of a system will be developed throughout this book, but the simplest model is displayed in Fig. 2.1, where a system is defined as having three elements, i.e.

- Input
- Process
- Output

In information systems, the *data* is the **input** and the *information* is the **output**. Figs. 2.2 and 2.3 show the examples of the previous section expressed as systems and throughout this book we shall use the word **'system'** as the process of providing *information* from *data*. Thus the stock control may be regarded as a **system** where *input* is provided in the form of issues and receipts. This input is used when the stock file is processed (possibly with the aid of a computer), to provide *output* in the form of management information. This model is particularly appropriate to all computer applications and to every useful computer program. However, the word 'system' has a broader interpretation and can be used in two specific contexts relating to computers, as we shall see in later chapters; first, to describe a program, and second, to describe the computer itself. As you will see in the next section the former is called a *software system* and the latter is the *hardware system*. There can also be *manual systems* which use neither hardware nor software.

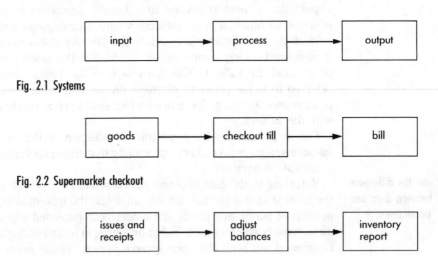

Fig. 2.1 Systems

Fig. 2.2 Supermarket checkout

Fig. 2.3 Stock control

HARDWARE AND SOFTWARE

The words hardware and software are frequently used in describing computers and computer systems. Like data and information, these words are best defined in terms of examples since rigid definitions are often difficult. In simple terms **hardware** is *equipment* and **software** refers to the *programs* used by the computer. Thus a disc drive is undoubtedly hardware, being a piece of equipment used by the computer. Other examples of hardware are the processor, a bar code reader and a printer, whereas every program written for the computer falls into the category of software. It is a common mistake to think that software only includes those programs purchased with the computer such as the operating system, a spreadsheet or a Basic language interpreter. In fact the true definition includes all of these plus any applications programs developed in an installation, or by a user, or obtained from any source.

The difficulty in these definitions can be seen by considering the programs provided on read-only memory (ROM) chips fitted into a microcomputer. In one sense they are hardware, being a piece of equipment, but in another sense could be software since they contain programs. Some people use the term **firmware** for these products and although the widespread use of this terminology has made the word respectable it is, as said in the discussion of data and information, far more important to understand the distinction than to be able to define the words.

Another point of confusion is the classification of, for example, a floppy disc or magnetic tape. Like the ROM chip it is apparently a piece of equipment which, for the sake of this discussion, may contain programs. This is really not worth pursuing as an argument because it is better to consider a disc simply as media.

TYPES OF COMPUTER

As we have already seen, within computing there are many examples of terminology which can be described as computer *jargon* rather than definitions. This is inevitable in such a new subject though it is important to make an attempt to be consistent whilst studying a subject at this level. A good example of this jargon is a study of the names used to describe the different types of computer, namely **microcomputer, minicomputer,** and **mainframe** computer. At this point we should define or, perhaps, explain these terms but it must be admitted that they are rather arbitrary categories of computer and that the classification of certain computers is often a matter of dispute.

Microprocessor

The best starting point is, perhaps, the term **microprocessor**. A microprocessor may be defined as a computer processor on a silicon chip, which has circuits imprinted on a small wafer of silicon. In some cases the whole computer can be on a single chip, hence the expression *single chip microcomputer*. It is more usual for the main processor to be on a single chip mounted on a circuit board with one chip containing the control and arithmetic units, and additional chips for the working storage, or memory, and for the control of data flow to and from the peripherals.

Microcomputer

A **microcomputer** is most easily defined as a computer which uses a microprocessor as its central processing unit. The microcomputer first appeared in Britain in desktop personal computers in 1979 with the Commodore PET, and also the British Nascom systems. Very soon schools started to use the RML 380Z, and the Sinclair ZX80 brought computers into the home, by mail order, for around £100. These computers had more power than the major systems of the earlier era and the home and business microcomputer market has developed as a major force from these beginnings.

All the early microcomputers were based on so-called *8-bit processors*, a term which will be explained in Chapter 3. The later (current) ranges of machines use processors described as *16-bit* which not only carry out their arithmetic a great deal faster than the 8-bit machines but are able to address a much larger working store. Typical among these computers is the IBM range of Personal Computers and a large number of machines based on the same type of architecture and described as *IBM compatible*.

Mainframe computer

The word **mainframe** is used to describe the large computer systems. Originally the idea of a mainframe involved a major computer configuration in an organisation which might have a number of smaller computers linked to it and serving it. This is still the true meaning, though the term is normally used to describe *any* large computer.

In the early days of the industry, there were just 'computers' with no real classification other than that some, like the IBM 1400 series, were designed for *business* applications, with others, like the IBM 7090 series and Atlas, designed for *scientific* applications. As the technology improved and processors became smaller, so the potential for more and more sophisticated systems evolved. Models such as the ICL 1900 range and the IBM 360 series had the ability to implement both data processing applications and large mathematical, 'number crunching' tasks, such as the calculations required for space travel and in nuclear physics. It became possible to implement more and more powerful computers. These original computers tended to be designed as large as possible in terms of capacity, or at least to be capable of expansion to the size of the largest systems available.

Minicomputer

During the 1970s, a number of companies realised that there was an enormous potential for a range of computers which would:

- be small in physical size;
- be cheaper than the giant computers on the market at that time;
- use cheaper, and perhaps slower peripherals;
- have limited upwards expansion;
- often be dedicated to a single application or range of applications rather than being 'general purpose' machines.

The price and performance of these machines in their special application areas compensated for their limitations in size. The mass production and consequent price reductions which resulted from the expanded markets began to make them a particularly attractive proposition both to the small organisations seeking their first computer and to the large organisations requiring a 'distributed' data-processing service with mini-computers in a number of user departments. These computers were, and still are, described as *minicomputers*.

Many people in the computer industry were quite puzzled by the term minicomputer and yet, rather like the fairy-tale of the 'Emperor's New Clothes', were loath to admit their lack of understanding of a term largely invented by the marketing people rather than by the computer specialists. One leading computer magazine wrote to a number of well-known manufacturers advertising minicomputers and asked for a definition of the term. It was hardly surprising to find that each manufacturer gave a *different* version. Putting all the definitions together they came up with the following composite description of a *minicomputer*:

❝ Aspects of the minicomputer ❞

1   The basic machine costs between £5,000 and £10,000.
2   The memory of the machines was usually organised in 'words' of 16–24 bits as opposed to the 32–, 48– and 64–bit word sizes of larger machines.
3   The maximum capacity of memory was usually less than that of a mainframe.
4   The peripherals tended to be slower and have smaller capacity than mainframes, and hence were cheaper.
5   The machines were often dedicated to multi-access applications, i.e. to controlling a large number of simultaneous users.
6   The price was less than that for a mainframe; a full system typically being in the range £30,000 to £50,000.

There were further complications in the use of the word *minicomputer* in that a range of small machines based on magnetic stripe cards had been introduced in the 1960s and had been marketed as 'mini computers' (two words). This interpretation is still used by a number of people in the industry. Furthermore, the machines at the top end of the *microcomputer* range are very often described in advertisements as *minicomputers*, partly to distinguish them from the home computers and small 8-bit machines, and partly perhaps because their capabilities match those of the computers previously given the name minicomputer.

Supercomputer

There is another class of computer, equally difficult to define precisely, called a **supercomputer**. These may be explained as machines produced with the following philosophy:

- The machine must run as fast as possible.
- The capacity should be as great as possible.
- Peripherals should be as fast as possible, consistent with the maximum capacity available.
- There is little or no restriction on price, i.e. *money is no object*.

This is almost a return to the original computers which were designed, of necessity, on the basis of these criteria before the marketing forces introduced the minicomputer. The *supercomputers* have a small but significant market, particularly in the area of number crunching, i.e. processing large volumes of numeric data. An example is the Cray.

In conclusion, it is important to remember that the labels microcomputer, minicomputer and mainframe computer only indicate a type of machine and are not hard and fast categories. Very often these terms are invented or used by people who write about computers or sell computers, rather than by people who design the machines, but this is almost inevitable as they are attempts to hit a moving target. No sooner has a name been established than the technology advances and the titles become obsolete.

The evolving terminology, with the microprocessor-based computers getting more and more powerful, refers to:

- 8-bit computers
- 16-bit computers
- 32-bit computers,

since these divisions themselves (which will be defined later) determine price, memory size and ultimately speed and performance. Office microcomputers are tending to be called *personal computers* or PCs and the top of the range models are referred to as *workstations*, such as the Sun and Apollo systems.

PERIPHERALS

The term **peripheral** will be explained at length in Chapter 4. It will be sufficient here to define peripheral as any device which provides input to, or receives output from, a computer system; examples are disc drives, the keyboard, printers and video display screens.

On-line and off-line processing

We use the term *on-line* to describe peripheral devices under the control of the processor of the computer, and *off-line* to describe devices not under direct software control. In many mainframe applications it is often convenient to use slow peripherals, such as graph plotters, in an off-line mode. For example, a long complicated drawing may output in digital form, typically to a magnetic tape which is then taken off the computer and loaded to the plotter which runs independently or off-line from the computer. This technique used to be more important – before the days of multi-programming computers which now allow a number of different tasks to run independently of one another. Before such computers it was common for most input and output to be carried out off-line.

❝ Reasons for off-line processing ❞

The other circumstance where off-line processing is used is where it is necessary to carry out operations *remote from* the computer, where no on-line connection to the computer is feasible. A good example of this is the regular stock-taking in a large supermarket where it is very common to see light-pen devices used. A typical such device has a light-pen, capable of reading bar codes, connected by a cable to a portable reader. This has connected to it a small numeric key-pad and a casette recorder, the whole unit being small enough to fit in a shoulder bag carried by a shop assistant. At specified times in the week an employee will go along the shelves in the shop and first use the pen to read a bar code attached to the shelf, which will be coded with the product number of the items. The assistant then counts the number of items on the shelf and enters the total on the key-pad. The code and the total are recorded on the cassette which, at the end of the stock-take, is removed from the unit and either posted to the computer centre for input to the computer or loaded direct to a reader in the form of a terminal connected 'on-line' to the computer via a telephone link. The computer will then process the data and provide information on the total value of the stock, the sales since the last stock-take and may possibly generate orders for replacement of the quantities sold.

REAL-TIME SYSTEMS

The term **multi-programming** was introduced in explaining the term *on-line processing*; another related expression is **multi-access**. Multi-programming refers to the ability of many computers to execute two or more programs at the same time and multi-access is the use of a number of on-line terminals to permit users at different, possibly remote, locations to make use of multi-programming to run a variety of independent tasks. In fact current computers do not obey two programs simultaneously but switch from one to the other so rapidly that, to the user, the execution appears simultaneous.

Before multi-access systems became common, most business applications had to operate procedures involving the collection of data in batches to be input in a single, typically weekly, computer run so that there was a built-in delay between the creation of the input and the generation of the output. This is known as **batch processing** and is still widely used as the most appropriate means of implementation for many systems; for example a payroll, where instant response is not required but reports are needed on a regular basis. The use of multi-access systems allows a large number of users to have access to a single shared file or database and input can be processed apparently instantaneously with no artificial delay. These are known as **real-time** systems and typical examples are the many reservation systems for sports and theatre bookings, airline and cross-channel ferry reservations, as well as many banking systems where accounts can be interrogated. This has led to the introduction of home banking services as implemented on Prestel by the Nottingham Building Society and the Bank of Scotland, as well as to the introduction of other on-line banking services such as Link cards and Connect Accounts.

The implementation of a real-time system has important hardware requirements which will be discussed in Chapter 6 but the minimum requirement is an appropriate on-line terminal, a connection to the computer system either by a simple wire (called **hard-wired**) or by a communications link (such as a telephone line). The computer itself will need, in the way of hardware, some form of communications processor and, for direct access to files, a magnetic disc store. The software requirements will be for a special program to handle the enquiries and to provide the response in real time.

Another environment in which real-time systems are common is with small computers in general and with personal computers in particular. Quite often a microcomputer is purchased to handle a single application, as for example in the use of information retrieval systems by insurance brokers who, when quoting for car insurance, can ask a client a series of questions prompted by the computer, such as the make and age of the car, the number of drivers, and so on. These responses are typed into the microcomputer which, after the last question, will provide a list of the insurance companies giving the most competitive rates.

CONTROL APPLICATIONS

> **Applications of the microprocessor**

Microprocessors, being so cheap, small and fast in operation, are ideally suited to the implementation of systems in the area of control applications. One of the earliest examples involved the domestic washing machine which could be *programmed* to carry out a predetermined sequence of operations under the control of the microprocessor. The video recorder is another familiar example in the home, where the ability to *programm* the machine to record several transmissions at different times and on a variety of channels is becoming more and more sophisticated.

An interesting extension of computer technology involving price reduction via mass production is that even moderately inexpensive video recorders can now be provided with a *light-pen* which can be used to read transmission times and channels from bar codes printed in the TV magazines and in newspaper adverts. It is also a measure of the complex operations involved in using a recorder that the average member of the public cannot cope with the *programmable* features without an aid such as the light- pen.

One interesting example of a domestic control system is the CD player. These devices did not appear on the market until well after the microcomputer revolution and cannot really be operated without a microprocessor-based control system.

A final application is the use of a microprocessor in the control panel of a motor car to control all the displays and to use the data to provide information on the efficiency of the driver. At least one luxury model employs a speech synthesiser to warn the driver of any detected problems, whilst another has the suspension under microprocessor control.

ANALOGUE AND DIGITAL DEVICES

> **Be able to distinguish between analogue and digital, continuous and discrete**

Historically, there were two distinct types of computer, analogue (alternatively spelt analog) and digital. Almost all computers today are digital devices but we can still divide the input devices into the two categories analogue and digital. **Digital** data is data which is purely *numeric* whereas **analogue** data usually involves an electrical signal where the voltage represents the input quantity. In statistical terms we speak of *discrete* and *continuous* variables. An example of a discrete or digital input is the keyboard of a microcomputer where the depression of a key causes circuits to be completed which send the processor a signal, coded in eight binary digits, corresponding to a *discrete* numeric value assigned to the character on the key. An example of an analogue input is a mouse, where the input is the movement of the device across a desk creating a voltage which influences the position of the screen cursor, or the use of a joystick which moves the weapon in games such as Space Invaders: this type of analogue input corresponds to a *continuous* variable.

This distinction can be well illustrated using modern word processing systems. Here the screen cursor may be moved, using *arrow keys*, a character or line at a time (digital; discrete). Alternatively the mouse can be used to move anywhere on the screen (analogue; continuous), but pressing the mouse button or a key will stimulate the program to approximate the position to a discrete character position. Another analogue device is the *scanner* which reads pictures or diagrams and loads them into the system in a digital form.

Another area where analogue and digital appear as terms is in the recording of time. For many years, all time recording was analogue, using the sweep of the hands of a watch or clock to represent time. But micro-chip technology has introduced a range of clocks and watches which display time in a digital form to an exact number of minutes, seconds or fractions of a second. This is a very good example to quote alongside computer input, as it has the same characteristics. In theory, a digital watch only gives a digital approximation to time, whereas an analogue watch is capable of achieving greater accuracy since it is not restricted to a fixed point. In practice, the precision of a digital watch is quite sufficient for most needs and we are in any case unable to read an analogue watch with the same accuracy. Exactly the same happens with many computer input devices.

APPLICATION PACKAGES

We shall study software in some detail in Chapter 15 and also take a close look at the subject of **application packages**. It is well worth introducing the term *application packages* at this early stage since throughout the book there will be a number of references to them. The use of an application package is an alternative to the writing of programs. Many small businesses cannot afford to employ a programmer, and individual users, more often than not, are not capable of writing programs. So, as an alternative, many firms and individuals *purchase* all the programs for their computer. An application package will include, in addition to all the programs, a full description of the operation of the program, user instructions and, where relevant, speciment documents. As well as the small business there are many large organisations which find it more economic to purchase application packages rather than to write their own applications, for some of the reasons given below.

Among the *advantages* connected with the use of applications packages are:

1   There is no need to employ a programmer or use a programmer's time to carry out the program development.
2   The program is ready immediately, there is no need to wait for it to be written.
3   The supplier of the application package is likely to be in a position to employ more skilled programmers.
4   It may be possible to get help or share experiences with other users of the package.

 Advantages and disadvantages of applications packages

There are, however, many *disadvantages* in the use of applications packages as compared with program development. Among the most important are:

1   The programs may be too general and not so immediately matched to the needs of the user.
2   It is difficult to discover if the program is exactly what is required by the business.
3   It may not be possible to adapt the program to the changing needs and growth of the company.

EXAMINATION QUESTIONS

SHORT QUESTIONS

Question 1
Distinguish between the terms 'multi-access' and 'multi-programming'. (part question)
(London AS Specimen)

(also)
Explain the terms multi-programming and multi-processing when used to describe different ways of utilising computer systems.   (Northern Ireland 1987)

Question 2
Distinguish between the terms on-line and batch operation as they affect the user of a computer system.   (Cambridge 1988)

Question 3
A newly formed computer manufacturer has decided to design, build and market a microcomputer aimed at the business user. List some of the key factors to be considered.   (London 1988)

Question 4
You have been asked to evaluate a microcomputer system for its graphics capability.

List *three* features which you would examine in performing the evaluation.

(London 1989)

Question 5

What is an analogue device? Indicate how data from such a device may be input into a digital computer.

(Northern Ireland 1988)

LONGER QUESTIONS

Question 6

What is meant by a real-time system and how does it differ from a conventional computer system? Give one example of a real-time system, clearly stating its hardware configuration and its software requirements.

(Welsh 1982)

Question 7

What are the major characteristics of a microprocessor?

Why are these characteristics of particular value in the field of control applications?

Describe a particular control application, which uses a microprocessor, and explain carefully the role of the microprocessor in this application.

(Welsh 1983)

Question 8

Typical configurations from the range of computer systems presently available are:

1   A micro-computer with cassette storage and a VDU for input/output.
2   A small mini- or a micro-computer with 'floppy' disc storage, a VDU and a printer.
3   A mainframe computer with magnetic tape and disc storage, several printers and approximately 100 VDUs distributed amongst several remote sites.

Discuss, in general terms, the limitations of these computer systems, together with typical applications for which they are used in industry and commerce.

(AEB 1982)

Question 9

What is meant by an application package? In addition to programs, what would you expect to be provided within such a package?

What are the advantages and disadvantages of implementing an application package compared with the development of a set of programs within a user's own data processing department?

(London 1984)

Question 10

Distinguish between multi-programming and multi-access. Explain how each of these concepts arose and what is the link between them. Discuss how the operating systems of a mainframe computer can accommodate both multi-programming and multi-access. Account for the fact that generally mainframe computers support both multi-programming and multi-access but the majority of microcomputers do not allow either, satisfactorily.

(WJEC 1987)

OUTLINE ANSWERS

It is not possible, at this stage of the book, to give comprehensive answers to all the questions since a detailed coverage of some of the material required will occur in later chapters and has only been introduced in outline here. It may well be worthwhile to look at these answers again after studying the whole book, and to expand them in the light of the additional material you will then have covered.

SHORT QUESTIONS

Question 1

Multi-access is the use of a number of on-line terminals to permit users at different, possibly remote, locations to make use of the computer's processor, whereas multi-programming is the ability of many computers to execute two or more programs at the same time. In practice, current computers do not obey two programs simultaneously but switch from one to the other so rapidly that, to the user, the execution *appears* simultaneous.

Multi-processing refers to the linking of two or more processors in a computer system. One example is the use of one processor for handling communications from the remote users, a so-called **front-end processor**, and a second processor, sometimes called a **number cruncher**, to execute the actual programs.

Question 2

The term on-line is used to describe peripheral devices under the control of the processor of the computer. This normally means, to a user, the use of a remote terminal in the form of a VDU, with a keyboard and, possibly, a mouse and in many cases a dot-matrix printer. It allows the user to interrogate or update files and to obtain a response or confirmation almost instantaneously in *real* time.

The term batch operation refers to the implementation of a computer system whereby data is collected in batches to be input in a single, typically weekly, computer run. There is a built-in delay between the creation of the input and the generation of the output. This is known as batch processing and is widely used as the most appropriate means of implementation for many systems, for example a payroll, where instant response is not required but where reports are required on a regular basis.

Question 3

Some key factors to be considered by a newly formed computer manufacturer in designing, manufacturing and marketing a microcomputer aimed at the business user are:

1 The first concern must be the availability of existing relevant business software as it would be unwise to spend money on writing the full range from scratch.
2 Point 1 almost certainly implies that the new firm must design the computer to be software-compatible with one of the major ranges, e.g. IBM-compatible.
3 The hardware must meet the needs of a business user, which means a professional, robust keyboard, and a screen display with a high quality definition.
4 There should be, possibly as an option, an internal hard disc drive of at least 20 Mb capacity and, for loading software, at least one floppy disc which, in the business sector, ought to be a 3½″ drive.
5 There need to be additional peripherals available, such as a range of printers and communications hardware.
6 Finally, the whole system should be put together in a *package* which gives the user a complete hardware configuration and, ideally, the essential software as well.

Question 4

Three features to examine in performing the evaluation of a microcomputer system for its graphics capability are:

1 The *resolution*, i.e. the number of pixels used to make up the picture.
2 The *availability* and *range* of colours.
3 The *compatability* with standard packages.

Question 5

Digital data is data represented in a purely numeric form. Computer scientists and statisticians would refer to this as discrete data since every quantity is represented as a whole number. Analogue data is the representation of data by some means which causes quantities to be measurable in another (analogous) medium which may take values in (what statisticians call) a continuous range.

An example of an analogue device is the representation of temperature by the length of a column of mercury in a tube, but the most common is the use of a sensor which represents the data as an electrical signal where the voltage represents the input quantity. Many microcomputer systems can receive analogue input from a joystick or games paddle. This is an electrical analogue device containing a variable resistor which can vary the input voltage which may be used to influence the position of data on the screen. This signal has to be converted, on input, to a digital representation of the quantities.

LONGER QUESTIONS

Question 6

Before the evolution of multi-access systems and multi-programming hardware and software, most business applications had to operate in a batch processing mode where the input was collected in a batch over a specified period and then input in a single computer run. This could be a daily, weekly, or monthly job and the batch process created a built-in delay between the creation of the input and the generation of the output. It is still the most appropriate means of implementing many systems, for example a weekly supermarket stock-check where instant response is not required.

Real-time systems use multi-access computer facilities or a dedicated mini- or microcomputer to allow users to have access to a file or files with a response such that input can be processed almost instantaneously, with no apparent delay.

The principal distinction between batch processing and real-time processing is that the response from a real-time system is immediate and processes one enquiry or transaction at a time, whereas a batch processing system processes a number of transactions simultaneously, with a scheduled delay between data capture and response.

One example of a real-time system is operated by a large chain of furniture retailers who maintain a complete stock file which can be interrogated by the salesmen in the shops using a Visual Display Unit whenever a customer wants to make a purchase. This displays on the screen, for the salesman, whether a particular item is available. Then, if the customer agrees to the purchase, their name and address may be keyed in at a terminal and the system prints the sales invoice and adjusts the stock level.

The hardware requirements of a real-time system include:

1 An appropriate on-line terminal, which may be a printing terminal or a visual display unit (VDU) or a microcomputer acting as an intelligent terminal.
2 Some means of connection from the terminal to the computer, which may either be a direct cable linking the two (a *hard-wired* system) or by a remote telephone link.
3 Some special communications processor, needed by the computer itself, which may be a small computer called a *front-end processor* or a device called a *multiplexer*.
4 A direct access file store, usually a magnetic disc.

A real-time system also has special software requirements in the way of a special program to handle the enquiries and to provide the response in real time. There may also be the need for a multi-programming operating system.

Question 7

It is necessary first to refer to the definition of what is meant by a microprocessor. This is, perhaps, best defined as a computer processor on a silicon chip. Alternatively, it is where the processor is on a single circuit board with one chip containing the control and arithmetic units, and where additional chips for the memory and for the control of data flow to and from the peripherals.

It is next worth explaining that a microcomputer is a small computer which uses a microprocessor as its central processing unit.

Control applications are where a computer is used to control a device or a machine or to monitor its operation. It is the cheapness, size and speed of microprocessors which make them ideally suited to the implementation of systems in this field.

A good example of a control application using a microprocessor is in the instrument panels of many modern motor cars. The processor controls all the displays and can also use the data from its sensors to provide information on the efficiency of the driver.

Question 8

A microcomputer with cassette storage and a VDU for input/output is limited in that reading of data from files will be very slow and, since cassette recorders were designed for sound reproduction (an example of analogue data rather than digital), input will not always be reliable and consistent.

Cassette-based microcomputers are not normally suited to business applications due to the limitations of file access. One environment in which they have been used is in the comparison of insurance quotations from a range of companies to aid a broker in advising a client. The program, and all the data, are loaded into the memory at the start of the day (or even left in overnight) and the enquiries can be handled entirely from memory with no access to the cassette store, thus providing a simple on-line system.

A minicomputer or a microcomputer with 'floppy' disc storage, a VDU and a printer may imitate most of the functions of a large (mainframe) computer. However it is likely to be limited by the capacity of the memory and the floppy disc, which may be as little as 100,000 characters and is unlikely to exceed 1 million characters. The printer is unlikely to operate faster than 100 or 200 characters per second.

Typical applications for a disc-based microcomptuer in industry and commerce are in word processing and also in the preparation of financial models using a spreadsheet.

A mainframe computer with magnetic tape and disc storage, several printers and approximately 100 visual display units distributed amongst several remote sites may have limitations in terms of cost and, depending on the level and intensity of activity at terminals, in terms of the speed of response.

A mainframe system with disc storage, several printers and 100 VDUs is well suited to the implementation of a real-time system for interrogation of a database.

Question 9

An application package is a program developed to carry out a particular application. It is usually purchased from a supplier, which may be a computer bureau, a software house or a retail shop.

An application package will include, in addition to the programs, a full description of the operation of the program, user instructions and, where relevant, specimen documents.

The advantages of implementing an application package as opposed to the development of a set of programs include:

1   No need to pay directly for a programmer's time.
2   Program is ready immediately on purchase.
3   May be using the skills of more expert programmers.
4   May be possible to get help from, or share experiences with, other users of the package.

The advantages of the development of a set of programs *within* a user's own data processing department as opposed to implementing an application package include:

1   The programs may not fit exactly the requirements of the business, having been generalised to maximise sales.
2   May be difficult to assess the worth of the program without implementing it fully in the company.
3   May not be possible to adapt the program to the changing needs and growth of the company.
4   A general loss of local control of the development of the program.

Question 10

The distinction between multi-programming and multi-access was explained in question 1. The link between them is that a multi-programming operating system is required to support multi-access.

The remainder of this question will be discussed in the study of operating systems (see Chapter 14.

GETTING STARTED

Chapter 2 described the nature of data and information and looked at possible definitions. It also started to indicate the potential of a computer system as a means of processing information. We shall now study the computer as a device, and we look first at the *central processing unit* and also at *memory*.

It can be assumed now, though this was not true before the microcomputer era, that all students will have seen and used a computer of some type, and so can easily relate this material to their own experience. However it is quite possible to use (and even to write programs for) computers over a long period of time and still not understand the basic principles or even the terminology in current use.

Chapter 2 also introduced and explained the idea of a *system*. In this chapter we shall begin to see that the computer is *itself* a system; for example, by understanding the concept of a stored program and by studying its method of execution it should become apparent that a computer program is a system which simply models another system. Later in the book we shall start to look at the means by which systems are studied and models designed.

The material in this chapter should be considered in three main sections. First, there is a study of the distinction between the functions of the central processor and the peripheral devices. The second main section is a study of the particular functions of the central processing unit (CPU) which is the environment in which the computer's memory operates. In this respect it is important to understand the functions of the special memory cells or registers within the control unit, the means by which data is transmitted within the central processing unit and the basic cycle by which program instructions are obeyed. The group of topics in the third section are concerned with the characteristics of memory, both in the physical sense and in the logical sense, and with understanding the essential terminology such as RAM and ROM. It can then be seen that several programs can exist in memory at the same time, with control passed between them by using the technique of interrupts.

ESSENTIAL PRINCIPLES

THE COMPUTER AS A SYSTEM

It is convenient to think of the computer as consisting of two basic elements, the central processing unit and the peripherals. The **central processing unit** (CPU) carries out the execution of instruction in the form of a stored program, while the **peripherals** can be classified in three groups: input, output and file storage. The first *input peripherals* were punched cards and punched paper tape but these can now be thought of as obsolete. The most popular current input devices are the keyboard and mouse. The *output peripherals* include printers and video screens. *File storage* includes magnetic tape, disc and floppy disc drives. It is often difficult to be specific about these categories when devices can be used in several different roles; for example a VDU has a keyboard for input and a video screen for output.

Fig. 3.1 shows the various elements presented in the same form as the system diagram in Chapter 2. We may therefore consider the computer as a system, with input from, say, a keyboard and output to, say, a printer, while carrying out processes within the central processor and the file store.

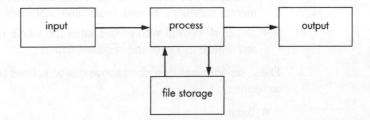

Fig. 3.1 The computer as a system

THE CENTRAL PROCESSING UNIT

The concept of the CPU and indeed the whole of the architecture of the digital computer is based on a proposed design from the 1930s by a mathematician, John Von Neumann. He defined the computer as having five basic parts: input, output, memory, an arithmetic unit and a control unit. These latter three are normally considered as forming the central processing unit and are shown in Fig. 3.2, though it is open to discussion as to whether the memory should be truly considered as part of the central processor.

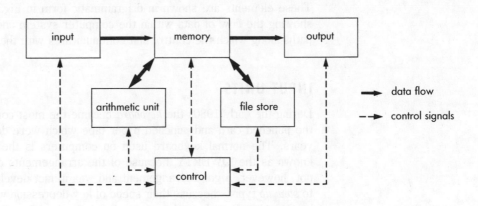

Fig. 3.2 The basic parts of a computer

Since the evolution of the microcomputer, the reduction in cost, the expansion in the capacity of memory, and the improvement in performance of other storage devices, it is common to consider a simplified model as shown in Fig. 3.3.

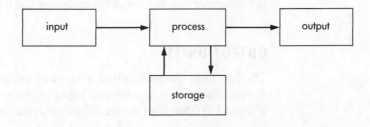

Fig. 3.3 Simplified model of computer system

THE BASIC ELEMENTS OF A COMPUTER

Computers were designed originally to meet the need to carry out complex mathematical computations faster than could be implemented with pencil and paper. In fact the first problems were concerned with missile trajectories and code-breaking during World War II. It is interesting to consider the requirements a *business* computer must possess if it is to imitate or model the functions of clerical workers.

When a clerk is sitting at an office desk, carrying out typical office duties, we may observe in the office:

- an 'in tray' where post, new instructions and data for processing are placed for action;
- an 'out tray' where the processed information will be placed for transmission to other departments of the organisation or to the outside world;
- work space, typically on top of the desk, with possibly a large writing pad and space on which to place documents and other materials for reference while working;

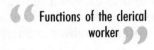
" Functions of the clerical worker "

- a desk drawer, or filing cabinet, or some other means of storing information, since any clerk would have far too much material for it all to be on the desk at the same time;
- a desktop calculator for arithmetical work too complex to be done quickly by mental arithmetic or with pencil and paper alone;
- the clerk himself who co-ordinates the whole operation, deciding what to do next and where to locate the required data.

These six functions described above can be related to their corresponding elements in the computer:

- Input
- Output
- Working store
- File store
- Arithmetic unit
- Control unit

Although we refer to *six* basic elements of a computer, many textbooks and some examination questions refer to *five* basic elements, by combining working store and file store as **storage**; some texts also combine input and output and refer to *four* elements. These elements are shown in diagrammatic form in Fig.3.2 above, with the solid lines showing the flow of data within the computer system and the dashed lines showing the paths along which the control unit communicates with the other elements.

INPUT UNITS

During the early 1980s the *keyboard* became the most common form of **input**, replacing the punched card and punched paper tape which were dominant for the previous thirty years. The normal keyboard used on computers is the standard typewriter keyboard known as the 'QWERTY' because of the arrangements of keys in the top row. This is not, however, a good arrangement and was in fact developed in the nineteenth century to *slow up* typists because their speed of key depression was faster than could be handled by the original mechanical typewriters.

Amongst the other common input devices are *bar code readers* (as used in libraries and supermarkets), *magnetic strip readers* as on credit cards and other plastic cards, *optical readers* (for reading printed text), *scanners* (for reading diagrams), *magnetic ink readers* (for cheques), *light-pens, touch sensitive screens* and the *mouse*. A future development may be speech recognition, though this is evolving only slowly so the ability to be able to talk to the computer to issue direct commands is still far away.

OUTPUT UNITS

The two most common output devices on computer systems are the *printer* and *video display*. There are many different types of printer, such as the *fast lineprinters*, operating at about 1,000 lines per minute, which are common on mainframe computers. For personal computers there are the slower and cheaper *character printers*, which operate at a range of speeds from fifteen to 400 characters per second and include dot matrix and daisy wheel printers. A growing market is that of the *laser printer* which uses photocopying technology to produce very high quality output. The prices of laser printers fell dramatically during the late 1980s, from £20,000-plus, to a range of models printing A4 size and costing from £1,500 to £3,000 for black print only. Video display devices can display text and/or graphics in colour or monochrome and alternative output devices include *graph plotters* and *audio response* or *speech synthesis*.

WORKING STORE

The working store is more commonly, though perhaps misleadingly, called *memory*, and in the machines of the 1950s and 1960s was referred to as *core store*. Another alternative name is IAS (*Immediate Access Store*) and any of these names may occur in examination questions.

Memory is used for two functions; first to store the *program* of instructions to be obeyed by the machine; second, and at the same time, to store the *data* being worked on by the program. The name *memory* is a little misleading in that, as with most computer systems, it is *volatile*, i.e. the data is lost when power is switched off which makes the name 'working storage' a little more meaningful.

It is the memory of the computer which is being measured when a model is described as 128K, a term to be explained in detail later, but for the moment it is sufficient to think of this as measuring the number of characters which can be stored within the computer; since K, in the context of computers, is a *kilobyte* and defined as 2^{10} or 1,024 characters, a 128K will hold about 128,000 characters.

FILE STORAGE

The memory is of a limited capacity. In early computers this was for economic reasons, since 1K of magnetic core memory would cost about £1,000. Microprocessor technology has now reduced this cost by a factor of £1,000, to less than £1 for 1K. An additional constraint, which has become of still greater importance, is that each memory cell, or word of store, has to be identified by a *unique reference*, called its *address*, and there is a limit to the number of such addresses available. In an 8-bit microcomputer this limit is normally 64K, and whatever the computer, there will be a finite limit to memory size. This can be thought of as analogous to the amount of data which can be visible on a working surface and, just as a clerk needs to use a filing cabinet, so the computer needs an additional store called a **file store**. Typical file storage media are *magnetic tapes, magnetic discs, floppy discs* and *Winchester discs*.

ARITHMETIC UNIT

The arithmetic unit was originally named by Von Neumann as the **mill**, a terminology which is still used by many people. More usually it is called the *arithmetic and logic unit* and is the part of the computer's processor where all the arithmetic operations are carried out. We shall see, again in a later chapter, that arithmetic is carried out by using logical functions.

The arithmetic unit has the following five *functions*:

❝ Functions of the arithmetic unit ❞

- Add
- Subtract
- Compare

and optionally
- Multiply
- Divide

It receives its input directly from special storage locations of the processing unit called **registers**.

CONTROL UNIT

The control unit gives a computer its particular characteristics. As will be explained later in this chapter in the section on the fetch − execute cycle, it examines the instructions stored in the program and causes them to be obeyed in the correct sequence.

The characteristic peculiar to computers is the ability to be *self-operational*, in that, having been presented with a set of instructions, known as the program, the computer can obey the instructions with no further need for human intervention until there is a requirement for interactive input. In obeying these instructions, as shown in Fig. 3.2 above, the control unit is in two-way communication with all the other devices so that, for example, it is able to send a message to a keyboard to receive a character, and then await a reply which indicates whether a response has been received, after which it can issue a command to another device for the execution of another instruction.

THE REGISTERS OF THE CPU

We have already seen that a *program* is a sequence of instructions interpreted and obeyed by the control unit in a set of smaller steps called the *fetch–execute cycle*. If we want to understand this cycle it is necessary to study the functions of some of the component parts or **registers** of the control unit and to study in outline the *format* of instructions within the computer. Computers are designed to obey only one language, which is their own special *machine code*, a language peculiar to each processor. The simplest example is a one-address language, similar to those used on the RML 380Z computer and the BBC Acorn. These languages will be studied in more detail in Chapter 12. We shall also discover how it is possible for programmers to write in languages such as Basic, Cobol and Pascal, which are so very different in structure and syntax from the machine codes.

In simple, one-address machine language the instructions are in two parts which are labelled:

operator   operand

The **operator** is the equivalent of a verb in a spoken language, while the **operand** is the equivalent of the object of a sentence.

Typical examples of such instructions are

LDA 400

which might specify that the accumulator register should be loaded with the character stored in memory location 400, and

JSR $D00

to implement a sequence change to the subroutine of instructions stored in memory location with the (hexadecimal) address D00; this means 'for the moment ignore the next instruction in the sequence and proceed instead to the instruction in 1024'. Chapter 12 will provide a more detailed study of machine and assembly languages, but it is worth now to make a brief study of the basic architecture of the CPU.

Many machine instructions and most operations within the central processing unit use special storage areas called *registers* which are special storage locations within the CPU or the control unit used to hold intermediate results or to assist in data manipulation. These are part of, and are physically located within, the CPU, which means that data from the registers can be accessed even faster than that in main memory. There are only a small number of registers, typically about sixteen, and their function is linked very closely to the machine language, some being used as a fast working storage and some being used for special functions, like storing a pointer to the next instruction to be obeyed. The examples given here are representative of typical registers and are not based on any one particular machine but combine the features of several.

Program counter

The program counter (PC) is also known as the **instruction register** (IR). It is sometimes called the **sequence control register** (SCR) and sometimes the **sequence register**, being a 'counter' used by the control unit to provide some means of knowing the whereabouts of the next instruction to be executed. The precise name varies with the make and model of the processor. Each memory cell is identified, like the lockers in a school or college or the houses in a street, by a unique numerical **address**. The sequence register stores the *machine address* of the location of the next instruction and is incremented as each program instruction is obeyed. If the instruction is a branch, or sequence change, as given in one of the examples above, it is executed simply by modifying the contents of the sequence register to contain the address of the new instruction, i.e. the *operand* of the instruction is copied into the sequence register.

Memory address register

When executing a machine language instruction the operand of the instruction contains the address of a memory location to be accessed. This value is copied from the program instruction in memory to a register called the **address register** or the **memory address register** (MAR) so that the load accumulator instruction given in the earlier example above would have the operand '400' copied into the memory address register.

Function register

Some important registers

Just as the address register holds the *operator*, the function register contains the operator of the instruction which is then decoded and 'obeyed' by the control unit.

Current instruction register

In some processors, the address and function registers are combined to form a single register called the current instruction register or CIR containing both operator and operand.

Accumulators

Accumulators are registers in the central processor used for intermediate storage for arithmetic calculations. They are analogous to the displayed results on a pocket calculator. If, for example, the machine were to be evaluating a simple arithmetic function such as

$$9 - 3 + 5$$

9 would be 'loaded' into the accumulator, then 3 would be subtracted, giving 6 in the accumulator. Finally 5 would be added to give the result 11 which is copied into the required memory cell. In general, all arithmetic operations are carried out using the accumulator as it is not possible to add directly the contents of two memory cells. Some early machines, often using a three-address language, did their arithmetic directly between memory cells and had no accumulator as such. This is not the method used in current microprocessors.

The memory data register

The memory data register is a register of the same size as a cell of memory and is used, like a buffer, to hold data during the transfer of data between memory and the registers.

Status registers

As well as the *working registers* described above, we shall see in a later chapter that there can be other registers. Each processor will have a set of status registers or **flags** which can be interrogated by machine language instructions. These flags are normally single binary digits and a number of status registers will be contained in a single register of, typically, eight binary digits. Examples include the *carry flag* which is set if the addition of two digits causes a *carry* and a *zero flag* set if the compare instruction or arithmetic operation just executed gives a *zero* result.

Bus

Bus is the name given to the connecting lines or communication channels along which the data and instructions between memory, registers and elements are transmitted. The word *bus* is derived from the latin *omnibus* with the idea that several sets of chips can be connected to the same bus and share the same communication channels. There will, typically, be three buses within the processor, the data bus, the address bus and the control bus. The *address bus* is used to send address information between the control unit and memory; the *data bus* is for transmitting the data; and the *control bus* is for transmitting signals from one component to another.

Processor clock

The speed of operation of a microprocessor is controlled by an internal electronic clock which sends out pulses at regular intervals. The Acorn BBC microcomputer uses a 6502 microprocessor which sends 2,000,000 pulses per second and so is described as having a 1 Megahertz clock; each pulse is referred to as a cycle so that the *cycle time* of the machine is 0.5 microseconds. The *execution time* of each instruction can be precisely measured in terms of cycles so that, for example, a sequence change instruction or JMP takes three cycles or 1.5 microseconds; an ADC or add with carry takes four cycles or two microseconds.

When a program is contained in the memory of a computer, it is executed by the control unit repeating a cycle of operations, which is sometimes called the fetch–execute cycle and sometimes called the fetch–decode–execute cycle. Let us take as an example a simple one-address machine language program to illustrate a simple addition of two digits and then study the fetch–execute cycle by tracing through the instructions.

Such a program might look like the sequence detailed below:

Address	Contents		Type	Interpretation
700	LDA	501	Instruction	load the accumulator with the contents of cell 501
701	ADD	502	Instruction	add to accumulator the contents of cell 502
702	STA	503	Instruction	store contents of the accumulator in cell 503
703	HALT	000	Instruction	end program
501	2		Data	the number 2
502	3		Data	the number 3
503	0		Data	the number 0

> **The fetch–execute cycle for the addition of two digits**

The cycle which is obeyed by the control unit can be broken down into the following steps:

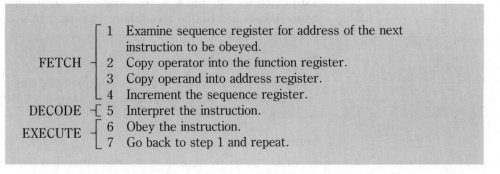

FETCH
1 Examine sequence register for address of the next instruction to be obeyed.
2 Copy operator into the function register.
3 Copy operand into address register.
4 Increment the sequence register.

DECODE
5 Interpret the instruction.

EXECUTE
6 Obey the instruction.
7 Go back to step 1 and repeat.

The decode operation is often combined with the execute to give the name *fetch–execute* cycle though the name *fetch–decode–execute–reset* is a common alternative. In the first four steps the instruction is *fetched* into memory and in the last three it is *executed*. It is a worthwhile exercise to study this further by tracing the execution of the four instructions in the program above.

The sequence register is initialised to contain 700, the address of the first instruction to be obeyed, before the execution commences. In the *first fetch cycle*, the memory cell 700 is examined, and the operator, which will be the machine code equivalent of the LDA or load accumulator instruction, is copied into the function register. The operand, 501, is copied into the address register and the sequence register is incremented to take the value 701. In the *execute cycle*, the contents of memory cell 501, the number 2, are copied into the accumulator.

The processing of the second instruction can be explained similarly. The sequence register now contains the value 701 and, after the fetch cycle, the sequence register is incremented to take the value 702. In the execute cycle, the contents of cell 502, the number 3, are added to the contents of the accumulator which will then hold the value 5.

In processing the third instruction, the sequence register is again incremented to 703, and the contents of the accumulator, which are 5, are copied into memory cell 503; but note that the accumulator will still hold the value 5. The operator of the fourth machine instruction specified a HALT instruction, the sequence register is incremented to take the value 704 and the operator causes the program to be terminated.

OTHER MACHINE CODE FORMATS

The simple language used in the machine code example given above employed a **one-address** structure, which means that each instruction uses one operand. Thus to add two numbers together three instructions were needed. If the section of program is thought as the evaluation of

alpha = beta + gamma

then the sequence of instructions is

" One-address language "

```
LOAD      alpha
ADD       beta
STORE     gamma
```

This is the type of machine code used in most microprocessors, including those in the BBC microcomputer, the RML Nimbus and the Acorn Archimedes.

In a **two-address** language, instructions have two operands so that the same program would be written

" Two-address language "

```
MOVE   alpha   gamma   setting gamma to the value of alpha
ADD    beta    gamma   adds in beta
```

A **three-address** language would implement this in a single instruction

```
ADD       alpha     beta      gamma
```

Another common type of instruction uses **zero addresses**, referring to CPU registers. Indeed many of the common microprocessors, though essentially one-address systems, use a special type of storage called a **stack** (see Chapter 13) and use many instructions which simply address the top of the stack. There are also instructions such as HALT which use no operand. It must be remembered that the machine language is peculiar to its processor and the programmer has no choice but to use the address structure of the language provided with the processor. Taking the 6502 processor of the Acorn BBC microcomputer and the Z80 processor of the RML 480Z and Sinclair Spectrum machines as examples, both are essentially one-address languages but also implement a number of zero address instructions within the language.

CHARACTERISTICS OF MEMORY

STORAGE OF DATA AND INSTRUCTIONS

All current computers are based on an implementation of the architecture of the 'Von Neumann' machine and assume that memory is divided into addressable units of equal size. These units are called **words** and each word can be identified within a program by its unique address which, within a computer, ranges from zero up to the limit of memory. This organisation of storage within memory has almost been taken for granted in the material presented so far. The so-called *8-bit microcomputers*, which include the BBC microcomputer and the RML 380Z, have as their unit of memory an 8-bit word or **byte** so that when such a machine is described as having 32K of memory it has $32 \times 1,024$ bytes, i.e. 32,768 bytes available to the programmer. The 16-bit computers, such as the IBM PC, the RML Nimbus and the ACT Apricot, also have words of eight bits but some operations group them together in two byte units each. Minicomputers and mainframe computers have, as mentioned earlier, larger words. For minicomputers, the word sizes are typically in the range sixteen to twenty-four bits, and for mainframes, thirty-two to sixty-four.

You may find it easier to think of memory as a long list, like pigeon holes in a letter rack. But memory is not accessed by searching through a long list of words. As we saw earlier in the chapter, the control unit has registers such as the instruction address register and by transmitting this through the address bus the relevant store location is addressed directly and its contents transmitted to or from the control unit using the data bus in a single machine cycle. Thus it is possible to transfer any word from memory to the control unit in the BBC microcomputer in one cycle, i.e. 0.5 microseconds. The time taken to access such a word of memory is often used as an alternative definition of **cycle time**. Since memory can be accessed in this random manner as opposed to linearly, it is commonly referred to as 'Random Access Memory' or RAM. A better interpretation of the expression RAM is to refer to the fact that every memory cell can be accessed in the same unit of time. This is a vital consideration in the implementation of machine language instructions.

The 6502 microprocessor, a typical 8-bit system, has a machine code with instructions which are a whole number of bytes, either one, two or three. The 1-byte instructions are zero-address instructions as described above. The 2-byte instructions have as operand a single byte where, for example, the instruction

LDA #7

will load the 8-bit accumulator or A-register with the value seven. The 3-byte instructions in the language use a 2-byte operand to contain the address of an instruction in memory.

First, notice that in all three instruction types the operator is a single byte. We shall find in Chapter 11 that one byte, of eight bits, can represent numbers in the range 0 to 255, thus these 256 distinct codes imply that the 6502 processor is able to support a total of 256 different commands in its instruction set. Secondly, notice that two bytes are used in the operands to address memory. The sixteen bits contained in two bytes can represent numbers in the range 0 to 65,535 only, so the maximum memory available on the 6502 is, theoretically, 65,536 bytes which is $65 \times 1,024$ or, more familiarly, 64K. The two bytes of a 16-bit address are often referred to as **page** and **line**; the page being the most significant byte and the line the least significant byte.

As a contrast, the 8086 16-bit processor, as used in IBM compatibles, uses registers of sixteen bits and so divides memory into sections of 64K bytes but has an address bus of twenty bits, which gives a memory limit of one megabyte, 1,000K or 1,048,576 bytes.

MEMORY ADDRESSING SYSTEMS

There are several other types of **memory addressing systems** which may be found in different computer systems:

Different memory addressing systems

• paged memory • virtual memory • cache memory • content addressable memory

Paged memory

It was demonstrated above that the two bytes of a 16-bit address can be referred to as page and line, with the page being the most significant byte and the line the least significant byte (these are the names always used, though it is grammatically incorrect). This is a simple example of the organisation of memory into sections, or *pages*, with the page just a convenient sub-division of the address. A second example is where a *page* number is used to select alternative pages of memory which, though occupying the same addresses, have to be selected as alternatives as required. One example is the implementation of sideways ROMs in BBC microcomputer, where both Basic, View and Pascal all occupy the same address range in memory but exist simultaneously on the main board and are selected as required by commands such as

```
*BASIC
*WORD
*PASCAL
```

Virtual memory

Virtual memory or virtual storage can be thought of as a further extension of the technique of paged memory. This is useful since many programs greatly exceed the physical size of main memory. Here the pages, containing parts of programs and data, are held on the backing store and read into memory as required. Thus, in effect, the computer regards part of its file store and all memory as a very large, possibly almost infinite, memory. The advantage to the programmer is that programs are less complex since memory limits are ignored. The main disadvantage is that programs can sometimes run very slowly if there is a great deal of activity transferring data from memory to and from the backing store.

Main memory will hold only a small number of pages and the designers of operating systems have invested a great deal of research into deciding how best to implement such a system to minimise the swapping of pages in and out of memory. The page size must be related to the physical block size on the backing store; for example if disc storage sectors hold 256 bytes then pages might be 1,024 bytes. The *virtual address* used by the program has to be mapped to the physical address in the main store, for which purpose the address is considered in two parts, page and word (or byte), as in Fig. 3.4.

A virtual memory system

Fig. 3.4

page no.	word no.

If, for example, the block size were to be 256 bytes, the least significant eight bits give the byte location within the page (if the block were 1,024 bytes then it would use ten bytes). A table has to be maintained in memory to map the pages of the program, either to a page in memory or to a backing store address. The start of the table in memory will be stored in a **base address register** and so the page number has to be added to this base address in order to locate its reference in the page table, from which is extracted either the actual location of the page in memory or its address on the backing store. This process is illustrated in Fig. 3.5. The table also holds **control bits** which specify whether the page is in memory or not, the access privileges, and whether it has been written to since it was last loaded.

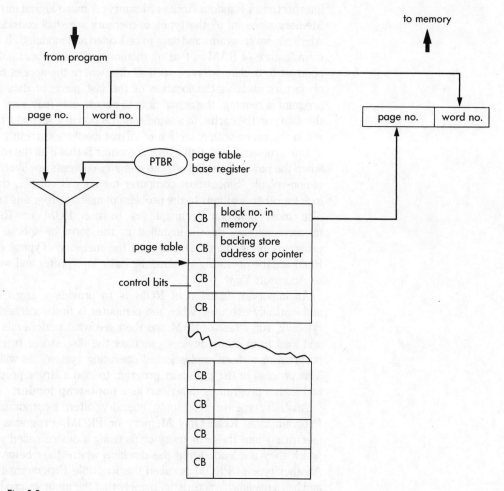

Fig. 3.5

The software designer of a virtual memory system needs to decide on a replacement policy for pages, i.e. when the required page is not in memory (known as a **page fault**) which page is to be overwritten in memory and, when altered, written to backing store. The best strategy is to select the **least recently used** (LRU) page, but since this takes a little additional time it is often abandoned for a **round-robin** or a random selection.

Cache memory

Cache memory is a special type of memory situated between the control unit and memory which, like the registers, is accessed at the maximum rate. It is directly analogous to virtual memory in that as memory cells are required, pages, which are referred to as sets, of typically four to sixty-four bytes are copied from main memory into the cache memory and then all accesses are to and from the cache. Access to cache memory is at the same speed as access to registers and, even with the swapping in and out of cache, this can make typical programs run up to ten times faster. The VAX 11/780, for example has an 8K byte cache divided into 512 sets of sixteen bytes each. Thus data is loaded from main memory to cache memory and used as required until replaced by another transfer from main memory.

Content addressable memory

This is a portion of memory where, instead of an address locating data, the value of a data item is used to locate an address. This is frequently implemented in a cache memory and could, for example, hold a table of data values and their memory addresses. By accessing the content addressable memory with a value, all entries in the table can be accessed simultaneously and the address returned instantaneously.

TYPES OF MEMORY

We have already introduced the term RAM to describe user accessible memory and it is interpreted as **R**andom **A**ccess **M**emory. A more logical interpretation is **R**ead **A**nd write **M**emory since, of all the types of memory we shall consider here, this is the only form which allows programs and data to be loaded and modified. It is also worth recalling that the main feature of RAM is that all memory cells are accessed in the same unit of time, in contrast to backing storage such as disc where the access time is variable and dependent on factors such as the location of the last piece of data accessed. However, when a program is running, the actual time to access data may vary from a single machine cycle if the data is in the cache, to a significant fraction of a second if the access involves replacing a set in the cache with a section of virtual memory currently located on a disc.

One problem faced with every computer is that if all the memory were to be RAM then, when the power is turned off, the memory contents are likely to be lost unless the memory is non-volatile. Since most computer memory *is* volatile, the manufacturers have had to look for other solutions to the problem of making programs and data available on power up. The most common technique is to use ROM or **R**ead **O**nly **M**emory and, in microcomputers, this is installed in the form of special chips which contain special programs permanently etched into the memory. Typical of the programs contained in ROM are the operating system, the Basic interpreter and word processing programs such as Acornsoft View.

An important function of ROM is to provide a small section of program which is automatically executed when the computer is first switched on. This small program will, typically, run a test of RAM and then see what peripherals are connected to the system and load from other devices, such as the disc store, from other ROM chips, a larger program or a more sophisticated operating system, as will be described in Chapter 14. This process of using a short program to load a larger program is called **bootstrapping** and such a program is described as a **bootstrap loader**.

Another type of read only memory often incorporated in a computer, is called **P**rogrammable **R**ead **O**nly **M**emory or PROM. Programs or data can be programmed electrically into these memory chips using a device called a **PROM programmer**, after which they are loaded into the machine where they behave in the same way as ROM. Another type of PROM is called the **E**rasable **P**rogrammable **O**nly **M**emory or EPROM and has a useful characteristic, namely that the memory can be erased by exposure to ultra violet light and then subsequently reprogrammed with a different set of data. This is most useful in the development of programs which are later to be mass-produced for ROM.

The term **volatile** was used earlier in the chapter in connection with memory. There is a particular problem with portable computers, such as the Tandy 100, which often have no file store and rely on data being retained in the memory. These can operate from torch batteries but also have a small internal battery which is charged up by the main batteries every time the machine is operated and can hold sufficient power to retain the contents of memory over several months.

PROGRAM-CONTROLLED INPUT–OUTPUT AND INTERRUPTS

The most straightforward method of communicating with peripherals is by **program-controlled input–output** by which the transfer of data to or from the peripheral is carried out under the constant supervision of the program. This might implement the following sequence:

1 Send byte to output device.
2 Await signal that transfer has been completed.
3 Repeat until no more bytes for transfer.

This technique has the disadvantage that the processor is monopolised by this transfer and in the case of a slow peripheral, for example a graph plotter, there would be a delay before any other task could be executed. This is one of the circumstances which gave rise to the use of **interrupts**.

INTERRUPTS

Interrupts may be considered as an extension to the fetch–execute cycle explained at the start of the chapter. A feature of most computers is the ability to carry out several tasks simultaneously, or for the processor to carry out a particular task until some *event* occurs, for example a key being depressed, a read or write operation being completed, an error detected or a program time limit being exceeded. This is carried out by a technique known as **interrupts** which makes use of special lines called *interrupt lines* in the control bus. These lines carry signals generated by processes or peripherals when an *event* occurs. These signals are detected by the control unit by the cycle which now becomes:

> *The technique of interrupts*

- Fetch
- Decode
- Execute
- Examine for interrupt

If an interrupt *has* occurred, the control unit, before carrying out the next fetch, stores the contents of the sequence control register (SCR) and then branches to a special program called the *interrupt service routine*. There may be a number of different ways in which an interrupt may arise and the interrupt service routine has access to a number of binary 'flags' which indicate the source of the interrupt and indicate the action to be taken. Since two or more interrupts occur simultaneously, each task is allocated a priority level and when the processing of the interrupt is complete, control passes to the task with the next highest priority.

Interrupts may be applied to the transfer of data in a manner totally independent of the main processor. This simply starts the transfer, which then continues *autonomously* until an interrupt is generated to indicate completion. One example is the ability of many word processing programs to print out one document whilst the operator is editing another; another example occurs with spreadsheet programs such as Excel where the calculation of results may be *interrupted* by a keystroke entering more data.

Another application is in process control where the processor can execute a program which is interrupted every time a new data item is detected, and returned to after the data has been processed.

DIRECT MEMORY ACCESS (DMA)

Both program-controlled and interrupt-controlled input–output require the active intervention of the processor in transferring data from memory to the I/O channel for the relevant device. With high speed peripherals this might both monopolise the processor and limit the speed of transfer. Therefore a third method, known as DMA (**D**irect **M**emory **A**ccess), has been devised. DMA is a separate module on the system bus which can receive a command from the processor and then carry out the transfer with no further intervention from the CPU.

The DMA controller needs just four pieces of information:

- Which device is required.
- Whether it is read or write.
- The start location in memory for the data involved in the transfer.
- The total number of bytes or words to be transferred.

It generates a single interrupt when the whole transfer has been completed. It will, naturally, impose one other restriction in that the data required for the operation will be *locked out* from other tasks during the transfer.

There are a number of alternative names for many of the registers and a great variety of implementations. Thus candidates should be prepared to recognise a variety of different names of the registers; they should also be thoroughly familiar with the registers and with the structure of the computer they are using.

EXAMINATION QUESTIONS

SHORT QUESTIONS

Question 1
What is understood by the term *virtual memory*?
Outline *one* technique that can be used by a computer system to manage virtual memory.

(London 1989)

Question 2
a) Explain what happens when a peripheral device requiring attention sends an interrupt to the processor.
b) Why do interrupts from different peripheral devices have different priority levels?

(Welsh and Cambridge 1989)

Question 3
Why is it usually necessary to have priorities associated with interrupt processing?

(AEB 1988)

Question 4
Distinguish between the terms *program-controlled* input–output and *interrupt-controlled* input–output.
Why might neither technique be suitable for handling high speed peripherals?

(London 1988)

Question 5
Describe the characteristics of RAM and ROM in a typical computer.

(Northern Ireland 1987)

Question 6
List three *different* types of software commonly found in read only memory (ROM). In each case indicate the suitability, or otherwise, of using ROM.

(London 1988)

Question 7
Explain briefly the term *virtual memory*. Describe *two* advantages from the user's point of view.

(AEB 1989)

Question 8
List the steps executed during:
i) the fetch phase, and
ii) the execution phase for an unconditional jump instruction.

(London 1988)

LONGER QUESTIONS

Question 9
a) Explain the terms main store, paged store and virtual store. Describe *one* advantage and one drawback of a virtual store system.
b) What is an *autonomous transfer* to a peripheral device? How can double-buffering allow transfers to take place in parallel with computing?
c) What is an *interrupt signal*? Give two reasons why an interrupt signal might occur.

(Oxford 1984)

Question 10
A microcomputer that is being used to control a laboratory experiment is expected to give its first priority to accepting and recording data from measuring instruments and is expected meanwhile to analyse the data.
Explain how this is possible and describe the main features of such a system.

(Cambridge 1984)

Question 11

a) Explain the nature and function of the following.

    i) Program counter (also known as sequence control register)
    ii) Memory address register
    iii) Memory buffer register
    iv) Instruction register
    v) Accumulator

b) In a simple computer the operation code and operand fields of each machine code instruction are both held in a single word. Use a flow diagram or pseudo code to describe the operations carried out during the fetch–execute cycle in terms of the contents of registers i) to v) of part (a). The explanation should include both arithmetic and branch (go to) instructions.

c) Describe the effect of i) logical, ii) arithmetic and iii) cyclic shift instructions on the content of the accumulator and explain how each type of shift differs from the others.

(Northern Ireland 1987)

OUTLINE ANSWERS

SHORT QUESTIONS

Question 1

Virtual memory is an implementation of paged memory used where programs exceed the physical size of main memory and the pages, containing parts of programs and data, are held on the backing store and read into memory as required. Thus, in effect the computer regards part of its file store and all memory as a very large, possibly almost infinite, memory.

One technique used by a computer system to manage virtual memory is to store a number of pages in memory indexed by a page address table which is consulted for every memory access. If the required bytes are not in memory then we have what is known as a page fault and one of the pages in memory, ideally the *least recently used*, is overwritten in memory by the required page after being written to backing store if it has been altered since read into memory.

Question 2

a) When a peripheral device requiring attention sends an interrupt to the processor, the signals are detected by the control unit and by the cycle which now becomes:

- Fetch
- Decode
- Execute
- Examine for interrupt

So when interrupt has occurred, the control unit, before carrying out the next fetch, stores the contents of the sequence control register and then branches to a special program called the interrupt service routine.

b) There are a number of different ways in which an interrupt may arise and the interrupt service routine has access to a number of binary 'flags' which indicate the source of the interrupt and indicate the action to be taken. Since two or more interrupts occur simultaneously, each task is allocated a priority level and when the processing of the interrupt is complete, control passes to the task with next highest priority. Otherwise a vital interrupt, for example an indication of a power failure or a message from an on-line monitoring system, might go unrecognised whilst other less-urgent tasks were completed.

Question 3

The need to have priorities associated with interrupt processing is covered in part b) of the previous question.

Question 4

With program-controlled input–output the transfer of data to or from a peripheral is carried out under the constant supervision of the program. As, for example, in implementing the following sequence:

1   Send byte to output device.
2   Await signal that transfer has been completed.
3   Repeat until no more bytes for transfer.

This technique has the disadvantage that the processor is monopolised by this transfer and in the case of a slow peripheral, for example a graph plotter, there would be a delay before any other task could be executed.

With interrupt-controlled input–output the transfer is initiated by the processor which is then free to undertake another task while awaiting the *interrupt signal* that the transfer is complete.

Both program-controlled and interrupt-controlled input–output require the active intervention of the processor in transferring data from memory to the I/O channel. With high speed peripherals this might both monopolise the processor and limit the speed of transfer, therefore a third method known as DMA (**D**irect **M**emory **A**ccess) has been devised. DMA is a separate module on the system bus which can receive a command from the processor and then carry out the transfer with no further intervention from the CPU.

Question 5

RAM or random-access memory is best described by the alternative interpretation of **R**ead **A**nd **W**rite **M**emory. It is the normal 'main memory' of a computer and holds the program currently being executed as well as all working storage connected with the program.

ROM or **R**ead **O**nly **M**emory is a means of storing programs permanently within memory. A typical application is the operating system of a microcomputer.

Question 6

Three different types of software commonly found in read only memory (ROM) are:

- the operating system;
- language interpreters or compilers;
- application packages.

ROM is ideally suitable for the basic operating system since it will then be immediately available when switching on power. The disadvantage is that a sophisticated operating system may require too much memory and so may not be appropriate to ROM. For example, the BBC computer uses very basic operating systems, for instance DFS and even ADFS, and these are quite appropriate to ROM, but a CP/M used on the RML 380Z has a skeleton system alone resident in memory with other facilities loaded into RAM as required. ROM could not possibly implement this without taking too large a share of the available memory.

Many small microcomputers have a Basic language interpreter in ROM. This is ideal for home computers where the only requirement might be to run programs written in Basic, but it is unsuitable for larger systems since it uses up large amounts of memory and so restricts what might be made available to other applications. It is more common on 16-bit micros to load the interpreters or compilers from disc.

There is no restriction, apart from memory limits, as to what may be stored in ROM. For example, a computer intended to run just one program could have that program loaded into ROM so that it would be executed automatically when switched on. This is ideal for special-purpose computers, particularly if intended to be portable and having no backing store. However its use is limiting in general purpose machines. One successful implementation is on the BBC microcomputer where applications such as View, ViewSheet, Quest, etc., are held in so-called *sideways ROM* which allows a number of applications to be held simultaneously in ROM and the operating system can select one or another as required.

Question 7

Virtual storage is a technique of dividing the memory requirements of a program into pages, with some being held on the backing store and read into memory as required. Thus the computer regards part of its file store and all memory as a very large capacity memory.

One advantage of virtual storage is that it provides a large range of addresses by providing a mechanism whereby an area of file store is treated as an extension of memory, so to the programmer, the memory seems almost infinite. A second advantage is that the programmer/user is hidden from any implementation details of segmenting or overlaying sections of the program.

Question 8

The control unit of a computer processes the instructions of a program by means of carrying out a cycle of steps called the fetch–execute cycle. Each computer can only obey its own special machine language peculiar to the processor and for this answer we shall assume a simple one-address language, similar to those used on the RML 380Z computer and the BBC Acorn. Each instruction in a one-address machine language has two components which are labelled:

operator   operand

An example of a control transfer instruction is:

JMP 345

which implements a sequence change to the instruction in memory cell 345, so that instead of executing the next instruction in the sequence the control unit obeys the instructions starting from cell 345. Assume also that the instruction is stored in location 700.

The fetch–execute cycle which is obeyed by the control unit can be broken down into the following steps:

FETCH
1 Examine sequence register for address of next instruction to be obeyed.
2 Copy operator into the function register.
3 Copy operand into address register.
4 Increment the sequence register.

DECODE
5 Interpret the instruction.

EXECUTE
6 Obey the instruction.
7 Go back to step 1 and repeat.

We can trace the steps for the JMP as follows:

1   Examine sequence register for address of the next instruction to be obeyed which will be 700, the address at which the JMP is stored.
2/3 Copy the operator from 700 (the binary pattern corresponding to JMP) into the function register and the operand (345) from 701 into the address register.
4   During this last step the sequence register is incremented to become 702.
5   Next interpret the instruction, i.e. recognise as JMP.
6   Obey the instruction so that the address register is copied into the sequence register which now contains 345.
7   Now repeat the cycle, and since the sequence register now contains 345, it is that location which will be examined for the next operator.

LONGER QUESTIONS

Question 9

a) Main store is another name for the memory, immediate access, or working store of the computer. It is that part of the computer's data store which is accessible by the CPU and normally holds programs and data which can be accessed almost instantaneously. Its main limitation is size and it needs to be supplemented either by file storage or by one of the other techniques mentioned in the question. A characteristic feature is that all the elements of memory are accessible by the processor in exactly the same time, irrespective of address. In early computers the memory was often considered to be part of the CPU, but these days it is considered as separate from the processor but, of course, distinct from the peripherals.

Paged store is one example of the organisation of memory into sections, or pages. This is normally achieved by considering the memory addresses to be sub-divided as, for example, the 6502 processor used in the BBC microcomputer, where the addresses refer to 256 pages of 256 bytes. Here the 8-bit address is divided into the high order four bits specifying the page and the low order four bits giving the location within the page, sometimes called a line. Taking a larger computer, the VAX-11 uses a 30-bit address with the most significant twenty-one bits giving the (virtual) page and the least significant nine bits specifying the byte within the 512-byte page.

The use of pages leads on to the technique of virtual memory, but with the pages in this case held on the backing store and read into memory as required. This enables the computer to regard part of its file store and all memory as a very large, possibly almost infinite, memory. One advantage of virtual storage to the programmer, particularly on a multi-user system, is that programs may be made less complex since memory limits can be ignored. One disadvantage is that, unless there is a very efficient and 'intelligent' paging algorithm, some programs may run very slowly since there will be a great deal of activity transferring data from memory to and from the backing store. If this was done without virtual memory, the program would be more complicated but the programmer would make it more efficient.

b) The main feature to be covered in an answer on autonomous transfers to a peripheral device is that a program initiates the transfer which is carried out independently of the main program and an interrupt is generated when the transfer is complete. This answer should also contain a reference to the description of interrupt handling as required by part c).

Double-buffering will be covered in Chapter 4, but essentially, it is a technique used with magnetic media such as tape or disc where, with reading for example, two successive blocks of data are held in memory in areas called buffers. The technique of autonomous peripheral transfers allows *reading* to one of the buffers to take place autonomously, or independently of the main processor, in parallel with *processing* the data in the second buffer.

c) An interrupt signal is a technique used to allow a computer to carry out more than one task, apparently, simultaneously. The interrupt signal is normally generated when either an autonomous process has been completed or an error or exception has occurred. On receipt of an interrupt signal the processor *interrupts* its present activity and is then in a position to process the interrupt or to decide which job has the highest priority. One type of *event* which generates interrupts includes the receipt of data from an input channel, which could be a keyboard or an on-line data-logger or a remote peripheral. A second example is the detection of an error in the system; a third example is the completion of some time interval limit on a process.

Question 10

Although primarily a question on interrupts, it is best to start by giving an explanation of the requirements of this system. There are no specific details of the actual experiment being monitored but we can expect that at regular, or irregular intervals a number of readings will be taken from the experiment, possibly 'pre-processed' by an analog/digital converter (see page 56). The data will be presented to the computer as input which can be regarded as no different to input from any other source. This data will have to be processed by the computer and then used for, possibly, three distinct functions:

1 To 'feedback' commands to the experiment.
2 To record the data on a file.
3 To provide a statistical analysis.

Ideally the system should be such that once set up and running there should be no need for a human operator to take any action. Data logging systems exist in many different forms and are used in a great variety of situations but for this question it must be assumed that the data must be processed almost immediately it is created. Some systems may have a large buffer which may allow data to be *queued up*, awaiting the attention of the computer, but this is not always feasible and, in particular, cannot be used when the computer is to use the data to control the experiment, e.g. to reduce power if some component registers strain or excessive load. One other aspect of data logging is that it is normally most important to have time as an input; in this context we say that the data is **time stamped**, i.e. as the data is recorded either the computer or the data logger adds to the readings a digital signal which gives the time since the start of the experiment.

As an example, consider the testing of the cables used at sea for towing, or for taking excessive strains in lifting gear. One way in which they are tested is to run a monitoring experiment where increasing loads are applied to a cable whilst a computer receives data from transducers measuring the load applied, the increase of length and the reduction in diameter. The computer may be required to shut off the experiment when the load reaches a critical value.

The three tasks mentioned above, plus a fourth, the actual receipt of the input data, may all be carried out simultaneously, but will have different priorities. The highest priority, for the reasons mentioned above, will be the input of data. Whatever other task is being processed will have to be interrupted to receive any new data sent from the experiment. Many computers have the ability to handle interrupts as part of their processor architecture so that the processor has the ability to carry out several tasks simultaneously, or to carry out a particular task until some 'event', for example data being received from an input channel or the completion of some time interval limit. The term **interrupt** is used and this feature makes use of special lines called interrupt lines in the control bus which carry signals generated by processes or peripherals when an **event** occurs. These signals are then detected by the control unit.

For the system required by the question, it may be assumed that statistical analysis of the data can take place and will be interrupted when input from a data channel is detected. The data will then be received by the program and written to the disc before control returns to the analysis. The order of priorities for the interrupt handler could be:

- Highest   data ready in the input channel.
- Medium   write data to the disc.
- Lowest   process the data.

Question 11

a)   i) The program counter, or sequence control register is used to store the machine address of the next instruction to be executed. When the instruction is a sequence change, as in one of the examples in this question, it is executed simply by modifying the contents of the sequence register to contain the address of the new instruction.

ii) The memory address register contains the address of the next memory cell to be used for a load or store instruction.

iii) The memory buffer register contains the data to be stored in a memory cell or, alternatively, is loaded with data retrieved from memory.

iv) The instruction register is used (when executing a machine language instruction) to contain a copy of the instruction currently being executed.

v) The accumulator is a register in the central processor used for intermediate storage in arithmetic calculations.

b)   The question assumes a simple computer with both the operation code and operand fields of each machine code instruction held in a single word. The operations carried out during the fetch–execute cycle can be broken down into the following steps:

FETCH
```
1  Examine program counter for address of next instruction to be obeyed.
2  Copy the instruction into the memory address register.
3  Copy operand into the memory address register.
4  Increment the program counter, to point to next instruction.
```

DECODE 5 Interpret the instruction.

EXECUTE
```
6  Obey the instruction.
   For a branch, the memory address register will be copied to the program counter.
   For an add instruction this might mean using the address in the memory address
   register to retrieve a byte from memory which is to be loaded into the memory buffer
   register then added to the contents of the accumulator.
7  Go back to step 1 and repeat.
```

c)   i) A logical shift moves data, typically left to right with the original rightmost bit *dropped* off the end and with a new high-order zero bit

so   10110001 shifts to 01011000

ii) An arithmetic shift works like a logical shift but leaves the leftmost (sign) bit untouched

so   10110001 shifts to 10011000

iii) A cyclic shift rotates the data so that the rightmost bit is re-inserted at the high
order end
so 10110001 shifts to 11011000

STUDENT ANSWERS WITH EXAMINER COMMENTS

Question 5

Describe the characteristics of RAM and ROM in a typical computer.

(Northern Ireland 1987)

> **❝This is a poor definition stating no more than is obvious from the name.❞**

RAM is random access memory it is the part of the processor which can
hold data for random access

ROM or Read Only Memory is a memory which can be read but not written

> **❝The definition is not strictly correct as random access is not really relevant in this context the only random element is that any element selected at random may be retrieved in the same unit of time.❞**

Question 6

List three *different* types of software commonly found in Read Only Memory (ROM).
In each case indicate the suitability, or otherwise, of using ROM.   (London 1988)

Three different types of software commonly found in Read Only Memory
(ROM) are:
  * the operating system
  * compilers
  * application programs

① The operating system needs to be in ROM so that the operator can be
given the correct instructions for using the computer.

② It is important to have in ROM, the compilers for languages such as
Fortran, Pascal and Cobol, otherwise all programs would have to be
written in machine code.

③ A third type of ROM would hold application programs like the company
payroll system.

① > **❝The operating system function is not one of giving instructions to the operator; it is only the basic system which is held in the memory, the other segments will be loaded from backing store as required.❞**

② > **❝Although Acorn produced a ROM compiler for PASCAL it is rare to implement compilers in this way and unknown for Fortran and Cobol, whose compilers are held in RAM due to their complexity.❞**

③ > **❝It is feasible to hold application programs in ROM but it is very rare apart from dedicated computer systems like POS devices; it is unlikely that a payroll system would be held in ROM.❞**

COMPUTER PERIPHERALS

GETTING STARTED

The term 'peripheral' was introduced and explained in Chapter 3 and the distinction between the central processor and peripheral was explained. The *peripheral* is any device which provides input or receives output from a computer system and the *central processor* is where the work is done, consisting of the main memory, the arithmetic unit and the control unit together with certain special registers.

Again it is assumed that all students will have access to a computer of some sort and should be able to relate the available peripherals to the three categories studied here. Even the very simplest home microcomputer has a keyboard providing input, a TV or monitor screen for output and a cassette recorder/player for file storage.

There are problems common to all these forms of input arising from the fact that whatever the device or technique used, the basic principle is that we have data in either *human-readable form*, like a sheet of writing, or in *machine-readable form*, like the barcode on a library book. Data needs to be converted into a digital signal to be understood by the computer. This digital signal will be coded in binary form using one of the codes to be described in Chapter 11. As the technology develops so we are able to get further removed from the crude coding of holes in cards or paper and to develop the facility to read characters and detect sounds.

Over the last few years of the 1980s most product packages incorporated barcodes, and supermarkets are gradually phasing out the keying in of prices at the checkout and implementing systems using readers for these barcodes. Humans have often yearned for the ability to converse with computers, either by speech or by handwriting. Although both are possible, they are, at present, limited, slow and expensive.

INPUT UNITS

OFF-LINE AUTOMATIC PREPARATION

ON-LINE INPUT SYSTEMS

OUTPUT DEVICES

DATA TRANSMISSION BETWEEN PERIPHERALS

ESSENTIAL PRINCIPLES

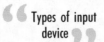
Types of peripheral device

There are a number of ways of classifying peripherals. For convenience in this chapter, they will be considered under their three main headings:

- Input peripherals
- Output peripherals
- File storage peripherals, with a fourth category
- Communications devices, also worthy of brief coverage.

In broader terms, peripherals can be considered in two groups:

a) Peripherals that act in some way as an extension to main memory.

b) Peripherals which transfer data to or from the outside world.

Examples of type a) are magnetic tape, disc and cassettes, and of type b) are printers, VDUs, keyboards and modems. Type a) devices always act in a *block* mode with no *individual* transfer of characters and will be the subject of the next chapter.

We shall look again at the input peripherals in the final part of this chapter, this time in the light of their role in the **capture** of data for an information system and consider the controls which may be applied to ensure that the data leaving the users in an organisation is the same as the data which finally arrives in the file store of the computer.

The emphasis at this level should always be on techniques or processing the data, the control of the data and specific applications. The mechanics of the devices, though quite interesting, are not so important and in any case change as new devices become available.

INPUT UNITS

In Chapter 3 it was stated that, in recent years, the keyboard has become the most common form of input, and has replaced the punched card and punched paper tape which had been the most widely used input peripherals techniques for the previous thirty years. This was a direct result of the introduction of the microcomputer and the growth of multi-access and real-time systems. It is interesting, historically, to remark that both these media date from the nineteenth century and were adapted for use by computers in the 1950s. For many years a succession of devices, notably key-to-tape and key-to-disc systems, were introduced and heralded as the replacements for cards and tape, but it was only an entirely new concept of computing, involving personal computers and VDU terminals, which saw their final demise. We can consider input devices under three main if arbitrary headings:

Types of input device

- Off-line keyboard data preparation
- Off-line automatic preparation
- On-line input systems

Some devices described here may be included under all three headings, according to the particular application considered. It is more important to understand the devices and their function, and to be aware of a range of appropriate applications, rather than to be too concerned about which is their most appropriate category.

Off-line keyboard data preparation is the traditional batch processing method, where data is entered from a keyboard by an operation which is solely for the purpose of transposing the data to some machine-readable form. When all the data has been prepared, the data is then read into the computer by a separate operation.

Off-line automatic preparation is similar to keyboard preparation but uses equipment which carries out the transcription automatically. For example, reading the magnetic ink characters from a batch of cheques and creating a file, reading data from a credit card and a point-of-sale terminal and creating a tape file. In these and many similar examples the file, as for keyboard preparation, can subsequently be read by the computer.

On-line input is the use of devices connected directly to the computer with a response to the input in real time. For example, the use of electronic mail from a computer terminal, the use of cashpoints terminals and the applications considered in Chapter 3 regarding process control and plant monitoring.

OFF-LINE KEYBOARD DATA PREPARATION

The traditional form of direct keyboard data preparation relied for many years on punched cards or punched paper tape, with data entered by an operation using a keyboard. This was carried out away from the computer and involved creating a file on some machine-readable form. This was referred to as **batch processing** and was, for many years, the only method available for processing data on the computer. Then things began to change. Firstly, the increased power of computers allowed multi-programming and multi-access, and secondly, the evolution of the microcomputer meant that the *idle time* of the machine no longer became so expensive. As a result of both these developments, computers or terminals could now be dedicated to **transaction processing** instead of *batch processing*.

The media which were used on the early computers, and indeed dominated computer input from 1950 until the late 1970s, were the punched card and the punched paper tape. Neither was designed originally for the computer; punched cards dating from the processing of the American census in 1890 and punched paper tape from the nineteenth-century telegraph industry. The most common form of punched card held eighty characters on a card which measured approximately 7½ inches by 3¼ inches. The characters are coded as holes punched in the twelve rows on the card; characters have one, two or three holes in a single column, making it a most inefficient code in terms of the size of the card and the reading speed.

The normal keyboard is a standard typewriter keyboard known as the 'QWERTY' keyboard because of the arrangement of keys in the top row. The data is entered onto the cards using a device called the card punch which normally has the 'QWERTY' keyboard. The early card punches had the keys connected directly to the drills so that each key depression punched a character directly onto the card. The modern card punches hold a complete card image, or more, in the 'memory' of the card punch, with the complete card being punched after all the data has been assembled. This can be done simultaneously with the keying of the data for the next card. These card punches allow corrections to be made by backspacing one or more columns and can implement a certain amount of data validation. The most common form of punched paper tape is the 8-track tape, using reels of tape one inch wide with characters coded with patterns of up to eight holes across the tape and contained in eight tracks along the length of the tape. It is worth noting that the code used on 8-track paper tape employed a 7-bit code plus a parity bit. This 7-bit code has been almost universally adopted as the ASCII code used internally in the memory and file store of computers.

> **The QWERTY keyboard**

The 'QWERTY' keyboard, mentioned above, has been adapted from the typewriter and was developed in the nineteenth century. It was designed to *slow up* the typists since early typewriters could not cope, mechanically, with the speeds of the operators. Thus, contrary to popular belief, the 'QWERTY' keyboard is *not* designed for efficiency and speed. Although a number of *better* designs have been developed, none has made a great impact. The alternatives include:

1 A **12-key keyboard**, used on early card punches. This had a rectangular keypad with four rows of three keys. Each character required several keys to be depressed simultaneously. This proved faster in operation but required extra operator training and is seldom seen now.

2 The **Maltron** keyboard. This was an entirely new layout, designed for efficiency and speed, with the keys divided into two, almost circular, sets arranged so that the operators hands have the minimum of movement. Although most people testing the system considered it an improvement, it has not proved popular and is very little used.

> **Alternatives to the QWERTY keyboard**

3 The **Microwriter** or **Quinkey** keyboard. This was designed with just five keys, one for each finger, plus one extra control key. It has many of the advantages of the 12-key keyboard, and was marketed as part of a cheap 4-user system operating on a BBC microcomputer to allow simple word processing. It was also marketed as a portable word processor, the Microwriter, but again has not been widely accepted, though undeniably a good keyboard system.

4 The **French equivalent of Prestel** uses home terminals with the letters of the alphabet set out in the sequence A B C D . . . Z. This is slow for large volumes of input but is the simplest for unskilled users.

Amongst the other keyboard input devices which have been used are key-to-tape systems, key-to-disc and key-to-floppy disc. These were all introduced at different points of time with the intention of replacing the punched card, but were outlasted by the punched card systems, mainly because of the amount of equipment already existing in organisations. All of these have now been superceded by the *on-line* input systems.

Key-to-tape systems use a keyboard to encode the data direct to magnetic tape and have special features to allow the data from several different tapes to be pooled or combined on a single tape for input to the main system. Key-to-disc uses a small multi-access minicomputer system to allow a number of operators simultaneously to enter data which can be validated by the processor before storing on a disc unit shared by all the operators. With key-to-disc, when all the data has been entered and verified for a particular application, the supervisor can issue a command which causes the data from all the individual operators to be copied to one medium, typically a magnetic tape, for input to the computer. Key-to-floppy disc, the most recent of the three, uses floppy discs instead of magnetic tape.

On many modern computer systems these methods have been replaced by a technique known as **direct data entry** (DDE). This can be implemented on any computer supporting multi-access and, effectively, implements key-to-disc input on the main computer itself. The data preparation operators log in to the computer using VDUs and enter the data to files on the backing store. After the verification operation there is no need to dump the files to another medium as they are already in the computer and are immediately available for the computer run.

OFF-LINE AUTOMATIC PREPARATION

The technique of off-line automatic preparation uses equipment to transcribe data automatically, creating a file which, as for keyboard preparation, can subsequently be read by the computer. Although a number of examples are given, it is not possible to give a complete list because new techniques are being developed all the time. Many of the devices mentioned under on-line input can be adapted for off-line preparation.

One of the main families of devices are those which read printed marks or characters and include the following:

- OMR   Optical mark recognition
- OCR   Optical character recognition
- MICR   Magnetic ink character recognition
- Bar code readers, including laser readers

Devices for off-line automatic preparation

Another family includes readers for the various types of card such as:

- punched cards
- kimball tags
- magnetic stripe coded plastic cards
- bar coded plastic cards

An increasing number of devices come under the heading of

- portable keyboard systems

The mechanics and detailed operation of these devices are not important, but we do need to study appropriate applications for each.

Optical mark reading (OMR) is the simplest of these techniques, using an optical mark reader which cannot read shapes but can detect black marks on white paper. One of the most familiar applications of mark readers is to read the answers to multiple-choice examination papers where the candidates answer each question by making a mark in a column corresponding to the chosen alternative answer; the answer sheets can then be read and marked by a computer. A similar system is used by shops for re-ordering stock by marking the quantities required on a pre-printed form.

Applications of the various devices

Optical character readers (OCRs) are devices designed to read text direct from the source document. Ideally they should read handwritten documents, but the most common use is in the reading of printed text generated from either a typewriter or a computer printer. OCR often uses **turnaround** documents where, for example, mail order companies or football pools firms use devices to read the code numbers of their clients from the returned forms and then use this data to maintain files of active customers.

Magnetic ink character readers (MICRs) are able to read the characters made up of thin lines which appear at the foot of cheques printed in an ink which is magnetisable. The readers operate by exposing the ink to a magnetic field and then the characters can be interpreted by detecting the magnetism of the ink. Batches of cheques are first encoded by a keyboard operator transcribing the amount in *magnetic ink* on the bottom of each cheque. The cheques can be processed automatically since the MICR device can read the amount, together with the account number and cheque number, and make the data available for processing.

Bar code readers are able to read the patterns of lines, called bar codes, which are familiar to many library borrowers. These appear in the front of books and are encoded on the plastic library card held by the borrower. When a book is loaned, a pen, called a light-pen, is wiped across the code on the borrower's card and then across the code on the book. The recording device then records the reference number of the borrower and the book number, and the librarian enters a further code to indicate whether it is a loan, a return or a renewal. This device can also be used *on-line* and, because of the technology becoming commonly used in the reading, is sometimes referred to as a **laser reader**. The device need not be expensive, and it is possible to purchase a simple light-pen which acts as a bar code reader for the BBC microcomputer for around £50. A growth industry in this area is the use of bar codes on virtually every product sold in shops so that readers in supermarkets can scan these bar codes at the checkout, creating bills more quickly, and with more detail, thereby making data available for stock movement, stock control and automatic re-order systems.

An earlier, cruder, system, originally widely used in shoe and clothing shops, was based on the use of **punched cards** as turnaround documents. For example, in the shoe trade cards can be placed in the boxes with the pairs of shoes and when the shoes are sold, the cards are returned to the supplier. The tags can be read by an off-line device and used to prepare a magnetic tape for input to the main computer run which can replenish the stock and also analyse sales over the whole country. Another application of punched cards going into the 1990s is in one of the major banks where branches hold a punched card with each cheque book stocked for customers. When a book is issued to a customer, the card is despatched to the computer centre and the reading of the batch of cards stimulates the printing of a new book.

A similar medium often seen in shops is the **Kimball tag**. This is also used by many clothing and shoe manufacturers and is attached to each garment or placed in its box. As with the punched card, when the item is sold, the tag is placed in the cash register. At the end of the day, all the tags are posted off to the supplier who then has a record of what has been sold and, as for the punched card, is able to implement an automatic re-order system to replenish stock. This is also particularly appropriate to stores with multiple branches who can carry out all the stock ordering centrally from the returned tags as well as being able to study sensitive fashion trends on a daily basis.

A number of systems exist for gathering input from various types of **plastic card**. One of the first examples was the credit card, embossed with details of the customers name and account number. This is used with a simple machine, embossed with details of the business, to print the details onto small multipart forms separated by carbon paper. These can be seen in many shops, restaurants and garages. The newer type of credit card is an example of a **magnetic stripe coded plastic card** which has a small magnetic stripe on the reverse. This can contain the account number, expiry date, and any other data decided on by the system designer. These cards can be read by a new type of credit card system used extensively in garages and increasingly in shops, where the magnetic stripe on the card is read and often combined with other data captured electronically, such as the cost of the fuel from a pump or the product data from a bar code reader. This same technology is used on phone cards, on the charge cards used to control the use of photocopying systems and also on rail tickets. In all these applications, data is written back to the card so that the number of phone (or other) units remaining can be decreased after each call (or use). **Bar coded plastic cards** were mentioned above as containing the details of library borrowers and could equally be applied to other systems.

Portable keyboard systems have evolved from the development of portable computers and may be considered as computers dedicated to a simple task with a program held in ROM. The devices are battery driven, and data can be entered from a keyboard and held originally on a magnetic tape cassette. But with the new technology, RAM is used, and when data capture is complete the device can be connected to the main computer, possibly by telephone link, and another program then transmits the data to the computer. One application of this is stocktaking in a shop, where the device may also incorporate a bar code reader; another application involves the use of such systems by meter readers in the gas and electricity services.

On-line input, as explained in Chapter 2, is the use of devices connected directly to the computer with a response to the input in real time. The most common device used in this context is the visual display unit (VDU) which has replaced the teletypewriter printing terminal. Modern microcomputer systems have great flexibility in VDU displays, including the use of graphics, to display a form or grid on the screen, and can also use colour and other special effects. However, there are a number of other devices which can be attached to a computer terminal, with the most important being the **mouse**. This is a small device used on the desk connected to the computer by a simple wire; it fits under the hand and normally has a roller ball underneath and perhaps three buttons on the top. This is used on the desk by being moved in four directions, with the movement being detected as equivalent to the four arrow keys on the keyboard. The buttons on the mouse can be programmed to be equivalent to three specific keys such as <return> <escape> and <copy>. The mouse is integral to most business microcomputers and is broadly similar to the joysticks or games paddles used on home microcomputers.

Some computers use touch sensitive screens where the user provides input by actually touching an area of the screen to select a required option which is frequently displayed as a small picture which is called an **icon**. The use of icons may be combined with the mouse to implement the most popular system for 16-bit microcomputers, the so-called **WIMP** environment, standing for *W*indows, *I*cons, *M*ouse, *P*ull-down menu (or *P*ointer).

Other examples of on-line input described elsewhere in the book include:

- Point of sale terminals
- Data logging devices including analogue to digital conversions
- The preparation of data as a by-product of processes

We may also include among the available on-line devices most of those described under the heading 'off-line' since, though it is usually more efficient and faster to use them in an off-line mode, they can be used on-line in appropriate applications. Graphical input can be provided by a **digitiser** or **scanner** device which can scan a picture, store it in a digital form in the computer and give an appropriate screen display. This picture can be tidied up by drawing lines or shading patterns with a mouse or with another type of light-pen which can, in effect, draw on the screen by passing over its surface. This is particularly useful in computer aided design (CAD) systems.

It is worth mentioning the use of a microcomputer as a terminal to larger systems. This allows some of the checking and editing of data to be carried out using a program within the microcomputer and is an example of the use of an **intelligent terminal**. Such an intelligent terminal could also have options to *spool* the computer output to a floppy disc or to transmit data from a disc file so that the time on-line is minimised. This is particularly appropriate in on-line enquiry systems such as TTNS (the on-line educational database system used in many schools) and commercial databases such as the British Library 'Blaise' system. In these applications a word processor can be used off-line to prepare the input and to edit the output from the computer.

One type of question which may appear in an examination is 'Give two input and two output devices you would expect to find in a computerised public lending library and state why each is appropriate to the system'. An answer could refer to the bar code for the borrower reference and book accession number and a keyboard for the input of requests to search for books or the entry of details of new books purchased. An alternative could refer to a bar code reader for loans and a video display terminal for enquiries and searches.

Verification

> 66 Verification is a key operation in eliminating errors 99

As we saw earlier, off-line keyboard entry introduces an extra step of transcribing the data from the source documents to the input media which is normally carried out by data preparation operators. These individuals will have no knowledge of the data and are trained to be very accurate in their work and so make only a small number of errors; but any one of these could cause major inaccuracies in the information produced by the system. Therefore an operation, called **verification**, is introduced in an attempt to eliminate these errors.

As a definition, verification is where data, input to any computer system, is re-entered by a second independent operator for machine comparison with the initial entry. It was developed initially for use with punched card data preparation systems, but has been adapted for use with all keyboard entry systems. With the key-to-disc system, for example, the data preparation operator keys in the data as specified on the source documents and it is then stored away on a file. The second operator is able to load the same file and re-enters the data in exactly the same form. The processor checks the keying, character by character, and reports any discrepancies for action to be taken by the operator, who may accept either version or re-type the character a third time.

It is possible to program the device to limit verification to a restricted set of the data fields since verification of descriptive data, such as customer name, as opposed to numeric fields, might be useful but may prove too expensive. For this reason, many computer programs show inaccuracies in names and addresses. It is important to remember that verification has no check on wrongly entered data due to badly written entries. Many people assume, wrongly, that any verified data must be totally accurate.

OUTPUT DEVICES

The two most common **output devices** on computer systems are print and video display. The mainframe and minicomputers tend to use *fast lineprinters*, printing 500 to 1,000 lines per minute. Microcomputers and computer terminals use the slower and cheaper *character printers* which include dot matrix printers. These form characters by the impact of an array of pins, typically 9×9, and can operate at speeds from fifty to 500 characters per second. Daisy wheel printers operate at speeds of fifteen to 200 characters per second, with characters on a revolving print wheel also struck against a ribbon. Most business applications tend to favour the *laser printer*, a device which became cheaper and cheaper through the latter part of the 1980s, dropping from £100,000 to £2,000. In this device complete pages are assembled by a processor, effectively a computer, within the printer and then the page is printed, with quality equivalent to a good photocopier. Laser printers can produce characters from a wide variety of print fonts and with great flexibility for graphics.

Video display devices can display text, graphics or both, and can be in colour or monochrome. Alternative output devices include graph plotters (though laser printers have taken over many of these applications) and also speech synthesis, which is much easier than speech recognition. There are programs available on several computers, including the Apple Macintosh, which can take text files and speak the words through a small loudspeaker on the terminal.

File storage

The maximum size of memory is always limited in terms of capacity. In the early computers the reason was cost, as 1K of magnetic core memory would cost about £1,000; microprocessor technology has now reduced this cost 1,000 times to less than £1 for 1K. Another constraint, more important now and which was introduced in Chapter 3, is that the number of words of memory which can be addressed is limited by the instruction format. We can explain this in terms of the amount of data which can be seen on an office desk. Just as a clerk needs to use a filing cabinet for surplus data, so the computer needs an additional store called a file store. Examples of file storage media, to be described in the next chapter, are magnetic tape, magnetic disc and floppy disc.

DATA TRANSMISSION BETWEEN PERIPHERALS

It is worth mentioning the *transmission* of data between the processor and peripherals as an important aspect of peripheral handling. In Chapter 3 it was said that a common means of storing characters in the memory is to use a word of eight bits, called a byte. Later in Chapter 11, we shall look in more detail at the coding of data as binary numbers, but the idea of a byte is sufficient for the moment to allow us to look at *serial* and *parallel* transmission of data. A good application of data transmission is the use of printers where, in serial transmission, there is effectively a single wire through which data is transmitted (though often four more for control signals) and the characters are transmitted one bit at a time. In parallel transmission there would be eight wires in parallel, with each of the eight bits making up a byte being transmitted down a separate wire.

Taking the BBC microcomputer as an example, we can look underneath the machine at the parallel printer port which has a 26-pin connector, though only ten are used; eight for data and two for control. The parallel connector is on the rear of the keyboard and has five pins, one for data and four for control. The extra pins in both serial and parallel ports are used to transmit signals, known as *flags*, which can be set to one or zero according to whether the relevant channel is ready or not to receive a signal.

Buffers

It is worth recalling the application of interrupts in the *autonomous transfers* of data using DMA. An alternative to autonomous transfers is the use of **buffers** where the data is read into an intermediate storage array within memory which is set aside for that peripheral. Some computer systems use a *double buffer* system where data can be processed from one buffer whilst further data is being transferred in or out of the other buffer.

Data communication

The use of on-line terminals demands some means of connecting the terminal to the computer. Possibly a simple wire for connections up to a few hundred metres within the same building or, for some systems, a fibre-optic cable for distances up to several thousand metres. Transmission over longer distances requires special equipment. A common form of data transmission for remote users is the use of the public and private telephone networks.

Telephone networks are designed to transmit sounds, which are *analogue* signals, whereas computers require (and most terminals generate) *digital* signals. It is therefore necessary to use devices called **modems** which are specialised analogue/digital converters. There has to be one modem connected between the terminal and the telephone link and another at the receiving end between the telephone and the computer. In some systems there is a special device called a **multiplexor** which can receive signals from a number of lines simultaneously, decode them into the individual enquiries and transmit the relevant responses.

With any transmission medium there can be loss of data, or the introduction of errors, between the transmitting and receiving modems and this data loss is likely to be greater, the faster the speed of transmission. The errors can be minimised by keeping the transmission rate within the capabilities of the medium.

There are two common modes of transmission: simplex and duplex, **simplex** means that data is transmitted in one direction only, whilst the **duplex** mode implements transmission in both directions simultaneously. There is another sub-division of the duplex mode into **full-duplex** and **half-duplex**, with half-duplex allowing transmission in both directions, but one after another as opposed to simultaneously. In half-duplex, at the end of each message there is a special signal which says, rather like a radio conversation, the equivalent of 'over and out' and then reverses the line to receive the response. The special codes which control the direction, check for the start and end of the message, and provide a simple check for errors, are referred to as the **protocol** of the system.

The maximum speed safely attainable on the public network is 300 bits per second duplex, often described as 300/300. A popular alternative is 1200/75 where the computer transmits at 1,200 bits per second but the terminal, normally some form of keyboard, transmits at seventy-five bits per second; the Prestel service operates at 1200/75. Speeds may be increased by the use of *dedicated private lines* which may allow 2400/2400, or by *special intelligent terminals* over the public network at 1200/1200. Modems allow remote access over very large distances and it has been shown that it is possible to get access to computers in other countries from public phone booths using a portable type of modem called an **acoustic coupler**. These are much used by journalists, and connect directly to the telephone handset rather than needing a special connection into the telephone socket.

Data capture

This is the first step in any information system and refers to the collection, capture and recording of the data which is to be input to the system. There are a number of topics which need to be studied under this heading including the equipment, described earlier in the chapter, the sources and detection of error by data entry validation and verification and the design of the man—machine dialogue and screen formatting for interactive systems.

EXAMINATION QUESTIONS

SHORT QUESTIONS

Question 1
Describe briefly an application for which a light-pen would be a suitable input device.

(London 1988)

Question 2
What methods of data capture or collection would you recommend as input to computer systems in each of the following situations:
a) Stock taking in a supermarket;
b) Recording the time of arrival and departure of employees;
c) Extracting money from a bank automatic cash dispenser?

Describe briefly the main features of each device you have mentioned.   (London 1988)

Question 3
A national opinion research organisation intends to distribute questionnaires to about 10,000 households. The recipients are to be asked to put their views on each of thirty statements into one of the five categories shown below:

> Strongly agree
>
> Agree
>
> Not sure
>
> Disagree
>
> Strongly disagree

Completed questionnaires are posted back to the research organisation.
a) Describe two different methods by which this data could be entered into the computer. Comment on the relative merits of each.
b) Select one of your methods in a) above and design the form which you would recommend the research organisation to use if it adopted your chosen method of entry.

(Cambridge 1988)

Question 4
Outline a method of employing double buffering for processing a serial file as input.

(AEB 1988)

Question 5
State **one** advantage and **one** disadvantage of using a dot matrix printer rather than a daisywheel printer. Give **two** reasons why many dot matrix printers contain a memory.

(AEB 1989)

LONGER QUESTIONS

Question 6

a) You have been delegated the task of selecting a new printer from a range of different options currently on the market. The machine has to serve a small network of microcomputers in your office. Software used includes a word processing package, database, spreadsheet and accounting packages. Assuming that cost is not a major constraint, list the features of the printers which you would investigate in your evaluation, and outline the criteria which you would use to make your selection.

(8)

b) Justify a choice of printer-type for the system as described, written as a report conclusion.

(2)

c) If it were envisaged that the network would be expanded in the foreseeable future, and that desk top publishing would be introduced as a further application, what differences could this produce in the conclusions of your report?   *(3)*

(London AS specimen)

Question 7

A graphic designer wishes to use a computer to assist in the design of regular patterns. These patterns may be used for tiling a floor, or for wallpaper or fabric designs.
a) Discuss suitable forms of communication between the user and the system, including examples of the different kinds of data and the devices used.
b) Describe the types of operation that the graphic designer could expect the computer system to perform.
c) Explain why this kind of system would normally be based on a standard software package. (Cambridge 1989)

Question 8

a) Give two examples of peripheral devices that are linked to a computer in each of the following situations:
    i) the retail trade
    ii) the office
b) Comment on the recent developments in speech recognition and speech synthesis and discuss a possible application of each.
c) Outline three methods of detecting errors in data capture. (Welsh 1984)

OUTLINE ANSWERS

SHORT QUESTIONS

Question 1

Light-pens are widely used in libraries to provide input concerning issues and returns. Each book has a bar code pasted onto part of the cover, typically inside the front cover, encoded with the accession number of the book. Each borrower has a plastic card containing a bar code giving the borrower's personal identity code. When a book is issued, or returned, the light-pen is passed over the code within the book and also over the code contained on the borrower's card; the library assistant keys in a code which indicates issue or return.

Question 2

a) For stock taking in a supermarket, the method of data capture recommended as input to the computer system is the use of a portable device incorporating a bar code reader. The stock-taking assistant would pass the light-pen over a bar code encoded on the shelf label and would then, after counting, key in the stock in hand using a small numeric keypad contained in the device. The data will be held within the memory of the device (or on an integral tape cassette) and after completing the stocktake, the device will be connected to the computer, possibly by a remote link. Alternatively the cassette will be sent to the computer centre for processing.
b) The recording of the time of arrival and departure of employees can be carried out in a number of ways. Essentially three pieces of data are required; the employee reference number, the time, and an indicator of whether it is an arrival or departure. There are a number of such time clocks which may be used by employees as they enter or leave their place of work. The data may then, at the end of the week, be entered into the computer using a batch processing run by key-to-disc or direct data entry.
c) The extraction of money from a bank automatic cash dispenser is captured by reading the account details from a magnetic stripe contained on a plastic card. The card is presented to the dispenser which then requests the personal identification number (PIN) from the customer, which is keyed in, followed by the sum required.

Question 3

a) Two different methods by which this data could be entered into the computer are keying in data from a form completed by the subjects, and the direct reading of documents by optical character recognition.

Keying in of data does not need special equipment in the nature of a document reader but requires the employment of operators, both for initial entry and for verification.

OCR is less costly on staff but is vulnerable to error if the subjects have creased or damaged forms or have used pens or pencils which make marks that cannot be detected by the optical reader.

b)　Fig. 4.1 shows a sample of the type that could be used for keyboard data entry.

Examination survey	strongly disagree	disagree	not sure	agree	strongly agree
1　This examination paper is easy!					
2　The questions are readable!					

Fig. 4.1 Examination survey

Question 4

A buffer is an array of memory used as intermediate storage to aid the transfer of data between the central processing unit and a peripheral device. Its role in input is to provide an area where a number of characters can be read or accumulated in memory with a single read statement, and then extracted one at a time as required. In the case of magnetic disc, for example, it would not be feasible to read each character from disc individually, so a complete block or sector, typically 256 characters, is read into a buffer and then the characters are 'read' by moving them one at a time from the buffer.

Two buffers are often preferable to one, particularly with access to files, so that data can be processed from one buffer whilst further data is being transferred in or out of the other buffer. This is very commonly used for both magnetic tape and disc systems on mainframe computers, since the time to access data in memory is literally thousands of times faster than retrieving data from disc.

Question 5

One advantage of using a dot matrix printer rather than a daisywheel printer is that it can produce graphics and a variety of print styles on the same document.

One disadvantage of using a dot matrix printer rather than a daisywheel printer is that for most models the quality is inferior and not even comparable, unless very slow speeds are employed.

Dot matrix printers contain a memory which can act as a buffer so that, say, 8K of print can be held in the buffer and printed independently of the computer which can then be used for other tasks. This not only speeds up printing but allows graphics to be assembled.

LONGER QUESTIONS

Question 6

a)　The features to be investigated in the evaluation of printers are:
1　**Print quality**, for example the print from dot matrix printers varies with the number of pins and even the best are inferior to laser printers.
2　**Character formation**, whether made from dots as in a matrix printer, or full characters as with a daisywheel or laser printer.
3　**Multi-part**, i.e. whether several copies can be printed at once, as with an impact printer.
4　**Fonts** or type style; early computer users were satisfied with any quality whatsoever, but the advances into areas such as word processing and desk top publishing have stimulated a demand for varying type faces or fonts within the same document.
5　**Letter quality**, i.e. whether the quality is equivalent or superior to that of a good typewriter and so acceptable for the word processing of mail. Some printers have a choice of two print modes, draft quality and letter quality.
6　**Speed**, in terms of characters per second.
7　**Graphics** capabilities.
8　**Flexibility**; for example is it suitable for one task only, such as good letter quality but no graphics, as with daisywheel printers, or good graphics but slow speed and indifferent letter quality, as with some dot matrix printers.

9 **Sheet feeding** in terms of single sheets, friction feed or sprocket feed.

10 **Capital cost** or what it costs to buy

11 **Running cost** or what it costs in ribbons, print toner, special stationery and maintenance.

12 **Compatibility** with standard packages; many programs support a range of printers by generating the correct control characters for fonts, features like italics and underline, and for graphics.

13 **Robustness**; some very cheap printers are ideal at home but would not last very long in an office.

14 **Reputation of the manufacturer** as a supplier of printers. At one time schools were all advised to buy a *British* printer from a manufacturer who had never made such a model before, instead of imported *named* models. Several of these caught fire in normal use!

b) Bearing in mind that the software used includes a word processing package, database, spreadsheet and accounting packages, and that cost is not a major constraint, the printer to serve a small network of microcomputers in an office would be a *high quality dot matrix printer*. It produces a good letter quality at medium speed and can produce several fonts, as well as being capable of both text and graphics.

c) If the network were to expand so that desk top publishing was introduced as a further application, then the additional expense of a *laser printer* with a 'post-fix' processor would be justified. It produces the best quality at high speed and can produce multiple fonts and features, as well as mixing text and graphics.

Question 7

a) Suitable forms of man/machine communication exist for a graphic designer using a computer to assist in the design of regular patterns. For tiling a floor, or for wallpaper or fabric designs, include a mouse, a keyboard and an optical scanner. The *mouse* could be used for freehand drawing, selecting designs from a palette and moving elements around the screen. The *keyboard* would be used to support the mouse where textual input is required, at the very least for giving a file name for saving a design. The *scanner* would be used to read a design from paper, which could then be edited on the screen using the mouse.

b) Some types of operation that the graphic designer could expect the computer system to perform were outlined in part a). However, specific to the design of regular patterns there would be features to select sections of a design using 'cut and paste' facilities and the ability to rotate and invert these sections.

c) This kind of system would normally be based on a standard software package because few users have the ability (or time) to write one, certainly not to the level of the standard packages. Furthermore, the demand for graphics design packages is so great that they can be sold in large quantities and so become relatively cheap.

Question 8

a) i) Laser readers for bar codes are increasingly used in the retail trade to identify goods at the point of sale. But the keyboard is still the most common device and many medium and large organisations use cash registers connected to a computer with the ability to retrieve the price and description of goods from a code number entered by the sales assistant.

Another medium often seen in shops is the Kimball tag, used by many clothing and shoe manufacturers with one attached to each garment. On completing a sale the tag is placed in the cash register and at the end of the day all the tags are posted off to the supplier who then has a record of what has been sold and is able to implement an automatic re-order system to replenish stock.

ii) Two examples of peripheral devices that are linked to a computer in an office are a keyboard and mouse for input, and a printer for tabulating reports.

b) It could be that speech recognition will be the future development which will make the greatest impact on computer applications, but this presents many more practical problems than the recognition of handwriting. Current systems are able to cope with sounds of varying pitch and quality and can be *customised* to recognise command words from an individual. An important application in this area is to give disabled people the ability to control equipment. Even the severely disabled with limited speech can get the machine to respond to grunts or, in extreme cases, the exhalation of breath.

Speech synthesis provides a lesser problem and is much further advanced, even being implemented on domestic microcomputers. Two possible applications are the ability to give instructions and to report errors verbally to an operator and, in primary education, to speak words for a spelling tuition program.

c) (Note that the material for this part is covered in the next chapter).

Three methods of detecting errors in data capture are:

i) Clerical checks – controls

ii) Data preparation checks – verification

iii) Software checks – validation

i) Clerical checks are procedures initiated by the user department to ensure that no records are lost, duplicated or inserted between the user department and the file store of the computer. The most common technique is the use of control totals where the source documents are accumulated in batches of an appropriate size. Some numeric data item which occurs in each record is designated as being for control purposes, and is totalled for all the items before being input to the computer. Each batch is given a serial number, called the batch number, which is transcribed on each input record, and the control total for the batch is recorded on a control slip which accompanies the batch. When the data is read by the computer, the batch totals can then be re-calculated by the input program. Any differences in the totals are displayed to warn that corrections are required.

ii) The most common data preparation check is verification where data, input to the computer system, is re-entered by a second independent operator for machine comparison with the initial entry.

iii) Perhaps the most common and important software check is the use of a *check digit* which is a mathematical method of checking numeric code numbers used with important code numbers (such as an employee number in a payroll system) which would cause difficulties if quoted wrongly.

5

DATA VALIDATION AND ERROR DETECTION

CLERICAL CHECKS

DATA PREPARATION CHECKS

SOFTWARE CHECKS

CHECK DIGIT VERIFICATION

DATA TRANSMISSION CHECKS

FAULT TOLERANCE

GETTING STARTED

Peripherals were studied in detail in Chapter 4 but there is one particular problem associated with input peripherals. It is that of ensuring that the data provided by the user is identical with that which is written to the file store of the computer, and which later appears on the output from the system. In this chapter we shall look at the validation and control procedures which may be incorporated in a data processing system, including validation, verification, the use of check digits, hash and control totals, type and range checking.

The five main groupings of these checks are:

- Clerical checks – off the computer
- Data preparation checks
- Software checks
- Data transmission checks
- Hardware checks

ESSENTIAL PRINCIPLES

CLERICAL CHECKS

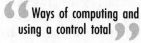

Useful clerical checks

These are procedures instituted by the user to ensure that no data is lost, duplicated or inserted into the input between the user and the file store of the computer. In some cases these checks can also provide a limited control against certain fields being corrupted. The main techniques in this area are:

- Document count
- Line count
- Sequence check
- Control totals
- Hash totals

Document count

Document count is probably the simplest check which can be applied to data and is a simple count of the documents or records entering, leaving or being processed by the system. It is sometimes carried out on the whole file, but more usually there is a subdivision of the documents or file into smaller batches to make it easier to locate any errors. A common technique is for each program to tabulate at the end of the run a simple statement of the number of records read, processed, deleted, written and printed.

Line count

A line count is an extension of the document count, where the number of lines on the source documents is counted. This is useful when each line on a document corresponds to a transaction or a record.

Sequence check

A sequence check is where all the source, or output, documents are numbered in sequence and the computer checks that each number occurs once and once only. In the ordering systems used in many organisations, including most schools, the order book has numbered forms. The goods are only paid for on quoting the number and there will be only one payment for each order number.

Control totals

The processing of control totals is a further extension of the document count. In this case it includes a **control total** which is computed and used as follows:

- The source documents are accumulated in batches of a suitable size, as large as possible but designed, from past experience, to have only a small chance of more than one error per batch.

- Some numeric data field which occurs in each record is designated as being for control purposes (a **control field**) and is totalled for all the items before being input to the computer. In a payroll this might be the total hours worked or, for an accounting system, the total amount of the transactions.

- Each batch is given a unique number, called the **batch number**, and this number is included as a field on each input record.

Ways of computing and using a control total

- The control total for the batch is recorded on a control slip which is processed along with the batch.

- A computer input record can be prepared from the control slips containing the batch number and batch control total.

- When the data is read by the computer, the batch totals are computed by the input program by adding up the values of the control fields on each input record. When all the records have been read, this total can be compared with the control totals read from the control slips.

- Any differences in these totals can be displayed and there may be a program option to tabulate all the batches which do not balance.

- All of the batch totals will be printed out for checking and will be kept and filed by the control clerks.

■ If there is only one error in a batch, the difference between the two totals should indicate which record has the error; in other cases it may be necessary to check through and compare the documents with the tabulation.

Hash totals

Another alternative is a non-numeric or 'inconsistent' item for the batch total. This does not give any control on quantity but does provide an easy identification of the error and is called a **hash total**. One example is the use of a product reference number of a date or simply a numeric item, such as quantity issued; a hash total applied to a stock control system might take the form of adding kilograms to cubic metres to units issued. Although the actual total may not have a physical interpretation it is nonetheless valid for control purposes.

The hash total can also be applied as an alphabetic item with each character being treated as its numeric equivalent. This can also provide an easy identification of any missing item. Hash totals can also be applied to on-line data entry systems where all the important items in an input record are added, and this hash total total is input as an extra item to check the validity of the whole record.

DATA PREPARATION CHECKS

The most common data preparation check is *verification*, which was described at length in the previous chapter. This is where data, input to the computer system, is re-entered by a second independent operator for machine comparison with the initial entry. Another important technique is the use of **check digits** (see p.65). This is a mathematical method of checking numeric code numbers used with important codes such as bank and building society account numbers which would cause difficulties if misquoted. These numbers will usually have an extra digit, called a check digit, added to the end of the number. Another example is the ISBN number allocated to every published book, providing a unique number for ordering and cataloguing. Yet another example is the VAT reference numbers allocated to each registered business.

Early electronic card punches and most electronic data entry systems have a programmable feature permitting the operator to enter the complete code number in the normal manner. If the system detects that the check digit appears to be wrong, a warning is given in the same manner as for any other verification errors.

Check digits themselves are not completely foolproof. If the number is obtained from a wrong source, is fraudulently quoted or simply read from the wrong line in a catalogue, it may be accepted as valid and the error will go undetected until the wrong account is credited or the wrong goods are delivered.

SOFTWARE CHECKS

The first procedure or the first program in any computer system should test the validity of the data. Such procedures, built into the program, are a vital part of on-line data capture systems. There is a lot in common between the validation of a complete file and the facilities available to test the individual records in an on-line data preparation system. Each field is checked against certain rules as it is keyed in and the operator has, instantly, the opportunity to over-rule, correct or amend any detected errors.

Validation may be carried out at two levels; firstly, the validation of individual records and secondly, as described above with the use of control totals and batch totals, checking the totality of the information submitted.

Validation of individual records is where each data item is examined by the program and checks are made on the data entered. The checks will have been devised and specified by the person who designed the program, probably the systems analyst, and will include some of the following:

■ Format checks
■ Range or limit check
■ Consistency
■ Sequence
■ Check digit

Format checks

These examine whether the format of the data conforms to that specified in the systems design, for example, numeric or alphabetic. In a particular program, the number of hours worked would have to be numeric, but a code letter would have to be alphabetic.

Range or limit check

This is a check to ensure that the data in a particular field lies within a given range, for example the month in a date must lie between one and twelve.

Consistency

Ways of validating individual records

Where two fields are linked in some way it is possible in some cases to check that the data entered in one field is consistent with that entered in the other. For example, if the month of a date is four, the day must be less than thirty-one.

Sequence

In some applications it is vital that the data is entered in a particular sequence; perhaps there are several divisions and data has to be submitted for each division in ascending sequence. There may then be a record number contained in one of the fields. In other applications it might presume that the data has already been sorted.

Check digit

This term was introduced under *data preparation* (see above) and is described in the next section.

CHECK DIGIT VERIFICATION

A **check digit** is a mathematical method of checking code numbers, in particular numeric codes. It ensures that the digits of a reference number satisfy some arithmetic relationship. It is best explained by looking step-by-step, at the procedure for a particular numeric field.

i) A set of numbers, called **weights**, is defined, one for each digit position.

ii) Each digit in the numeric field is designated as the **check digit** and the total of these products is accumulated.

iii) One or more of the digits in the field is designated as the **check digit** and computed for the purpose of making the weighted sum of the products divisible by a specified prime number, usually eleven.

iv) Every time a reference number is input to the system, the complete code number is entered, including the check digit, and the calculation described above is carried out to prove the number valid.

This system will check against the accidental mis-typing of a code number or the errors in transcribing onto the source document, but it has no control on the complete misquoting of a valid number. For example, someone quoting their father's bank account number instead of their own.

AN EXAMPLE OF THE USE OF A CHECK DIGIT

A five-digit number, 23496 is to have a check digit appended using weights 1 2 4 8 5 10 modulus 11.

We compute the sum of the products of weights:

$$1 \times 2 + 2 \times 3 + 4 \times 4 + 8 \times 9 + 5 \times 6$$

$$= \quad 2 \quad + \quad 6 \quad + \quad 16 \quad + \quad 72 \quad + \quad 30$$

$$= \quad \underline{126}$$

We append a check digit **n** to the field and, since it will have a weight 10, we require,

$$126 + 10n$$

to be a multiple of 11.

If we take n = 5, then $126 + 50 = 176 = 16 \times 11$ and the complete, valid code number is

$$\underline{234965}$$

If the code number 234965 were to be misquoted as 234956 the calculation would be:

$$1 \times 2 + 2 \times 3 + 4 \times 4 + 8 \times 9 + 5 \times 5 + 10 \times 6$$

$$= \quad 2 \quad + \quad 6 \quad + \quad 16 \quad + \quad 72 \quad + \quad 25 \quad + \quad 60$$

$$= \quad \underline{181}$$

dividing by 11 we have $181 = 16 \times 11 + 5$ and the check fails.

This demonstrates quite effectively how check digits detect a simple transposition error.

The following categories of error may occur in the recording of numeric data:

i) Transcription — e.g. 3 for 8

ii) Transposition — 234956 for 234965 as above

iii) Omission — 23965 for 234965

iv) Commission — 2345965

v) Random — no pattern

Thus the check digit system is ideal when codes are used in isolation from a catalogue or list and a suitable choice of weights will guard against 100% of the simple errors of types i) to iv) above.

On some occasions the computed valid check digit turns out to be 10 and will not fit into a single digit position. What happens then? There are a number of possibilities which have been tried, including:

■ Avoiding such numbers, which means that code numbers have to be issued with these exclusions in mind. This is often seen in banks and building societies where new account numbers are issued from a list with valid check digits 0–9.

Using the check digit for verification

■ Using another symbol like X or A. This can cause problems in some programming languages since it is mixing letters with numbers.

■ Using zero again; but this is dangerous, since zero is then used for 0 and 10 and can lead to failure to detect some errors.

■ Allowing an extra digit; in this case it would be better to go over to a two-digit check digit system and use modulus ninety-seven, that is divide the number of the products by ninety-seven instead of eleven (ninety-seven being the largest two-digit prime number).

DATA TRANSMISSION CHECKS

Checks used for data transmission

There are three types of check we need to study in the detection of errors during the transmission of data between different peripherals or different parts of the system:

■ Parity
■ Reader checks
■ Transfer checks

Parity

Parity was first introduced with punched paper tape, and since then has been used on most magnetic media as well as within the memory of the computer. Each storage unit (byte or word) is made up of binary digits which are either 0 (zero bits) or 1 (one bits). Parity systems use an extra bit in each storage unit to make the total number of 1-bits (i.e. 1s) in the unit *odd* (for a so-called **odd parity** system) or *even* (for an **even parity** system) as a simple safeguard against any loss of bits due to machine faults. This is a binary version of check digit verification.

To take an example, if the binary pattern for an 8-bit word on an even parity system were

1 0 1 0 1 0 1 0 1

we can count five 1-bits and four 0-bits, and since the number of 1-bits is not even, the word would fail the parity check implying that the data had been corrupted. Alternatively, suppose the byte storing the pattern

1 0 1 1 0 1 1 0

were to be used in an even parity system. Since it contains five 1-bits, then being an odd number the parity bit will be set to one and the number would be stored as:

1 1 0 1 1 0 1 1 0

Another implementation of parity takes the bits from several consecutive bytes and generates an additional byte with parity bits for each position. This is often called

longitudinal parity and is just one example of what are called *check sums*, a byte which contains a mathematical check on the group which precedes it.

When data is read by the computer, most devices employ some form of **reader checks** where, typically, in addition to the reading station there is a checking station where data is read for a second time and the two versions are compared. In the case of optical character recognition and magnetic ink character recognition, the reader may examine the characters in separate halves, each of which is sufficient for identification and ensures that the two halves represent the same character.

Similar to the reader checks, many devices employ **transfer checks**, often in the form of a standard **read after write** check to guard against hardware failure. Thus as each record is written to the relevant media, after writing out it is automatically read back in again to compare with the version in memory, thereby checking the accuracy of the write operation.

FAULT TOLERANCE

The detection and/or correction of hardware errors during a computer run is commonly referred to as fault tolerance. Since we cannot expect perfection in any hardware system, faults will occur from time to time and methods have been devised to provide a certain amount of tolerance to such faults.

We shall see in Chapter 6 that a common form of fault tolerance involves physical procedures such as keeping copies of the files, ideally in a separate location, so that disasters such as flood, fire, theft or sabotage may destroy the hardware or media but still allow the data to be recovered. The simplest example of this is the making of regular back-up copies of discs and floppy discs. This should be familiar to all students of programming who need to make regular back-ups of programs in case of disc failures, loss of files, etc. In a live system, where loss would be catastrophic, such as an airline booking system or a bank processing cashpoint transactions, the program itself takes regular back-ups at specific instances called **checkpoints**. This means that if a failure occurs the program can be restarted from the checkpoint rather than from the beginning.

The hardware implementation of fault tolerance involves the *duplication* of both processes and hardware. One method, known as **cold standby**, uses a second processor which can be brought into use in cases of failure; this could be done by an operator throwing a switch and may not recover all the data. Another implementation uses two independent processors, one nominated as the prime host for a process and another as the **back-up** or **slave**, both processors having a copy of the process. At various times the process meets a *checkpoint* and is copied to an alternate host, so if the prime machine fails, the second machine takes over from the last checkpoint. The system is reliable, but is slowed by dumping at the checkpoints. Recovery can be slow if the checkpoints are far apart as it will involve re-loading the master files and duplicating all the processes carried out since the last checkpoint by using the input data which will have been dumped to another file.

If an installation has two or more processors, this system works most efficiently because they can work on *different* programs at the same time and use their own disc space or even their own disc to avoid a common backing store being a source of problems. One refinement, though more costly, is where both the main and alternate CPUs execute the same program, effectively simultaneously in a system referred to as **hot standby**. This is shown in Fig. 5.1. Although it duplicates *processing*, it is *faster* because no checkpoints are needed and the second CPU is fully up-to-date and can resume processing immediately. This is a case of hot standby and uses an arbitration processor to decide which one, if either, is at fault. Although this ties up two processors, with the evolving technology, the processor may well be the cheapest hardware element in the system, and so it is also

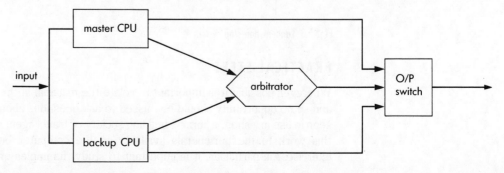

Fig. 5.1

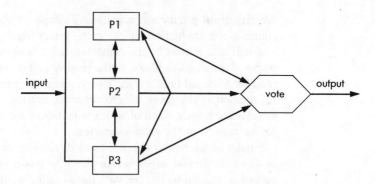

Fig. 5.2

common to use three processors with a 2–1 voting arrangement as shown in Fig. 5.2. All three will share the virtual memory and the processes must produce checkpoints without specifying an alternate processor. The system may have a number of independent processes and the operating system assigns programs to processors as required and will detect and bypass any faulty unit.

One of the first, and best-known, examples of a fault tolerant system is the **tandem non-stop system** which uses two to sixteen processors, and duplicates nearly everything using multiple data paths. The two bus controllers for each processor are independent of each other, every device is connected to two controllers attached to different processors. Disc stores are identical images of one another so that there is always more than one copy and at least two paths for any data in the system. The operating system forces every processor to send a status message to all others at regular intervals, say once each second, and if a processor fails to do so it is declared to be unavailable for service. Each process is allocated a prime and back-up processor. If these are X and Y, a disc on X 'mirrors' that on Y and if X fails, Y resumes from the checkpoint and another processor, say Z, now becomes back-up as Y becomes the prime processor.

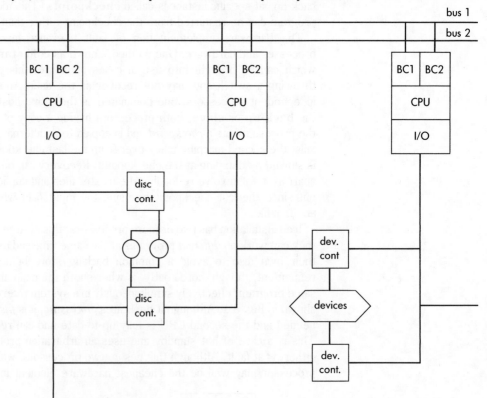

Fig. 5.3 Tandem non-stop system

PRACTICAL STEPS

Wherever possible it is important to relate the material in this chapter to live applications and so no opportunity should be missed to ask questions about the use of any peripherals seen in use in a shop, a library, building society or travel agent. It is important also to relate this work to the peripherals available on the computer being used for programming exercises; in particular, it is important to study the implementation of buffering.

EXAMINATION QUESTIONS

SHORT QUESTIONS

Question 1
The data capture process for a mail order company begins when a standard form is filled in by a customer and sent to head office. The order forms are received and batched by data control, and the data is then keyed to floppy disc before processing. Give examples of the types of error likely to occur, and of means by which they might be prevented from entering the system.
(London AS Specimen)

Question 2
Calculate a check digit for the reference number 85431 using a suitable algorithm   (3)

Now transpose two digits and show that your algorithm detects an error.   (2)
(London 1988)

Question 3
Describe briefly *three* different kinds of error which can occur due to the *input* of faulty data.

(AEB 1989)

Question 4
Explain how the inclusion of a parity bit in a sequence of bits can greatly minimise the risk of an undetected error arising when the sequence is transmitted.
(Northern Ireland 1988)

LONGER QUESTIONS

Question 5
An insurance office has an enquiry terminal which customers can use if they require an immediate quotation for the renewal of their car insurance. Some of the questions which appear on the screen are shown below.

a)   What checks would you expect the program to make on the data, as it is entered?

Annie's Insurance Company

1. Name?

2. Address ?

3. Date of birth?   4. Sex?

5. Number of complete years driving?

6. Make of car?

7. Model of car ?

8. Size of engine (cc) ?

9. Year of manufacture ?

b) The form of the questions is not very helpful and may lead to inconsistent responses. Re-design the layout and wording so that fewer misunderstandings will occur.

(Cambridge 1987)

Question 6

a) In computer-based systems, code numbers are often used primarily in order to identify items. Describe briefly four requirements which code numbers should satisfy.

b) What is a check digit? Which of the following are valid ISBN codes? (International Standard Book Number using modulus 11 with ascending weights 1, 2, 3 . . . 10 from the right-most digit.)

085 012 452 2
090 543 538 X
009 154 961 2
009 154 971 X

c) Distinguish between data verification and data validation and explain why such procedures are not sufficient to ensure the correctness of computer output. Describe briefly other checks which can be used.

(Northern Ireland 1988)

Question 7

Read the following passage about an electronic funds transfer system then answer the questions given below:

A chain of shops has installed terminals for electronic funds transfer at the point of sale (eft/pos). The eft/pos system provides three basic functions. It verifies a customer's identity, authorises the payment and transmits the data required for money to be transferred from the customer's bank account to the shop's bank account. Each terminal installed in the shops is *on-line* to a *fault tolerant* mainframe computer which manages the whole system and is itself connected to the computers belonging to participating banks.

To use the system for making a payment a customer's plastic card which stores data on a magnetic stripe is read by the eft/pos terminal. Cards are issued by the customer's bank. The terminal reads a number from the card. This is the issuer identity number which identifies which bank issued the plastic card. Software then connects the terminal via the central mainframe computer to the computer belonging to the customer's bank where details of the customer's account are stored.

To verify identity the customer has to enter a personal identification number (PIN) on a keypad connected to the terminal. An encrypted version of the pin is stored on the magnetic stripe on the customer's card and this is transmitted to the customer's bank's computer by the central mainframe. The transaction can continue only if the number entered, the number stored in the computer and the decrypted number from the card all match.

Details of the transaction are entered by the shop assistant. Payment is authorised by the customer's bank's computer if the customer's credit limit is not exceeded.

The terminal prints a receipt and the total money is debited from the customer's bank account and credited to the shop's bank account which may be stored on a third computer belonging to the shop's bank. All data is transferred among the various computers using a packet switch stream (PSS) service.

a) Explain the meaning of the terms in italics. Give *one* reason why each of these features is desirable in this system. *(4)*

b) Draw a diagram showing the relationship between the shop's terminals and the three computers mentioned in the passage. *(3)*

c) State *three* advantages for the shop and *two* advantages for the customer when eft/pos is used. *(5)*

d) Suggest a reason why the PIN stored on the customer's card needs to be encrypted. *(1)*

e) Discuss briefly one danger in the system other than loss or theft of the customer's card. *(1)*

f)   Identify *two* elements in the system for which secrecy is essential.   (2)

g)   Describe briefly the method by which PSS sends data from one computer to another.   (4)

(AEB 1989)

Question 8

a)   Explain, with the aid of suitable examples, the concept of 'the quality of data'. State two ways in which data may have become of 'poor quality'.

b)   Distinguish carefully between verification and validation of data and briefly describe one example of each process.

c)   Discuss the effectiveness of verification and validation in ensuring the accuracy of data.   (AEB 1985)

OUTLINE ANSWERS

SHORT QUESTIONS

Question 1

The mail order company is using order forms batched by data control before keying to floppy disc for processing. Assuming of course that the data on the forms is correct, the two main categories of error likely to occur are the loss or duplication of complete forms and keying errors on individual fields.

The loss or duplication of complete forms can be guarded against by employing batch totals. The problems with individual fields can be guarded against in two ways, firstly with verification, the re-entry by a second operator, and secondly with validation checks on the fields, particularly the use of check digits on key fields like the customer reference number and on the product code.

Question 2

In order to append a check digit to the five digit number, 85431 using weights 1 2 4 8 5 10 modulus 11 we compute the sum of the products of weights:

$$\begin{aligned} & 1 \times 8 \; + \; 2 \times 5 \; + \; 4 \times 4 \; + \; 8 \times 3 \; + \; 5 \times 1 \\ = \; & \quad 8 \quad + \quad 10 \quad + \quad 16 \quad + \quad 24 \quad + \quad 5 \\ = \; & \underline{63} \end{aligned}$$

We append a check digit which when multiplied by ten and added to sixty-three gives a multiple of eleven. Eight is appropriate, so the complete, valid code number is 854318.

If the three and four were to be transposed, the code number would be quoted as 853418 and the calculation would be:

$$\begin{aligned} & 1 \times 8 \; + \; 2 \times 5 \; + \; 4 \times 3 \; + \; 8 \times 4 \; + \; 5 \times 1 \; + \; 10 \times 8 \\ = \; & \quad 8 \quad + \quad 10 \quad + \quad 12 \quad + \quad 32 \quad + \quad 5 \quad + \quad 80 \\ = \; & \underline{147} \end{aligned}$$

this is not divisible by eleven which shows that the check fails and detects the transposition error.

Question 3

Three different kinds of error which can occur due to the input of faulty data are:

1   Misquoting of a code number which may be detected by a check digit.

2   Misalignment of data which may be picked up by a format check.

3   Misquoting or misreading a character, e.g. 5 for S, I for 1.

Question 4

The letter A coded in ASCII is 65 decimal or 100 0001. If it were to be distorted in transmission and received as 100 0101 it would now appear as E. This might be something of a problem in, for example, the recording of GCE or GCSE grades. If it were to be encoded with even parity it would be transmitted as 0100 0001, the high order bit being the parity bit and the number of 1-bits is two. If received as 0100 0101 it would have an odd number of 1-bits (in fact three) and the error would be detected.

LONGER QUESTIONS

Question 5

a) The validation checks for an insurance office enquiry terminal for customers to use in obtaining an immediate quotation for the renewal of their car insurance, could include:

1 Date of birth must be numeric and checked for valid range, for example month must be 1–12, and day must be consistent with month, for example less than thirty-one days if month is four.

2 Sex must be one of two possibilities.

3 Number of complete years driving must be numeric and feasible, for example ninety-nine must be wrong, eighty might be wrong.

4 Size of engine must be numeric and checked for range, perhaps 500 to 4,000.

5 Year of manufacture must be checked for range, could be this year but rejected if less than some extreme, say 1945 and queried if less than, say, 1960.

6 Finally, once the complete screen has been entered, there should be a question on the form 'is this correct?' giving the user the opportunity to amend the entries.

b) Most of the questions could lead to inconsistent or incorrect responses. The numbers seem to be irrelevant and the wording could be redesigned along the lines set out below but each ought to have the field limits defined:

1 Name ought to be divided into surname and first names, and could also have a sub-field for title (Mr Mrs Dr)

2 Address ought to allow for several lines and isolate postcode which could be used by the program to identify the home area which is used to decide the premium due

3 Date of birth needs to indicate that we require dd/mm/yy

4 Sex needs to indicate the possible responses, i.e. m or f

5 Number of complete years driving could indicate a two-digit limit

6 Make of car may influence premium and so must make an exact match, there should therefore be a help key or a pull-down or super-imposed menu to select the make required

7 Model of car could be selected as for make

8 Size of engine should indicate number of digits

9 Year of manufacture should, like size of engine, indicate number of digits and both could be cross-referenced against make and model

10 Adding an accept/reject response to allow the customer to change one or more fields

A possible revised screen layout is shown below.

Question 6

a) Among the requirements which code numbers should satisfy are:
Expandable to allow for additional items to be entered
Unique so that each code number refers to one item only
Concise, as brief as possible whilst satisfying the other requirements
Meaningful so that parts of the code may indicate properties of the item; we call this a *facet code*
Consistent with current and present systems
This part of the question will be considered in Chapter 16

b) A check digit is a mathematical method of checking numeric code numbers used with important codes where problems would arise if the code were to be misquoted. These numbers have an extra digit, called a check digit, added to the end of the number. Examples are the ISBN number allocated to every published book, providing a unique number for ordering and cataloguing, and the VAT reference numbers allocated to each registered business.

For 085 012 452 2 we compute:

$$10 \times 0 + 9 \times 8 + 8 \times 5 + 7 \times 0 + 6 \times 1 + 5 \times 2 + 4 \times 4 + 3 \times 5 + 2 \times 2 + 1 \times 2$$
$$= 0 + 72 + 40 + 0 + 6 + 10 + 16 + 15 + 4 + 2$$
$$= 165 = 15 \times 11 \quad \textbf{a valid code}$$

for 090 543 538 X we compute:

$$10 \times 0 + 9 \times 9 + 8 \times 0 + 7 \times 5 + 6 \times 4 + 5 \times 3 + 4 \times 5 + 3 \times 3 + 2 \times 8 + 1 \times 10$$
$$= 0 + 81 + 0 + 35 + 24 + 15 + 20 + 9 + 16 + 10$$
$$= 210 = 19 \times 11 + 1 \quad \textbf{an invalid code}$$

For 009 154 961 2 we compute:

$$10 \times 0 + 9 \times 0 + 8 \times 9 + 7 \times 1 + 6 \times 5 + 5 \times 4 + 4 \times 9 + 3 \times 6 + 2 \times 1 + 1 \times 2$$
$$= 0 + 0 + 72 + 7 + 30 + 20 + 36 + 18 + 2 + 2$$
$$= 187 = 17 \times 11 \quad \textbf{a valid code}$$

For 009 154 971 X we compute:

$$10 \times 0 + 9 \times 0 + 8 \times 9 + 7 \times 1 + 6 \times 5 + 5 \times 4 + 4 \times 9 + 3 \times 7 + 2 \times 1 + 1 \times 10$$
$$= 0 + 0 + 72 + 7 + 30 + 20 + 36 + 21 + 2 + 10$$
$$= 198 = 18 \times 11 \quad \textbf{a valid code}$$

c) *Data verification* is where data, input to the computer system, is re-entered by a second independent operator for machine comparison with the initial entry. *Data validation* is where each item of data is examined by the program and checked, for example for format, range, consistency and check digit.

Other checks which can be used are procedures to make sure that no data is lost, duplicated or inserted into the input between the user and the computer. In some cases these checks can also provide a limited control against certain fields being corrupted. The main techniques in this area are:

- Document count
- Line count
- Sequence check
- Control totals
- Hash totals

Question 7

a) *On-line* means that each terminal is connected directly to the mainframe computer so that any data entered is transferred instantaneously to the file store of the mainframe and any response comes back in *real time*. The scenario states that the system i) verifies a customer's identity, ii) authorises the payment and iii) transmits the data required for money to be transferred from the customer's bank account to the shop's bank account, none of which could be carried out in any mode other than *on-line*.

A *fault tolerant* mainframe computer is one which has built-in hardware and software features for the detection and/or correction of hardware errors during a computer run where, for example, the program takes regular back-ups of both memory files at specific instances called checkpoints so that if a failure occurs the program can be restarted from the checkpoint rather than at the beginning.

It is a desirable feature in this system because transactions such as the authorisation of payments and transfer of funds from the customer's bank account to the shop's bank account must not be lost in the event of a machine fault or breakdown.

b)   Fig. 5.4 is a diagram showing the relationship between the shop's terminals and the three computers.

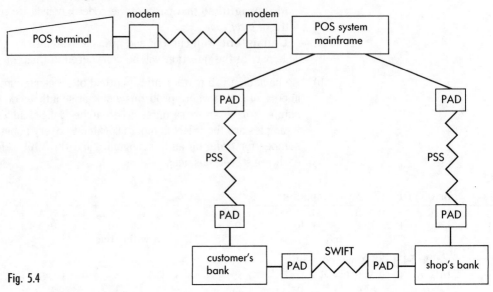

Fig. 5.4

c)   Advantages for the shop when eft/pos is used include:
    1 Immediate transfer of funds to the shop account.
    2 No danger of cheques bouncing as customer creditworthiness is checked before the sale is complete.
    3 Sales may increase because customers will be able to buy on impulse without having to carry cash.
    Advantages for the customer when eft/pos is used include:
    1 No need to carry cash or a cheque book.
    2 If the plastic card is lost or stolen the fraudulent use is limited whereas a stolen credit card could be used many times over in a short space of time to run up a large debt.

d)   The PIN stored on the customer's card needs to be encrypted to prevent it being unscrambled for fraudulent use.

e)   Dangers in the system include loss or theft of the customer's card and the fact that a breakdown due to loss of power, perhaps from storm damage or strike, could render the whole system inoperable and the shop might have to close until it was restored.

f)   Secrecy is essential in preventing a shop assistant gaining additional information about a customer's account and also to prevent a customer from obtaining access to the shop account.

g)   PSS is a *packet switching system* on a public network available for the transmission of data between computers. It differs from the simpler Datel systems by transmitting data at high speed in 'packets' of 128 bytes over a computer-controlled network. The packet is encoded with a unique address of the sender and the address of the recipient whose hardware PAD or *packet assembler/disassembler* will decode it into its original format.
    Examples of British systems are the British Telecom PSS, the clearing banks' SWIFT system and the SITA system used by airlines.

Question 8

a)   The quality of data refers to the accuracy and completeness of the data entering the computer. Amongst the ways in which data may have become of poor quality are incorrect initial *recording*, a clerk writing the wrong customer number by mistake, errors in *transcription*, where the data is copied from one source to another, and *transmission errors*, where data is copied electronically from one device to another.

b) Keyboard entry involves the introduction of an extra step of transcribing the data from the source documents to the input media and this may introduce a small number of errors. Thus an operation, called *verification*, is introduced to attempt to eliminate these errors where data, input to a computer system, is re-entered by a second independent operator for machine comparison with the initial entry. It was developed initially for use with punched card data preparation systems, but adapted for use with all keyboard entry systems.

Validation is a software check on data where each data item in a record is examined by the program and checks carried out which have been devised and specified by the systems analyst. These are likely to include format checks to examine whether the format of the data (perhaps numeric or alphabetic) conforms to that specified in the systems design, a range or limit check to ensure that the contents of a particular field lie within an expected range, consistency if two fields can be linked logically in some way, and the use of check digits on important numeric fields.

c) The effectiveness of verification is limited in that if an item is obtained from a wrong source, is fraudulently quoted or simply read from the wrong line in a catalogue, it will be accepted as valid and the error will go undetected.

The effectiveness of validation is limited by the ingenuity of the systems designer to devise sufficient tests.

FILE STORAGE

TYPES OF PERIPHERAL

BASIC FILE TERMINOLOGY

TYPES OF COMPUTER FILE

CHARACTERISTICS OF MAGNETIC TAPE

BATCH FILE PROCESSING

DEMAND PROCESSING

DIRECT ACCESS STORAGE DEVICES

VARIABLE LENGTH DATA

INDEXED FILES

FILE SECURITY AND FILE RECOVERY

GETTING STARTED

We have already seen that there are two types of storage used on computer systems, memory, which includes ROM and RAM, and file store or backing store. This chapter describes the most popular file storage peripherals and some of the techniques for organising the data in files. It is worth remembering that **memory** is closely linked to the processor and can be accessed almost instantaneously; however the capacity is relatively small, has a finite limit, and is organised in cells of equal size, with each cell identified by a unique number called its address. A **file store**, or **backing store**, is used to store data *outside* the central system. It appears to have an almost infinite capacity but allows access to any required data item in less than a second, though even this is 100,000 times slower than the access of data in memory.

In studying the use of peripherals and particularly in preparation for examination questions it is most important to relate them to the file storage peripheral of a *specific* computer and also to a range of live applications.

ESSENTIAL PRINCIPLES

TYPES OF PERIPHERAL

In Chapter 4 there was an attempt to classify peripheral devices. Another possibility is to consider them to be divided into two groups:

1   Those that act in some way as an extension to main memory.
2   Those that transfer data from/to the outside world.

Typical examples are:

- Magnetic tape, disc, drum, bubble, cassettes
- Display terminals, lineprinters, VDUs and modems

The first group generally act in a **block** mode with characters aggregated for transfer. The second group typically process individual characters, though there are exceptions to this rule. It is this second group which will be introduced in this chapter.

The most common file storage devices are magnetic tape cassettes, reel-to-reel magnetic tape, tape cartridge systems and magnetic disc devices, which may be either EDS (exchangeable disc store), FDS (fixed disc store) or floppy disc and bubble memories. The organisation of the data in file store varies between devices according to the characteristics of the media, but data is normally stored in units, called blocks. On disc, for example, data is stored in *sectors*, typically containing 256 bytes and, in order to allow direct access to any sector, each sector has a numerical address. Just as with memory, high-level languages allow us to ignore how the data is physically represented and to design a data structure suited to the application being implemented.

Some early computers used punched cards and punched paper tape and the first small business computers, called visible record computers (VRCs), used large cards. These were about A4 size with data stored in text form on one side and on the reverse side encoded in a magnetic strip. These were called **magnetic stripe cards**, but the most common current devices are:

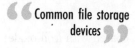
" Common file storage devices *"*

- **Magnetic tape cassette** using standard audio cassettes. This is a very cheap and slow system, only really appropriate on home, games-orientated computers.
- **Reel-to-reel magnetic tape** system, normally using ½-inch tape similar to video where the tape is read from beginning to end.
- **Tape cartridge systems** which, though similar in some respects to cassettes, have a shorter length of tape in a continuous loop. Probably the best known and first of these devices was the Sinclair **Microdrive** system; another system is called **floppy tape** and on microcomputers these can be even cheaper than floppy disc.
- **Magnetic disc**. This is a metal disc, or set of discs, on which data is stored in concentric tracks to allow any record to be read by direct access. In EDS the discs are contained in removable cartridges so that a file appropriate to a system can be loaded as required. With FDS, the disc file is retained on-line all the time. A cheap form of FDS appropriate to microcomputers is called the **Winchester Disc**, giving capacity of 10–40 million bytes.
- **Floppy disc**. This is a flexible disc, which is comparatively cheap, with drives priced from £70 upwards. It is very popular, allowing direct access on small computer systems with capacity from 100K to 2 million bytes.

BASIC FILE TERMINOLOGY

There are four important definitions concerned with file processing. These should be understood before proceeding, though they are in everyday use and have already occurred in this text.

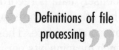
" Definitions of file processing *"*

- A **file** is a collection of records containing related data organised in a manner suitable for retrieval and processing.
- A **record** is a sub-division of a file containing the set of data associated with one transaction or subject, assembled in a specified format. In modern systems terminology this is also called an **entity**.

- A **field** is an item of data within a record which has been identified as required for processing. In modern systems terminology this is also called an **attribute**.
- A **character** is an element within a field which may be a letter, a digit, a punctuation symbol, a control code or a graphics character. It is best to consider a character as being the result of a single key entry from an input keyboard.

As an example of a file, consider the payroll of a company. The *file* would be the complete set of data covering every employee; a *record* would contain all the information on one member of staff; its *fields* could include surname, first names, salary, etc. Each digit in the salary and each letter in the name is a *character*.

TYPES OF COMPUTER FILE

There are a number of names, referring to file types, which are used in most information systems:

- The **master file** is the principal file in a system which contains the current state of the system. For example, employees and their 'year to date' salaries paid. It is kept up to date by regular processing with transaction files.

❝ File types ❞

- The **transaction file**, which is sometimes called a **movements** file. This contains all the transactions or changes to be made to the records or entities in the master file of the system. It often exists in several different forms during processing; for example, an unsorted input file, a validated version of the same, a sorted version used in the update, and a journal file of processed transactions. Some of these may well be used for their specific purpose and then, quite possibly, not retained.
- A **reference file** is a file with records of a permanent nature which may be read during a computer application but will not normally be amended. An example might be customers' names and addresses. This may be the master file in another system.
- The printed output from a computer run is called, for consistency, a **print file**.
- A **work file** or **scratch file** is the name given to a magnetic tape or disc which is used during the execution of a program but is not retained. Alternative names are **common tape** or **common disc**.

CHARACTERISTICS OF MAGNETIC TAPE

Magnetic tape, the cheapest medium, is a mylar plastic tape coated with iron oxide; the standard width is ½-inch on reels up to 2,400 feet. The data is recorded in **frames** across the tape, with each frame consisting of a number of magnetised spots positioned in one of a number of tracks or channels (usually nine, sometimes seven) across the tape, as shown in Fig. 6.1. The 9-track tape system uses eight tracks to store the bits of a single byte with, in addition, as a check, a parity bit as was described in Chapter 5. It is processed by being passed across the read/write heads of the tape drive, at a constant speed, typically 200 i.p.s. (inches per second).

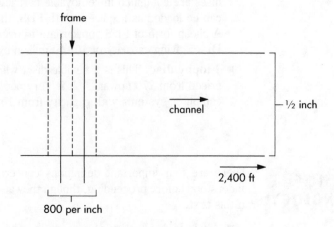

Fig. 6.1

The term **packing density** is used as a measure of how densely data is recorded on magnetic tape. The original density was 200 frames per inch, but other standards such as 550, 800 or 1,600 frames per inch have existed and 6,250 is now commonplace. These are often written as 800 b.p.i. or 6,250 b.p.i. standing for bits per inch meaning bits per inch in

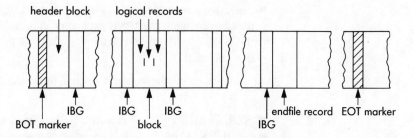

Fig. 6.2

each channel. Magnetic tape, in common with all magnetic media, can only be read or written when moving at full speed. Hence for tape, the data is written in blocks, separated by 'inter-block gaps' of up to about an inch to allow for the time it takes for the tape to accelerate to full speed and decelerate to rest between accessing blocks of data. This is illustrated in Fig. 6.2. A data block may contain a single record but, more usually, contains a number of records collected together in memory and written to tape in a single operation. The term **physical record** is often used in place of block, particularly in the context of tape, in which case the term **logical records** is used in place of record.

When a tape is loaded onto a tape drive, the operator winds the beginning part of the tape around the take-up spool, like loading 35mm film in a camera. Because of this handling it is unreasonable to expect to record data right from the start of the tape, so there is a **beginning-of-tape marker** (BOT marker) which in some systems is a transparent section and in others a piece of reflective foil. In either case this can be detected by a photo cell to locate the start of the data. There is a similar **end-of-tape marker** (EOT marker) close to the physical end of the tape, and the operating system detects this if an attempt is made to read or write over this marker.

A typical transfer rate for magnetic tape is 200 inches per second so, with a packing density of 6,250 characters per inch, this gives, theoretically, a transfer rate of 6,250 × 200 or 1,250,000 characters per second. However this is only the transfer speed for a complete block, once located and moving at full speed. It is important, in this context, to study past examination questions at the end of the chapter which represent typical examination questions on magnetic tape. In the answers, cover in detail the necessary material on effective transfer rates and tape capacity.

An inhibition to processing is the **seek** time needed to find the required block of data on a tape, as the medium is totally sequential in structure. The worst case could be several minutes if the tape needs to be rewound or moved forwards from the start to the end. Many systems do not allow a backwards search, only a full rewind and forwards skip, therefore data searches need to be organised into the same sequence as the tape.

MAGNETIC TAPE FILE ORGANISATION

Each file starts with a special record called a **header record** or **label record**. This will have a different structure to the data on the main file, and may contain a number of fields, including a code identifying the record as a header label, the symbolic name of the file which will be read and checked by the program before any record is processed. Other fields may include the creation date, retention period and generation number. Files are also terminated by another special record, called the **endfile** record, which will contain a special code which is searched for and, like the EOT marker, which can be detected by the program as it reads the data records. This can be illustrated by a sample statement taken from a Cobol program:

READ CUSTOMER RECORD AT END PERFORM TOTALS.

which shows how a high-level language can execute a specified procedure when the end of the file is located. The endfile record can also contain record counts and control totals for the file. Therefore, when a file is created, the control total is written to the endfile record and when read by a subsequent program, the control total is recalculated as each record is read. This is then checked when the endfile record is detected, a condition often referred to as **at endfile**.

As stated above, because of the way it is read, magnetic tape can only be accessed **serially**, that is, by starting at the beginning of the tape and reading through every record in the sequence it was written. So direct access to records is not feasible because:

■ It may take up to three minutes to locate an individual record

■ Selective over-writing by reading a record, backspacing and re-writing, is not possible because the block gaps vary in length. Therefore updating a file requires the complete file to be read and copied out to a new tape with the amendments now included

As a consequence, the records on magnetic tape are organised in one of two ways, either:

■ SERIALLY — in a random unsorted sequence
■ SEQUENTIALLY — in a specified sequence which is determined by the contents of a particular field or fields called the **sort key**

Magnetic tape used to be of great importance and was, before the development of cheaper disc, the most widely used storage medium, but is now mostly restricted to archive and other long-term storage. It is a useful medium for transferring data between machines because tapes have common standards and the same tape can be read on two computers of different manufacturers. However there is no in-built **security** to prevent access to confidential data. Improvements in magnetic technology have resulted in great increases in packing density (by a factor of thirty), but over the same period the reading speeds have changed only from about 100 to 200 inches per second. Thus the magnetic technology has improved but not the physical characteristics. While it is necessary to read and write tape in blocks, the block can be varied, even within a program, and is not fixed, as happens for magnetic disc. The data buffers must be large because it is not possible to stop within a block and the nature of tape demands quite long gaps between data blocks (usually ½-inch) to allow tape to start and stop. Furthermore, if the read-after-write check detects an error, it assumes it to be due to a bad portion of tape. It then treats the portion of the tape as an extension to the inter-block-gap and attempts to write again. It is this feature, which is invisible to the user, but logged by the computer's operating system, which causes the variation in gaps and prevents the implementation of direct access.

BATCH FILE PROCESSING

The process of amending any file is called **updating**. Amendments may include adding new records, deleting records, replacing a record or amending the contents of some of the fields within records. In serial files, which means virtually all tape-orientated systems and many disc-based applications, there will be four distinct operations, called **program segments** or **modules**:

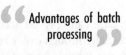
Program segments

■ VALIDATE and edit the input transaction file
■ SORT the transactions into the same sequence as the master file
■ UPDATE the master file with the transaction file
■ TABULATE the updated file

The relationship between these segments is shown in Fig. 6.3. The validation of input data is carried out as described in Chapter 5 and then written to a tape or disc file. A sort program will normally be provided as part of the standard software (it is even an instruction in the Cobol language) and will arrange the data in the sequence required for the update program, for which a design is given in Chapter 7. After all this, the complete file, or specified subsections, can be tabulated.

Virtually all serial file systems contain this segment structure whether implemented on magnetic tape or magnetic disc. This mode of operation is called **batch processing**. Its characteristic is that all input data is collected together and processed as a batch at regular periods; typical applications are stock control and payroll. This was historically the first mode of processing when it was orientated around magnetic tape file storage. Indeed it was the only method available until magnetic disc became cheap enough to use more widely. It is still the most appropriate processing method for many applications, even using disc, but its main disadvantage is the inability to access, instantaneously, a given record, in order to provide the answer to a query.

There are a number of *advantages* of batch processing, including:

Advantages of batch processing

■ Many applications are best implemented in this manner.
■ Use of magnetic tape is often cheaper than disc or other media.
■ The programming of this type of application is simpler than direct access and can make use of automatic program generators.
■ No manual intervention or dialogue is required.

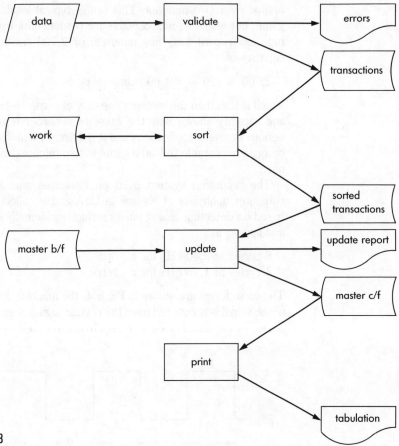

Fig. 6.3

DEMAND PROCESSING Transactions are processed in the random order in which they arise, 'on demand' and in 'real time' with the operator waiting for a response. Common examples are airline and theatre ticket reservation systems, cashpoint transactions with banks and order processing. It is also sometimes called **transaction processing** as it concentrates on individual transactions rather than on batches of data. It needs direct access storage devices and the response may be measured in seconds, but may appear immediate in most applications, even though thirty to sixty users may be 'on-line' at the same time.

Demand processing is the only feasible implementation for many applications but it has the disadvantage that if user activity is high, then the response may be slow, and that if an immediate response is required then the system may be inefficient. Many demand processing applications will be based on a large number of on-line terminals with a *multi-programming operating system*.

Key fields

An important term in all file processing is key field, which in a serial file is the same as the **sort key** and determines the sequence in which the records are to be sorted. In a direct access file stored on disc, an individual record can be retrieved by a simple calculation on the key field to locate the sector containing the required record. This is called a direct access addressing algorithm and the key field is then called the **access key**.

Magnetic tape cassettes

Before leaving magnetic tape it is worth looking at the cassette systems used on many small microcomputers, which can be regarded as a small edition of magnetic tape. They use the standard ¼ inch audio cassettes which are not well suited to *digital* recording, and *parallel bit* recording would need a precision not appropriate from such a cheap device. These normally operate at 120 characters per second, so if it is required to load a program of 15K or 15,000 characters, the time taken will be:

$$\frac{15,000}{120} \text{ seconds}$$

$$= 125 \text{ seconds}$$

or just over two minutes. This is the typical loading time for a sophisticated computer game, but would be unacceptable for reading data from a file in a major application. A C90 tape can record forty-five minutes, or 2,700 seconds, on each side and so has a total capacity of

$$2,700 \times 120 = \underline{324,000 \text{ characters}}$$

which is less than the memory capacity of some 16-bit microcomputers. This transfer rate and capacity shows why the cassette recorder is unsuitable as a peripheral device for serious business applications and is only really suitable for home computers where it might be quite acceptable to load a game in two minutes and where large files are unlikely to be used.

The recording system used on cassettes was specified at a conference for home computer hobbyists at Kansas in USA and is called the **Kansas City** standard. This is based on detecting analog pulses, which incidentally can be heard as a high pitched sound and appear as:

8 cycles at 2,400 Hz for a   one
4 cycles at 1,200 Hz for a   zero

The wave forms are shown in Fig.6.4; the machine samples at 'mid-bit' time and the timing of the signal is recovered from the regular signal at each mid-bit instant. Recovering a clock buried in the data is called an **isochronous** (self clocked) transfer.

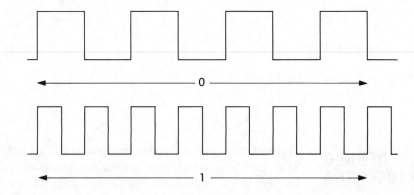

Fig. 6.4 Kansas City standard; waveforms

Tape streamers

Another device worth mentioning is the tape streamer which is a cartridge device used in small systems to take 'backups' of Winchester discs.

DIRECT ACCESS STORAGE DEVICES

The most common devices are the exchangeable disc storage (EDS), fixed disc storage (FDS), magnetic drum and floppy disc, and another device called the data cell which uses magnetic card. An emerging device is the CD-ROM which uses the technology of the compact disc and provides one hour of digitally recorded sound but has been adapted for computer input.

Magnetic discs

Unlike tape, magnetic discs (apart from the 5¼-inch floppy discs) spin continuously so there is no start/stop delay. They have inter-block gaps but, since the discs can be manufactured to a greater precision, they are much smaller and the more rigid nature of the physical medium allows a higher packing density of data. All discs have their data recorded in concentric circles, not spiral as on a gramophone record. Each **track** is divided into a number of **sectors** separated by inter-block gaps.

Fixed head discs have a read/write head for *each track* and so moving between tracks is only a matter of electronic switching. This gives far more rapid access to the track, but there is a small delay known as **search time** or **rotational latency delay** to wait for the required sector to pass beneath the head; on average, this delay is a ½ revolution. FDS units usually have non-removable discs and are met in high performance systems as it is expensive to maintain so many heads in alignment.

The heads of high-speed EDS and FDS devices 'fly' above the surface through the spinning boundary of air adjacent to the discs, so they must be designed with an aerofoil sector. Mechanically, the heads must also be lifted from the disc when it is not spinning to avoid *head crashes* on the magnetic surface. The standard EDS device provides one read/write head per surface which accesses all the tracks, and the time required to move the head from track to track is called the **seek time**. There is also a rotational delay once the track is located.

Example of EDS storage

The figures quoted are an approximation of a well known EDS system and are sufficient to illustrate speeds and capacity.

Exchangeable disc stores have a number of metal discs, from one to eleven but more usually six or eleven, each coated with iron oxide like magnetic tape and all contained in a cartridge or disc pack. The standard eleven disc system records data on twenty surfaces of the eleven discs, the two outer surfaces being used only for protection. The system can address 200 tracks on each surface, and each track has fifteen sectors storing up to 512 characters giving a total capacity of:

$$20 \times 200 \times 15 \times 512$$
$$= 30,720,000 \text{ characters}$$

often expressed as 30 Mb or 30 megabytes.

The disc revolves at a fixed constant speed, typically forty times per second. Therefore the *capacity* of one track is

$$15 \text{ sectors} \times 512 \text{ characters} = 7,680 \text{ characters}$$

and the *transfer rate* during a read or write is

$$40 \times 7,680 = 307,200 \text{ characters per second}$$

which is usually expressed as 307,200 ch.p.s.

There will be at least one read–write head for each surface, and it is convenient here to think of a single head for the surface. The heads are connected to a single mechanism which moves across the surfaces, rather like a comb with all the heads moving together in a single unit.

These systems will normally have not 200 but 203 tracks, with three unused but held in reserve, so that when an error occurs on one track, the operating system will automatically take the track out of use and use one of the spares instead. The user is usually totally unaware of this recovery process which is handled entirely by the disc operating system. This will be discussed further in Chapter 14.

When data is written to the disc it writes a complete block or sector. Thus if only ten bytes were to be required, they will still occupy the space allocated for the full sector which may be 512 characters. The operating software will, for many machines, allow the sectors to be accessed in logical units of one, two, four or eight sectors. These units are sometimes called **buckets**. Unfortunately the terms record, sector, block and bucket can vary a little between different manufacturers, though the principles of the storage are similar in virtually every disc storage device.

Disc access time

We have seen that the time taken to read information from a sector is made up of the following elements:

Reasons for taking time in reading information from a sector

- **Seek time**, to move the disc head to the required track.
- **Latency**, the time taken to select the required disc head, i.e. which surface is required.
- **Search time**, to locate the required sector, which means waiting while the disc revolves to the required position.
- **Transfer time**, for the actual read/write operation.

Taking typical figures, relating to the example used above, to illustrate the times, we have

- **Seek time** varying with the number of tracks to be passed over; the minimum will be 0 (no movement), the maximum, typically 80 ms. (0.080 sec to move from the centre track to the outermost), with an average of 40 ms.

- **Latency** is effectively almost 0 but typically 1 or 2 ms. and constant for all transfers.
- **Search time** again could be zero but in the worst case would have to wait for a complete revolution of the disc which with a speed of 40 revolutions per second could take one fortieth of a second or 0.025 sec giving a minimum 0, maximum 25 ms. and average 12.5 ms.
- The **transfer rate** has already been computed as 307,200 ch.p.s.

To summarise, we can compute the time taken, in milliseconds, to access a particular record:

	Min.	*Av.*	*Max.*
Seek	0	40	80
Latency	2	2	2
Search	0	12.5	25
TOTAL	2	54.5	107

Therefore the total average access time is 54.5 ms. and the maximum access time is 107 ms.

Disc cylinders

On EDS and FDS each disc surface will have the same number of tracks and its own read/write head. Some of the more expensive systems have more than one head for each surface, with the heads spaced out evenly over the surfaces. All the heads are fixed to a single comb-like mechanism so that movement of any one head causes the complete set to move together over the corresponding tracks on each surface.

On systems with a single head per surface, when the head mechanism is at rest, the heads may access one track from each surface. This set of tracks form what is known as a **cylinder** and the tracks in any cylinder are all of identical radius and lie one below each other. The disc sectors are numbered in sequence from track zero on surface zero through one complete cylinder before proceeding to the next. Sequential files are organised so that each complete cylinder is processed in turn to minimise disc head movement. Where a disc uses more than one head per track, there will still be a single head mechanism and the cylinder still refers to the set of tracks accessible with the heads at rest, though physically it may look like several cylinders, one inside the other. It is most important to understand this **cylinder concept**.

Disc file access

Disc files may be processed

- with **serial access** in the same manner as for magnetic tape when the transfer rate will be comparable to tape;
  or
- with **direct access** which is often, misleadingly, called random access since 'random' normally implies selection by chance but here it means the processing sequence demanded by the data is random.

We may see from the example of a calculation of access time that using direct access we are normally able to locate and read any record within about 0.1−0.2 sec., which is quite satisfactory for demand processing. Individual records for direct access may be located by a number of techniques including:

- Use of a key field, with either a field or a number within a field, giving the exact sector address.
- Address generation using an arithmetic algorithm taking the key field and computing the sector address.
- Use of an index.

Disc file organisation

The various methods of access to disc sectors can be adapted to implement a number of alternative strategies of file organisation, of which the most common are serial, sequential, random, indexed, indexed sequential and linked file organisation. We can now apply some of the techniques already discussed and summarise the methods as follows:

- **Serial** organisation is where records are unsorted and stored one after another, in a similar manner to magnetic tape. The usual way in which a record is accessed is to read the complete file until the one required is located.

" Strategies for file organisation "

- **Sequential** organisation is similar to serial but has the records sorted according to a specified key field. The access to a record may involve reading through the file until the desired record is located. As the records are in sequence, a missing record is more quickly detected once its position in the file is passed. Alternatively access may be by a technique called **binary search** where the middle record is examined and the file then divided into two halves successively until the wanted record is located.

- **Random** organisation is where the records are stored in unique sectors according to some characteristic or to the contents of a 'key field'. A specified record on the disc may be accessed directly by using a set of rules called an **addressing algorithm** in what is often referred to as random access, but ought really to be called direct access. However, random organisation is an acceptable term and is so-named because in computing the sector address, the records on the file appear to be stored at random intervals and it is not possible to tabulate the complete file without having a complete list of keys. This can be thought of as similar to the storage of books on the shelves of a library, where each book will be stored on a shelf according to a classification code and a borrower may walk direct to the shelf and select the required book, which will be stored alphabetically within the category. A complete tabulation of books in accession number sequence is only really feasible by using a separate index, called the library accession register.

- **Indexed** organisation uses direct access but maintains an additional file or index relating each key to its sector. In the case of a large file there may be several indexes; an initial coarse index selects the relevant finer index.

- **Indexed sequential** file organisation is an indexed file where the records are stored in sequence but use the key field to compute the cylinder which contains the record. Within the cylinder there will be a finer index to locate the individual records. It therefore allows the program direct access to a record as well as allowing a complete tabulation if required. This overcomes the problem where, in order to access a group of related records in a serial file, it may be necessary to read the complete file. In a direct access file, access to related records may be slow due to an excessive amount of disc head movement caused by the *random* organisation of the file.

- **Linked files**, sometimes called **chained files**, are set up initially as sequential files but each record contains a field which specifies the sector address of the next record. This is ideal for cross-referencing in an information retrieval system. An extension to this technique uses several such sequences of addresses to allow retrieval in more than one sequence. This is called a **multilist** and an example is a company which might wish to access its orders file firstly in customer sequence, to see what products have been delivered to a customer, and then in product sequence, to list all the customers purchasing a particular product.

To summarise:

Organisation	Access
Sequential or **Serial**	Access much be SERIAL; minimises seek time and so optimises the run time for a large volume of transactions. Impractical for demand processing.
Random	Requires direct access and allows demand processing. Inefficient for a large transaction file. Does not permit a complete file tabulation.
Indexed	A compromise; allows sequential and direct access. Direct access may take two or three times longer than for random organisation, but allows flexibility of access to the same file: i) DIRECT for update or enquiry ii) SERIAL for long tabulations iii) SELECTIVE for information retrieval.

There are a number of factors to be taken into account when deciding which disc access strategy to adopt. One measure which is often applied is **hit rate**, which measures the proportion of master records accessed by transactions in a particular run. For example, a payroll run may access all the records except those of employees who left during the year and could have a hit rate of 98 per cent and thus be ideal for serial access, whereas a weekly run to amend the master file with new employees and incorporate changes to the records of existing staff might have a hit rate of only 1 or 2 per cent.

Update of direct access files

Recall that when updating a serial file on magnetic tape, a second copy has to be made as individual records cannot be written back to the tape. However, when using magnetic disc we are able to read and write sectors and update individual sectors using the following steps:

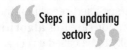

Steps in updating sectors

- Read from disc the block or sector containing the transaction
- Extract the record from the block within memory
- Amend the master record in the memory
- 'Pack' the record back into the block held in memory
- Re-write to disc the block containing the master record

There are a number of problems associated with direct access processing:

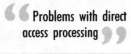

Problems with direct access processing

1   When a record is deleted it is not, in fact, deleted from the disc but a 'delete marker' is written to the disc and this may reserve the same space as an active record.
2   Unexpected growth in the activities of some part of the system may cause the overflow of assigned disc areas.
3   In the absence of other procedures, any update to a record over-writes or destroys the original version of the record and so a change may be irreversible.

Direct access files have to be copied, from time to time, to another disc or, quite often, to magnetic tape in a process called **dumping**. This may allow:

- Restart after a system failure;
- Checking procedures for audit and control;
- Reassignment of disc areas.

A multi-access system may also make a copy of all the transactions which occur between dumps to another 'journal' file which can be used with the dump to repeat update procedures and restore the file to its state at the failure. This can be done on a **file generation** strategy where three or more versions are retained; the latest version is called *son*, the one before is called *father* and the oldest of the three is called *grandfather*. The existence of these allows the repetition of any run after a hardware or software failure.

Fixed disc storage

The need to purchase the removable disc packs has led towards a standardisation of the majority of EDS systems, but this is not the case for Fixed Disc Storage (FDS). All systems use surfaces, tracks, cylinders and sectors, but the devices can be further divided into **fixed head** and **moving head** systems. The moving head systems work the same way as EDS, but the fixed head devices use one head for each individual track. There is a middle ground where each head accesses a group of adjacent tracks to minimise the disc head movement time.

Drum storage

This was the first type of file store and consists of a rotating drum coated on the outer surface with magnetisable material and organised with tracks on the outer surface. Processing may be considered to be the same as for a fixed head disc, with access generally much faster than EDS (no seek time), e.g. 5 ms., with transfer rates up to 1.5 million characters per second. However capacity is limited compared to disc, and drum storage is rare in modern computers.

Floppy discs

The floppy disc was developed originally to provide a cheap file storage device for small business computers. The original discs were contained in an 8-inch square plastic sleeve but were soon superceded by the 5¼-inch disc; this in turn is being overtaken by the 3½-inch disc which, although still called a floppy disc, is contained within a rigid plastic case. There have been at least two other 3 inch type discs, including the one on the Amstrad PCW computers, but none has gained the popularity that comes from widespread use on different models of computer. This is the only way in which the price of disc drives and the discs themselves can be reduced. The 5¼-inch disc has a case with a slot for read/write access, a hole for the spindle, and a hole to locate a hole within the disc which marks the start of the track. The disc rotates within the sleeve at about 300 r.p.m. or five times per second. Unlike EDS and FDS systems, and also the original 8-inch floppy discs and the newer 3½-inch systems, the disc does not rotate continuously but stops for a short time after each read/write and starts rotating again when the next access is encountered. This gives a further delay with a motor start time of about one second. The standard forty-track disc used on a BBC microcomputer has:

- 40 tracks per surface
- 10 sectors per track
- 256 bytes per sector
- Disc capacity is then $40 \times 10 \times 256 = 102,400$ bytes, usually referred to as 100K.
- Average access time is 0.75 sec.
- Data transfer rate of 12.8K bytes per second once the sector is located

Alternative systems use eighty tracks, two-sided discs and double density recording to increase the number of bytes per track to more than a million bytes per disc. The 3½-inch systems have a similar capacity. It is almost a paradox that the smaller discs can achieve a higher packing density because their rotation has greater predictability or precision.

Winchester discs

A Winchester disc, also called a **hard disc**, is a moving head disc which is not normally removable. The disc and the heads are assembled in a unit in clean conditions. They are designed for the more expensive end of the microcomputer market and are much cheaper than standard FDS systems, have greater density, but smaller total capacity. The typical capacity is 32 Mbytes (32 Megabytes or 32,000,000 bytes) and these drives are fitted as standard in most 16-bit business microcomputers. Unfortunately, manufacturers have started referring to such computers as having a 32 Mbyte memory, which is quite misleading as we have seen that memory is something quite different.

When the Winchester discs first appeared in the mid 1980s the cost was in the region of £3,000, but by 1990 the price had dropped by a factor of ten. It is now possible to buy for less than £300 a device called a **hard card**, which is a Winchester disc printed on a circuit board containing the disc controller. The board can be mounted quite simply into many microcomputers.

CD-ROM

The CD-ROM or **optical disc** uses laser technology, adapted for computer input, and holds, say, 600 million bytes of information, which is the equivalent of about 200,000 pages of A4 text. It is a read only device but would be ideal to store the applications program library or a large, static database.

VARIABLE LENGTH DATA

In many applications there are alphanumeric fields which can vary in length between records. For example, the surname may be as short as two letters for a Mr On or twenty to thirty characters for a long double-barrelled name. This provides a problem in systems design since, if the maximum field length is much greater than the average length, then setting a fixed field size equal to the maximum length will result in a great deal of wasted space. Various techniques have therefore been devised to use fields of *variable length*, of which the most common are:

- To put additional bytes in front of the field holding a *counter* specifying the number of characters contained in the field.
- To use a *special character* to indicate the end of the field.

■ To start the field with additional bytes containing a *pointer* in the form of a number indicating the position of the start of the next field.

All of these strategies use additional characters and require additional processing but save overall storage space and so may reduce the time required to read a file. If a record has one or more variable length fields, the record itself may also be of variable length. Variable length records may also arise from having a variable number of fields in the record. Take, for example, a school library system; the sixth form and staff may be allowed up to fifteen books, but on average only borrow four or five. A possible record structure might include:

■ Borrower reference
■ Borrower's name
■ Books allowed
■ Total books issued

then for each book

■ Book reference
■ Date issued

In this application, the length of the record will vary with the number of books on loan.

Processing variable length records

The techniques required to deal with variable length *records* are similar to those mentioned above for variable length *fields*. In general, a record of variable length will always be split into two parts:

1 A *fixed length part*, containing the fields of fixed length which occur in every record.
2 A *variable length part*, containing the variable length fields and the fields which either do not occur in all the records or which occur in variable numbers.

The way in which these are processed include:

■ Using a field in the fixed length part, giving the number of characters contained in the record or the number of repetitions of a group of fields

■ Using a special character to indicate the end of the record

■ Including a field in the fixed length part containing a pointer to the position of the start of the next record

If the file is to be sorted, the sort key must be in the fixed length part as must be the key field for direct access. In general, software for variable length records is highly complex and may be both more costly and limited in facilities.

INDEXED FILES

The elements of the organisation of **indexed files** can be studied with the aid of a particular example used in an examination set by the Cambridge Board and shown in Fig. 6.5. This question deals with the organisation of a large file of variable length records held on disc and subject to frequent insertions and deletions. The file occupies a number of blocks, some of which contain records, some of which contain the index, and the rest of which are free. The records in the file are not stored in any particular order, but each has a key field by which it is referenced. After the last record in each block there is an end marker, so the blocks have a variable number of variable length records separated either by end of record markers or by the use of pointers. The end marker mentioned above is used to detect the end of the last record in the block.

The index consists of two parts, a **primary index** which occupies a single block, shown as block 1 in the diagram, and a **secondary index** occupying several blocks, represented by blocks 15, 33 and 49. The secondary index contains an entry for each record in the file, consisting of a copy of the record key field and the number of the block in which the record is stored. Each block of the secondary index contains a count of the number of entries in it, followed by the entries, and all the entries in the secondary index are held in ascending order of key. The primary index block contains the block number of the *first free block* (or −1 if there are none) and a count of the secondary index blocks, followed by an entry for each block in the secondary index. These entries consist of the highest key referred to in that secondary index block, together with its block number, and they are held in ascending order of key.

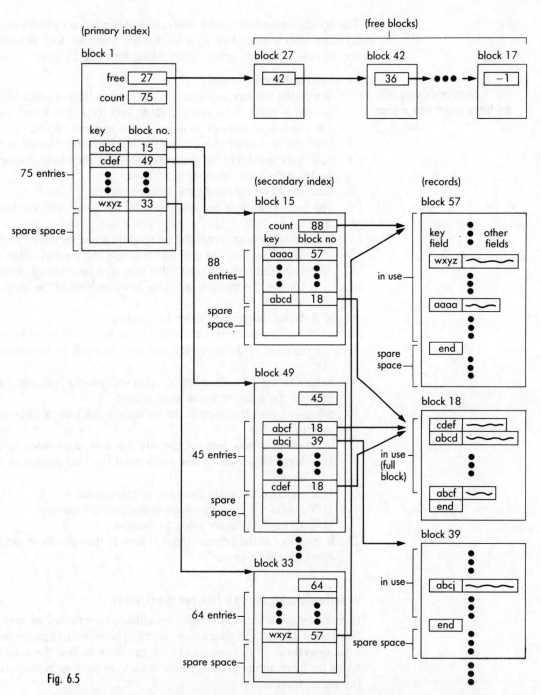

Fig. 6.5

Each free block contains a single entry, the block number of the **next free block, or −1** if there is none, to form a chain starting with the first free **block** referred to in the primary index. This last sentence, taken from the question, **needs a little more** explanation; it is a simple example of a linked file structure. If it is **necessary to create a new block then** the primary index indicates that block 27 is the **first one available and, on being taken** into use, the 'first free' pointer will be replaced **by the pointer from block 27, i.e. 42,** to indicate that the first free block is now 42.

To illustrate the means of **access, assume we wish to retrieve the** record with key 'abcj'; the steps are as follows:

1 Load the primary index
2 Search **the primary index until a key greater** than or equal to 'abcj' is found; **remembering that these are stored in** ascending sequence, in this case it would be **'cdef'**
3 **Load the secondary index using the** block number located in the primary index; in this **example it will be block 49**
4 Search the **45 entries in block** 49 for the entry for 'abcj' which, as can be seen, has a block number of 39
5 Load block 39 and look for the key 'abcj'
6 The record can now be retrieved for processing

The question asked for a brief description of the actions which may need to be taken when a record with a given key is to be deleted from the file, including consideration of the special cases that may arise. Again taking this step by step:

Steps in deleting from the file a record with a given key

1   Load the primary index
2   Search the primary index until a key greater than or equal to that of the record to be deleted is found. If no entry greater than the key is found, then there is an error in that there is an attempt to delete a non-existent record
3   Load the secondary index using the block number located in the primary index
4   Search the entries in the secondary index for the required entry: if it is not found then we have the same error as in 2 above
5   Load the block containing the desired record
6   The record can now be removed from the block, and the block written back to the disc
7   If the block is now containing no records it can be added to the free list
    7.1 Write the block to disc with a single entry equal to the previous free pointer
    7.2 Load the primary index (this may well be retained permanently in memory)
    7.3 Change the free pointer to the block address of the block to be added to the free list
    7.4 Write the primary index to the disc
    Notice that new entries are added to the head of the free list and so will be the first to be removed. This last-in first-out structure will be described as a stack in Chapter 14.
8   Return to the secondary index which will, almost certainly, be retained in memory
9   Remove the entry to the deleted record
10 Subtract 1 from the count in the secondary index block and write the secondary index back to the disc
11 If the count is now zero we can add this secondary index block to the free list
    11.1 Write this block to disc and amend the free pointer as described in 7.1 to 7.3 above
    11.2 Remove the entry from the primary index
    11.3 Subtract 1 from the count in the primary index
    11.4 Write the primary index to the disc
12 If the count in the primary index is now 1, then the file is empty and a report to that effect should be given

Overflow problems and file reorganisation

In maintaining any indexed system, on adding a new record we may reach the stage where there is insufficient space for a new record to be added to a particular block; this is referred to as **overflow**. In the example of the previous section the solution would be simply to divide the block into two, using a new block from the free list and creating an extra entry in the higher level index.

For an indexed sequential file and some other structures there is an alternative strategy in that all these 'overflow' records are written to a single block within the same cylinder, known as the *overflow block* or the *overflow sector*. If there is an overflow in the overflow block, entries will be added to yet another special area, known as the *overflow cylinder*.

After a large number of insertions and deletions there may be an excessive number of records in the overflow areas and there will be a utility operation to copy all the records in sort-key sequence to a sequential file. This sequential file will then be read back and used to create a new indexed sequential file with the overflow areas empty and sufficient gaps left in each block to allow for insertions.

Hierarchical file structures

One other file structure which should be investigated is the hierarchical structure used in Prestel and Viewdata systems. In this structure, each record can be linked to one or more lower level records in a tree-like structure. As implemented in Prestel, there is a general index on page one and this is linked to a number of other pages such as Sport, Travel, Microcomputing and Education. Each of these allows access to records at an increasing level of detail by displaying finer and finer indexes until the desired record is located.

FILE SECURITY AND FILE RECOVERY

As a final topic in this chapter we should touch on the problems of file security. With magnetic tape systems there is a well-defined and well-known system of retaining file generations. Thus referring back to Fig. 6.3 we see there are three principal files in use:

- The transaction file
- The input master file
- The new master file

It is normal to retain at least three versions of the input master file and these are referred to as three *generations*, and named as grandfather (the oldest), father and son (the most recent). Each week, son is used as the input master and the result of the update will be a new son; the old son becomes father, father becomes grandfather and the previous grandfather is re-cycled as a work tape. If the transaction files are retained over the same period, it means that if a file is lost, becomes corrupt or unreadable, or an error in the system is detected, then we can go back to an earlier generation of master and run it with the relevant transaction file to **recover** the lost or corrupt file. This same process can be adopted for serial processing systems on EDS or floppy disc.

For real time systems a **snapshot** dump of the master file is taken at regular prescribed intervals, usually to magnetic tape, and all the transactions between dumps are also written to a transaction backup file. These will normally be retained on a similar 'generation' system to the serial systems so that in the event of a failure the master file can be re-loaded from the previous dump and all subsequent transactions repeated from the transaction file. This process is essential in any real-time or multi-access system.

PRACTICAL STEPS

As with all aspects of hardware it is important to relate the material in this chapter to actual devices in use in schools, colleges and in business. A useful source of material are the equipment manuals, furthermore it is important to take every opportunity to see equipment demonstrated when visiting any company. It is useful to see *demonstrations* of filing systems, for example how Prestel and reservation systems are used in a local travel agency.

It is important to realise that the study of past examination questions reveals that the terms serial and sequential are often used for the same structure and this is not uncommon for terminology throughout this subject. At least one computer manufacturer advertises its machine with 32 Mbytes of memory, referring to the internal hard disc. The only remedy is to be in a position to understand fully the concepts and background to the subject and not be put off by the occasional unconventional use of jargon.

EXAMINATION QUESTIONS

SHORT QUESTIONS

Question 1
What is meant by 'hit rate' in the context of file processing? How does it influence the choice of file organisation? (Northern Ireland 1988)

Question 2
Why are logically consecutive sectors of a disc sometimes not stored in physically adjacent sectors? (NEAB 1988)

Question 3
Describe *each* of the following types of file organisation:

i) Serial file

ii) Sequential file

iii) Random file

Suggest a situation in which *each* type of file would be the appropriate choice. In *each* case indicate briefly how records can be saved and retrieved.   (Welsh AS 1989)

Question 4

Suggest *three* distinct reasons why a large food warehouse should use an indexed sequential organisation for their stock file in an on-line computerised stock control system.

(AEB 1989)

Question 5

In the context of disc or tape storage, explain what is meant by the blocking of records. Give *one* reason why blocking is used.   (AEB 1988)

Question 6

Explain why a magnetic disc needs to be formatted before it can be used to store data. What is the function of the directory which is created on the disc?   (London 1989)

Question 7

a) Before a floppy disc can be used for the first time it must usually be *formatted*. Explain briefly what this involves and why it is necessary.

b) A disc is formatted and has files written to it using a particular computer system. Why may it be difficult to read the contents of the disk using a different make of computer?

c) What are the main benefits of having two floppy disc drives on a microcomputer that has no other forms of backing storage?   (Cambridge 1988)

LONGER QUESTIONS

Question 8

A magnetic tape is 2,400 feet long and can hold 1,600 characters per inch.

a) Calculate the theoretical maximum storage capacity of the tape.
   Note: 12 inches = 1 foot.

For a particular application, the data is held in fixed length records of 200 characters each with several records per block. Each inter-block gap occupies half an inch.

b) Assuming that only the blocks of records and the inter-block gaps are held, what items of information, other than the data of the records, would normally be held on the tape?

c) Calculate the storage capacity if
   i) 4 records
   ii) 16 records
   are stored per block.

d) What factors might influence the choice of the number of records stored per block?

(Cambridge 1988)

Question 9

Magnetic tape is used as a backing storage medium on mainframe computers.

a) In this context describe, with the aid of diagrams,
   i) A format in which data may be stored on magnetic tape, including the form and purpose of the beginning and end of tape markers
   ii) The way in which a magnetic tape drive operates, including the effect of the write permit ring

b) A particular magnetic tape drive records data at 1,600 bytes per inch, the read/write speed of the tape is 75 inches per second and the inter block gaps are 0.5 inch.
   i) Calculate the transfer rate of this tape drive.

ii) Calculate the effective transfers rates in reading a file of 1 megabyte held in

1   512 byte blocks
2   1,024 byte blocks
3   2,048 byte blocks
4   4,096 byte blocks

You may assume the tape continues to travel at read/write speed over the inter-block gaps.

c)   What practical limitations might there be in increasing the block size?

(AEB 1984)

Question 10

A credit card company currently operates its computer system in both on-line and batch processing modes. When customers use their credit cards in order to make purchases, a copy of each sales voucher is made out by the shop assistants and is returned to the credit card company by post. A customer master file is maintained by daily processing of the sales vouchers in batch mode. Once each month the master file is processed to produce a statement for each customer, also in batch mode. The statements list every transaction which has taken place since the last statement was printed, the outstanding balance, the interest charged, and the minimum payment due from the account holder.

a)   State *six* items of data that must be recorded at the time of purchase.

b)   Describe the likely structure of both a master file record and a transaction-file record.

c)   Outline *four* batch processing activities which will have to be carried out upon the customer master file in addition to that described above.

d)   Describe *one* real-time activity, involving the customer master file, which might be carried out under the present system.

e)   State a suitable file organisation for the customer master file and justify your choice.

f)   Due to the limitations of the present system, the company has decided to investigate the use of point-of-sale terminals. Describe *two* advantages of such a development from the point of view of the company.   (London AS 1989)

Question 11

a)   Describe what is meant by a sequential file structure. Give the advantages of this type of file structure.

b)   A library keeps a file containing details of the books borrowed by users. Records in the file include the following fields:

- Books identification number
- User identification number
- Date user borrowed
- Date book returned

This file is used to answer queries such as: 'list all the users who have borrowed a given book'. Suggest a suitable file organisation and describe how the file be processed to deal with the above query.   (London 1985)

Question 12

A file of data stored on a magnetic tape consists of 10,000 records, each containing 280 characters. The tape density is 560 characters per inch and there are 1-inch gaps between each block. Each record is stored in a separate block. When at rest in the middle of an inter-block gap the tape takes 0.01 seconds to reach the start of the next block. It also takes an equal amount of time to stop the tape. At full speed the tape travels at 100 inches per second. The usable part of the 2,400-foot tape is approximately 27,000 inches.

a)   i) How many records could the magnetic tape hold?

     ii) If only one block of data is read and processed at a time, how long will it take to search the file for all records containing a particular keyword? (You may assume that computing time is negligible compared with tape travel time.)

iii) What would be the advantages of storing more than one record in a block?

b) If the file is unordered, describe how a second magnetic tape could be produced from the first which contains the same records sorted on a particular field. You may assume that several magnetic tape drives are available.　　　　　　　　(Cambridge 1983)

Question 13

a) Describe the following methods by which files on a direct access storage device may be organised:
　i) serial
　ii) indexed sequential
　iii) random (or direct)

b) For each of the following files state with reasons the organisation you would use:
　i) A stock file to be accessed from an on-line terminal
　ii) A payroll file

c) Before a random file can be created it may be necessary to specify the following parameters.

$$\text{Block packing density} = \frac{\text{Number of records to be allocated per block}}{\text{Number of records a block could hold}}$$

$$\text{Cylinder packing density} = \frac{\text{Number of home blocks per cylinder}}{\text{Total number of blocks per cylinder}}$$

Explain the relevance of these two parameters.

d) It is sometimes necessary to reorganise a random file after much use. What circumstances give rise to the need for reorganisation and what is the effect of the reorganisation upon the file and access to it?　　　　　　　　(AEB 1984)

OUTLINE ANSWERS

SHORT QUESTIONS

Question 1
Hit rate measures the proportion of records in file, accessed in a particular run. It influences the choice of file organisation in as much as for a high hit rate, batch processing is the most appropriate, whilst for a low hit rate, direct access would be recommended.

Question 2
This question could be answered in two different ways and it is hard to predict what is being sought by the examiner. One possible reason why logically consecutive sectors of a disc might not be stored in physically adjacent sectors refers to the storage of records in 'cylinders' so that two consecutive records could be on different surfaces.

The other reason is that the file might be indexed sequentially and so consecutive records might be in entirely different parts of the disc, with one contained in an overflow sector or even an overflow track.

Question 3
i) A **serial** file is where records are unsorted and stored one after another. The normal way in which a record is accessed is to read the complete file until the one required is located. A typical example is the transaction file of data entered into a batch processing system.

ii) A **sequential** file has the records sorted according to a specified key field. Again, access to a record may involve reading through the file until the desired record is located but as the records are in sequence a missing record is more quickly detected once its position in the file is passed. An example of an application is the master file of a payroll system or any master file with a high hit rate during processing.

iii) A **random** file has records which are stored in particular sectors according to some characteristic or the contents of a 'key field'. Records are accessed directly by using a set of rules called an addressing algorithm. An example of a situation where a random file would be used is any type of seat reservation system where direct access would be essential and sequential access might not be relevant.

Question 4

A large food warehouse should use an indexed sequential organisation for their stock file in an on-line computerised stock control system for the following reasons:
 i) Direct access will be required for on-line enquiries
 ii) Sequential access will be required for stock tabulations
 iii) Indexed sequential files have flexibility in allowing additional records to be inserted

Question 5

Data organised in disc or tape storage is in units called blocks containing several records which are read or written together.

One reason why blocking is used is to speed processing by minimising the number of physical accesses to the tape or disc.

Question 6

A magnetic disc needs to be formatted before it can be used for a number of reasons, firstly to erase any data or random magnetisation of the disc, secondly to mark the position of the various tracks and sectors, thirdly to number or label sectors for subsequent access and lastly to create a (blank) directory on the disc.

Disc files are stored using a system broadly similar to an indexed file of variable length records. The directory holds the name of each file plus other information such as its length and position on the disc.

LONGER QUESTIONS

Question 7

a)   The functions of formatting a floppy disc were described in the previous answer.
b)   A disc formatted on one system might prove difficult to read on a different make of computer since the number of tracks may be different. Also the number of sectors per track may differ and furthermore the operating system may organise the directories differently on the two computers. Finally the method of recording the data might be different.
c)   The main benefits of having two floppy disc drives on a microcomputer that has no other forms of backing storage are that the on-line storage capacity is doubled and also files may be quickly copied or 'backed up' from one disc to another. In most systems it is essential to keep a disc with operating system routines loaded all the time and this may reduce the on-line work space.

Question 8

a)   The tape length is 2,400 feet or $12 \times 2,400 = 28,800$ inches
     The theoretical maximum storage capacity is $1,600 \times 28,800 = 46,080,000$ characters
     Note: 12 inches = 1 foot.
b)   Apart from the blocks of records and the inter-block gaps, the tape will also hold header and trailer labels, the former holding the file name, creation date, generation number, retention period etc.
c)   With packing density of 1,600 characters per inch, a fixed length record of 200 characters occupies 0.125 inches and each inter-block gap occupies half an inch.
     i) with 4 records per block, the block size is $(4* 0.125) + 0.5 = 1''$
         so the tape holds 28,800 blocks of 4 records each
         or a total of 115,200 records
     ii) with 16 records per block, the size is $(16* 0.125) + 0.5 = 2.5''$
         so the tape holds $(28,800/2.5) = 11,520$ blocks of 16 records each
         or a total of 184,320 records

d) The factors which might influence the choice of blocking factor (number of records stored per block) are:
 i) Maximise the blocking factor to minimise number of reads
 ii) Minimise the blocking factor to reduce memory use
 iii) Using disc we consider sector size to minimise the unused space

Taking this last point, if the disc sectors are 512 characters:

1 record per block uses 200 characters in each 512 character sector wasting 312 or 61%
2 records per block uses 400 characters in each 512 character sector wasting 112 or 22%
3 records per block uses 600 characters in pair of sector wasting (1024−600) = 424 or 41%
4 records per block uses 800 characters in pair of sector wasting (1024−800) = 224 or 22%
5 records per block uses 1,000 characters in pair of sector wasting (1024−1000) = 24 or 2%

Question 9

a) Data is stored on magnetic tape in a number of magnetised spots **frames** across the tape, with each frame positioned in one of a number of tracks or channels (usually seven or nine) across the tape (refer to Fig. 6.1).
 Magnetic tape can only be read or written when moving at full speed, hence data is written in blocks, separated by inter-block gaps which allow for the time it takes for the tape to accelerate to full speed and decelerate to rest between accessing blocks of data(refer to Fig. 6.2). Data blocks may contain a single record but, more usually, contain a number of logical records collected together in memory and written to tape in a single operation.
 Each file will start with a length of blank header tape terminated by a beginning of tape marker − a physical mark which is detected by the drive. When a tape is loaded it will be wound on to this marker, the file will start with a special record called a header record which will normally contain a number of fields including the name of the file, version number and creation date, which will be read and checked by the program before any record is processed. The tape file will be terminated by another special record called the endfile record which will contain a special code which is detected by the program as it attempts to read the data and there will be, in addition, an end of tape marker which can also be detected during a read operation. The endfile record can also contain record counts and control totals for the file.
 The drive operates by reading a reel of tape from a feed spool to a take-up spool at about 100 inches per second. Unlike audio systems, there are two tape reservoirs between the spools and the read−write heads where the tape is contained in a vacuum in a long loop to allow for a smooth feeding past the heads at this speed also to allow for a quick stop and start which could not be achieved from a spool. There will be three elements in the read− write mechanism: erase, write and read, so that in a write operation the previous data is erased, the new data written and then immediately read back as a check. The write permit ring is a ring of metal or plastic which, when fitted to the tape spool will set a switch on the drive mechanism which can physically prevent data being written to the tape.

b) i) The transfer rate, as quoted by manufacturers, would simply reflect the speed of 75 inches per second and 1,600 bytes per inch. This gives:
 $75 \times 1,600 = \underline{120,000 \text{ characters per second}}$

 ii) 1 megabyte is 1,024,000 bytes and these will occupy
 $1,024,000/1600 = \underline{640'' \text{ of tape}}$

 1) With a block size of 512 bytes there will be 2,000 blocks
 2,000 inter-block gaps take 1,000″ tape
 Total tape length = 640″ + 1,000″ = 1,640″
 Total reading time = 1,640/75 seconds
 Effective transfer rate for the 1mB file
 $$= \frac{1,024,000 \times 75}{1,640}$$
 $$= \underline{46,829 \text{ characters per second}}$$

2) With a block size of 1,024 bytes there will be 1,000 blocks
    1,000 inter-blocks gaps take 500″ tape
    Total tape length = 640″ + 500″ = 1,140″
    Total reading time = 1,140/75 seconds
    Effective transfer rate for the 1mB file
    $$= \frac{1,024,000 \times 75}{1,140}$$
    = 67,368 characters per second

3) With a block size of 2,028 bytes there will be 500 blocks
    500 inter-block gaps take 250″ tape
    Total tape length = 640″ + 250″ = 890″
    Total reading time = 890/75 seconds
    Effective transfer rate for the 1mB file
    $$= \frac{1,024,000 \times 75}{890}$$
    = 86,292 characters per second

4) With a block size of 4,096 bytes there will be 250 blocks
    250 inter-block gaps take 125″ tape
    Total tape length = 640″ + 125″ = 765″
    Total reading time = 765/75 seconds
    Effective transfer rate for the 1mB file
    $$= \frac{1,024,000 \times 75}{765}$$
    = 100,392 characters per second

iii) The practical limitation in increasing the block size is the amount of memory that is available to store the blocks. If there were to be two tape files, one input and one output, and there were double buffers for each then this means there must be enough memory for four blocks to be held at the same time. Thus, if the block size were 4K, then 16K of memory would be used.

Question 10

a) Items to be recorded at the time of purchase are:

- Customer reference
- Total amount
- Shop reference
- Goods purchased
- Date
- Customer signature

b) A transaction record might contain:

- Shop reference
- Customer reference
- Date
- Total amount
- Indicator to specify sale, credit or payment received

The requirements for the customer master file are not entirely clear from the question. First of all the file will contain fixed data for the customer, it is likely that this is what was meant by **master file**:

- Customer reference
- Customer name
- Customer address
- Credit limit
- Balance brought forward

but it also indicates that a record is stored for each transaction in the month for processing at the end of the month in a customer master file:

- Shop reference
- Date
- Total amount
- Indicator to specify sale, credit or payment received

c) The four batch processing activities to be carried out on the customer master file are:

- Data entry
- Data validation
- Sorting by customer reference
- Merging into the file of transactions for the month

d) One real-time activity could be the answering of a query from a shop at the time of purchase to see if the customer has sufficient credit for a purchase.

e) Customer master file ought to be indexed sequentially to allow real-time enquiries as well as the batch processing described above.

f) Installation of point-of-sale terminals able to read the magnetic stripe on a credit card would allow direct input to the system and cut out the data entry and validation stages. In addition, the master file could be interrogated at the time of the sale to check validity of the sale against credit limit and to check that the card is not reported lost or stolen.

Question 11

a) A sequential file structure is where records which are unsorted are stored one after another, with the records sorted according to a specified key field. The way in which a record is accessed is to read through the complete file until the desired record is located.

Among the advantages of this type of file structure are that it is a simpler strategy to program, the retrieval of records is faster for applications with a high hit rate and, compared to serial files, it is more efficient since searching through a file for a particular record may be quicker. This is because once the position where the record *would have been located* has been reached, we will know it is missing *without* reading the remainder of the file.

b) There are a number of possibilities for this answer. For current borrowings, the simplest would be to have a sequential file of borrowers; queries requiring a list of all the users who have borrowed a particular book could be made by a serial search through the file. If, however, there are a large number of such searches to be made, the sequential file structure will be much too slow. Furthermore, there is an ambiguity in this question in that it *could* refer to a complete historical record of readers over a period. It would therefore be best to maintain a *separate* file containing just the fields:

- Books identification number
- User identification number

This could either be maintained as a *sequential file* with a batch processing type update and accessed as a serial search or, more likely, as an *indexed sequential file*. This would give direct access to the first borrowing of a particular book, and all subsequent borrowings would be quickly accessed from the same cylinder.

An even better answer would be to use a *linked structure* where the file structure would be:

- Books identification number
- User identification number
- Pointer giving address of next borrowing of this book

A pointer would be added to the main book file giving the address of the record giving the first borrowing of the book.

Question 12

a) i) Each block has 280 characters
    The tape density is 560 characters per inch
    Thus each block takes ½ inch
    There are 1-inch gaps between blocks
    Each block thus requires 1.5 inches
    Usable tape length is 27,000 inches
    Maximum number of records is 27,000/1.5 = 18,000

ii) As computing time is negligible compared with tape travel time we may assume that with buffering, the read statements are issued so quickly that the tape never slows down but runs at maximum speed for the full 10,000 records.

The file occupies $10,000 \times 1.5 = 15,000$ inches

Time to search all records at 100 inches per second is $15,000/100 =$ <u>150 seconds</u>

or 2.5 minutes

iii) The advantages of storing more than one record in a block would be that the file would take less space and be read quicker. For example, writing a block of ten records would use 5 inches for the block and 1 inch for the gap, so that ten records would require 6 inches and 10,000 records would only use 6,000 inches and be read in 60 seconds.

b) Assume that we have, in all, four tape drives available. The procedure then is:

1 The records from the unordered file will be read into memory until the memory is full and then sorted into the prescribed sequence.

2 This set of sorted records is called a 'sorted string' and is written to one of the spare magnetic tape drives.

3 Another 'memory full' of records is read in and a sorted string produced.

4 The process is continued until the complete file has been processed into sorted strings which are written alternately to two of the work tapes.

5 The operator is instructed to remove the input tape and replace it with a work tape. There are now two input tapes with sorted strings and two other drives with work tapes to use as output.

6 The next phase is to merge the first string from each of the two input tapes and create a new string, twice as long as one of the output tapes.

7 Step 6 is repeated, writing the new sorted strings alternately to each of the output tapes until the complete file has been processed, giving half as many strings, each doubled in length.

8 Steps 6 and 7 are repeated until there is just one sorted string containing the complete file.

There are other strategies which will allow sorting with three or more tapes.

Question 13

a) i) *Serial files* were explained in the answer to question 1.

ii) *Indexed sequential file organisation* is an indexed file where the records are stored in sequence but which uses the key field in place of a primary index to compute the cylinder or the block which contains the secondary index for that record. The file is initially set up in sequence but with gaps for insertions. It therefore gives the program direct access to a record as well as allowing a complete sequential tabulation if required.

iii) *Random*, or *direct organisation*, is where the records are stored in particular blocks according to some characteristic or the contents of a key field. Access to a record on disc uses a set of rules called an addressing algorithm. This is the organisation appropriate to on-line interrogation of files such as order processing or reservations for travel or entertainments.

b) i) A *stock file* to be accessed from an on-line terminal needs direct access in order to answer a query in real time.

ii) A *payroll file* is a batch processing application where almost every record will be accessed in each run, since all employees will be paid. Therefore serial or sequential organisation is the most appropriate.

c) *Block packing density* specifies the amount, or percentage, of space to be left in each block, since it computes the proportion of the block to be filled with records.

Cylinder packing density similarly computes the proportion of blocks to be used within a cylinder in setting up the initial file.

d) A random file will need to be organised from time to time, especially after a large number of insertions and deletions. There may then be an excessive number of records in the overflow areas which may slow the access to records in direct access mode.

There will be a program utility to copy all the records in sort-key sequence to a sequential file. This sequential file can then be read back and used to create a new indexed sequential file with the overflow areas empty and sufficient gaps left in each block to allow for insertions as computed from the parameters described in part c).

STUDENT ANSWERS WITH EXAMINER COMMENTS

Question 1

What is meant by 'hit rate' in the context of file processing? How does it influence the choice of file organisation? (Northern Ireland 1988)

❝It is the proportion of records not the number.❞

❝Sequential is the correct term, serial is unsorted sequential means ordered by a particular key field.❞

> Hit rate is the number of records in file, accessed by a program. It influences the choice of file organisation because if the hit rate is high we would use serial and for low hit rate indexed sequential organisation would be recommended.

❝Indexed sequential is possible but direct access should be specified and random organisation for direct access would be better.❞

Question 2

Why are logically consecutive sectors of a disc sometimes not stored in physically adjacent sectors? (NEAB 1988)

❝Not really incorrect but the two answers given earlier are better. Some operating systems, including those on a number of microcomputers are implemented in this way.❞

> Logically consecutive sectors of a disc might not be stored in physically adjacent sectors because when the file was created there might not have been much space left and the sectors might have had to have been chosen from different places scattered all over the disc.

Question 3

Describe **each** of the following types of file organisation?
  i) serial file
  ii) sequential file
  iii) random file

Suggest a situation in which **each** type of file would be the appropriate choice. In **each** case indicate briefly how records can be saved and retrieved. (Welsh AS 1989)

❝Serial files are unsorted.❞

❝This mixes up *sequential* with *indexed sequential*, part (i) was describing sequential.❞

> i) a *serial* file has records which are sorted and stored one after another serially on a magnetic tape. An example is the daily issues of a stock control system.
>
> ii) a *sequential* file has the records organised on disc with an index, therefore it is often called *indexed sequential*. An example of an application is the customer file used during processing orders received.
>
> iii) a *random* file has records which are stored at random on a disc to allow real-time access. An example of a random file is the master stock file used during processing issues and receipts.

❝The definition of random file is poorly expressed and the example is wrong. A master stock file used during processing issues and receipts would also need regular tabulations so indexed sequential is needed.❞

CHAPTER 7

STRUCTURED PROGRAMMING DESIGN

GETTING STARTED

The earlier chapters have concentrated on the hardware of computer systems and how it provides an environment for the programs or software. In this and the following chapters we shall look at the design, development, testing and documentation of programs. It is not the function of this book to cover the details of how to program in a high level language or to cover the coursework element of the syllabus. This would need a separate text and would need to concentrate on a single language and possibly even on the implementation of that language on one particular computer, because although languages such as Pascal are well defined and, for the most part, independent of machine, the use of editors and the mechanics of running the programs do vary considerably. If Basic is used, then a book is required for that implementation alone, because BBC Basic, for example, is very different to RML Basic or Microsoft Basic or any other implementation. The evolution of high level languages, the relative merits and choice of language will be dealt with in Chapter 8. Here we shall concentrate on the general principles of program design and on what is known as **structured programming**. This will be attempted in a 'language independent' manner since, as we shall see later, all the major logical constructs are available in most modern high level languages.

It is often difficult to convince students of one important truth in the study of programming, namely that 'the mechanics of the programming language are relatively simple'. Unfortunately most people learn a new language at the same time as they learn the techniques of program design and so confuse the difficulties of program design with the study of the language and write 'unstructured' programs. In this chapter we shall first concentrate on the elements of good design and only then examine how these can be implemented in a high level language program.

ELEMENTS OF PROGRAM DESIGN

TOP-DOWN PROGRAMMING

ERRORS IN PROGRAMS

PROGRAM TESTING

THE STAGES OF PROGRAMMING

PROGRAM TESTING AND DEBUGGING

STRUCTURED PROGRAMMING CONCEPTS

MODULAR PROGRAMMING AND STRUCTURED PROGRAMMING

ESSENTIAL PRINCIPLES

ELEMENTS OF PROGRAM DESIGN

Programming is essentially a practical subject and the principal means of learning the subject is by writing a number of programs. However, there are several topics which are important to study; for example, the types of structure to use, the characteristics of good program design, efficient program testing and the documentation to be provided. The task of program design is similar to using a toy construction set like Meccano or Lego where you have all the components and the nuts and bolts to hold them together, but after you have assembled the model the result may not look like what was intended and may not run as was intended. If this happens it is wrong simply to blame the kit or the diagrams or the instructions, or even yourself. The remedy is to take the model apart and to try again, being more careful with the methods of construction.

An experienced model builder knows that certain parts should be assembled first and others added later. This chapter will show some methods used by the experienced designer of computer programs. There is no one method put forward as the best; some are better than others and it is good practice for a programmer to try a number of methods to see which suits an individual and which method is best suited to particular applications.

We can illustrate some of the principles by looking at an example of a program to print the marks scored in examinations, in order to give an analysis of marks over a whole school. In this case we would need to cater for the situation where it may be necessary to list all the grades in one subject, an analysis of all the grades in every subject, or the performance of a particular candidate.

Bottom-up structure

The main characteristic of most program design strategies is 'where to start'. In the **bottom-up** approach, for example, the smaller, more crucial sections of the program are written first. These are then joined together to produce larger program blocks, which in turn are joined to one another to form larger blocks until the job is finished. This method makes it easy to understand what is going on and in the past was a very popular design. However, it suffers from a major drawback, in that it is very easy to create errors in logic which are not obvious initially and are sometimes not discovered until the complete program has been run live for some time. This is because the programmer does not always step back and take a detached view of the complete environment of the program.

One application which suits the bottom-up approach is where a computer is used to monitor and control some device or experiment. Here it may be advisable to start by writing and testing the small part of the program which communicates with the device, to check the interface, *before* developing the remainder of the program which carries out the analysis and communicates with the user. Another simple example, often adopted by programmers, is to write the central part of the print routine to print the output in a rough and ready format in order to check the essential elements of the output *before* tidying up the format to include alignment, headings, page footers and page throw routines.

Top-down structured programming

This is the most widely advocated method of program design and is the main method used by professional programmers. Its essential feature is a *tree structure*, or *hierarchical design*, illustrated by the same mark tabulation which could be specified first as:

1   Initialise the variables and open the files
2   Print the mark analysis
3   Close down the files and stop

Indeed in the Cobol language this could simply be written as:

```
PERFORM STARTUP
PERFORM PRINT-THE-MARKS
PERFORM CLOSE-DOWN
```

and in Pascal it could be coded as:

```
startup
print_the_marks
close_down
```

This does not mean that statements such as STARTUP, or PRINT-THE-MARKS are contained within the Cobol language, or similarly, that startup, print_the_marks and close_down are within Pascal. Each of these refers to procedures or routines which the programmer will have to write to carry out the operations required.

To use a language more familiar to many students, in BBC Basic, this could be coded as:

PROC_startup
PROC_print_the_marks
PROC_close_down

Each of these is then specified in the program by a statement enclosed within
DEF PROC . . .ENDPROC

There are a great variety of names which have been used for these program sub-divisions, varying between programming language and evolving with time. Unfortunately, examination candidates may need to be aware of many of the names since different examiners may have different prejudices. The most common are procedure, subroutine, function, sub program and module.

Terminology for program divisions

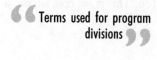
Terms used for program divisions

- **Procedure** is the most meaningful and, perhaps, the most common name.
- **Module**, which evolves from the strategy of **modular programming**, is a technique of developing large programs in small self-contained modules which is often, but not necessarily, the same as the **top-down** approach described in this chapter.
- **Subroutine**, or sub-routine, is the name used in the earliest popular high level programming language, Fortran, and has since been widely adopted by many programmers.

There are two types of *procedure*, which in Fortran and other languages are distinguished by having two different names, namely **subroutine** and **function**. In this context the main program should be called the **main routine**.

- **Function** is a procedure which returns a specific value for a variable, for example in Basic TAN(X) is a function which computes the tangent of X. There can also be **user functions** defined within the program. There are languages, such as **Forth**, and **functional programming** languages such as **ML** and **Miranda**, where the whole program is made up of nested function calls.
- **Subprogram** is, these days, a more unusual name which means, in effect, the same as procedure.

TOP-DOWN PROGRAMMING

Top-down design for computer programming is the design of a program from the top level of logic down to the fine detail, step by step; i.e. starting from the broad level of detail shown for the mark analysis program with a broad overview and then expanding the main module into lower and lower levels of detail. This structure is often illustrated as a tree as shown in Fig. 7.1. However this representation often hides one important aspect of modular programming, namely that the same module may be called from *more than one* branch of the tree. The routes down the tree are called **branches**, the modules are called

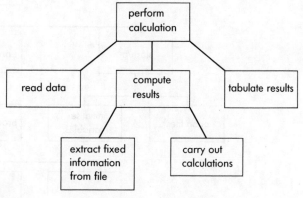

Fig. 7.1 Tree structure

nodes, and the lowest level of module is called a **root node.** The relationship between connected nodes is described by referring to the upper node of a connected pair as the **parent** and the lower level as its **descendants.** This is the reverse of nature, in that a tree structure in computing is normally illustrated as growing 'downwards' instead of upwards.

Structured programming languages such as Pascal implement procedures in exactly this hierarchical manner so that if a routine at the bottom of one root wishes to call or use a routine in another branch, then the request is passed up the tree and back down another set of branches.

A top-down design has a major *advantage,* that a change of any part of the program only affects those parts logically below it, often relatively few, and so the amount of additional amendment is minimised. In addition, it is very easy to divide the program design between several programmers and it should produce fewer causes of error, with the result that programs are produced quicker and with greater accuracy.

The main *disadvantages* of this approach are:

- When the program is executed, additional time is taken to pass a request from one module to another. In some real-time applications this delay may cause timing problems and a different method may have to be used.

> **Disadvantages of the top-down design**

- If space is at a premium, for example fitting an application into a 8K ROM chip for a microcomputer, then the extra instructions to implement a subroutine structure may take too much space.

- Finally, this strategy is often unpopular with programmers trained in an unstructured approach. This is because it requires a vastly different approach to program design and needs to be implemented *before* any coding is attempted. This is, of course, not a valid reason for avoiding the top-down approach.

Further example

Fig. 7.2 shows a more complex example which illustrates one of the most common program segments in commercial programming, the update of a serial file. The transaction file has three record types; an insertion, a deletion and an amendment; the master file and the transaction file are both sorted in the same sequence. The lowest level of routine is not shown for all branches but left as an exercise to complete.

> **ERRORS IN PROGRAMS**

When a program has been written, it cannot be expected to be correct and the programmer needs to locate and correct all the errors. These errors fall into two categories: **syntax errors** and **semantic or logic errors.** Syntax errors are the mistakes made in the actual grammar of the language, for instance the following short Basic program contains several syntax errors:

```
10 IMPUT X, Y
20 SET Z = X + W
30 DISPLAY Z
```

In line 10, the word INPUT is incorrectly spelt as IMPUT, in line 20 SET should be LET and in line 30, the statement DISPLAY is from Cobol and should be PRINT. Also, even

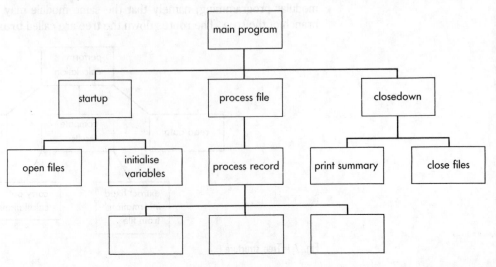

Fig. 7.2 Update of a serial file

with these corrections, the program will fail to run because line 20 attempts to add X and W and W has not been defined.

Some high-level programming languages, including Pascal and Cobol, demand that every variable is declared at the start of the program and its **type** and **size** specified, in which case the use of an undeclared variable would result in a syntax error.

PROGRAM TESTING

When modular programming is employed it becomes much easier to *trace, step through* or, *debug* programs. This is because each calling routine can be instructed to print a message announcing that the procedure call has taken place and values of certain crucial variables can be displayed. In addition, since each routine is completely independent of every other, they can be written and tested in isolation. As a result rewriting a routine should have virtually no effect on any other routine. This type of design strategy is vital to major applications since program maintenance is faster, cheaper and more reliable; it is also much easier for a programmer to maintain programs written by a colleague.

The most important point is that any program must have a defined structure, and the more well-defined the structure the easier the program will be to write, test, debug, and maintain. The testing of a program should commence with a **dry run** or **walkthrough**, where the programmer simulates the execution of the program using pencil and paper, partly to check the program and partly to determine the expected output from the actual test run. We shall return to this topic later in the chapter.

Logic errors in programs

Two of the most common causes of **logic error** in a program are:

1 Execution of one part of the program causes a variable used by another part of the program to be modified to a value which is not valid or not anticipated, causing an error such as an endless loop.
2 A logic branch from part of the program executes a routine, but the return point is not the same as the calling point because some conditional, or IF, statement bypasses the correct return statement. Thus the sequence of operations is not as desired under all conditions.

THE STAGES OF PROGRAMMING

THE JOB OF A PROGRAMMER

Programming is not just the writing, or coding, of program statements, but consists of a number of steps to see a project through:

- Identifying the requirements
- Designing the data structure, file layout and test data
- Using flowcharts or some other technique to specify the algorithm
- Writing the actual computer instructions
- Testing the program and correcting any errors
- Completing the program documentation

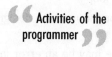 Activities of the programmer

Identifying the requirements

It is necessary to determine exactly what information is required from the program. In the business environment this responsibility is carried out by an individual known as a *systems analyst*, whose job will be defined and discussed in a later chapter. In many cases, particularly with small tasks, there may be no systems analyst as such, and the program will be designed by the programmer. In either case it is vital for the program requirements to be determined completely and unambiguously before the program design is commenced.

It is important to realise that it is impossible to write a good program until it is established precisely what the program should do and exactly what is available for the program to achieve it with.

Designing the data structure

Data structures, in particular, stacks, queues and trees, will be studied in Chapter 13. In designing the program we need to select the best form for data and files. It is good practice to decide at the same time to design test data, that is a specimen set of inputs to test that the program design is good and that the files are processed correctly.

Specifying the algorithm

There are several stages in this specification:

- Constructing a data flowchart showing the environment of the program, as in Fig. 6.3.
- Drawing a structure chart showing the main modules on a single sheet of A4 paper. The purpose of this is:
  - to show that the linkage of the modules is logically correct
  - to provide a basis for writing the computer instructions
  - to form an essential part of the documentation.
- Completing the program structure chart to provide a full program specification. Finally, creating a detailed design of the algorithm by expanding the structure chart either as a top-down design, a program flowchart, a set of decision tables or some alternative. There should be no change in logic between this and the simpler version. It is often worth drawing two simple versions which work differently. This will often show the best method(s), which may be a combination of two different approaches.

> Stages in specifying the algorithm

Writing the program instructions

The program design must now be coded into the desired programming language with the programmer writing the **source program**, and in Chapter 9 we shall see that this will need to be processed to provide an **object program** which actually executes the design. In theory, having completed the analysis and design stages, then the program should work in whatever language is chosen and on any computer. However, in practice, the particular language or operating system might not support or provide all the required functions, or it may be that the version of the language available may be non-standard and so the programmer may need to amend the design. Any machine-dependent features introduced must be carefully documented and, if possible, restricted to a small number of named modules which can easily be replaced if transferring to another computer.

PROGRAM TESTING AND DEBUGGING

After coding the program, however good the design, it is unlikely to be 100 per cent correct and so it must therefore be thoroughly tested to locate any errors. A program error is called a **bug**, (hence the term **debugging**). The bug may come from a number of sources:

- Within the program design as a logic error
- An error in coding
- A peculiarity of the particular implementation of the language, for example initial values or the value of a control variable at the end of a loop
- There may be idiosyncrasies of the operating system or the machine design, for example the precision of a calculation
- Even if working to the specification of the design, there may be an error in that it is not what the user wanted or expected, so that there is an error in the overall systems design

> Sources of a bug

It is virtually impossible to test a program under all the conditions which may be encountered. Some of the reasons why this is impossible are as follows:

- It could take far too long and be too expensive in terms of computer time.
- The range of possibilities involved and the various combinations of possible errors may not be predictable.
- However good the design and the coding, there may just be something the systems analyst or program designer was not told.

The more complex the program, the greater the problems in locating all the errors. Nevertheless these problems can be minimised by developing and testing the program in smaller modules. If each module works correctly on its own, then the problem must lie in the way they link together, i.e. their *interface*. Finding the bug within a module is usually straightforward, but finding an interface problem may be more difficult without efficient documentation. A common means of program proving is the use of a **dry run** where the program is **traced** step-by-step to predict the outcome of a live test run.

PROGRAM DOCUMENTATION

Documentation will be covered fully in Chapter 9. It cannot be emphasised too strongly that the majority of the documentation should be complete *before* programming is commenced. The completion of documentation after the testing stage will involve noting amendments made to the design during the coding and testing, and the documentation of test data, dry runs and the test results.

STRUCTURED PROGRAMMING CONCEPTS

On the first computers, all programming had to be carried out in machine language. It is therefore hardly surprising that as high-level languages first became available, programmers were more interested in completing a task than studying the most efficient or elegant methods of writing programs. In addition, the early programming languages (for example Fortran II, which was the first widely used language, and the original version of Basic, which dates from the late 1960s) were designed for ease of programming rather than for programming style. It was not until the 1970s that programmers started to think more seriously about well structured programs and elegant design.

The term **structured programming** was first used to describe the three elementary sequence control structures for logical flow within a program. These are often called sequence, iteration and selection.

> *Elementary sequence control structures for logical flow within a program*

- **Sequence**, refers to the normal flow of logic from one statement to the next in physical sequence.
- **Iteration**, or **looping**, refers to the repetition of a group of instructions until a particular condition is satisfied; this comes in two forms *do while* and *repeat until*.
- **Selection**, or **decision**, is used to describe the structure where the program logic selects its next instruction on the basis of a decision on the value of some quantity within the program.

While the principles of structured programming were evolving, programmers began to appreciate the merits of dividing programs into a number of smaller, self-contained and independent procedures or modules. This not only allowed more than one programmer to collaborate and work independently on the same application, but enabled an installation to identify and collect together a library of procedures to be used in more than one program. This is called **modular programming** and must be studied alongside structured programming.

Sequential algorithms

Sequence is the simplest and most obvious of the structured programming constructs, being the normal flow of logic from one statement to the next in sequence. Most programmers, when learning a new language, start with a simple program which will read data, carry out a calculation and then print results, as shown in the flowchart in Fig. 7.3.

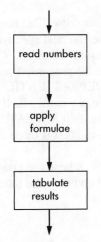

Fig. 7.3 Sequence flowchart

As an example of a sequential program, take the calculation of a 15 per cent rate of VAT to be added to the selling price of some goods. The program can be broken down into the following steps:

1 Read the VAT-free price
2 Compute the VAT
3 Add VAT to give selling price
4 Print the selling price
5 End

Each step is carried out just once in the sequence listed and at step 5 the program is terminated.

Iteration algorithms

Iteration means the repetition of a set of instructions a specified number of times, or until, or while, a particular condition holds. As a simple example, take the reading of a set of data, perhaps for the VAT calculation shown under 'sequence', and terminate the program by entering a price of zero. Then print four copies of a tabulation.

The two forms of iteration are shown in Figs. 7.4 and 7.5. These present the two distinct forms of the iteration construct which are called **DO WHILE** and **REPEAT UNTIL**. Although both are necessary in order to implement the full range of algorithms, it

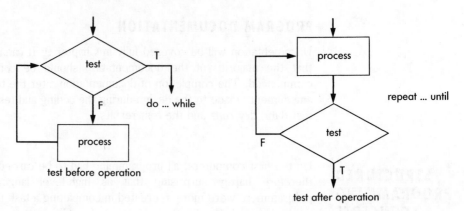

Fig. 7.4 Do While   **Fig. 7.5 Repeat Until**

is unfortunate that not every programming language has statements giving a direct translation of both constructs. Thus the programmer has to use a little inventiveness in the writing of programs. For example, BBC Basic only implements REPEAT UNTIL, and DO WHILE is achieved only with some ingenuity.

From Figs. 7.4 and 7.5, the principal distinction between DO WHILE and REPEAT UNTIL is that

- DO WHILE tests the condition before the instructions in the loop are executed
- REPEAT UNTIL performs the loop once before the test is carried out.

The following illustrates the looping constructs by taking, as an example, a variable length record in a library system. Here there is a record for each book, and this record contains a field which specifies how many readers have borrowed the book. The variable length part of the record has a variable number of fields recording the reference codes of the readers.

A procedure is required to tabulate the borrowers for a particular book. This requires a loop and, whichever construct is used, it is necessary to examine the field specifying the number of borrowers and then to repeat the loop the required number of times. With the DO WHILE loop we test to see if any more borrowers are to be processed and then execute the loop to process the next borrower. With the REPEAT UNTIL loop a borrower is processed and then the test is made to see if there are any more left. If a book has *no* borrowers then the DO WHILE will perform correctly, but with REPEAT UNTIL the program would attempt to tabulate a (spurious) reader before the test is made and this would be a logic error.

An example of a DO WHILE loop is the procedure given below, where the program is required to request how many copies of a tabulation are required and then the tabulations are produced one at a time in a loop:

1   Input the number of copies (call this N)
2   Set 'copies remaining' to N
3   WHILE the 'number remaining' is greater than zero
4   Print (next) copy
5   Decrease 'copies remaining' by 1
6   END LOOP

This is written in a shorthand which may be called **pseudo-code** and is an alternative to flowcharting. The usual format is to number instructions 1, 2, 3 etc. and then to use a top-down approach in expanding the steps, so that 2 would be expanded to 2.1, 2.2, 2.3 and 2.3 to 2.3.1, 2.3.2 etc. as shown below:

1
2
        2.1
        2.2
        2.3
                2.3.1
                2.3.2
        2.4
3

The text used at each step is left to the style of the designer but at the top level it tends to be free format text. As the design gets further and further refined so it gets closer to source program statements. This technique will be used throughout the book and there have already been examples in Chapter 6 specifying the access to records in an indexed file.

For an example of REPEAT UNTIL, we consider a procedure to accept a number to specify the month in a date which, of course, must be an integer in the range 1–12:

```
1   REPEAT
2           Input the month number
3               IF month number is invalid print a message
4   UNTIL valid month has been accepted
```

Notice the indentation of instructions within a loop which is a common convention used to clarify the logic.

The selection construct

Selection, which is illustrated in Fig.7.6, is implemented in most high-level programming languages as an IF statement. It allows a program to decide between two alternative courses of action according to the result of some condition of data or some calculation carried out within the program. There was one example in the previous section in the REPEAT UNTIL illustration. Most well structured languages implement decisions in the form

```
IF . . .
        THEN . . .
        ELSE . . .
```

to select the two courses of action.

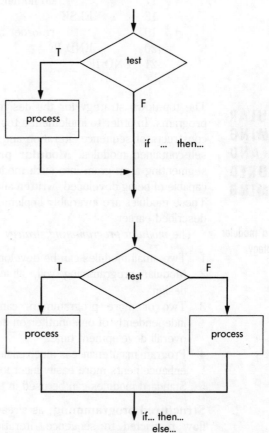

Fig. 7.6 Selection

The procedure which might be adopted at the heart of a system to process customers' orders provides an example of a selection algorithm which might have the following steps:

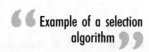
Example of a selection algorithm

```
1   Read the new order
2   Read the customer record with balance owing
3   Compute new balance by adding in value of order
4   IF value of order < credit limit
```

```
 5   THEN
 6           process order
 7           update customer record
 8   ELSE
 9           print "order refused"
10   END IF
```

It is possible with all of the sequence control structures to *nest* them or include one within another. A different order processing procedure which checks to see if stock is available and initiates re-order procedures is given as the next example:

❝Another order processing procedure ❞

```
 1   Read the number requested by the order
 2   Read the current balance of stock
 3   IF stock balance < number requested
 4   THEN
 5           process order
 6           decrease balance
 7   ELSE
 8           IF stock balance > 0
 9           THEN
10                   assign balance to customer
11                   set balance to zero
12           ELSE
13                   print "out of stock" report
14           END IF
15           IF re-order has been made previously
16           THEN
17                   do nothing
18           ELSE
19                   re-order from supplier
20           END IF
21   END IF
```

MODULAR PROGRAMMING AND STRUCTURED PROGRAMMING

❝Reasons for a modular programming strategy ❞

The top-down strategy for the design of programs can be applied to the design of all programs. In order to implement a top-down design, and also to make the best use of the constructs of sequence, iteration and selection, it is necessary to develop programs in self-contained modules. **Modular programming** is the technique of subdividing or segmenting a program into such modules, each of which has a defined interface and is capable of being developed, written and tested, independently of the rest of the program. These modules are invariably implemented as procedures, functions and subroutines, as described earlier.

The *modular programming strategy* can be justified for the following reasons:

1   Two small modules can be developed in less time than one large module.
2   Modular programming will, almost certainly, lead to a more efficient program design.
3   Two or more programmers can be employed to work at the same time but independently of one another on different modules of the same program to speed the overall development time.
4   Program maintenance is much easier since logic errors can be more easily detected and enhancements more easily incorporated.
5   Standard modules can be used in two or more programs.

Structured programming, as already observed, is the design of programs with logic flow restricted to sequence, iteration and selection and incorporating independent subroutines, procedures or modules. The other characteristic which will be explored in Chapter 9 is that structured programs do not use the GOTO statement since this is the statement which causes most logic errors. The major problem with this statement is that if we write, in Basic for example,

GOTO 2000

which executes a branch to the statement number 2,000, then when we look at statement

2,000 we have no idea how this statement can be reached, what the code represents and how we return to the calling statement. In structured and modular programming, each module has one entry point and one exit and is self-contained in executing a specific task. The principles are best studied from examples drawn from past examination questions.

EXAMINATION QUESTIONS

SHORT QUESTIONS

Question 1
Distinguish between *iteration* and *recursion*. Why are both useful to a programmer? Give **one** example of the use of iteration and **one** example of the use of recursion in programming. (Welsh AS 1989)

Question 2
It is often claimed that one advantage of programming in a high-level language is that the source code is portable. Explain what is meant by portable source code.
In practice, high level language programs are seldom portable. State why this is the case and explain how a programmer could avoid the problem when portability is important. (NEAB 1989)

Question 3
Briefly describe the process of program development known as 'top-down design'
(Northern Ireland 1987)

Question 4
A language supports the IF . . . THEN . . . ENDIF construct.
Explain how the following statements would be executed. In particular, show how the value of the Boolean expressions would be determined.
i) IF a>40 THEN PRINT "TOO LARGE"
ENDIF
ii) IF (a = b) AND ((j>k) OR (m=n)) THEN PRINT "OK"
ENDIF

Illustrate your answers with the example values:
a=3, b=3, j=7, k=9, m=8, n=8. (NEAB 1988)

Question 5
i) Describe what is meant by 'top-down design' as applied to program development.
ii) Describe *two* advantages a programmer gains from the use of this technique in developing a new program.
iii) Describe *two* benefits the maintenance programmer gains when working on programs which have been developed using top-down design. (NEAB 1987)

LONGER QUESTIONS

Question 6

a) Write brief notes to describe the following program design strategies:
   i) Top-down design and stepwise refinement
   ii) Bottom-up design
   Describe *one* advantage of each of these methodologies.

b) Describe *one* feature of a programming language which assists the implementation of a top-down design.

c) Describe briefly *five* examples of software which assist in the development of computer programs. In each case explain why the example you have described is helpful. (AEB 1988)

Question 7

A game which uses a coin is played between two players, P (the payer) and R (the receiver), as follows. The coin is tossed. If it is a head, P pays R one penny and the game is over. Otherwise, it is a tail, and the coin is tossed a second time. If it is a head this time, P pays R two pence and the game is over. But if it is another tail, the coin is tossed a third time. If it is now a head, P pays R four pence and the game is over. If it is still a tail, the coin is tossed again. This continues, doubling the payment each time a tail is tossed, until a head is tossed, at which point P pays R and the game is over.

a) Write a program in a programming language of your choice which will simulate the playing of the game 1,000 times and will print the mean payment made by P to R. (You may assume the existence of a pseudo-random number generating function, but you must provide a specification of what it produces.)

b) A table is required to show in addition how many of the 1,000 games ended in a payment of one penny, of two pence, of four pence, and so on. Describe how your program would need to be changed to produce this. (Cambridge 1984)

Question 8

a) Explain why many programming languages have both FOR and WHILE constructs to program loops. Under what circumstances would each be used? Show how the FOR construct may be programmed using a WHILE loop.

b) Give *two* reasons why an incorrectly programmed loop may never terminate. How could the TRACE facility of a debugging system be used to ensure a WHILE loop iterates the correct number of times?

c) Two integers may be multiplied by repeated addition. Using a WHILE loop, give an algorithm for such a multiplication. Explain how you would dry run this algorithm. Carry out such a dry run for two values 4 and 6. (NEAB 1988)

Question 9

A graph plotter can be programmed with instructions to:
1 Raise the pen (no mark)
2 Lower the pen (mark)
3 Move the pen in a straight line from its present position to specified (x, y) co-ordinates.

Make, and explain, any assumptions about any features of the plotting system not defined by the question, so that, with the help of a flow diagram, or otherwise, you can explain how to construct a program for this plotter which draws a figure in the centre of a sheet of paper consisting of

a) a square with its sides of length two units parallel to the x and y axes;
b) a square centred at the same point with its diagonals parallel to the axes and its sides passing through the corners of the first square. (Oxford 1984)

Question 10

Two sequential files *A* and *B* contain records of a fixed length with key values in ascending order. The two files are to be merged to form a single file *C* containing the same records with the key field values in ascending order. Each of the files *A* and *B* is terminated by a dummy record with a huge key field value, represented by *hugekey*. File *C* is to be terminated similarly. Apart from the dummy records, all the key field values are supposed to be different from each other; it is therefore an error if any record in file *A* has the same key field as any record in file *B*.

Describe in detail an algorithm for a program to carry out the merge.

(Cambridge 1986)

Question 11

A magnetic tape transaction file contains the following fields:

■ Account number
■ Transaction code
■ Value

The transaction file to be used to update the master file in a way determined by the transaction code is as follows:

Tranaction code	Transaction type	Action
R	Receipt	Value is added to balance
P	Payment	Value is subtracted from balance
D	Delete	The corresponding master file record is to be deleted, provided the balance is zero

Note that

1   Both files have been sorted into ascending account number order
2   For a particular account number there may be many payment and receipt transactions but only one delete transaction, and the delete transaction, if present, will always follow any other transactions for that account number
3   Each file is terminated by a dummy record containing a 'high value' account number

Construct a flowchart, or a pseudo-code description, for a program to perform this update process.   (AEB 1984)

Question 12
Under the rules of tennis, one player serves to the other. The server's score is given first, the other second. The first three points won by a player take his score to 15, 30 and 40. If he wins a fourth point before his opponent wins a third he wins the game. If both players win three points before either win a fourth, the score is called deuce. Then the player who wins the next point has the advantage. If the player who has the advantage wins the next point he wins the game. If he loses, the score returns to deuce.

a)   Describe a computing system which could be operated by a scorer to record and display the score during the game.
b)   With the help of a flow diagram, or otherwise, explain how the program for the system would operate.   (Oxford 1984)

OUTLINE ANSWERS

SHORT QUESTIONS

Question 1
Iteration means the repetition or looping around a sequence of instructions, recursion is where a procedure calls itself. Both terminate on some specified end condition.

Both are useful to a programmer, iteration occurs in almost every program since if a program were to be a simple sequence of instructions it would probably not be worth programming. The essence of a program is to abstract or generalise the process in some way so that it may be implemented as a repetition of these instructions. Recursion is useful in that it often provides a more elegant and more efficient implementation of a loop.

Taking as an example, the computation of n! for a positive integer, this could be programmed in BBC Basic as a loop:

```
    fact = 1
    FOR i = 1 to n
          LET fact = fact* i
    NEXT i
```

and as a recursive function

```
    DEF FNfact(n)
    IF n = 1 THEN fact = 1 ELSE fact = n* FNfact (n-1)
    = fact
```

Question 2

Portable source code means that a source program can be taken from one machine and run directly on another.

The question states that in practice, high-level language programs are seldom portable. This is *not* strictly true in the case of languages implemented to an agreed standard like Iso Pascal, Ada, Fortran 77 or Ansi Cobol but is usually the case for ill-defined, non-standardised languages such as Basic or for languages which use special hardware. Programs are also not portable if it is required to change languages.

If portability is important, programmers can avoid the problem by restricting the language only to standard elements and by implementing the complete program by structured programming constructs, which means that it will minimise the problems of translation to a new machine or even to a new language.

Question 3

Top-down design means specifying the design of a program from the top level of logic down to the fine detail, step by step, that is starting from a broad level of detail and then expanding the main module into finer and finer levels of detail. The structure is often illustrated as a tree shown in Fig. 7.1.

Question 4

i) IF a>40 THEN PRINT "TOO LARGE"
   ENDIF
   In this case if a takes a value greater than 40 then the message 'TOO LARGE' will be printed.

ii) IF (a=b) AND ((j>k) OR (m=n)) THEN PRINT "OK"
    ENDIF

This program has a more complex condition, firstly it evaluates (a=b) which will have the Boolean value **true** if a=3 and b=3. It then examines ((j>k) OR (m=n)) which is broken down into (j>k) and (m=n), if j=7 and k=9 then (j>k) has the value **false** and if m=8 aand n=8 then (m=n) has the value **true** so ((j>k) OR (m=n)) has the value **true** OR **true** so ((j>k) OR (m=n)) has the value **true** thus (a=b) AND ((j>k) OR (m=n)) breaks down to **true** AND **true** which is **true** so the program will print the message OK.

Question 5

i) Top-down design as applied to program development means specifying the design of a program from the top level of logic down to the fine detail, step by step.

ii) Advantages a programmer gains from the use of top-down design in developing a new program are:
   1 The improved structure will speed the process of obtaining a logically correct program
   2 It is very easy to divide the program design between several programmers

iii) Advantages a maintenance programmer gains from the use of top-down design in developing a new program are:
   1 The clarity of design will make it easier for the programmer to make amendments subsequently or even to allow another programmer to maintain the program
   2 The features of top-down design are that a change of any part of the program only affects those parts logically below it, often relatively few, and so the amount of additional amendment is minimised

LONGER QUESTIONS

Question 6

a) i) Top-down design and stepwise refinement have been covered in the answers to previous questions.

ii) Bottom-up design means taking the lowest level of detail first and after completing the design, building the overall structure around it. This has the advantage that if the program is orientated around some special technique, such as monitoring a piece of equipment or implementing some special mathematical technique, then the most important part of the program is checked out first.

b) An important feature of any programming language which assists the implementation of a top-down design is the ability to define subroutines and functions.

c) Examples of software which assist in the development of computer programs are:
1 An editor to assist the entry and amendment of source programs and test data files
2 A compiler to translate the program to object code
3 A linker to combine the object code modules into executable code
4 An animator to trace the execution of the program
5 A file dump utility to verify the output

Question 7

We assume there is a random number function with the following specification:
RND(N) where N is a positive integer returning a random integer uniformly distributed in the range 1 to N so that RND(2) gives 1 and 2 with equal chance.

a) In order to simulate the playing of the game 1,000 times, the following is the top level of logic:
1 Set totals to zero
2 Loop for game = 1 to 1000
3   Play game
4   Add payment to total
5 End of loop
6 Print average

The only step which needs an extensive expansion is step 3, play the game, which would also be best implemented in a program as a procedure

3.1 Set payment to 1
3.2 REPEAT
3.3   Toss coin
3.4   IF tail then double the payment
3.5 UNTIL head thrown

It is seen that we remain in this loop until a head is thrown. If there is a head the first time we exit the loop with payment set to 1, from then on payment is doubled each time the loop is executed. This gives the final version as:
1   Set totals to zero
2   Loop for game = 1 to 1000
3   Play game
3.1   Set payment to 1
3.2   REPEAT
3.3   Toss coin
3.4   IF tail then double the payment
3.5   UNTIL head thrown
4   Add payment to total
5   End of loop
6   Print average

b) To print a table to show, in addition, how many of each of the possible outcomes occur over 1,000 games we need to accumulate the occurrences in an array, this could be done in one of two ways:
i) We could use the array count, to store the occurrences of each outcome, so, for example, count(8) stores the number of times 8 is paid out, but this is not an efficient use of the array because only a small number of elements would be used because the only outcomes are: 1 2 4 8 16
ii) We could store the number of times the coin was tossed, from which the payout can be very easily calculated, this uses the elements: 1 2 3 4 5

The revised algorithm is:

```
1       Set totals to zero
1.1         Set total to zero
1.2         Set the array Count to zero
2       Loop for game = 1 to 1000
3       Play game
3.1.1       Set payment to 1
3.1.2       Set throws to 1
3.2         REPEAT
3.3             Toss coin
3.4             IF tail thrown
3.4.1               THEN
3.4.2                   double payment
3.4.3                   add 1 to throws
3.4.4               END IF
3.5         UNTIL head thrown
4       Add to totals
4.1         Add payment to total
4.2         IF throws < 20
4.3             THEN
4.4                 Add 1 to Count (throws)
4.5             ELSE
4.6                 Add 1 to Count (20)
4.7         END IF
5       End of loop
6       Print average = total/1000
7       Print frequencies
7.1         set payment to 1
7.2         LOOP for throws = 1 to 20
7.3             IF Count (throws) > 0 Print payment & Count(throws)
7.4                 double payment
7.5         END LOOP
```

There is one unresolved problem in this design, in the tabulation we loop from 1 to 20, and in defining the array we will have to make some assumption about the maximum payment, which is related to the maximum sequence of tails thrown. As a precaution against error, if the sequence is longer than 20 it is taken as 20 for the frequency distribution in step 4 but will still contribute its full value to the average.

Question 8

a) Many programming languages and all languages with a full implementation of structured programming have both FOR and WHILE constructs for the implementation loops, because FOR implements a REPEAT … UNTIL and tests for completion only after executing the loop, whereas WHILE tests for completion before executing the loop.

A FOR loop is used to repeat a block of statements a required number of times, for example

for i:= 1 **to** 10 **do**

A WHILE loop is used to repeat statements until a condition is reached:

while difference >0.0001 **do**

A FOR construct may be programmed using a WHILE loop as illustrated below for the same example:

i=0

while i<10 **do**

begin

    i:=1+1; etc.

b) If a loop is incorrectly programmed, it may become an infinite loop, if the end condition is incorrectly defined. One example is:

for i:=1 **to** n **do**

with n having the value 0 and so i will progress from 1 to 2 to 3 and so on and never reach 0.

Another example is:

```
x:=1
while x <> 100
begin
x:= x + 2; etc.
```

so that x never reaches 100 but skips from 99 to 101.

The TRACE facility of a debugging system can be used to ensure a WHILE loop iterates the correct number of times either by counting the number of iterations or, if the TRACE facility allows, displaying the value of the control variable at each iteration to prove that the loop works correctly.

c) The following algorithm shows how two integers, n and m, may be multiplied by repeated addition. It assumes both are positive but if negative numbers are allowed the signs would be processed separately.

```
1   set prod to 0
2   set i to 0
3   while i < m
4           add n to prod
5           add 1 to i
6   end while
```

Dry run this algorithm. Carry out such a dry run for two values 4 and 6.

The dry run may be set out as below:

step	i	n	m	prod	test
0		6	4		
1				0	
2	0				
3					true
4				6	
5	1				
3					true
4				12	
5	2				
3					true
4				18	
5	3				
3					true
4				24	
5	4				
3					false

Question 9

From the information in the question we can assume either the existence of three procedures or that we may write three procedures. These will be called, in this answer,

- raise – to raise the pen
- lower – to lower the pen
- move (x, y) – to move the pen in a straight line to (x, y)

It may be best to provide two additional procedures so that the origin can be moved and plotting can be carried out relative to the new origin. This may be provided within the system but if it is not, it is comparatively straightforward to write two procedures:

- origin (p,q) – to move the origin to (p,q)
- move (x,y) – to move to the point (x,y) relative to the origin (p,q)

a) For a square at the centre of the paper with sides of length two units parallel to the x and y axes, if we can move the origin to the centre of the paper then the co-ordinates of the corners will be (1,1), (−1,1), (−1,−1) and (1,−1):

1   compute position of the centre of the paper for the new origin
2   move origin to the centre of the paper
3   lift pen
4   move to position (1,1)
5   lower pen
6   move to position (−1,1)
7   move to position (−1,−1)
8   move to position (1,−1)
9   move to position (1,1)
10   lift pen

b)   For a square centred at the same point with its diagonals parallel to the axes and its sides passing through the corners of the first square then we first use geometry as in Fig. 7.7 to deduce that with the origin at the centre of the paper then the co-ordinates of the corners will be (0,2) (−2,0), (0,−2) and (2,0). The algorithm then becomes:

1   compute position of the centre of the paper for the new origin
2   move origin to the centre of the paper
3   lift pen
4   move to position (0,2)
5   lower pen
6   move to position (−2,0)
7   move to position (0,−2)
8   move to position (2,0)
9   move to position (0,2)
10   lift pen

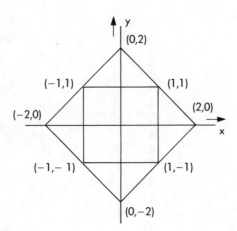

Fig. 7.7

Question 10

Whatever the method chosen to describe the algorithm the best initial approach is to define some terminology and then to write a specification using this notation. We shall use *A* and *B* to refer to the files, recordA and recordB to refer to the records read from those files, and KeyA and KeyB to refer to the contents of the key fields. There is a flowchart solution in Fig. 7.8 and a top-down solution using pseudo-code below:

1   open the files
2   read a record from each file
3   REPEAT
4   REPEAT
5   copy B to C as long as KeyB < KeyA
6   copy A to C as long as KeyA < KeyB
7   UNTIL KeyA = KeyB
8   write recordA to C
9   IF KeyA is not equal to hugekey print an error and READ A
10   UNTIL KeyA (= KeyB) = hugekey
11   close the files

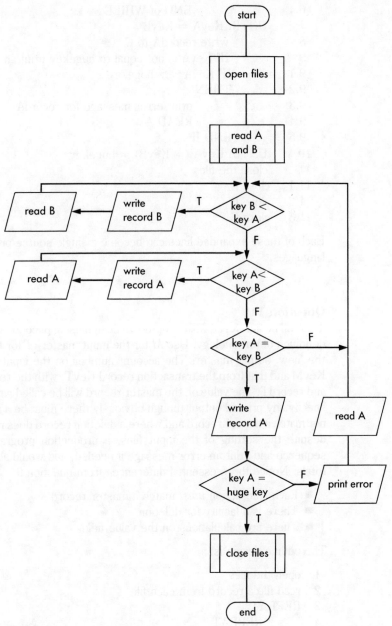

Fig. 7.8

This can be expanded:

1	open the files
1.1	open A
1.2	open B
1.3	open C
2	read file a record from each file
2.1	read A
2.2	read B
3	REPEAT
4	REPEAT
5	copy B to C as long as KeyB < KeyA
5.1	WHILE KeyB < KeyA
5.2	write recordB to C
5.3	read B
5.4	END of WHILE
6	copy A to C as long as KeyA < KeyB
6.1	WHILE KeyA < KeyB
6.2	write recordA to C
6.3	read A

6.4	END of WHILE
7	UNTIL KeyA = KeyB
8	write recordA to C
9	IF KeyA is not equal to hugekey print an error and READ A
9.1	IF KeyA <> hugekey
9.2	THEN
9.3	print error message for recordA
9.4	READ A
9.5	END IF
10	UNTIL KeyA (= KeyB) = hugekey
11	close the files
11.1	close A
11.2	close B
11.3	close C

Each of these expanded lines can become a single source program line in most high-level languages.

Question 11

This will be answered with a top-down design using pseudo-code, and again we start with a definition of terminology. Use M for the input master, T for the transaction file, and N for the 'new' output master. The account number on the input master record will be called KeyM and that from the transaction record KeyT, with the records referred to as recordM and recordT. The value on the master record will be called *balance*. This program does not specify any printed output though obviously there must be a report where transactions do not match a master record and where a deletion record does not have a zero balance. Also, despite the sorting of the input files, a production program would still check for the sequence and print an error message if needed, and would also print details of the control totals. Notice three essential differences from question 9:

- Each transaction *must* match a master record
- There is a facility for deletion
- There are calculations on the value fields

The outline design is:

1	open the files
2	read file a record from each file
3	REPEAT
4	REPEAT
5	copy M to N as long as KeyM < KeyT
6	report errors as long as KeyT < KeyM
7	UNTIL KeyM = KeyT
8	IF KeyM is equal to 'high value' write record M otherwise process transactions
9	UNTIL KeyM (= KeyT) = 'high value'
10	close the files

This can be expanded:

1	open the files
1.1	open M
1.2	open T
1.3	open N
2	read file a record from each file
2.1	read M
2.2	read T
3	REPEAT
4	REPEAT
5	copy M to N as long as KeyM < KeyT
5.1	WHILE KeyM < KeyT
5.2	Write recordM to N
5.3	Read N

5.4	END of WHILE
6	report errors as long as KeyT < KeyM
6.1	WHILE KeyT < KeyM
6.2	print no record for KeyT
6.3	read T
6.4	END of WHILE
7	UNTIL KeyM = KeyT
8	IF KeyM is equal to 'high value' write recordM otherwise process transactions
8.1	IF KeyM = 'high value'
8.2	THEN
8.3	write recordM to N
8.4	ELSE
8.5	process transactions
8.5.1	WHILE KeyM = KeyT and code <> 'D'
8.5.2	IF code = 'R'
8.5.3	THEN
8.5.4	add value to balance
8.5.5	ELSE
8.5.6	subtract value from balance
8.5.7	END IF
8.5.8	READ T
8.5.9	END WHILE
8.5.10	IF KeyM = KeyT (code will be 'D')
8.5.11	THEN
8.5.12	IF balance = zero
8.5.13	THEN
8.5.14	READ M (implements the delete)
8.5.15	ELSE
8.5.16	print "Cannot delete recordM"
8.5.17	END IF
8.6	END IF
9	UNTIL KeyM (= KeyT) = 'high value'
10	close the files
10.1	close M
10.2	close T
10.3	close N

Again it is a relatively trivial step to translate. Each of these expanded lines can become a single source program line in a high-level language.

Question 12

This needs to be restricted simply to the rules in the question so we ignore first and second services, scores for games and sets, etc. There is more than enough to think about in an examination without providing extra problems over and above the specification.

a) In describing a computing system which could be operated by the scorer, all we need is a simple device to indicate which of the two players won the point and a simple display of the score on a video screen, though a spoken response would be even better. The mouse is ideal because all that is needed is a two-state input like 'A' or 'B' for server or non-server.

b) The program design can be expressed in pseudo-code:
   1 Initialise the scores
   2 Play until 6 points or 'game'
   3 IF leader has only won three points perform deuce
   4 Print winner

In writing such a program, which will be illustrated in Chapter 8, there will be a look-up table to translate the scores from 0, 1, 2 and 3 to love, thirty and forty. There will also be a procedure to 'play a point', i.e. receive the code of the winner and convert it to 1 for the server or 2 for the receiver so that their names and points scored can be held in arrays.

The procedure will then be expanded as:

1	Initialise the scores
1.1	Set scores to zero
1.2	set points to zero
2	play until 6 points or 'game'
2.1	REPEAT
2.2	give score
2.3	play point
2.4	add 1 to points played
2.5	add 1 to winner of point
2.6	UNTIL points = 6 OR winner has scored 4
3	IF leader has only won 3 points perform deuce
3.1	IF winner has 3 points
3.2	THEN
3.3	REPEAT
3.4	set scores to 0
3.5	PRINT "Deuce"
3.6	play point
3.7	set winner to 1
3.8	PRINT "Advantage"
3.9	play point
3.10	add 1 to score of winner
3.11	UNTIL score of winner is 2
4	Print winner

CHAPTER 8

HIGH-LEVEL PROGRAMMING LANGUAGES

GETTING STARTED

In Chapter 7 we looked at the concepts of structured programming and modular programming which were then applied to the design of structured programs to match a problem specification. In this chapter we shall look at **high-level languages**, or third generation languages, and how they support the constructs of structured programming. Most examinations at this level involve a great deal of practical programming work, usually with a project. The language chosen for this work will be studied in much greater depth than can be undertaken in this book. Here languages can only be studied in general terms to illustrate and compare their structures, and to consider their appropriateness to particular types of application.

ALGORITHMS

THE CLASSIFICATION OF LANGUAGES

THE COMPILATION PROCESS

THE CASE AGAINST BASIC

LANGUAGE EXAMPLES

CHARACTERISTICS OF HIGH-LEVEL LANGUAGES

ESSENTIAL PRINCIPLES

ALGORITHMS

We may define an algorithm as a set of *unambiguous* rules which specify the method of *solution* of a problem in a *finite* number of steps.

The term algorithm has already been used in this book and the concept of an algorithm is very important to a programmer since all computer programs should match exactly all of the characteristics identified in the definition. When a computer program is written to solve a problem we are instructing a machine to solve the problem by specifying a set of rules in the form of a **program** of instructions which, because they are being obeyed by a machine, have to be unambiguous and reach the required solution in a finite number of steps. Thus it can be said that the job of a programmer is the design and implementation of algorithms. In Chapter 9 we shall look at other means of describing algorithms since programmers need to have means of putting such descriptions on paper to clarify their own ideas, to demonstrate to a colleague how a particular task has been or is to be coded in the chosen language and also as a convenient means of documentation of a finished program or system.

All the top-down designs and the pseudo-code examples in Chapter 7 are examples of algorithms. However, programs exist which may not complete in a finite number of steps. For example, the operating system of a microcomputer has a procedure in a loop which tests to see if a key has been depressed; this could run indefinitely, or until a power failure or machine fault.

THE CLASSIFICATION OF LANGUAGES

In Chapter 3 there were a number of references to **machine code** or machine language and we studied the execution by the control unit of a simple machine language program. It is important to get a picture of the range of languages used on computers and to group them into categories. The common categories are shown below:

66 Categories of language 99

- Machine languages ⎤
- Assembly languages ⎦ Low-level languages
- High-level languages
- Program generators
- Specialised languages
- Functional languages

In general terms low-level languages are peculiar to the computer or processor on which they execute and thus are **machine-orientated**. High-level languages aim at being independent of machine and are **programmer-orientated**, while program generators and specialised languages are **applications-orientated**. In this chapter there will be an attempt to explain and justify these definitions as they relate to high-level languages and to provide some examples of program statements in popular languages.

Fourth generation languages

There is an alternative classification which is becoming more commonly applied to languages:

66 A generation classification 99

- Machine code languages are referred to as first generation languages.
- Assembly languages are referred to as second generation.
- High-level languages are referred to as third generation.

The term fourth generation language (4GL) is applied to the full range of program generators and user-orientated languages where, in many cases, the language is used to generate object code in a third generation language. Another type of fourth generation language is based on an application package, such as the spreadsheets Logistix or Lotus 1–2–3, or on database packages such as dBase or Oracle, and allows the user to create procedures in a special language; these instructions are often called **macros**.

Functional languages and imperative languages

The languages used by readers are likely to be Basic, Pascal, Fortran, Cobol, Modula-2 or C, all of which are imperative languages, that is the program is a list of instructions with the constructs of sequence, selection and iteration. Functional languages, like ML, Miranda and Hope, build up the procedures as sets of function calls, and the basic method of running a program is to execute a function which calls other functions which call lower level functions, and so on. The programmer builds up a library of functions on the backing store and so works in what is referred to as an **environment** where the standard supplied functions are augmented by locally-written functions to suit the range of applications being programmed.

Statements in functional languages look very different to those in imperative languages and look more mathematical. For example the following three functions are valid in ML:

```
(*positive, tests whether an integer is positive
      type positive : int → bool
*)
fun positive (i:int) = i>0;
(* even, tests whether an integer is divisible by 2
      type even : int → bool
*)
fun even (i:int) = (i mod 2 = 0);
(* poseven, tests whether an integer is positive and even
      type poseven : int → bool
      uses functions positive and even
*)
fun poseven (i:int) = (even (i) andalso positive (i));
```

Miranda has a feature which allows the evaluation of what are called 'list comprehensions'.

[x^2 | x ··[1..]; odd x] – list of all odd squares

Functional languages can be applied to a wide range of problems, including all those of imperative languages but are also applicable to the simulation of other languages being used, like BNF which will be studied later, as a **meta-language**.

The need for high-level languages

As will be shown in Chapter 12, there is a great deal of study to be undertaken in mastering a low-level language, since both the machine architecture and the language structure need to be covered. A simple program example which might take about 100 statements in a high-level language, if required in a low-level language, might well take many months or even years of study of assembly language before programming could be attempted. This was the problem facing all programmers in the 1950s; hence from the early days, languages were devised to enable programs to be written in a **problem-orientated** manner. The earliest examples allowed the direct evaluation of formulae, replacing the need to write several hundred lines of machine code or assembly language to carry out arithmetic procedures. A full list of advantages and disadvantages of high-level languages is given at the end of this chapter.

The evolution of high-level languages

The first examples of the design of high-level languages were referred to as **autocodes**, and usually just consisted of assembly language macros, or subroutines, which could be used to generate code for useful operations like arithmetical calculations or data transfers between the CPU and peripherals.

Almost as soon as computers became generally available, IBM initiated a project to devise a high-level language for the programming of mathematical applications, with a special emphasis on **for**mula **tran**slation. This resulted in the development of the language **Fortran**.

The next major development was the setting up of an international committee to devise and agree on standards for an 'algorithmic language' which was called **Algol**. This was, in many respects, similar to Fortran, but with a better design and structure. In order to satisfy the needs of non-mathematical, data processing-orientated applications, another committee was set up, about the year 1960, to specify a **C**ommon **B**usiness **O**rientated **L**anguage which became known as **Cobol**. Cobol became the most widely used programming language, and even today is second only to Basic.

The implementation of Cobol was effectively the end of a phase where languages were classified as either scientific or commercial. Around 1965, IBM developed a language called **PL/1** intended to combine the features of both Fortran and Cobol. In Dartmouth College, in America, another new language was devised, based on some of the simpler features of

Fortran but also allowing data handling. This was intended to allow students to write computer programs with the minimum of tuition and without requiring a great expertise or understanding of computers. The language was christened **B**eginners **A**ll-purpose **S**ymbolic **I**nstruction **C**ode or **Basic**.

Around 1970 a new language was devised, based initially on the ideas of Algol but with a greatly improved structure and with additional capabilities. This was called **Pascal**, and it is widely promoted by colleges and universities as an ideal language for program design. It was the first of the current trend of devising languages for their structure rather than for their appropriateness to particular applications.

Among the many other popular high-level languages are:

❝ Popular high-level languages ❞

- CORAL for real-time control
- FORTH a structured functional-type language which implements so-called threaded code
- LISP for list processing
- ADA a major enhancement to Pascal

THE COMPILATION PROCESS

It is important to remember that computers can only understand instructions in their *own* machine code and so, if the programmer wishes to write in another language, it is necessary for a translation process to be carried out. In the case of assemblers, the process is relatively simple in that each assembly language instruction normally generates a single machine language instruction. However with high-level languages, a statement in Fortran such as:

$$D = SQRT(B**2 - 4*A*C)$$

or COBOL statements of the type:

WRITE PRODUCT-DETAILS

cannot be so readily translated and have to be handled by a program called a *compiler* which is a far more complex process. We will return to the assembly process in Chapter 12.

A **compiler** is a program which translates a **source program** written in a high-level language into an **object program** in a target language which is, in the majority of cases, in machine code. At the same time as carrying out the translation, the compiler will detect and report syntax errors in the source code. The function of a compiler is illustrated in Fig. 8.1, related to high-level language compilation on the VAX/VMS system where, as on many systems, file names are made up of two parts, the file name and an extension. The extension is used to indicate the file type, so that PROG.FOR is a Fortran program, PROG.PAS is Pascal etc. The compiled program has the extension OBJ, the compilation listing LIS, and the linked, executable program, EXE. The language written by the programmer is called the **source program**, the output from the compilation is called the object program. In the case of a compiler it is better to refer to the language produced by a compiler as a **target language** because in many cases it is not machine code but an intermediate language or even another high-level language. Any examination question on the functions of a compiler will normally require a definition of high-level languages and the ability to contrast them with low-level languages.

When using a compiler there will be two distinct *inputs* to the program:

- The source program in the high level language.
- Compiler directives which are commands to the compiler to determine the form of output required and to select options available.

The *output* from the compilation process may include the following options:

❝ Output from the compilation process ❞

- A tabulation or listing of the source program.
- A list of syntax errors.
- A storage allocation map.
- A printed version of the object program.
- A cross reference list of variables used.
- A machine code version of the object program, which may either be in memory, on the file store, or both.

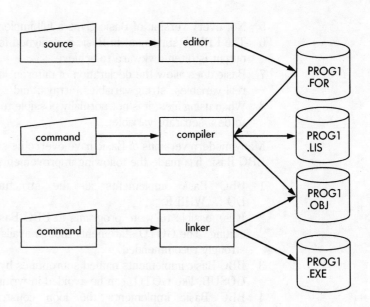

Fig. 8.1 High-level language
compilation on VAX VMS

Program development and testing with a compiler

Several stages and a number of distinct pieces of software are required and used when
programs are developed and tested using a compiler system with a high-level language:

- A **text editor**, or possibly a word processor, to create, amend and edit the
  source program.

- The **compiler** system to compile individual program modules or segments.

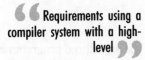
Requirements using a
compiler system with a high-
level

- A **linker**, which is a program that combines the compiled segments into a single
  executable object program.

- A **program loader** which retrieves the object program from the backing store
  and commences execution.

The programmer is often hidden from these individual programs in that the compiler
system may provide a composite command or **macro** which carries out compilation,
linkage, loading and running. At the program-testing stage there may be additional
requirements:

- Again, a **text editor** to create and amend test data.

- To assist program testing, many systems provide what is known as a **test
  harness** which allows the program to be tested under *controlled conditions*,
  thereby enabling the program to be halted at specified points, variables to be
  examined, or alternatively for the program to be **traced** (that is the generation of
  a display of the sequence of the instructions as executed).

THE CASE AGAINST BASIC

Basic was also designed originally to make the most of what were, at that time, the novel
features of multi-access computer systems. For instance, instead of having a computer
dedicated to a *single* user, a *whole group* could access the computer from a laboratory
containing a number of terminals. The simple syntax not only allowed non-specialist
programmers to use the language but, when microcomputers evolved, it was possible to
write an interpreter program for Basic which could be loaded and resident in the memory
of even the smallest computers. All this has made Basic, without doubt, the most widely
used computer language. At the same time it is the most universally criticised high-level
language. Much of the criticism is little more than prejudice against the language used in
schools and home computers, but there are a number of quite valid criticisms:

1 In Chapter 7 we established the importance of structure in the implementation of
   programs. Not all the constructs are available in many versions of Basic.

Criticisms of basic

2 Basic tends to be orientated around statements with line numbers and is dependent on
   the use of the GOTO statement.

3 Very few versions of Basic give a satisfactory implementation of subroutines, but use a
   statement GOSUB which refers to a line number rather than named procedures.

4 The only looping construct used in most versions of Basic is FOR ... NEXT.

5 Not every version of Basic gives a full implementation of IF ... THEN ... ELSE.
6 The PRINT statement in Basic is designed for ease of use, and formatting of printed output is often awkward to achieve.
7 Basic does allow the declaration of different data types. The only **types** available are real variables, string variables, arrays, and sometimes integers.
8 When using files, it is not normally possible to define a record structure; each field has to be a separate variable.

Many modern versions of Basic have overcome some of these criticisms, and in particular BBC Basic has made the following improvements to 1–5 above:

1 BBC Basic implements all the structured programming constructs except DO ... WHILE.
2 It is possible to write programs in BBC Basic which only use the line numbers for editing. The GOTO statement, though available, *can* be ignored, and this practice is strongly recommended.
3 BBC Basic implements named subroutines by the use of a DEF PROC statement and GOSUB, like GOTO, can be avoided in writing programs.
4 BBC Basic implements the loop construct REPEAT ... UNTIL as well as FOR ... NEXT (some others implement DO WHILE with a WHILE ... WEND construct.
5 BBC Basic does give a full implementation of IF ... THEN ... ELSE.

If all these improvements are used fully, and GOTO and GOSUB are ignored, then it is possible to write well-structured programs in BBC Basic. The major criticism of Basic is that, by its design, it tends to make it too easy to write unstructured programs.

LANGUAGE EXAMPLES

It is worth making a brief comparison of the manner in which the structured programming constructs are implemented in some common high-level languages, namely Pascal, Fortran and Cobol. All of these support structured programming, though in the case of Fortran it is necessary to use the latest version **Fortran 77** which has been enhanced to allow the additional structures.

- **Subroutines** These are implemented as an integral part of Pascal, being declared, either in a procedure statement or as a function, and then simply called by name. All versions of Fortran implement named subroutines, and functions and subroutines are invoked by a CALL statement. Cobol programs are written with all the procedure division statements in named paragraphs and these can be called as subroutines using the PERFORM verb

- **Selection** This is implemented as an IF statement in Pascal. Fortran 77 and Cobol both support the construct of IF ... THEN ... ELSE ...

- **Iteration** This has three main forms in these languages
  1 an indexed FOR or DO statement like the Basic statement FOR I=1 TO 100
  2 REPEAT ... UNTIL
  3 DO ... WHILE
  Pascal implements all three of these. Fortran 77 only implements the indexed DO, but many Fortran compilers implement a non-standard enhancement which gives a DO WHILE.
  Cobol has a PERFORM verb which allows the implementation of both the indexed loop and the REPEAT UNTIL, as illustrated by the following examples:
  PERFORM STOCK-CHECK VARYING I FROM 1 BY 1 UNTIL I=100.
  PERFORM STOCK-CHECK UNTIL PRODUCT= PRODUCT-REQUIRED

- **The declaration of data types** This is mandatory in Pascal and Cobol where every variable must be declared and specified as to size and format, i.e. real, integer, alphabetic, etc. However Fortran, like Basic, only requires variables to be defined which do not conform to the default types integer and real

CHARACTERISTICS OF HIGH-LEVEL LANGUAGES

The principal *characteristics* of **high-level languages** can be identified as follows:

- The languages are not machine-dependent.
- The statements have been designed to relate to the requirements of anticipated applications.
- The languages are implemented on a variety of different machines.
- There is a well defined syntax, and often internationally agreed standards.
- Programs are relatively easy to write.
- The source programs are normally readable and readily understood by another programmer.

The majority of application programs are written in high-level languages and it is important to identify a list of *advantages* of high-level languages:

- The languages aim at (but do not always achieve) **machine independence**, which makes for ease of translation between computers.
- Programs can be written in much less time.
- Writing high-level language programs needs no detailed knowledge of the machine.
- Program testing takes less time.
- Programs are usually easier to read by other programmers and can be made self-documentary.
- A number of standard programs are available in most high-level languages.
- There is a great deal of expertise available to help high-level language programmers if assistance is required.
- There are a number of programming aids in the way of development tools for high-level language programming.
- In business it is easy to recruit trained programmers for the popular high-level languages.

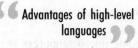

Advantages of high-level languages

We can identify a number of *disadvantages* in using high-level languages, of which the more important are:

- The object program may be less efficient in its use of memory and in its execution time, as compared to the same program written in a low-level language
- Some high-level languages are suited only to a particular range of problems or application areas
- High-level languages are usually subject to complicated grammatical rules
- The facilities available for tracing and debugging during program testing are often poor and thus program testing can be a lengthier process
- Each program has to be compiled, which introduces an additional operation which takes time, including machine time

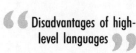

Disadvantages of high-level languages

The attributes of scientific and commercial languages

High-level languages for **scientific** applications have the following requirements:

- Ease of coding mathematical formulae
- Floating point arithmetic
- High precision in arithmetic

The requirements for languages for **data processing** applications are:

- The ability to handle individual characters
- Facilities for record and file processing
- Ease of formatting of output

The future of high-level languages

In the evolution of high-level languages there has been a move away from the languages which concentrate on making programming easier as the main objective, towards a concentration on the structure of the language and its suitability to structured programming. The language Ada is the 'state of the art' in this respect and may become the most important high-level language of the future.

A recent development in the family of fourth generation languages is the appearance of **specification languages** which have evolved from the earlier family of **program generators**. Here the source language allows the user to specify the requirements of a problem or application either as a list of statements or in response to a series of questions or queries. The specification is then translated into a program, which may be in a low-level language but is often in a high-level language, which can then be modified to come even closer to the system requirements.

The drawback of such languages is that they can tend to generate object code in a third generation language, such as Cobol. This is much less efficient and may have less satisfactory screen displays and user dialogue than that which would be written by a programmer. However, this code may be used as a first rough version or **prototype** to test the systems procedures before refining or re-writing the code in a final production version. The inefficiency of code, however, may not be a problem since, on modern computers, memory is cheap and plentiful and the speed of execution is such that even drastic inefficiencies may be tolerable.

PRACTICAL WORK

The questions in this chapter depend on an understanding of a high-level programming language. It is not sufficient to consider the practical work as simply a means of passing the practical element of the course. Instead practical work must be used in conjunction with the material in this chapter to provide illustrations of structured programming and modular design. These may then be included in examination answers.

One of the problems arising from the widespread use of home microcomputers is that many people learn programming in an unstructured manner and are reluctant to *reform* their approach, though the benefits, as outlined in this chapter, greatly outweigh the effort needed to adopt a new design strategy. Briefly, structured programming leads to programs which will work more quickly and are easier to follow by other programmers needing to make subsequent amendments.

EXAMINATION QUESTIONS

SHORT QUESTIONS

Question 1
a) State *three* features which distinguish a high-level language
b) Describe what is meant by 'block- structured' with reference to high-level languages.
c) Give an example of a block- structured language.   (London AS 1989)

Question 2
Explain what is meant by the *scope* of a variable in a block-structured language. Explain how a variable may not be in scope throughout the whole of the procedure in which it is defined.   (AEB 1989)

Question 3
A program written in a high-level language was compiled with no errors reported and ran to completion. Although output was expected, none was produced. Give *three* distinct reasons why this may have occurred.   (London 1988)

Question 4
State *one* advantage of compilation and *one* advantage of interpretation as methods of translating computer languages.   (AEB 1987)

Question 5
Name and state the function of *three* software tools which might be used in the creation of a source program and its conversion to an executable form.   (Northern Ireland 1989)

Question 6

Give *three* reasons why there are so many high level computer languages.

(AEB 1987)

Question 7

In a particular programming language, a procedure SWAP, which interchanges the values of two variables X and Y, has been declared as:

```
DEF PROC SWAP(X,Y)
      LET T:=X
      LET X:=Y
      LET Y:=T
ENDPROC
```

[*This is rather a strange language, it appears to be BBC Basic but uses := for the assignment. Also BBC Basic would not work this way as it does not allow parameters to have their values changed within a procedure.*]

a) Write down a statement which could be used within a program to interchange the values of two variables called FIRST and SECOND which are of the same data type as X and Y. Explain what happens when your statement is executed.

b) Explain why the statement
   CALL SWAP(A + 1,7)
   would cause problems.

c) Assuming that the language allows it, explain why it would be better to declare the variable T as a local variable in the procedure definition. (Cambridge 1988)

Question 8

Below is a program written in a language which allows procedure calls.

In this language, parameter values are copied into a procedure when it is called. There is no mechanism for transferring values out of a procedure via parameters.

```
A = 1
CALL PROCEDURE example (A)
PRINT "After Procedure example, A = " A
END {of program main body}

DEFINE PROCEDURE example (F)
PRINT "Initially, in Procedure example, F = " F
F = 2
PRINT "Then, in Procedure example, F = " F
END {of Procedure example}
```

[*This is obviously intended to be BBC Basic, which does not allow parameters to have their values changed within a procedure though the CALL and DEF procedures are slightly different.*]

a) i) Write down, in order, the output this program would produce.
    ii) What result would you expect if the statement *PRINT F* were added immediately before the END in the main body of the program? Explain your answer.

b) The use of parameters in this language is restricted. By making reference to a real or invented programming language, give an example of one other method of passing parameters which you would find useful, showing clearly the context in which it could be used. (Cambridge 1988)

LONGER QUESTIONS

Question 9

In a named high-level language show how loops can be organised to
i) Handle multiple sets of data
ii) Repeat until a condition is met
Using relevant examples, explain how one- and two-dimensional arrays can be defined and show how the elements in each can be accessed. (Welsh 1984)

Question 10

Some high-level languages have specifications conforming to internationally agreed standards, but it is quite common for individual suppliers to provide extensions to these standards.

Give an example of an extension to a language standard and state one advantage and one disadvantage of this practice. (Northern Ireland 1989)

Question 11

a) Give *three* examples of statements which control the path of execution in a high-level language program. Explain how this affects the choice of test data.

b) A school is computerising its file of pupil records. Each record must contain the following information: name; address; date of birth; number of subjects studied; subjects studied; year in school; marks for each subject; and sex.

Design a suitable pupil record, and show how the file of records can be accessed using a high-level language.

Describe how the various fields in the records can be updated. Which type of file would you choose to store these records? Justify your choice. (WJEC 1983)

Question 12

a) What advantages are provided by using subroutines during program development? What advantages may be gained by using local as opposed to global variables in a subroutine?

b) It has been stated that one aim of designing a high-level language should be to allow for easy comprehension, i.e. it should be possible to read other people's programs more as one would a novel and less as one does an examination set book, than most current programming languages permit one to do.

For any high-level language that you know, show how its form can be used to assist comprehension. (London 1984)

Question 13

a) i) Describe and justify three features of a high-level programming language which make it particularly suitable for use in business applications.
   ii) Describe and justify three features of a high-level programming language which make it particularly suitable for use in scientific applications.

b) Distinguish carefully between those statements in an assembly language which have a one–one correspondence with machine code instructions and those that do not, giving examples where appropriate.

c) Give three distinct reasons why high-level languages are often preferred to assembly languages. (AEB 1985)

Question 14

a) Write brief notes on each of the following processes which are carried out when developing a program in a high-level language:
   i) algorithm design, either flowcharts or pseudo-code
   ii) correction of syntax errors
   iii) detection of logical errors

b) Discuss the importance of program segmentation and state why it is desirable to have subroutines with parameters. (AEB 1984)

OUTLINE ANSWERS

SHORT QUESTIONS

Question 1

a) Features which distinguish a high-level language are:

- the languages are not machine-dependent;
- the statements have been designed to be programmer-orientated;
- there is a well defined syntax, and often internationally agreed standards.

b) Block-structured, with reference to high-level languages, refers to the characteristic that variables have **scope** and also have **local lifetime**. Scope means that variables are defined as an active only in the routine in which they are defined and any routines local to that routine, and so variables with the same name can be used in different routines with different scope. Local lifetime means that variables local to a routine use storage which can be released after completion of the routine, for use by variables in other routines. Thus, in the case of arrays, for example, the total size may be much bigger than the total storage available.

c) Examples of block-structured language are Algol and Pascal.

Question 2

The scope of a variable in a block-structured language is the aggregate of the procedures or routines in which it is available.

A variable may not be in scope throughout the whole of the procedure in which it is defined if a variable of the same name is defined as local to a procedure within the scope of the original declaration.

Question 3

A program written in a high-level language may compile with no errors reported and run to completion but produce no output even if some was expected for the following reasons:

- though syntactically correct it may be semantically incorrect, in other words the statements may be valid in the high-level language but there could still be logic errors;
- there might be errors in the test data and files supplied;
- there might be an operating error in running the wrong version of the program or supplying the wrong files;
- there might be an error in the prediction of results from the test run or in the design of the test data.

Question 4

An advantage of compilation is that the resulting object program is in machine language and will run faster than interpreted code.

An advantage of interpretation is that the program will run immediately without compilation and so can reduce the time taken in program development and testing.

Question 5

Software tools which might be used in the creation of a source program and its conversion to an executable form are:

- a text editor to create, amend and edit the source program;
- the compiler to translate individual program modules or segments;
- a linker to combine the compiled segments into a single executable object program;
- a program loader to retrieve the object program from the backing store and start execution;
- a test harness to implement program testing under controlled conditions, enabling the program to be traced and halted at specified points to examine variables.

Question 6

There are a great many high-level computer languages for the following reasons:
- Different languages are suited to different applications, for example Cobol for business, Fortran for mathematical and engineering applications
- As computing has developed, so the needs have changed, Pascal evolved when programmers realised that language structure was more important than application orientation
- Hardware developments have lead to new requirements, e.g. Basic for on-line terminals and microcomputers, Coral for real time, and Ada for multi-tasking

Question 7

a) A statement which could be used within a program to interchange the values of two variables called FIRST and SECOND is
      CALL SWAP (FIRST,SECOND)
    When this statement is executed the variables FIRST and SECOND are copied to the local variables X and Y of the procedure SWAP, after implementing the swap via the temporary storage area T when the new values of X and Y are copied back to FIRST and SECOND on executing the ENDPROC.

b) The statement CALL SWAP (A+1,7) will cause problems because on returning from the subroutine on executing the ENDPROC the copy back to "7" cannot be executed as it would amend a constant, similarly the copy to "A + 1" is undefined. The output parameters must be variables and not constants or expressions.

c) It would be better to declare the variable T as a local variable in the procedure definition, to avoid corrupting a variable T in the calling routine, or any other part of the program.

Question 8

a) i) The program would produce the following output
          Initially, in Procedure example, F = 1
          Then, in Procedure example, F = 2
          After Procedure example, A = 1
    ii) If the statement PRINT F were added immediately before the END in the main body of the program the output would become:
          Initially, in Procedure example, F = 1
          Then, in Procedure example, F = 2
          After Procedure example, A = 1
          2

    This is because F is a global variable and so is accessible in both the main program and the subroutine.

b) It is not completely obvious what was intended by the examiner in referring to another method of passing parameters. Most high-level languages implement the passing of parameters in the manner of the sample program but allow the parameters to be modified within the subroutine. Another possibility is to pass parameters by the use of GLOBAL variables, but perhaps what was sought is the use of a stack in the context of a low-level language where variables can be pushed into the stack in the calling routine and popped out in the subroutine.

LONGER QUESTIONS

Question 9

Taking BBC Basic as an example of a high-level language, in handling multiple sets of data we assume that we know how many sets are to be read and this is stored in a variable called *number* and the loop will be in the form
    FOR set = 1 TO number
      INPUT ...
    NEXT set
to illustrate repetition. Until a condition is met consider another way of handling multiple sets of data where it is assumed that after each set has been read and processed using a procedure_ PROC_process, the user is asked, via a procedure PROC_yesno, if there is more to be processed. In this case the loop will be in the form

```
REPEAT
  INPUT ...
  PROC_process
  PRINT "Any more data";
  PROC_yesno
UNTIL answer = "NO"
```
In Basic both one- and two-dimensional arrays have to be defined using DIM statements. Take as examples the storage of the names of thirty pupils in an array *name$* and their marks in ten subjects in an array called *marks*, then they will be defined in a DIM statement of the form:
```
DIM name$(30), marks(30,10)
```
within the program, the name of the seventh pupil can be accessed by reference to name$(7), and their mark in subject 3 by reference to the element marks(7,3).

Question 10

Pascal, Cobal, Ada and Fortran are amongst the high-level languages whose specifications conform to internationally agreed standards. Taking Fortran, for example, there have been a number of standard versions, including Fortran II, Fortran IV, Fortran 66 (referring to the year rather than a serial number) and Fortran 77. A new version, possibly Fortran 88, was debated during the 1980s and due for acceptance in the early 1990s. Fortran 77 was a great advance and implemented some of the constructs of structured programming and character handling missing from earlier versions, but still had many omissions and lagged far behind Pascal as a structured language.

In order to meet the needs of programmers, most compilers of the 1980s implemented a number of extensions which became widely, though unofficially, accepted as the 'de facto' standard. One of these was the implementation of DO WHILE, for example:
```
DO WHILE (X.NE.0)
   . . . .
END DO
```
The advantage of this is that it provided most programmers with a glaring omission from the standard Fortran 77 language. The disadvantage of this practice is that programs no longer conform to the accepted standard and may not be portable. The example of the Fortran DO WHILE is one which is probably justified since language standard committees often debate without agreement over many years. In general it is a bad practice as it leads to the situation which exists in Basic where there is no standard language between manufacturers and, worse still, Basic programs are often not portable between different models of computer produced by the same manufacturer.

Question 11

a) In giving three examples of sequence control statements in a high-level language program, we should refer to the standard constructs of structured programming which are sequence, selection, iteration and procedures. Taking BBC Basic as the language chosen for the examples and ignoring sequence, which is the trivial case of passing from one statement to the next, we have:

- *Selection* is implemented by an IF statement, for example:
  ```
  IF X>Y THEN PRINT X ELSE PRINT Y
  ```
  which will print the larger of the two variables X and Y.

- *Iteration* has two possibilities in this language:
  ```
  FOR counter = 1 TO 10
        PRINT stock (counter)
  NEXT counter
  ```
  which will loop and print 10 values from the array stock
  ```
  REPEAT
        Z = GET
  UNTIL Z = 32
  ```
  which is a delay loop which will execute continuously, examining the keyboard until the space bar is detected.

- *Subroutines* are implemented by *procedure* definitions and calls. For example, if it is decided to implement the above delay loop by a subroutine, it would be defined as follows:

```
DEF PROC_get_space
LOCAL Z
PRINT "Press space bar to continue"
REPEAT
Z = GET
UNTIL Z = 32
ENDPROC
```

and then whenever within the program it is required to stop the process until the space bar is pressed then we use the statement

```
PROC_get_space
```

In explaining how this affects the choice of test data it is important that sufficient items of test data are used to ensure that in running the test, every logic path is executed at least once.

b) A problem with this question, and with many others of its type, is that we do not have sufficient information to give a full answer. We need to know school size, range of number of subjects, and the purposes for which this file is to be used. However, if all this information were to be included, then the question might become impossibly long to read. Therefore in such questions where there is a little doubt, it is *vital* to *state* any assumptions made in the answer so that, even if it is not exactly what the examiner had in mind, credit will be given.

There are two points to emphasise in the structure of the pupil record; firstly, there is a need to include an extra field as an identifier containing a pupil reference number since name may not be unique; secondly, this will be a variable length record dependent on the number of subjects studied. The record therefore needs to be divided into fixed and variable length parts. Thus the structure of the pupil records could be:

pupil reference	numeric code
name	alphanumeric
address	alphanumeric
date of birth	numeric
year in school	numeric
sex	M or F
number of subjects studied	numeric

Then for each subject:

subjects studied	subject code
marks for each subject	numeric

As an alternative, the address could be a variable length field, or the record could be made fixed length by allowing sufficient space for the maximum number of subjects which could occur. For the purposes of this question we will assume that variable length records are used, although in many schools the maximum number of subjects may be well defined. Even then it could still be the case that with options, subdivisions and resits, a variable length record is essential.

There are four program statements which we need to mention here but they may differ between the various languages and possibly the different models of computer used. In the examination each candidate would, obviously, use instructions from the language used in the practical part of the course. The statements which would need to be illustrated are:

- Open the files
- Write a record
- Read a record
- Close the files

Describing how the various fields in the records can be updated cannot really be separated from a consideration of the type of file used to store the records and its organisation and access. Pupils will be identified by their reference number, their record will be retrieved, updated and rewritten to the disc. Three possible file organisations will be considered here:

1 *Sequential organisation* with the file sorted on pupil reference number
2 *Random organisation* using an index to store the disc sector addresses for each pupil reference
3 A *linked file* with the records held in sequence but with an extra field in each record to give the address of the next

Let us assume that there is wide variation in the number of subjects studied. A *variable length* record structure would then be best. If we also assume that the main use of the file will be in batch processing, to tabulate or enter marks for a class, and that there is no need for direct access to an individual pupil record, then the *sequential organisation* will prove best. The justification of this choice will be partly on the nature of the processing and partly on the difficulties of maintaining variable length records in a direct address mode.

Question 12

a) The advantages provided by using subroutines during program development are:

1 More than one programmer can collaborate and work independently on the same application

2 An installation is able to identify and collect together a library of procedures to be used in more than one program

3 Two small subroutines can be developed in less time than one larger routine

4 The use of subroutines and modular programming leads to a more efficient program design

5 Program maintenance is easier since logic errors can be more easily detected and isolated to a specific subroutine

The difference between local and global variables in a subroutine is that local variables are declared as local or private to the subroutine itself and are independent of variables of the same name used in other subroutines. The advantages which may be gained by using local instead of global variables in a subroutine include:

- Names can be duplicated between several routines

- When amending a program, use of a new local variable can avoid the possibility of corrupting a variable used elsewhere

- We may use the same name for variables of two different types in two different routines

- When a program is compiled, in some circumstances it may be quicker or more efficient to access a local rather than a global variable

- In a block-structured language such as Pascal, the space used by local variables can be released for use by other variables when the subroutine is not active. Hence, particularly with arrays, a program has, potentially, more variable space than if all the variables were global

b) Some of the principal points to note in designing high-level language programs in such a way as to assist comprehension are:

- Inserting comments to obtain the function of key lines of code

- Providing a list of variables and procedures in comments at the start of the program

- Giving meaningful names to the variables adds to the ease of comprehension

- Adopting a modular structure makes a program easier to follow, particularly if modules are given meaningful names

- IF statements are often more readable if they use logical variables, particularly if they have meaningful names

- It is possible, in most high-level languages, to nest IF statements; this should be limited to three, or at most four levels

- Statements should be made more readable, where relevant, by inserting extra spaces

- Programs can be made more readable by inserting spaces at the start of lines to indent statements within a loop or within the two blocks of code within an IF ... THEN ... ELSE statement

- Multiple- line statements are best avoided unless they themselves add to the readability

- Complex arithmetic formulae are often best split into several steps

Question 13

a)   i) Three features of a high-level programming language which make it particularly suitable for use in *business applications* are:

     1   The ability to handle individual characters within fields; for example, if a postcode is used as a field then the first two characters can be extracted to identify the postal area

     2   Good facilities for record and file processing; for example, in a payroll system a complete record can be read or written by a single READ statement instead of by enumerating all the fields each time

     3   The ease of formatting of output so that reports can be tabulated in columns, right- or left-hand margins justified and decimal points aligned as required

   ii) Three features of a high-level programming language which make it particularly suitable for *scientific applications* are:

     1   Ease of coding mathematical formulae so that, as was originally conceived for Fortran, equations can be incorporated within the source program for direct evaluation

     2   Floating point arithmetic so that, by working to a number of significant figures with an exponent, a very wide range of numbers can be processed

     3   High precision of arithmetic, allowing data types of double or even quadruple the normal eight-digit precision

b)   Most statements in an assembly language have a one-to-one correspondence with machine code since in essence, assembly instructions are a symbolic representation of machine code. Most assembly language systems have a 'library' of subroutines or procedures which can be incorporated into programs. The way in which they are invoked is by commands which have the same form as assembly language statements; since each one, on assembling, is replaced by the instructions of the subroutine, they are called *macros*. Typical examples are macros for opening and closing files, also for reading and writing records.

c)   Three reasons why high-level languages are often preferred to assembly languages are:

     1   High-level languages aim at (but do not always achieve) machine-independence which makes for ease of translation between computers

     2   Programs can be written and tested out in much less time than for low-level languages

     3   Writing high-level language programs needs no detailed knowledge of the machine so that the programs are usually easier to read by other programmers and can be made self-documentary

Question 14

a)   i) An algorithm is a set of unambiguous rules which specify the method of solution of a problem in a finite number of steps. To specify an algorithm design with flowcharts we carry out the following steps:

- Draw a data flowchart showing the environment of the program within the system

- Draw an outline program flowchart showing the main modules on a single sheet of A4 paper. This will show that thee linkage of the modules is logically correct, will be the basis for writing the computer instructions, and will form an essential part of the documentation

- Draw the detailed program flowchart

A similar approach could be adopted with a top-down design to create an algorithm in pseudo-code.

   ii) Syntax errors are errors in the grammatical structure of the source language. They will be detected during compilation when a list will be generated for the programmer, and will be corrected using the text editor. A program will not normally compile until it is completely free of syntax errors. However, this does not in any way guarantee that it is free from logical errors.

   iii) The detection of logical errors should start at the program design which, if carried out with efficiency, will minimise the number of errors in the program. After coding the program, however good the design, it is unlikely to be completely correct and so it must be thoroughly tested to locate any errors or bugs. It is virtually impossible to test a program under *all* the conditions which may be encountered during live running. This is partly due to the time required for such complex and exhaustive tests and also because of the wide range of possibilities involved and the unpredictable nature of the combinations of unlikely errors. The more complex the program, the greater the problems in locating all the errors. However, these can be minimised by developing and testing the program in smaller modules. The key, however, to efficient program testing is the thorough design of test data to test every logical path.

b) Program segmentation is the subdivision of programs into a number of smaller, self-contained and independent procedures or modules:

   i) Allows more than one programmer to work on the same application
   ii) Exploits the fact that two small modules can be developed in less time than one large module
   iii) Almost certainly leads to a more efficient program design
   iv) Reduces program maintenance time
   v) Allows standard modules to be incorporated in programs

When calling on subroutines, parameters are used to transmit data between the subroutines and the calling routine. This allows much greater flexibility in the design of subroutines which can then be more general. The alternative to the use of parameters is to use global variables which have the problem that the names must match in both routines. The two techniques may be contrasted by comparing GOSUB and PROC: the GOSUB statement relies on global variables but PROC can use either global variables or parameters. A restriction in BBC BASIC does not allow parameters to be changed within the procedure so that parameters can be used for input but not output.

DUTIES OF DATA PROCESSING STAFF

DATA PROCESSING STAFF

THE NEED FOR DOCUMENTATION

DOCUMENTATION IN COURSEWORK AND EXAMINATIONS

FILE SPECIFICATIONS

SYSTEM OUTPUT

GETTING STARTED

In this chapter we shall study a series of **job descriptions** for the various staff in a computer department. However, the number and variety of posts varies considerably from one organisation to another, as indeed does the reporting structure; for example, some organisations have programmers and systems analysts in separate departments and others have them mixed together in project teams.

The second topic relates to one of the most neglected aspects of programmer training, that of **documentation**. A program which is *not* documented is normally of little use to anyone except the programmer, and even then only during the relatively short time when the details remain in the memory of the programmer.

There are several diferent categories of documentation which need to be identified, though the content and techniques may overlap:

- **The program specification** or design, usually provided by the systems analyst for the programmer
- **The program documentation**, usually provided by the programmer for use by other programmers in maintenance or enhancement of the program
- **User instructions**, provided by the systems analyst assisted by the programmer to help the user
- **Operator instructions**, also provided by the systems analyst assisted by the programmer

ESSENTIAL PRINCIPLES

DATA PROCESSING STAFF

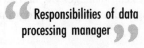

Staff involved in data capture and preparation

A number of computer staff are involved in the various stages of data capture and preparation:

- Data preparation operators
- Data control clerks
- Computer operators
- Systems analysts
- Applications programmers

Data preparation staff are responsible for the actual transcription of data from source documents to the machine-readable input media.

The **data control clerks** are responsible for the interface between the users and the computer operators. Normally, data will be entered on the relevant input documents, which are then sent from the user department to the data control department. Here the staff will carry out a cursory inspection of the data to check for feasibility, completeness and legibility, before passing to the data preparation staff and finally to the computer operators. Data control clerks will also be responsible for the batch totalling which will be described later in this chapter. After the computer system has been run, they will also be responsible for checking the output for feasibility and completeness, as well as for the correctness of the control totals, before returning to the user.

The **computer operations staff** are responsible for all aspects of the computer hardware operations, including the handling of media containing input, output and files. The **systems analysts** and the **applications programmers** are responsible for designing and programming the implementation of the controls, as described below.

Data processing manager

The D.P. manager is responsible to top management for the introduction and maintenance of computer-based systems.

- **Responsibilities**

The main responsibilities are:

1) To define and control the budget and resources for all the data processing department
2) To advise management on the choice of all data processing equipment, on the enhancement or replacement of the existing installation, and on the purchase of microcomputer systems
3) To advise management on the specification, selection and implementation of applications software
4) To interpret the policy and needs of the management of the organisation and to suggest worthwhile areas for future computer applications within the organisation
5) To plan in conjunction with the various users within the organisation, the implementation of projects, and to ensure integration with other existing and planned systems.
6) To provide justification, and to obtain approval for, new systems products and production work on existing applications
7) To deploy staff within the organisation between the development of new systems products and production work on existing applications
8) To set up, and enforce, both methods standards and performance standards
9) To arrange staff recruitment and training, in conjunction with the personnel department, and in addition to establish and maintain a career structure for all staff in the department
10) To control and co-ordinate the resources in the various subsections of systems design, programming and operations
11) To keep abreast of developments in the field of data processing and to ensure that the same holds true for all relevant staff

Responsibilities of data processing manager

Senior systems analyst

A senior systems analyst will be responsible to either the D.P. manager or, possibly in a large organisation, to a chief systems analyst for the analysis and design of existing systems and the design and justification of computer-based systems.

■ **Responsibilities**

1) To make an appraisal of the information needs of the organisation in some area or areas defined by management, and to specify the information which is required to meet the current and expected needs of the organisation

2) To design information systems to meet the requirements as defined in 1) above, and to provide an outline plan, including environmental diagrams, systems flow charts, file and input/output layouts, as well as supporting narrative specifications

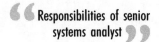
Responsibilities of senior systems analyst

3) To provide estimates of the time, cost, and resources required to develop and implement any of the proposed systems

4) To provide estimates, in conjunction with user departments, of the benefits of any proposed new system over the existing situation

5) To submit justification reports relating to any proposed system, thereby enabling the data processing manager to obtain approval by management

6) To control the progress of all projects under development

7) To monitor and continually to re-appraise the effectiveness of all installed systems for which responsibility has been delegated

8) To design, document and enforce standards for all aspects of systems work

9) To supervise a team of systems analysts working on a variety of projects

Systems analyst

A systems analyst will be responsible to the senior systems analyst for the detailed design of part, or the whole, of a computer based system.

■ **Responsibilities**

1) To take part in the fact-finding for any feasibility study

2) To examine the requirements of any new or existing system, and to define in detail the requirements for input, outputs, and files

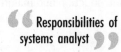
Responsibilities of systems analyst

3) To prepare adequate documentation for the programmers to implement the design

4) To assess volumes and frequencies of input, output, and files, as a basis for time and cost estimates for the system

5) To collaborate with the internal and external auditors, Customs and Excise, and other authorities in the incorporation of adequate controls within the systems design

6) To design, in conjunction with both users, programmers, data preparation and computer operations staff, the forms for data input and output

7) To provide detailed specifications for any off-computer clerical procedures

8) To provide a system operations manual to standards specified within the organisation for all staff concerned in the implementation of any design

9) To check and validate by program test runs, systems trials, and the observation of live test runs, in order to ensure that the system meets the required specification

10) To supervise, if required, any junior staff assisting in all or some of the above duties

Senior programmer

The senior programmer will be responsible to the data processing manager or, in a large organisation, to the chief programmer for the planning, writing and testing of all programs.

■ **Responsibilities**

1) To advise the senior systems analyst on the feasibility and efficiency of the proposed program suite and, when required, to assist in its design

2) To produce an overall schedule for the programming and testing of each job, and to examine and maintain progress schedules

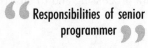
Responsibilities of senior programmer

3) To supervise the testing, correction and linking of all programs and, if required, to supervise the final system test, which may involve pilot and parallel running

4) To direct the maintenance of any operational programs requiring amendment or correction

5) To liaise with the computer manufacturers in matters concerning software queries and programming developments

6) To decide on the selection of appropriate high-level or low-level programming language, and the use of standard commercial program packages and other applications and systems software

7) To code any part of the program which is beyond the capabilities of junior programmers or where special expertise or efficiency is required

8) To ensure the completion of all necessary documentation and, in particular, to provide adequate computer operating instructions and to check the user documentation

9) To allocate work and supervise programmers for whom direct responsibility is given

Programmer

Programmers are responsible to the senior programmer for the detailed flowcharting, writing and testing of application programs in a selected language

■ Responsibilities

Responsibilities of programmer

1) To finalise the structure of files and data based on the documentation supplied by the systems analyst

2) To draw detailed flowcharts, decision tables, top-down designs or structure diagrams

3) To code, write, desk check and test applications programs

4) To design a program structure using modules of manageable size

5) To design and document test data and expected results and to check all possible logical paths of the program

6) To provide a comprehensive test of all applications programs

7) To complete the preparation of full computer operating instructions for all applications programs

Operations manager

The computer operations manager is responsible to the data processing manager for the day-to-day control of the operation and maintenance of the hardware (and possibly the systems software) in the computer installation.

■ Responsibilities

Responsibilities of operations manager

1) To establish and maintain standard techniques for operating

2) To advise both management and the systems analysts on the feasibility, cost and practicability of any proposed system

3) To estimate the cost of work to be done in the installation, and to report on the actual costs of tasks run

4) To schedule both the data preparation and loading of jobs on the equipment

5) To set up, and control, the libraries of programs and data files, and to supervise appropriate security arrangements

6) To schedule the hours when equipment will operate and to liaise with the maintenance organisation

7) To ensure that records of equipment usage and operational efficiency are adequately and efficiently maintained

8) To ensure the availability of adequate supplies of magnetic tapes, discs, stationery and other media

9) To arrange reciprocal stand-by facilities for emergency use in the event of failure or possible unexpected peaks

10) To ensure that the optimum use is made of the systems software and operating systems

Computer operations shift supervisor

A computer shift supervisor will be responsible to the computer operations manager for the supervision of the computer operators on a shift.

■ Responsibilities

Responsibilities of computer operations shift supervisor

1) To supervise and assign duties to the various staff operating the computer

2) To maintain a log of equipment usage and faults detected in hardware and software

3) To arrange and monitor the introduction of new production jobs

4) To assist in the training of staff in operating the equipment and to establish and enforce standard procedures
5) To assist the programmers in the production of job instruction sheets
6) To watch for, and suggest, system changes to improve operating efficiency
7) To call the appropriate maintenance engineers when any equipment malfunctioning occurs

Computer operator

The computer operators are responsible to their shift supervisor for the operation of the equipment to which they are assigned.

■ **Responsibilities**

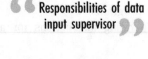
Responsibilities of computer operator

1) To assemble all necessary input and output materials for the various jobs
2) To set up, clean, and operate the equipment
3) To maintain records of machine utilisation and malfunctioning in the designated log books
4) If required, to direct and assist in training junior operators
5) To undertake first-line fault finding and equipment maintenance

Data input supervisor

The data input supervisor is responsible to the operations manager for the day-to-day supervision of data preparation.

■ **Responsibilities**

Responsibilities of data input supervisor

1) To supervise all of the staff involved in the entry and verification of data
2) To assign data preparation operators to jobs and plan operations
3) To keep within overall job schedules
4) To maintain records of the progress of jobs through the data preparation section
5) To maintain records of speed and accuracy of individual operators to ensure the maintenance of standards
6) To train staff in operating the various items of equipment
7) To ensure that adequate stocks of stationery are maintained
8) To advise the systems analysts, where required, on forms and input screen design
9) To report on the breakdown or malfunctioning of equipment

Data control supervisor

This post may be responsible to the operations manager in some installations for the control of data *within* the computer installation, but is usually *outside* the operations area.

■ **Responsibilities**

Responsibilities of data control supervisor

1) To assign tasks to, and supervise, data control clerks who:
   a) check the accuracy of input and output documents;
   b) record and agree control information
2) To control the progress of work from the originating department, through the computer installation to its final destination
3) To arrange the re-running and correction of computer jobs as directed
4) To maintain written records of all work for audit purposes

THE NEED FOR DOCUMENTATION

In the remainder of this chapter we shall study the importance of program documentation; firstly, because it is of the utmost importance to all programmers, and secondly, since it is a prime requirement for all practical and project work carried out for examinations.

Good documentation is essential for any developed program for the following main reasons:

Needs for documentation

1) To allow the user to ensure that the program design meets the requirements of the stated objectives
2) To give the programmer a full understanding of the requirements of the program
3) To prove that the proposed program design is logical and complete
4) To enable subsequent corrections and amendments to be implemented with maximum accuracy and efficiency

CONTENTS OF A PROGRAM DOCUMENTATION FILE

We shall first look at the various elements of a **program documentation file**. We shall justify and specify the format of each part since it is imperative that all are included in practical work. Furthermore, documentation should be commenced and, for the most part, completed *before* programming is started.

- Title page
- Program abstract or outline
- Environmental systems flowchart
- Narrative description
- Algorithm specification
- File specifications
- Program input
- Program output
- Test data and expected results
- Sample output
- Program listing
- Operating instructions
- Development record
- Amendment record

Title page

This should contain the name of the program, the name of the system, the installation if relevant, the name of the programmer, and the date written. There may also be other items, such as program reference number, the name of the systems analyst or project leader, etc. Most programs, particularly those being marketed, should have a short (six to eight characters) name which is both meaningful and suitable for use as the file name on the program disc.

Program abstract or outline

This might also appear on the title page. It is a brief statement describing in two or three sentences, or a small paragraph, the main function and objectives of the program.

Environmental systems flowchart

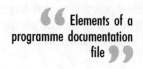
Elements of a programme documentation file

This will, if the program is a segment within a data processing system, be a systems flowchart or data flowchart showing the relationship between the program and the rest of the system. A typical example of a data flowchart is given in Chapter 6, in Fig. 6.3. If it is a 'stand-alone' program, it is still important to include a simple data flowchart to show the inputs, outputs and files for the program.

Narrative description

This is important because, despite the many types of chart available to specify the program, there is inevitably a need to provide part of the specification in narrative form. This will complement the flowcharts and other design aids and contain a level of detail which may not be possible in flowcharts, decision tables and top-down designs.

Algorithm specification

This will be a flowchart, a structure chart, a top-design, a decision table or some other technique to give a precise, step-by-step definition of the algorithm.

File specifications

These give the format of data on the files, including the structure and contents, and is normally represented in a tabular format which is likely to include, for each file, the file reference, the file name, medium, record type (fixed or variable length), access method, record length, number of fields and a description of each field. The *field description* will include the field name, length, description and type, coding system for the field, the range of values and number of repetitions.

Program input

This will be specified in a manner similar to the files, since in modern systems the majority of input comes either from an interactive keyboard or from a file. If it is from a file, having been transcribed from some other input media, its format will be specified as described above; but if the input is from a keyboard, then the best form of documentation is a diagrammatic representation of the screen, showing what the user would see on being requested to enter data. This can often be produced directly from the screen by a software screen dump.

Program output

This will normally be print or screen display. In the case of the screen display, as for the input, a sketch or pictorial representation of the output containing typical values is the best form of documentation. The alternative is to use a standard gridded form, such as graph paper with rectangles corresponding to each screen position. These forms should be complemented by a specification of each field, tabulated as for the files, on a special form specifying the field name and description, position, length, field type, type of display (where relevant, what colour, what character font and whether any special feature is to be used, e.g. flashing, underlined or emphasised), range of values and number of repetitions. For printed output, the output specification would be the same, but the screen might be twenty-five lines of eighty columns, and the print, typically, sixty-six lines of 132 characters, which would occupy a much larger form.

Test data and expected results

These will contain the specification of the input data (including files where relevant) for a full test run, together with the expected results, the output from the test run and a 'justification' of the expected results. That is, for arithmetical programs, the calculations which would be carried out to achieve the results, and for a file-processing program, a reconciliation of the reason for each output file record and an explanation of any screen display or printed output. It is important to design test data meticulously to test, if possible, every logical path in the program.

Sample output

In addition to the test data results, sample output can be included for a new user wishing to learn about running the program, thereby giving a test run to emulate. Sample output will also be useful for a programmer making amendments to the program which must still be consistent with the original test run, and will serve as a check when implementing the program on another computer.

Program listings

These should be a tidy listing of the final working version of the source program together, if compiled, with the results of the compilation. It is always good practice to annotate the listings with comment statements as explained in Chapter 8. Where possible this should be produced with the assistance of a word processing program to give a tidier listing.

Operating instructions

These will be written in simple terms for the novice user and operator, bearing in mind that the operator may know nothing about programming but must have all the necessary information to run the program.

Development record

This will be built up as a journal or log, listing the various test runs, their degree of success and the action taken before the next test. In an organisation, this is often presented on a pre-printed form and its use made compulsory for all programming staff.

Amendment record

This will be used when the program has been taken into live usage and will record any changes made to the program or the specification.

DATA PROCESSING STAFF INVOLVED IN DOCUMENTATION

A number of the computer staff who may be involved in the various stages of *documentation* including systems analysts, programmers, project leaders, data control clerks and computer operators.

The **systems analyst** is responsible for investigating the requirements of a computer system and documenting the design of the program for the programmer to implement.

The **programmer** will be responsible for implementing the design of the systems analyst and adding the additional elements which arise during program development, such as the actual test data and sample output, the program listings, the operating instructions and the development record. In small organisations, the programmer will also take on the responsibilities of the systems analyst, but should carefully distinguish between the two stages of development and complete the design before commencement of the programming.

The job of **project leader** exists in large organisations. He or she has the responsibility of supervising a team of analysts and programmers involved in the development of a large system or a number of related projects.

The duties of a **data control clerk** were explained earlier; their particular responsibilities for a computer system will need to be specified in the program documentation.

The **computer operator**, or in the case of a small organisation the user, will need to receive full documentation of the media requirements, the input format and the action to be taken in the case of error and exceptions.

DOCUMENTATION IN COURSEWORK AND EXAMINATIONS

The topics studied in this chapter are of particular importance where there is assessed coursework as part of the examination. Written papers may also include questions on the need for, and content of, documentation, to be answered from the theoretical viewpoint. In addition, if an examination question has a requirement to write a complete program or subroutine, there will almost certainly be marks to be gained from documentation; furthermore, it is likely that marks will be lost if the documentation is omitted. The extent of such documentation will be limited by the time available in the examination, but the items which could be included are the program abstract, an environmental systems flowchart, a brief narrative account, the file specifications, the input and output specification and, if possible, the test data and expected results rather than just a program listing. These items may take a little time to present, but need to be included not only to gain the marks allocated but to assist in clarifying your thoughts in designing the program. They will also help the examiner to follow the program.

The project itself is likely to be a fully working and documented program and, as such, must contain *all* the sections described earlier in this chapter. There will be a definite apportionment of marks for this documentation and candidates will get a poor mark if they omit to present documentation, *even if the program works perfectly*.

Because the program documentation is designed, in part, to aid program development, it is vital that as much of the documentation as possible is completed *before* programming is commenced. The following can normally be completed *before* the first line of source program is written:

- Title page
- Program abstract
- Environmental systems flowchart
- Narrative description
- File specifications
- Program input and output specifications
- Test data and expected results

and only the following should be left until *after* the program has been written and tested:

- Sample output
- Program listing
- Operating instructions
- Development record

It is therefore strongly recommended that *all* the items in the first list are prepared and checked *before* starting to write the source program, not only to save time but to ensure a satisfactory program design. The excuse heard many times over by every teacher supervising coursework, 'I can't start the documentation yet because the program is not working', is neither acceptable nor justified.

Documentation of systems

In the case of a data processing system which may consist of a number of individual program segments, each program will be documented individually. In addition there will be an overall description of a system, full system flowcharts, details of the structure of the files used throughout the system and common to a number of programs, together with documentation of the precise hardware requirements.

The documentation of such a system may well be in two main parts; the *systems documentation* and the *operating instructions*.

FILE SPECIFICATIONS

One of the most important sections in any documentation file is the one giving the *file designs*. This not only provides a working plan for the writing of the program, but also regards the file design in a logical manner and clarifies the thought processes in the system design.

One feature of computer programs generally is that they need a rigid specification of the format of the files, whether of fixed or variable length. The *fixed length records* with a fixed structure can be represented very easily in a tabular format. The information which needs to be specified for each file includes the following:

> " Information needed for each file "

System name, to relate the file to the overall system

File Reference, which is likely to be the symbolic name used by the program

File name, which is normally the name given to the file by the operating system

File medium, normally tape or disc

Record type, which is fixed or variable length

Access method, which could be sequential, serial direct, or indexed etc.

Record length, in bytes

Number of fields, then for each field:

Field number, an optional serial number to identify the individual fields

Field name, which is the symbolic name for the field used within the program

Field length, normally measured in bytes

Field type, whether character, integer, logical or real etc.

Field description, which is a small amount of text describing the function of the field

Coding system, this may be needed where the field contains a specific code, e.g. record type or an abbreviation

Value range, specifying the minimum and maximum values or the set of valid field contents

Repetition factor, which specifies the number of occurrences if the field is an array

These lists are not necessarily exhaustive and the method of presentation is normally determined by an installation standards manual which will almost certainly specify a standard form for the presentation of this data.

A SAMPLE FILE

Take, as an example, the design of a very simple wages file with the following fields:

Surname
Initials
Sex
Title
Employee number
Grade
Tax code
Tax paid this year
Gross pay to date this year
Monthly salary
Total deductions per month

We may take the following headings as the minimum documentation needed to be specified for each field:

Field title
Field name

Format
Description
Coding system

> **Documentation needed for each field**

- **Field title** This could be, for example, 'Quantity in Stock'. This gives a concise explanation of the contents of the field and could be combined with the description.
- **Field name** This should be the same as used in the programming language.
- **Format**. This is often expressed in a notation similar to the Cobol language PICTURE statement and specifies the field size, type and format. It is usual to use 9 to indicate numeric data; A to indicate alphabetic; and X to specify alphanumeric or free format. Thus A999 indicates a field of size 4 characters of which the first is a letter and the last three are numeric digits. As a shorthand, we use X(24) to indicate twenty-four characters and A(10) to indicate ten alphabetic characters. This notation is worth adopting whatever language is being used.
- **Description** This will be a brief explanation of the field, which may be an expansion of the title and could be optional where the title is self-explanatory.
- **Coding system** This may need explanation where, for example, we have a field such as SEX where we may use 'M' for male and 'F' for female, or there may be a more extensive coding such as subject studied by a pupil.

The documentation may be set out as shown below:

SYSTEM OUTPUT

The two main types of output are *hard-copy*, i.e. print, and *screen display*. In the case of the screen display, rather as for the input, a sketch or pictorial representation of the output containing typical values is the best form of documentation. This may be complemented by a specification of each field tabulated as for the files, on a special form. The form should contain the following items for each displayed field:

> **Items for each displayed field to be included on special form**

- **Field name** The symbolic name for the field used within the program
- **Field position** The line and column numbers where the field is displayed
- **Field length** Measured in characters
- **Field type** Whether character, integer, or real number
- **Field description**
- **Type of display** i.e. where relevant, what colour, what character font and whether any special feature is to be used, e.g. flashing, underlined or emphasised
- **Value range** Specifying the minimum and maximum values or the set of valid field contents
- **Repetitions** To specify the number of occurrences and the vertical and horizontal displacements

PRACTICAL EXAMPLES

There are many examples of program documentation in schools, colleges, businesses and the shelves of shops supplying computer software. It is important to supplement this chapter by examining critically some examples of published documentation, identifying their deficiencies and recommending areas for improvement.

EXAMINATION QUESTIONS

SHORT QUESTIONS

Question 1
The documentation developed for applications software includes:

- A user manual
- An operations manual
- A system specification

State clearly the purpose of *each*.

(Northern Ireland 1989)

Question 2

State and explain the action of *four* commands you would expect to find in a general purpose text editor. (London 1988)

Question 3

List *three* elements found in each of:
1) A program flowchart
2) A system flowchart (Northern Ireland 1989)

Question 4

a) Why do software projects require documentation? Suggest *two* reasons.
b) Name *three* different documents associated with software projects and describe briefly their specific function. (AEB 1989)

Question 5

Large central computer installations which serve many users employ operators as well as programmers and other staff.
List *four* functions carried out by computer operators. (Northern Ireland 1989)

Question 6

What is the main purpose of a 'data dictionary'? (Northern Ireland 1989)

Question 7

a) Describe the main tasks in producing a suite of computer programs, from the initial definition of the problem to be solved to the release of the programs for use.
b) What forms of documentation should be produced for a suite of programs? What are the functions of such documentation? (Cambridge 1988)

LONGER QUESTIONS

Question 8

a) Describe the principal features of each of the following:
1) System design documentation
2) The user manual
b) 'An interactive program should behave in a way meaningful to the end user for any type or volume of input'.
Discuss the implications of this objective for program design. (AEB 1987)

Question 9

State the main purposes of *program documentation*. Discuss how program documentation can be produced, and also indicate the consequence of using programs with and without adequate documentation. Give one simple example to illustrate your answer. (WJEC 1983)

Question 10

a) Write a brief note on each of the following processes which are carried out when developing a program:
i) Program design
ii) Program writing
iii) Program documentation
b) Describe how you would *test* a program which is designed to read from a keyboard, in a random order, a number of transaction records each with several fields, to update a master file with these records causing several master file records to be modified and also to print an analysis of the transaction records. (AEB 1985)

Question 11

A computer program is needed, to keep records of the pupils in a school. Their names, dates of birth, dates of entering and leaving the school, successes in sport and athletics, contributions to school clubs and societies, subjects taken and examination results should be recorded, and preserved after they have left the school.

a) Describe the instructions for using the system which should be given to the people who have to operate it.

b) Describe the documentation which should be provided for those who have to maintain the software without help from the original programmers.

c) What safeguards would be needed to prevent corruption of data, and how should they be provided?

c) What limitations on access to the system should there be, and why?   (Oxford 1985)

Question 12

Describe the functions of the following personnel in a computer installation:

a) Project leader
b) Systems analyst
c) Programmer
d) Data control clerk
e) Computer operator   (AEB 1983)

OUTLINE ANSWERS

SHORT QUESTIONS

Question 1

A user manual provides the instructions necessary for the user to provide input and interpret output from the system and also to enable the user to gain the maximum benefit from the system.

An operations manual is provided to give instructions for the installation, maintenance and operation of a package.

A system specification provides a full specification of the requirements of a system to be implemented by the systems designer and programmers.

Question 2

A general purpose text editor used for program entry or for preparation of documentation will have a range of commands including:

load	to retrieve a document from the disc
save	to store a document on disc
print	to obtain hard copy
search	to locate a specified portion of text
cut	to *cut* out a selected portion of text to the paste buffer
paste	to insert the text from the paste buffer

Question 3

1) A program flowchart will contain boxes to specify operations, decisions, loops and logic flow.

2) A system flowchart will show program modules, files and data flow.

Question 4

a) Software projects require documentation to provide a specification for the programmer writing the program and also to assist the maintenance programmer at a later stage.

b) Documents associated with software projects include:

- Program specifications to document the logic of a program
- File layout to specify the content and format of the records
- Input and output layouts to specify the user interface

Question 5

Functions carried out by computer operators include:

- To assemble all necessary input and output materials for the various jobs
- To set up, clean, and operate the equipment

- To maintain records of machine utilisation and malfunctioning in the designated log books
- If required, to direct and assist in training junior operators
- To undertake first-line fault finding and equipment maintenance

Question 6

A data dictionary is created by the systems analysts as part of the specification of the system to identify the records and fields in the files included in the systems design.

Question 7

a) The main tasks in producing a suite of computer programs are:

- Identify the requirements
- Design the data structure, file layout and test data
- Use flowcharts or some other technique to specify the algorithm
- Write the actual computer instructions
- Test the program and correct any errors
- Complete the program documentation

b) The documentation to be produced for a suite of programs could include:

- The program specification or design, usually provided by the systems analyst for the programmer
- The program documentation, usually provided by the programmer for use by other programmers in maintenance or enhancement of the program
- User instructions, provided by the systems analyst assisted by the programmer to help the user
- Operator instructions, also provided by the systems analyst assisted by the programmer

LONGER QUESTIONS

Question 8

a) 1) System design documentation provides a full specification of the requirements of a system determined from the systems analysis to specify what is to be implemented by the programmers.

2) The user manual provides all the instructions necessary for the user to provide input and interpret output from the system and also to enable the user to gain the maximum benefit from the system by explaining all the features and options.

b) [*Questions of this type are often difficult to answer since the quotation is usually invented by the examiner who may have a specific point in mind and it can be hard to predict what is expected. This part is not strictly on documentation but on user friendly program design so only an outline answer is given.*]

The design of the input/output dialogue for an interactive program should be implemented in such a way as to predict every possible input by the user or response to the prompts from the system. All the machine responses must be fully documented but in addition should be readily understood by the user by providing intelligible text, rather than obscure messages such as:

INVALID RESPONSE
INPUT ERROR TYPE 1
BAD DATA

The quotation refers to both type and volume of input; type refers to the response of text instead of numbers and volume means not restricting the input to a fixed size, for example, a program to compute the average of ten numbers is practically useless whereas a relatively simple change will allow the program to run for N numbers where N is input by the user.

This answer could be further expanded to include good and bad examples of dialogue.

Question 9

The purposes of program documentation are:

1 To allow the user to ensure that the program design meets the requirements of the stated objectives
2 To give the programmer a full understanding of the requirements of the program
3 To prove that the proposed program design is logical and complete
4 To give the user a full record of all the options available within the program
5 To give the operator complete and unambiguous instructions for entering data and running the program
6 To enable subsequent corrections and amendments to be implemented with the maximum accuracy and efficiency

The contents might include:

- Title page
- Environmental flowchart
- Algorithm specification
- Input and output design
- Sample output
- Operating instructions
- Program abstract
- Narrative description
- File specifications
- Test data and expected results
- Program listing
- Amendment record

Program documentation can be produced by being handwritten or typed but is best produced by the programmer using either a word processor or a simple text editor of the form used to enter high-level language programs. Some computers even allow charts and diagrams to be created and printed, but it is most likely that these will be hand drawn.

If a program is well documented, it will receive all the benefits listed in the first part of the question in that, before programming is commenced, it will have been clearly demonstrated that the program does the required job. The user is then able to gain maximum benefit from the program by running it correctly and by using every option. If the requirements change, or if errors are located, then the program can be amended more efficiently when the programmer has a well-documented design to follow.

Without documentation, it is possible that the programmer will not have received all the requirements of the program and may not have produced the optimum program design. The user may not be aware of al the possibilities of the program and, worse still, may not even use it properly. If it is desired to amend the program, or if bugs are located, then without documentation, it might almost be quicker to rewrite the complete program rather than to incorporate amendments.

An example of good documentation is the Clwyd Technics word processing program EDWORD. This provides not only a reference manual but a self-instruction guide for new users, as well as a number of items of support material, such as sample documents.

As an example of bad documentation, consider a one-off program written to carry out some calculations and stored on a disc with no documentation or instructions. It is likely that six months later, not even the programmer will remember what the program was intended to do.

Question 10

a) i) Program design involves fact-finding to establish the requirements of the application, documentation and analysis of the findings, then the production of a program design, normally as a set of flowcharts or a top-down design.

ii) Program writing is the implementation of a design in the required source code to produce a well-structured program. The testing and design of test data are also an important part of the writing of a program.

iii) Program documentation is carried out in part at the design stage, and in part during writing and testing. The contents of a program documentation file are outlined in the answer to the previous question.

b) The essence of program testing is to run the program with test data designed to check out every logical path in the program. In this case we need to supply a specimen input form with a number of transaction records to be typed in from the keyboard in a random order. The question states that each has several fields, and we must assume that the program will validate these fields. Thus we must ensure that each possible error is represented on the test data as well as each possible combination of error. There must also be a sufficient quantity of valid records to test the updating of the master file, including records which update one, two and three or more master file records to be modified. Finally in testing the print routines, every message should occur at least once and the end of page routines should be tested similarly.

Question 11

Many of the items of documentation are useful to programmers, operators and users and so there can be some overlap in these sections.

a) The requirements of this part could be interpreted in two ways, dependent on the type of computer. For a mainframe computer system, the people who have to operate it would be the staff employed as computer operators. In a small company or department using a microcomputer, the 'people who have to operate it' could be the users themselves.

The operating instructions must contain all the necessary information to run the program and should include the hardware requirements, the file media, the type of input and the required form of stationery to be loaded on the printer. In the case of the microcomputer system or any application where the operator supplies the input, there must be a full specification of the requirements and the responses required for interactive input. In addition, the test data and expected results might be useful in testing out the program before attempting a live run.

b) The documentation which should be provided for those who have to maintain the software without help from the original programmers should include the environmental systems flowchart. This will show the relationship between the program and the rest of the system and also the inputs, outputs and files for the program. The documentation should also include a narrative description to complement the specification of the algorithm either as a flowchart, a top-down design or a decision table. There will also be full file specifications, program input and output specifications including interactive keyboard and (as for the operators) the test data and expected results (in this case so that any modifications can be shown to provide the same output). On enhancing or correcting the program it is equally important to provide additional test data to demonstrate the correctness of any new logical paths. There should also be some sample output, program listings, a development record and an amendment record.

c) The safeguards needed to prevent corruption of data were covered in Chapter 3. They should include input verification, validation and control, control totals on files and the maintenance of back-up copies of the main files. These procedures should be well documented by the systems analyst and implemented by the operators.

d) The access to the files on any computer system must be rigidly controlled since the information is as important a resource to the organisation as any of its equipment or other assets. In particular, looking at the example given here, it would be undesirable if pupils could access the system and alter their own records, or those of their friends. As a further consideration, a recent Act of Parliament, the Data Protection Act, puts legal requirements on any organisation to maintain the confidentiality of data showed on their computer systems.

Question 12

a) The *project leader* has the responsibility of supervising a team of systems analysts, applications programmers and other staff involved in the development of a computer system, or a number of related systems or projects. The job tends to exist only in the larger organisations.

b) A *systems analyst* is responsible for investigating and documenting the requirements of a computer system, for creating and documenting the requirements of a computer system, for creating and documenting the design of the new system and its programs, and for monitoring the implementation of the programs as well as the systems procedures.

c) A *programmer* is responsible for the writing, testing and documentation of the programs designed by the systems analyst. In small organisations the programmer may also have to take the responsibilities of the systems analyst.

d) A *data control clerk* provides the channel of communication between the user departments and the operators.

e) A *computer operator* is responsible for loading the file media on to the computer and for providing the appropriate input, either from a keyboard or from the media being used.

STUDENT ANSWERS WITH EXAMINER COMMENTS

Question 3
List three elements found in each of:
i) a program flowchart;
ii) a system flowchart. (Northern Ireland 1989)

> 66 The program flowchart should not contain program statements but the logical steps which can be converted to the program; furthermore the GOTO statement should be avoided in programs and can only be shown on a flowchart as a flow line. 99

```
A program flowchart contains IF statements, FOR loops and GOTO
statements.

A system flowchart shows the computer system, that is the memory the
input and the output units.
```

> 66 This confuses a system flow chart with a diagram of a computer hardware system. 99

Question 5
Large central computer installations which serve many users employ operators as well as programmers and other staff.

List *four* functions carried out by computer operators. (Northern Ireland 1989)

> 66 The reference to loading the punched cards is poor as these are rarely used these days. 99

> 66 Operators should never be allowed to amend programs; apart from not being a skill they are likely to possess, it could be a serious breach of security. 99

```
Functions carried out by computer operators include:
1  to load the punched cards into the computer
2  to set up, clean, and operate the equipment
3  to amend programs if there are errors
4  to repair faulty equipment
```

> 66 With the exception of first-line maintenance of terminals and microcomputers, it is far more likely that the repair of faulty equipment would be carried out by the suppliers or manufacturers on a maintenance contract. 99

CHAPTER

10

THE STRUCTURE OF LANGUAGES

GETTING STARTED

In this chapter we shall continue the theme of high-level languages introduced in Chapter 8. It is easy to take programming languages for granted, and indeed many people whose first introduction to computing is a study of a high-level language, particularly Basic, are not aware that the computer does not understand the particular language but needs it to be translated. In this chapter we shall look at two such translation processes, after a brief study of the concepts of compilation and interpretation. In that context we shall note the distinction between logical, syntax and execution errors.

On the practical side of compiler design it is important to realise that high-level languages have to have a very rigid structure if a translation program is to be written and in *Backus Naur Form* and *syntax diagrams* we shall see two ways of specifying programming languages. After studying the specification of languages we can take an overview of the major sections of a compiler, with an introduction to lexical analysis, syntax analysis, parsing and code generation. As a specific technique we need to study *reverse polish* notation as a means of conversion of expressions to object code.

ESSENTIAL PRINCIPLES

In Chapter 8 we saw that a **compiler** is a program which translates a source program written in a high-level language into an object program in a target language which is, in the majority of cases, in machine code. With most high-level languages, including Fortran, Algol, PL/1, Cobol and Pascal, there is no alternative to the use of a compiler. However, Basic was designed with a much simpler syntax and in many implementations, particularly on microcomputers, uses an interpreter instead of a compiler.

In its simplest form, an **interpreter** holds the source program in memory, with each instruction examined in logical sequence, then interpreted and executed. This is a software analogy of the fetch–execute cycle. The principal advantage, familiar to all users of Basic, is that programs can be executed instantaneously by simply typing a command such as RUN. The main disadvantage is that instructions have to be translated or interpreted every time they are executed, so that in the short Basic routine:

```
300   LET S = 0
310   FOR I = 1 TO 100
320   LET S = S + I*I
330   NEXT I
340   PRINT S
```

which computes the sum of the squares of the numbers one to 100, each instruction will be translated 100 times. In contrast, if a compiler were used there would be a *single* translation and the program would, in theory, execute much faster. Of course in practice there are often other considerations. Take, for example, the routine:

```
200   FOR I = 1 TO 100
210   PRINT I,I*I
220   NEXT I
```

which tabulates the squares of the numbers one to 100. It is possible that executing the PRINT statement, whether it uses a printer or screen, would slow up the execution to such an extent that the translation time is negligible by comparison. Another more striking example is that of interactive input where the waiting for a response from the user makes any loss of execution speed quite negligible. It is important to realise that Basic does not have to be run using an interpreter; there are many versions of compiled Basic on the market.

In most interpreter systems, rather than retaining the complete source code in memory, the keywords, such as FOR, PRINT and NEXT are **tokenised**, which means they are translated into a single byte to save memory and speed execution. A table of such tokens will be found in the programming manual of the computer systems and will be referred to again in Chapter 13.

There is an important distinction between syntactical, logic and execution errors.

Syntactical errors

Syntactical errors are errors in the grammar of the language. These may be simple spelling errors, for example writing IMPUT instead of INPUT, or less obvious errors in, for example, the construction of complex conditions in an IF statement. As we have already seen, the compiler, at the same time as carrying out the translation, will detect and report syntax errors in the source code. An interpreter will leave the error undetected until the program is run in, when it will be reported as the interpreter attempts to execute a syntactically incorrect statement. This shows another distinction between compilers and interpreters: a *compiler* will scan the complete program and detect every syntax error, enabling all to be corrected before a second compilation. An *interpreter* will only find one error on each run, and furthermore, will only detect syntax errors in the logical paths tested by that run.

Logic errors

Logic errors are errors in the construction which, though grammatically correct, do not achieve the required objective. A classic example, given here in Cobol, but readily translated into any other language, is:

IF TRANS-TYPE IS NOT EQUAL TO "A" OR TRANS-TYPE IS NOT EQUAL TO "B"

THEN PERFORM AMEND-MASTER.

This statement, as is indicated from its structure, appears to say exactly what would be expressed in spoken English, namely that if the variable called TRANS-TYPE has any value other than A or B then a procedure called AMEND-MASTER is to be executed. In fact what happens is that when TR-TYPE is "A" then it is not equal to "B" and so AMEND-MASTER is executed, and the same will happen if TR-TYPE is "B". The logically correct version of this statement is:

IF TRANS-TYPE IS NOT EQUAL TO "A" **AND** TRANS-TYPE IS NOT EQUAL TO "B"

THEN PERFORM AMEND-MASTER.

and AMEND-MASTER is only executed when TRANS-TYPE is niether "A" nor "B". Logical errors can only be detected by running the program with specially designed data, known as *test data*, for which the expected results are known with certainty, and then running and correcting the program until these results are actually achieved. Thus the test data must be designed so that during the test, which might need several runs, every logical path is executed at least once.

Execution errors

Execution errors, or **run time errors** as distinct from logical errors, are really errors in the design of the program. They will have been written in syntactically correct statements, and given a correct logical implementation, but are not in accord with the requirements of the program. This is a problem of poor systems analysis and design and is the result of a programmer sitting down to write the program without determining exactly what the *user* requires of the program.

Program development and testing aids

There are a number of software aids which can be used in the testing and debugging of high-level language programs. The most popular and often the simplest testing aid is the incorporation of extra print statements within the source program to provide a trace of the execution by tabulating important variables at key points. These **debug** prints will not only help in the detection of logical errors, but in a positve way will prove the accuracy of the program.

BACKUS NAUR FORM

English, or indeed any spoken language, as has been demonstrated, is not sufficiently precise to specify computer programs. They are likewise unsuited for the definition of programming languages for which the syntax must be specified in concise, unambiguous terms, and for these reasons a number of special languages have been devised for the purpose of defining other languages. These are called **meta-languages** and one example is Backus Naur Form or BNF which is named after two of the pioneers of the subject.

" Structure of BNF "

The structure of BNF is very simple, being composed of a list of statements of the form:

"left-hand side" ::= "right-hand side"

Where it is convenient to interpret the assignment operator "::=", which is known as a **meta-symbol**, as meaning 'is defined by'. The language is made up of a collection of statements, called **meta-components**, in which new elements of the language are defined one at a time by appearing on the left-hand side of one or more statements. They are defined in terms of previously defined meta-components.

There are other elements which may appear in a BNF statement: the basic elements of the language, such as digits, letters of the alphabet, arithmetic operators, punctuation marks and other characters, do not require definition and are called **terminal symbols**. This may be illustrated by the simple statement:

" Terminal symbols "

<point> ::= .

where the meta-component <point> is defined as the terminal symbol".".

Meta-components, which are also called **syntactic variables**, are distinguished by being enclosed in angle brackets. More complex statements can be constructed by using the meta-symbol " | " to separate alternatives. As an example, the statement:

 Syntactic variables

<sign> ::= + | −

is equivalent to the pair of statements:

<sign> ::= +
<sign> ::= −

in defining <sign> as being either '+' or '−'. As a further example, the statement:

<digit> ::= 0 | 1 | 2 | 3 | 4 | 5 | 6 | 7 | 8 | 9

defines the meta-component <digit> as being any one of the symbols 0–9 and

<letter> ::= A | B | C | D | E | F | G | H | I | J | K
          | L | M | N | O | P | Q | R | S | T | U | V | W | X | Y | Z

defines <letters> as being any of the upper case letters A to Z.

The early versions of Basic restricted variable names to a single letter or a letter followed by a digit, string variables were restricted to a letter followed by a $ so that A, X3 and P$ were allowed, but AA or P31 or K1$ were not. We can represent these definitions as:

<numeric variable> ::= <letter> | <letter> <digit>
<string variable> ::= <letter> $
<variable> ::= <numeric variable> | <string variable>

BNF and recursion

Recursion in programming is the technique where a procedure has the ability to call itself. In BNF, it is where a statement is defined in terms of itself, as is best illustrated by an example:

 Recursion

<variable list> ::= <variable> | <variable list>, <variable>

The first possibility is that a variable list is just a variable. The second possibility is that a variable list is a previously defined variable list, followed by a comma and a variable; e.g. X, being a variable, is also a valid variable list and X,Y,Z is a valid variable list because:

X is a variable list
X,Y is a variable list (X) followed by a comma and a variable
X,Y,Z is a variable list (X,Y) followed by a comma and a variable

Similarly we may define an integer by:

<integer> ::= <digit> | <digit><integer>

so that a digit alone, for example, 4, is a valid integer; a two-digit number, such as 24, is a digit followed by an integer, as is any longer string of digits. As another example:

<fraction> ::= .<digit> | <fraction><digit>

which can be usefully combined with:

<signed integer> ::= <sign><integer>
<real number> ::= <signed integer> | <signed integer><fraction>

This will allow the definition of real numbers of the form:

+23.45   −77   +0.1

but will not permit 23.45 as it has no sign or +.1 as there must be a digit before the decimal point. The sign restriction can be removed by the revised defintion:

<sign> ::= + | − | null

where null is a terminal symbol.

Defining program statements

As stated above, BNF is used principally in the specification and definition of program statements, for example in Basic:

<Print statement> ::= PRINT <variable list>

or in Pascal

<Statement> ::= <Simple Statement> | begin <Statement list>end
<Statement list> ::= <Simple Statement> | <Statement list> ;
                                            <Simple Statement>

The use of syntax diagrams

Use of syntax trees and diagrams

There are several alternatives to the use of BNF, two of which are illustrated in Figs. 10.1 and 10.2. The **syntax tree**, Fig. 10.1, expresses the definitions in a hierarchical format so that the diagrams can be examined from the top downwards, either to clarify the format of a statement or to check the syntax of a particular statement. The **syntax diagram**, Fig. 10.2 shows an alternative representation which is often used in textbooks and programming manuals for the Pascal language.

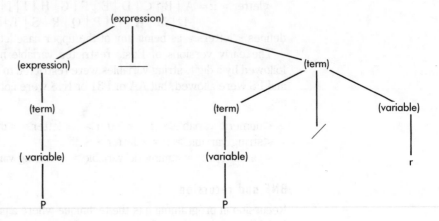

Fig. 10.1 The syntax tree

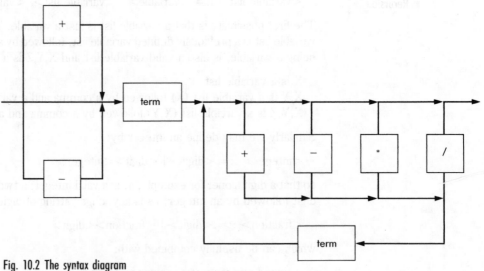

Fig. 10.2 The syntax diagram

THE MAJOR SECTIONS OF A COMPILER

The compilation process may be considered to be made up of three main steps:

- Lexical analysis
- Syntax analysis
- Code generation

Lexical analysis

Steps in the compilation process

Lexical analysis is an editing or tidying up process which takes place before the more detailed syntactical analysis is commenced. One operation implemented at this stage of the analysis is the changing of the source code into a form independent of the input device; at the same time, redundant spaces and embedded comments are removed. There can also be some editing of multi-line statements and multi-statement lines. This may well be a lengthy stage but speeds up the later processes since it separates the 'housekeeping' operations from the main processing. Another operation which can be carried out at this stage is the replacement of the names of variables, either with a shorter name, or with a reference in a table of names.

Syntax analysis

Syntax analysis is where the grammar and structure of the source program is analysed to identify the instruction keywords, constants and variables, etc. This is carried out in a manner corresponding to the language defintions in BNF, discussed earlier in this chapter, where the statements may be considered as nested blocks. An IF statement in Basic may be defined as:

IF <condition>THEN <compound statement>
           ELSE<compound statement>

and

<compound statement>::=<simple statement> |
<simple statement>:<compound statement>

There will then be further analysis at lower and lower levels until the complete program has been analysed. This operation is also referred to as **parsing** and produces an output which can be further processed at the code generation stage, as well as identifying and listing errors in the syntax of the source program. One common technique in syntax analysis is the conversion of arithmetic assignment statements into a 'Reverse Polish' notation. This will be discussed later in this chapter. It not only provides a syntax check on the expresion but generates an alternative form of the statement more suited to code generation.

Code generation

The code generation phase takes the parsed code and generates the object program as the final output from the compilation process. This phase may well make use of one or more symbol tables or dictionaries which identify the interpretation of keywords, variables and statement labels.

Optimisation is an additional operation which can be included at the code generation stage, where the object code is examined and manipulated to produce code which is more efficient, either in its length or in the number of object program statements.

REVERSE POLISH NOTATION AND THE CONVERSION OF EXPRESSIONS

A characteristic common to nearly all high-level languages is the ability to express arithmetic statements in a form similar to the following statement in Basic:

X = A *(B + C) / D

If this were to be carried out in a one-address code or on a pocket calculator then the sequence of opertions would be

LOAD   B
ADD   C
MULTIPLY   A
DIVIDE   D
STORE   X

> Reverse Polish notation

The standard arithmetic notation is called **infix**, with the operators placed between operands, for example (B+C). In Reverse Polish notation, the expression given above would be expressed as:

X A B C + * D / =

The operators are always given after the operand, hence the expression '**postfix**' notation. Expressions are evaluated according to the following rules:

1   Scan the expression left to right
2   Apply each operator in turn to the two operands which precede it
3   The result of each operation is to be regarded as a single operand

The evaluation of X A B C + * D / = will thus be

add B to C
multiply the result by A
divide that result by D
store the result in X

This is exactly the sequence in which the statements of the object program would be generated, hence the importance of Reverse Polish in the implementation of compilers. Notice that the operators are in the same sequence as in the original expression:

$$X = A * (B + C) / D$$

There are a number of algorithms which have been defined to carry out this conversion from infix to postfix notation, one of which is given in the next section.

Conversion of expressions to Reverse Polish

The algorithm described here takes the infix expression which is scanned once, from left to right, and generates the postfix expression. It does so using a temporary work area where items can be inserted and removed on a last-in-first-out basis which we shall later refer to as a stack. First we need to identify the precedence of operators, but to do this we need to be aware of an operator called the **unary minus**, which to be distinguished from the normal or **binary minus** will be characterised by the symbol $\sim$. The binary minus operates on two operands, as in $(P - Q)$, whereas the unary minus has a single operand as in -5, which we shall write here as ~5. Compilers usually restrict the unary minus to appearing only immediately after an opening bracket or an =, as in

$$V = -W + Z$$

or

$$I = J ^ (-N)$$

and this operator has the highest priority and we can summarise the priorities:

operator	precedence
=	0
+ −	1
* /	2
^	3
~	4

The algorithm may be defined as follows:

```
1   WHILE input characters remain
2   obtain next character
3   IF character is an operand add to output list
4   ELSE
5       WHILE operator is not of higher precedence than last put into the stack
6           remove latest operator from the stack
7           output operator removed from stack
8       END WHILE
9       add the operator to the stack
10  END IF
11  END WHILE
12  WHILE operators remain in the stack
13      remove latest operator from stack
14      output operator
15  END WHILE
```

This can be extended to cope with brackets simply by adding five to the precedence of all operators after detecting an open bracket, and subtracting five when a close bracket is found. This algorithm may be implemented in BBC Basic as below:

```
10    PROC_polish
99    END
1000  DEF PROC_polish
1010  REM = = = = = = = = = =
1020  DIM P (80)
1030  REM P stores the precedence of operators in the stack
1040  C$="+*^~=− /( ) "
1050  L1=0:L2=0:C=0:L$="":P$=""
1060  REPEAT
1070    E$=GET$
1080    UNTIL E$<>" "
1090  REPEAT
```

```
1100    PRINT E$;
1110    IF E$=" ( " THEN C=C+5
1120    IF E$=" )" THEN C=C−5
1130    J =INSTR (C$, E$)
1140    REM IF an operator add to list of symbols
1150    IF J=0 THEN L$=L$+E$
1160    IF J>0 AND J<8 THEN PROC_operator
1170    REPEAT
1180      E$=GET$
1190      UNTIL E$<>" " OR ASC(E$) =13
1200    UNTIL ASC (E$)=13
1210  L$=L$+P$
1220  PRINT 'L$
1230  ENDPROC
1500  DEF     PROC_operator
1510  REM     =============
1520  IF J>4 THEN J=J−5
1530  R=C+J
1540  REPEAT
1550    IF P$<>"" AND R<=P (LEN(P$)) THEN L$=L$+LEFT$ (P$,1):
                              P$=RIGHT$ (P$,LEN(P$) −1)
1560    UNTIL P$="" OR R>P(LEN (P$))
1570  P$=E$+P$
1580  P (LEN(P$)) =R
1590  ENDPROC
```

To test the algorithm it may be run with the example used earlier in the chapter to give the following:

```
>RUN
X=A* (B+C) / D
XABC+*D/=
```

and taking a more complex example:

```
>RUN
Z=C − (A + B* (D−E/F)^G) *H+ (I − (J*L+M) ^ (~N))
ZCABDEF/−G^*+H*−IJL*M + N ~ ^−+=
```

To trace this program, we may include the following 'de-bug' print which tabulates the input character, the output string, the stack and the precedence of operators in the stack.

```
1195   PRINT TAB(5) ;L$;TAB(20) ;P$;TAB(35) ; :
       FOR I=LEN(P$) TO 1 STEP −1:PRINT " ";P(I);:NEXT I:PRINT
```

```
>RUN
X       X                       0
=       X               =       0
A       XA              =       0
*       XA              *=      2 0
(       XA              *=      2 0
B       XAB             *=      2 0
+       XAB             +*=     6 2 0
C       XABC            +*=     6 2 0
)       XABC            +*=     6 2 0
/       XABC+*          /=      2 0
D       XABC+*D         /=      2 0

XABC+*D/=
```

EXAMINATION QUESTIONS

SHORT QUESTIONS

Question 1
Convert the following infix expression to postfix (Reverse Polish) and show how the postfix expression may be evaluated using a stack.

$(3 * 4 + 5) - (1 + 6/3)$ (AEB 1988)

Question 2
Write down the Reverse Polish form of the following expression:

$u/v - w * (x + y) - z$

State *briefly* what feature of Reverse Polish form makes it useful when an arithmetic expression is to be evaluated.   (Cambridge 1983)

Question 3
A list of names consists of a sequence of at least one name. Names are separated by commas and the list is terminated by a full stop. A name consists of a sequence of letters or digits commencing with a letter. Write a definition of a list of names in extended Backus Naur Form.   (Irish 1987)

Question 4
The following part of a language defines an arithmetic expresion in Backus Naur Form (BNF):

<expression> ::= <term> | <expression> + <term> | <expression> − <term>
<term> ::= <variable> | <term> * <variable> | <term> / <variable>
<variable> ::= a | b | c | d

Show that a + b*c is a syntactically correct expression in this language.

(AEB 1988)

Question 5
a)   When the following infix expression is converted to Reverse Polish (postfix) notation a unique solution is produced although the infix expression is ambiguous. State what this unique expression is, and explain how it is produced.

   $X \uparrow 3 * (Y \uparrow (3 + Z))$

b)   Why is it common for a computer to convert an expression to Reverse Polish notation before evaluating the expression.   (London 1988)

LONGER QUESTIONS

Question 6
A <Freight train> consists of one or more <Locomotive>s at the front, followed by zero or more <Wagon>s and then one <Guard's van>, with zero or more <Locomotive>s at the rear.

a)   Write down rules in Backus Naur Form (BNF) to define a <Freight train>, explaining the notation you use.

b)   A string of the letters L, W and G, terminated by a full stop, is used to represent a <Freight train>; for example, LWWWWWWG. Describe in detail an algorithm for a program, or write a program of your choice, to input a string and output either that is a valid representation of a <Freight train>, or if it is not, what is wrong with it.

c)   Design a set of strings to act as test data for your program. For each string explain what purpose it serves in testing the program.   (Cambridge 1985)

Question 7
The following is a formal partial description in BNF of the syntax of a programming language.

   <program>   ::= <line> cr { <line> cr } END
   <line>   ::= [<line no] <statement>
   <line no>   ::= <digit> { <digit> }

```
<statement>      ::= <assign> | <if> | <goto> | <read> | <print>
<assign>         ::= <var> : = <exp>
<op>             ::= + | – | * | /
<integer>        ::= <digit> { <digit> }
<var>            ::= A | B | C | D | E | F | G – – – – | Z
<if>             ::= IF <var> <comp> <var> THEN <line no>
<comp>           ::= > | < | = |≥ | ≤
<goto>           ::= GOTO <line no>
```
Note: [ ] brackets denote an optional string of symbols
      { } brackets denote repetition of a string of symbols an arbitrary number of times,
      inlcuding none.
      Statements have the same meaning as in other languages with similar facilities; cr
      denotes 'carriage return'.

a) Draw a tree diagram or obtain a derivation to demonstrate that the following is a
   correctly formed <line>.
     40 IF A = B THEN 8

b) Write a fragment of program in the above language, which has the same meaning as
   the following pseudo-code:
   IF A + B > 10 THEN SET X TO P + Q $*$ (R – S) OTHERWISE SET X TO A + B

c) *Outline* the functions of the lexical analyser of a compiler.　　(Northern Ireland 1987)

Question 8

The form of arithmetic expressions in a particular programming language is defined by the
following rules.

```
<expression>     ::= <term> | <expression> <addop> <term>
<term>           ::= <primary> | <term> <mulop> <primary>
<primary>        ::= <identifier> | <constant>
<identifier>     ::= <letter> | <identifier> <letter>
<constant>       ::= <digit> | <constant> <digit>
<addop>          ::= – | –
<mulop>          ::= * | /
<letter>         ::= a | b | c | d | . . . . .  | x | y | z
<digit>          ::= 0 | 1 | 2 | 3 | 4 | 5 | 6 | 7 | 8 | 9
```

a) i) For each of the following, indicate whether or not it is a valid expression. For those
      which are not valid, explain why.
      half-baked
      farthing=1/4
      hammond
      m45+a6
      –2
      minutes+hours*60
   ii) The rules do not allow parentheses to be used to enclose subexpressions. Suggest
       how one or more of the rules could be modified to allow for this.

b) i) Write down the Reverse Polish form of the following expression.
      jones–sandra*(claire–gareth)–frank/dan*bryn
   ii) Describe in general terms how an interpreter could, during execution of a program,
       evaluate the expression from the Reverse Polish form.　　(Cambridge 1989)

Question 9

The following production rules attempt to define a fairly wide class of 'ordinary' decimal
numbers:

```
<number> ::= <sign> <unsigned integer> <point> <unsigned integer>
<sign> ::= + | –
<unsigned integer> ::= <digit> | <digit> <unsigned integer>
<digit> ::= 0 | 1 | 2 | 3 | 4 | 5 | 6 | 7 | 8 | 9
<point> ::= .
```
The rules do not allow:

a) numbers without a sign (e.g. 27.32)

b) integers, with or without a sign (e.g. 4. –6)

c) numbers without an integer part or without a fractional part (e.g. $-40.,.72$)

Rewrite the rules so that numbers a) to c) are allowed. (Cambridge 1986)

Question 10

The following rules, in BNF, define a \<list\>
1 \<list\> ::= \<begin\> \<end\> | \<begin\> \<contents\> \<end\>
2 \<contents\> ::= \<item\> | \<item\> \<separator\> \<contents\>
3 \<item\> ::= \<object\> | \<list\>
4 \<object\> ::= a | b | c | d | e |
5 \<separator\>::= ,
6 \<begin\> ::= (
7 \<end\> ::=)
For each of the following, state whether it is a valid \<list\> and, if it is not, give a brief explanation of why it is not.

  i) a
  ii) ()
  iii) (((dab)))
  iv) (c,a,b,b,a,g,e)
  v) ((( ),b,(e)),d)
  vi) (((a,(c),e),(( ))) (Cambridge 1986)

Question 11

a) Indicate the processes that occur in the translation of a high-level language statement to an executable form. At what stage is Reverse Polish notation used?
b) Convert the following assignment statements into Reverse Polish notation, showing the intermediate steps in each case:
  i) $a = (bc + de)/(ac - fe)$
  ii) $b = abc + d(e^n + fg)$
each variable is denoted by a lower-case single letter variable name.

c) By considering the statement
  $a = (bc + de)/(ac - fe)$
indicate how the assignment can be achieved in an assembly language with the aid of a stack. (WJEC 1984)

Question 12

a) Outline the major functions of a *compiler*. Why would an installation hold two compilers for a particular language?
Distinguish between a compiler and an interpreter, giving one advantage of each.

b) What is the purpose of BNF (Backus Naur Form) notation, and of syntax diagrams?
    A real number can be expressed in one of two forms, for example:
  i) 123.456,
  ii) 1.23456 E02
In the first form there can be several digits before and after the decimal point. In the second form only one digit precedes the decimal point, which is followed by several digits followed by E and two further digits. Express rules to define these real numbers in *both* of these forms. (WJEC 1983)

OUTLINE ANSWERS

SHORT QUESTIONS

Question 1

The Reverse Polish form of

$(3 * 4 + 5) - (1 + 6/3)$

is

$3\ 4\ *\ 5\ +\ 1\ 6\ 3/+-$

This expression may be evaluated using a stack by the following steps taking the symbols in the Reverse Polish string one at a time:

PUSH 3
PUSH 4
Multiply top two on stack and PUSH result
PUSH 5
Add top two on stack and PUSH result
PUSH 1
PUSH 6
PUSH 3
Divide top of stack into second and PUSH result
Add top two on stack and PUSH result
Subtract top of stack from second and PUSH result
Stack now contains result of the expression

Question 2

The Reverse Polish form

$u/v - w * (x + y) - z$

as can be verified from the program given in the chapter, is

$u\ v\ /\ w\ x\ y\ +\ *\ -\ z\ -$

Reverse Polish form is useful when an arithmetic expression is to be evaluated because the operators and operands can be processed in a single scan since it requires no brackets and there is no concern for hierarchy of operators.

Question 3

A list of names consists of a sequence of at least one name. Names are separated by commas and the list is terminated by a full stop. A name consists of a sequence of letters or digits commencing with a letter. Write a definition of a list of names in extended Backus Naur Form.

\<list of names\>	::= \<name\> | \<name\> , \<list of names\>
\<name\>	::= \<letter\> | \<name\> \<letter\> | \<name\> \<digit\>
\<letter\>	::= A | B | C | D | E | F | G | .... | Z
\<digit\>	::= 0 | 1 | 2 | 3 | 4 | 5 | 6 | 7 | 8 | 9

Question 4

Taking the string a + b*c.

a b and c all satisfy	\<variable\>::= a | b | c | d
b satisfies	\<term\>::= \<variable\>
b*c satisfies	\<term\>::= \<term\> * \<variable\>
a satisfies	\<term\>::= \<variable\>
b satisfies	\<expression\>::= \<term\>
a + b*c satisfies	\<expression\>::= \<expression\> + \<term\>

Question 5

a)   The expression

$X \uparrow 3 * (Y \uparrow (3 + Z))$

converted to Reverse Polish notation becomes

$X\ 3 \uparrow Y\ 3\ Z + \uparrow *$

The conversion is undertaken by scanning the infix expression from left to right and generating the postfix expression using a stack as a temporary work area for operators. Any longer explanation (such as given in the chapter) is not feasible in a short question.

b) Compilers normally convert expressions to Reverse Polish notation before evaluating the expression because the postfix form can be directly translated into object code.

LONGER QUESTIONS

Question 6

a) Using BNF as defined in the chapter we may define:
   <Engine> ::= <Locomotive> | <Locomotive> <Engine>
   this defines the one or more <Locomotive>s at the front
   <Body> ::= <Guard's van> | <Wagon> <Body>
   this gives zero or more wagons and a <Guard's van>
   <Freight train> ::= <Engine> <Body> | <Freight train> <Locomotive>
   this allows zero or more <Locomotive>s at the rear

b) The algorithm may be expressed as follows
   1 IF first character not L THEN Error
   2 ELSE
   3   WHILE character = L
   4   IF more input THEN read character
   5   ELSE set character to Z
   6   END WHILE
   7   WHILE character = W
   8   IF more input THEN read character
   9   ELSE set character to Z
   10   END WHILE
   11 IF character not G THEN Error
   12   ELSE
   13   WHILE more input and Error not set
   14   read character
   15   IF character not L THEN error
   16   END WHILE
   17 END IF
   18 END IF

c) We can set out the test data as follows

Test String	Purpose
XWWWG	Invalid first character
WWWGL	No locomotive at front
LWWWG	One locomotive at front
LLWWWG	Two locomotives at front
LLLWWWG	More than two locomotives at front
LG	No wagons
LWG	One Wagon
LWWG	Two wagons also no locomotives at end
LWWWWG	More than two wagons
LWWWGL	One locomotive at end
LWWWGLL	Two locomotives at end
LWWWGLLLL	Several locomotives at the end
LWWWWL	No guards van
LWWWW	
LXWWG	Invalid characters at various points
LWXWG	
LWWWGX	

The set of strings given above are designed to test all the possible errors and also all the types of valid train. The set could be reduced as there is some duplication but each string tests a separate condition.

Question 7

a) The statement
      40   IF A = B THEN 8
   satisfies

                         \<line\> ::= [\<line no] \<statement\>
            where 40 satisfies
                  \<line no\> ::= \<digit\> { \<digit\> }
                          4   0

and   IF A = B THEN 8   satisfies
\<statement\>   ::=

                    \<assign\> | \<if\> | \<goto\> | \<read\> | \<print\>
\<if\>   ::=   IF \<var\> \<comp\> \<var\> THEN \<line no\>
                        IF A   =   B THEN 8

b) Using the specified language, the pseudocode:
       IF A + B > 10 THEN SET X TO P + Q * (R − S)
       OTHERWISE SET X TO A + B
    would be implemented as:
        C = A + B
        IF C > 10 THEN 1
        X = C
        GOTO 2
     1 X = R − S
        X = Q * X
        X = P + X
     2 next sentence

c) The lexical analyser of a compiler edits and tidies up the source code before the more detailed syntactical analysis is commenced. Source code is changed into a form independent of the input device, redundant spaces and embedded comments are removed and there is editing of multi-line statements and multi-statement lines to speed up the later processes. Also the names of variables can be replaced with a reference in a table of names.

Question 8

a) i) half and baked both satisfy   \<identifier\>
          half-baked satisfies   \<expression\>
          fathing = ¼ **fails** since = is not in the character set
          hammond satisfies   \<identifier\>
          m45 + a6   **fails** since \<letter\> can only be followed by a \<letter\> or +−*/

          −2   **fails** since − can only follow a letter or a digit

          breaking down minutes + hours * 60
          minutes and hours satisfy   \<identifier\> , \<primary\> and \<term\>
          60 satisfies   \<constant\> and \<primary\>
          hours * 60 satisfies   \<term\> ::= \<term\> \<mulop\> \<primary\>
          minutes also satisfies   \<expression\> ::= \<term\>
          minutes + hours * 60   \<expression\>\<addop\> \<term\>
   ii) We could redefine:
          \<expression\> ::= \<term\> | \<expression\> \<addop\> \<term\> |
                                       (\<expression\>)
          \<term\> ::= \<primary\> | \<term\> \<mulop\> \<primary\> | (\<term\>)

b) i) The Reverse Polish of
              jones − sandra * (claire − gareth) − frank/dan*bryn
       is jones sandra claire gareth − * − frank dan/bryn * −
   ii) Expressions in Reverse Polish can be evaluated according to the following rules:
       1   Scan the expression left to right
       2   Apply each operator in turn to the two operands which precede it
       3   The result of each operation is to be regarded as a single operand
       Adapting this to an interpreter with a stack the rules can become:
       1   Take the expression one symbol at a time
           (where symbols are either operands or arithmetic operators)
       2.1 Place each operand on the stack
       2.2 Apply each operator to the two operands on the top of the stack
       3   Place result of the operation on the stack

Question 9

a)   Numbers without a sign can be represented simply by altering the definition of sign to allow a null sign:
<sign> ::= + | − | null

b)   Integers, with or without a sign (e.g. 4, −6), can, similarly, be represented by
<integer> ::= <sign> <unsigned integer>

c)   To allow numbers without an integer part or without a fractional part we add two additional definitions to that given for number:
<number>::= <sign> <unsigned integer> <point> <unsigned integer>
<number> ::= <sign><unsigned integer> <point>
<number> ::= <sign> <point> <unsigned integer>

Question 10

The following rules, in BNF, define a <list>
1   <list> ::= <begin> <end> | <begin> <contents> <end>
2   <contents> ::= <item> | <item> <separator> <contents>
3   <item< ::= <object> | <list>
4   <object> ::= a | b | c | d | e
5   <separator> ::= ,
6   <begin> ::= (
7   <end> ::=)

For each of the following, state whether it is a valid <list> and, if it is not, give a brief explanation of why it is not.

i): a
    This is not a valid <list> since every <list> starts with a <begin> and ends with an <end> and these are uniquely defined as (and)

ii): ( )
    This is a valid <list> since it satisfies
    <list> ::= <begin> <end>

iii): (((dab)))
    This is a valid <list> as although enclosed by a <begin> and <end>, in parsing for <contents>, (((dab))) satisfies
    <list> ::= <begin> <contents> <end>
                   (((dab))   )

    ((dab)) satisfies
    <contents> ::= <item>
    <item>   ::= <list>
    <list>   ::= <begin> <contents> <end>
                       (dab)   )

    (dab) also satisfies
    <contents> ::= <item>
    <item>   ::= <list>
    <list<   ::= <begin> <contents> <end>
                       (dab   )

    dab needs to satisfy
    <contents> ::= <item | <item> <separator> <contents>
    <item>   ::= <object> | <list>
    <object>   ::= a|b|c|d|e
    <separator> ::=,

    where dab is in fact <object> <object> <object> which does not match the definition.

iv): (c,a,b,b,a,g,e)
    This is a valid list since it satisfies
    <list> ::=<begin> <contents> <end>
    where c,a,b,b,a,g,e satisfies
    <contents> ::= <item> | <item> <separator> <contents>

```
<item>    ::= <object> | <list>
<object>  ::= <a|bπc|d|e
```

c is an <item> and so <contents>
c, a is <item> <separator> <contents> etc.

v): ((( ),b,(e)),d)

((( ),b,(e)),d) satisfies
```
<list>    ::= <begin> <contents> <end>
              (     ((),b,(e)),d     )
```

(( ),b,(e)),d satisfies
```
<contents> ::= <item> <separator> <contents>
               (() ,b,(e))   , d
```
and, d is valid for contents from
```
<contents> ::= <item>
<item>     ::= <object>
<object>   ::= a|b|c|d|e
<separator>::= ,
```

(( ),b,(e)) satisfies
```
<contents> ::= <item>
<item>     ::= <list>
<list>     ::= <begin> <contents> <end>
               (     (),b,(e)     )
```

( ),b,(e) satisfies
```
<item>     ::= <list>
<contents> ::= <item> <separator> <contents>
                ()        ,   b, (e)
```

b, (e) satisfies
```
<contents> ::= <item> <separator> <contents>
                 b         ,       (e)
```

b satisfies
```
<item>     ::= <object>
<object>   ::= a|b|c|d|e
```

(e) satisfies
```
<contents> ::= <item>
<item>     ::= <list>
<list>     ::= <begin> <contents> <end>
                   (     e     )
```

e satisfies
```
<contents> ::= <item>
<item>     ::= <object>
<object>   ::= a|b|c|d|e
```

(vi): (((a,(c), e),(())))
This is invalid since there are six opening brackets and only five closing brackets.

Question 11

a)   The processes that occur in the translation of a high-level language statement to an executable form are lexical scan, syntax checking and code generation. Reverse Polish notation is generated during the syntax check and used during the code generation.

b)   i) a =(bc + de)/(ac − fe)
        converted into Reverse Polish notation is
        abc*de*+ac*fe*−/=
        The conversation can be traced using the program listed in the chapter to give the following intermediate steps:
        The input string to the program will be
        a = (b*c+d*e)/(a*c−f*e)

Character	Output	Stack	Precedence in stack
a	a		0
=	a	=	0
(	a	=	0
b	ab	=	0
*	ab	*=	7 0
c	abc	*=	7 0
+	abc*	+=	6 0
d	abc*d	+=	6 0
*	abc*d	*+=	7 6 0
e	abc*de	*+=	7 6 0
)	abc*de	*+=	7 6 0
/	abc*de*+	/=	2 0
(	abc*de*+	/=	2 0
a	abc*de*+a	/=	2 0
*	abc*de*+a	*/=	7 2 0
c	abc*de*+ac	*/=	7 2 0
−	abc*de*+ac*	−/=	6 2 0
f	abc*de*+ac*f	−/=	6 2 0
*	abc*de*+ac*f	*−/=	7 6 2 0
e	abc*de*+ac*fe	*−/=	7 6 2 0
)	abc*de*+ac*fe	*−/=	7 6 2 0

b)   (ii) $b = abc + d(e^n + fg)$

converted into Reverse Polish form notation is

$bab*c*den \uparrow fg*+*+=$

Again the conversion can be traced with the program from the input string:

   $b = a*b*c + d*(e \uparrow n + f*g)$

to give the following intermediate steps:

Character	Output	Stack	Precedence in stack
b	b		0
=	b	=	0
a	ba	=	0
*	ba	*=	2 0
b	bab	*=	2 0
*	bab*	*=	2 0
c	bab*c	*=	2 0
+	bab*c*	+=	1 0
d	bab*c*d	+=	1 0
*	bab*c*d	*+=	2 1 0
(	bab*c*d	*+=	2 1 0
e	bab*c*de	*+=	2 1 0
↑	bab*c*de	↑*+=	8 2 1 0
n	bab*c*den	↑*+=	8 2 1 0
+	bab*c*den ↑	+*+=	6 2 1 0
f	bab*c*den ↑ f	+*+=	6 2 1 0
*	bab*c*den ↑ f	*+*+=	7 6 2 1 0
g	bab*c*den ↑ fg	*+*+=	7 6 2 1 0
)	bab*c*den ↑ fg	*+*+=	7 6 2 1 0

c)   The statement gave

   $abc*de*+ac*fe*−/=$

in Reverse Polish. The Reverse Polish string can be processed at the code generation stage by the following general procedure:

1   WHILE symbols left
2   IF symbol is an operator
3   THEN apply to top two elements in stack
4   store result in stack
5   ELSE store symbol in stack
6   END IF

Question 12

a) A compiler is a program which translates a source program written in a high-level language into an object program in a target language which is, in the majority of cases, in machine code. In Chapter 8 we listed the major functions of a compiler which is one approach to this type of question. An alternative is to describe the stages of lexical analysis, syntax analysis and code generation as described in this chapter.

   An interpreter holds the source program in memory with each instruction examined in logical sequence, then interpreted and executed. This is a software analogy of the fetch–execute cycle. The principal advantage is that programs can be executed instantaneously by simply typing a command such as RUN. The main advantage of a compiler is that instructions do not have to be translated or interpreted every time they are executed.

b) BNF and syntax diagrams can be used in defining other languages and for the syntax analysis of source program statements.

   The BNF definition of these real numbers can be developed as follows:

   <point> ::=

   <exponent> ::=E

   <sign> ::=+|−|null

   <integer> ::= <digit>|<digit> <integer>

   <fraction> ::=.<digit>|<fraction><digit>

   <signed integer> ::=<sign> <integer>

   <real number>::=<signed integer><fraction>|

   <integer> <fraction> <exponent> <integer>

   <integer>

   i) 123.456 conforms to

   <signed integer> <fraction>

   (ii) 1.23456 E02 conforms to

   <integer> <fraction> <exponent> <integer> <integer>

NUMBER SYSTEMS AND BOOLEAN ALGEBRA

THE BINARY NUMBER SYSTEM

THE OCTAL NUMBER SYSTEM

THE HEXADECIMAL NUMBER SYSTEM

SIGN AND MAGNITUDE NOTATION

TWO'S COMPLEMENT REPRESENTATION

ONE'S COMPLEMENT REPRESENTATION

FLOATING-POINT NUMBERS

LOGIC AND BOOLEAN ALGEBRA

GETTING STARTED

In this chapter we shall look at the way numbers are represented and manipulated within the computer. There have been many different number systems used through history. The **Roman system** is familiar to most people, with counting starting:

I II III IV V VI VII VIII IX X

Roman numerals were used for many centuries in many cultures. Lengthy resistance to change actually held back the development of mathematics in many countries. The system now used universally is that which is often referred to as the **Arabic** system, so called because it reached Europe through the Arab world, though it is believed that it is more likely to have come from India. It uses just nine digits plus a zero. This was an innovation, as some earlier systems did not use a zero. Numbers are decoded by interpreting each digit as powers of ten in descending order from left to right. Thus

3495

is interpreted as

$3 \times 1000 + 4 \times 100 + 9 \times 10 + 5 \times 1$

Fractions are represented by powers of 1/10 separated from the integral part by a full stop, called the decimal point, so that

0.9345

is interpreted as

$$9 \times \frac{1}{10} + 3 \times \frac{1}{100} + 4 \times \frac{1}{1000} + 5 \times \frac{1}{1000}$$

The use of ten as the radix in number systems is partly due to us having ten fingers on which to count, and also because ten is a convenient size. It provides a reasonably compact representation of numbers whilst enabling us to memorise multiplication tables which might prove less manageable in, say, base sixty. The radix ten has some disadvantages, however, in that it is not divisible by three and so even the simplest calculations can result in recurring decimals. A good case can be made for the use of twelve as a base, as it divides by two, three and four or alternatively eight or sixteen as powers of two. These latter representations need to be studied since they are widely used in computers. The systems needed for study in this text are denary, binary, octal and hexadecimal.

The other main topic in the chapter is that of **Boolean algebra** and the design of the basic logic gates used in computers. This will lead on to circuit design, for example the implementation of binary addition.

ESSENTIAL PRINCIPLES

THE BINARY NUMBER SYSTEMS

The major advances in the evolution of computers came after designers concentrated on two-state devices, for example memory cells in an on-off representation, rather than on attempts to control mechanical counters (like the mileage recorder in a car) which can come to rest in one of ten different positions. Two-state devices were implemented by holes punched in cards and paper tape, by the direction or level of magnetisation on magnetic media, and also by the contact made by the depression of a key on a keyboard. These two states are represented by zero and one and the numbers in a computer are represented by strings of zero and one in a radix two or **binary** notation. Thus

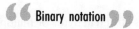 **Binary notation**

10010110

represents

$$1 \times 128 + 0 \times 64 + 0 \times 32 + 1 \times 16 + 0 \times 8 + 1 \times 4 + 1 \times 2 + 0 \times 1$$
$$= 128 + 0 + 0 + 16 + 0 + 4 + 2 + 0$$
$$= 150$$

This demonstrates the most obvious method of converting a number from binary to decimal. A more usual method is to use a nested multiplication as illustrated below by the same example.

$$((((((1 \times 2) + 1) \times 2) + 0) \times 2) + 1) \times 2) + 1) \times 2) + 1) \times 2) + 0$$

This can be represented as an algorithm:

1 Set N to Q
2 WHILE characters left
3   Multiply N by 10
4   Read character
5   Add character to denary
6 END WHILE

This method can be applied to any conversions between various radices, by subsituting a different value for ten in step three.

THE OCTAL NUMBER SYSTEM

Although numbers are stored internally as binary digits (bits), this is not an appropriate mode for display or printing out. One method of representing binary numbers is to group the bits in threes, from the right-hand end and write a single digit for each group. These digits will be from the set 0,1,2,3,4,5,6,7 and represent the number in radix 8, or **octal**. Thus in the 12-bit number:

110101010011

 Octal number system

we group the digits as

110 101 010 011

and write   6 5 2 3   as the octal number.

To convert an octal number to binary we simply reverse the process so that

5 4 6 3
becomes
101 100 110 011

Octal was used extensively in the early computers where memory often represented characters in a 6-bit form and these characters could be expressed as two octal digits.

THE HEXADECIMAL NUMBER SYSTEM

Another frequently used system uses radix sixteen and is known as **hexadecimal**. It uses as its digits:

0 1 2 3 4 5 6 7 8 9 A B C D E F

where A is used to represent the denary number ten, B represents eleven, C represents twelve and so on with F representing denary fifteen. As with octal, it is used to represent binary numbers by grouping the bits, this time in fours, from the right-hand end and write a single digit for each group. Thus in the 12-bit number:

110101010011

we group the digits as

1101 0101 0011

and write   D 5 3   as the hexadecimal number.

Conversion of a hexadecimal number to binary is the reverse process so that

E 7 A 9

becomes

1110 0111 1010 1001

Hexadecimal is used in computer systems where memory is stored in bytes or multiples of eight bits, where each byte can be expressed as two hexadecimal digits.

Hexadecimal and octal are also used as an intermediate step in conversions between binary and decimal. For example, returning to the earlier conversion, 10010110 in binary is 9 6 in hexadecimal or $9 \times 16 + 6 = 144 + 6 = 150$

SIGN AND MAGNITUDE NOTATION

As we have already seen, three bits can represent the numbers zero to seven, four bits can represent zero to fifteen, so it therefore follows that five bits can represent zero to thirty-one and eight bits can represent zero to 255. Once we allow the operation of subtraction to take place, there needs to be some means of representing negative numbers. The most obvious method is to use the first, or most significant, bit to represent a sign, with the usual convention 0 for + and 1 for −, and the remaining bits are used to represent the value, hence the name **sign and magnitude** representation. The full range for a 4-bit word is:

0000	+0	0001	+1	0010	+2	0011	+3
0100	+4	0101	+5	0110	+6	0111	+7
1000	−0	1001	−1	1010	−2	1011	−3
1100	−4	1101	−5	1110	−6	1111	−7

Arithmetic operations are carried out with the magnitude separately from the signs. A complication is introduced, however, in that since the computer works with a fixed word length, there can be an **overflow** condition as a result of some operations. Take for example:

```
  1 0 1 1 0 0 0
  0 1 1 0 1 1 0
1 0 0 0 1 1 1 0
```

Working with 8-bit registers, with one bit for sign and seven bits for magnitude, there is an extra **carry** digit at the end of the word which indicates the overflow. This is usually stored in a special register which can be examined by a machine code program instruction to cause a branch to an error routine if the overflow indicator is set.

Magnitude subtraction can also provide an overflow condition detected as an overflow of the "**borrow**" digit. This indicates that the sign of the answer is to be reversed and the subtraction is to be taken the other way round. For example:

```
  1 0 0 1 1 1 0
− 1 1 0 0 1 0 1
  1 1 0 1 0 0 1
```

borrow   1 1 1
indicating overflow

```
1 1 0 0 1 0 1
1 0 0 1 1 1 0
0 0 1 0 1 1 1
```

borrow 1 1 1 1 answer −0010111

This corresponds to $78 − 101 = −23$. An alternative algorithm is to reverse each of the bits of the original answer:

Reversing 1 1 0 1 0 0 1 gives 0 0 1 0 1 1 0
and adding 1 gives 0 0 1 0 1 1 1

In representation of r bits, the largest positive number which can be represented has (r−1) 1's and this has the numerical value $(2^{(r-1)}-1)$; similarly, the smallest negative number has the value $-(2^{(r-1)}-1)$. For example, in an 8-bit representation, the largest positive number is +1111111 which is $2^7 - 1$ or $(128 - 1)$ and the smallest negative is −127. Notice that both 00000000 and 10000000 can represent zero, and it is conventional to refer to 00000000 as +0 and 10000000 as −0. Therefore with eight bits, the 256 patterns are used to represent 127 positive numbers, 127 negative numbers and two zeros.

TWO'S COMPLEMENT REPRESENTATION

The most common form of representing negative numbers in binary is given the name **two's complement**. If the representation uses r digits, as with sign and magnitude, the least significant (r−1) digits store the value of positive numbers. Negative numbers are stored by subtracting their magnitude from $2^{(r-1)}$. For example, in an 8-bit representation, +77 would be represented as 0 1 0 0 1 1 0 1 and −77 would be represented as $2^7 - 77$ or 256 − 77 which is 179 or 1 0 1 1 0 0 1 1.

The simplest way of deriving the two's complement is:

> **Two's complement representation**

1 Change all ones to zeros and zeros to ones
2 Add one

so 0 1 0 0 1 1 0 1 changes to 1 0 1 1 0 0 0 0; adding 1 gives 1 0 1 1 0 0 0 1.

This is the same operation as was described for determining the result of an overflow in subtraction for two's complements. It is important to notice that, although the representation of positive numbers is the same as for sign and magnitude and a one in the most significant digit indicates a negative number, the representation of negative numbers is different to that for sign and magnitude. As an example, the pattern 1 0 0 0 0 0 0 1 represents a negative number, its magnitude is the complement of   1 0 0 0 0 0 0 1   which is 0 1 1 1 1 1 1 1 or 127

thus   1 0 0 0 0 0 0 1   represents −127
and similarly   1 0 0 0 0 0 0 0   represents −128
so that the full range is −128 to +127. Taking a 4 bit word, the full range is:

0000	+0	0001	+1	0010	+2	0011	+3
0100	+4	0101	+5	0110	+6	0111	+7
1000	−8	1001	−7	1010	−6	1011	−5
1100	−4	1101	−3	1110	−2	1111	−1

ONE'S COMPLEMENT REPRESENTATION

There is a second complement representation of binary numbers which is called **one's complement** which is, for an r digit representation, a subtraction from $(2^{(r-1)} - 1)$. This, being one less than that used in two's complement, means that the conversion is simply the step of converting the ones to zeros and the zeros to ones, i.e. complementing the individual bits. Thus we have:

> **One's complement representation**

	+1	0 0 0 0 0 0 0 1	−1	1 1 1 1 1 1 1 0
	+64	0 1 0 0 0 0 0 0	−64	1 0 1 1 1 1 1 1
	+127	0 1 1 1 1 1 1 1	−127	1 0 0 0 0 0 0 0
also	+0	0 0 0 0 0 0 0 0	−0	1 1 1 1 1 1 1 1

So the range is the same as for sign and magnitude, though the actual representation differs from both sign and magnitude and two's complement. Taking a 4-bit word, the full range is:

0000	+0	0001	+1	0010	+2	0011	+3
0100	+4	0101	+5	0110	+6	0111	+7
1000	−7	1001	−6	1010	−5	1011	−4
1100	−3	1101	−2	1110	−1	1111	−0

FLOATING-POINT NUMBERS

A common representation of *denary* numbers, particularly on electronic caluclators and in the output from programs written in Basic, is the *exponent form*. Here the numbers are expressed in two parts, first a decimal number, usually between 0.1 and one and second a power of ten. This is often written as in the following example:

0.2689 E 3 which represents 0.2689×10^3 or 268.9.

The same method is used within computer systems to represent numbers in binary and is referred to as **floating point** to distinguish it from the more common **fixed point** where numbers are represented by a fixed number of digits after the decimal point. As an aid to understanding we may consider fixed point as rounding numbers to a fixed number of places of decimals, with floating-point as a representation to a given number of significant figures. The fraction is usually referred to as the **mantissa** and the value of the power as the exponent. In the example above, 0.2689 is the mantissa and three is the exponent.

In binary there is a similar notation, again best illustrated by an example. The number 27¼ could be expressed in fixed point binary as 11011.01 but in binary floating point form this will be $0.1101101 \times 10^{101}$. It is important to realise that all three of these numbers are expressed in binary, not only the mantissa, 0.1101101 and the exponent 101, but also the power ten which is equivalent to denary ten.

An important technique used with floating point is **normalisation** or **normalised form** which represents the mantissa as a number with zero before the point and, except in the representation of zero, a non-zero digit immediately following the point. Floating point numbers are always 'normalised' before storing within the memory of the computer which makes sure that numbers are stored to their maximum precision.

As an example, *multiplication* of floating point numbers is carried out by the following steps:

> **Steps in multiplication of floating point numbers**

- Normalise both operands
- Multiply the mantissas
- Add the exponents
- Normalise the result

The arithmetic unit of the computer will usually carry out its arithmetic to a greater precision, typically double length, before normalising the result for storage in order to minimise the loss of accuracy during the operation.

Division of floating point numbers is equally simple and carried out by the following steps:

> **Steps in division of floating point numbers**

- Normalise both operands
- Divide the mantissas
- Subtract the exponents
- Normalise the result

Addition and *subtraction* are, rather strangely, a little less straightforward:

> **Steps in addition and subtraction of floating point numbers**

- Normalise the operand of larger magnitude
- Change the representation of the other operand so that the two exponents are the same
- Add (or subtract) the mantissas
- Normalise the result

The *advantages* of floating point representation are

> **Advantages and disadvantages of floating point representation**

- Ease of use
- Automatic scaling
- A large range of values
- May represent both integers and fractions

The disadvantages are

- Loss of precision
- Arithmetic operations may be slower
- There may be a loss of control of accuracy

LOGIC AND BOOLEAN ALGEBRA

We have seen that the binary number system is a convenient method of expressing and manipulating arithmetic data. We shall see that this is closely linked to the subject of logic where binary digits may be used to represent logical quantities called **propositions**. These can be further combined to form compound propositions which, in turn, may be simplified by a set of rules which form what is known as **Boolean Algebra**, named after the Mathematician George Boole. A Boolean variable may take either of two values, **true** or **false**, which can also be represented by a one and zero. These variables can be manipulated by a number of operators of which the simplest is the function **NOT** which operates on a single variable. One method used to define Boolean functions is the **truth table** as illustrated below:

Truth table

The function **NOT**	Input	Output
	A	NOT A
	0	1
	1	0

The other operators take two inputs and produce a single output as can be illustrated for the two most common, **AND** and **OR**:

The function **OR**	Input		Output
	A	B	A OR B
	0	0	0
	0	1	1
	1	0	1
	1	1	1

The function **AND**	Input		Output
	A	B	A AND B
	0	0	0
	0	1	0
	1	0	0
	1	1	1

Another use of truth tables is in the proof of theorems in logic, for example to establish that AND is 'associative', i.e. that it satisfies:

(A AND B) AND C ≡ A AND (B AND C)

This can also be expressed as below using . as the operator

(A.B).C ≡ A.(B.C)

Notice the use of ≡ to signify 'is equivalent to' in these relations.

Input			Output			
A	B	C	A.B	(A.B).C	B.C	A.(B.C)
0	0	0	0	0	0	0
0	0	1	0	0	0	0
0	1	0	0	0	0	0
0	1	1	0	0	1	0
1	0	0	0	0	0	0
1	0	1	0	0	0	0
1	1	0	1	0	0	0
1	1	1	1	1	1	1

THE OPERATORS NAND AND NOR

Two additional operators are important in the design of computers, these are NAND and NOR. **NAND** is a representation of **not and** while **NOR** is **not or**, as defined below:

The function **NOR**	Input		Output
	A	B	A NOR B
	0	0	1
	0	1	0
	1	0	0
	1	1	0

The function **NAND**	Input		Output
	A	B	A NAND B
	0	0	1
	0	1	1
	1	0	1
	1	1	0

Adequate sets of connectives

All the Boolean operators or **connectives** can be defined in a Venn diagram as shown in Fig. 11.1, the two regions A and B correspond to the two inputs A and B, and these divide the diagram into four areas corresponding to the four possible combinations of those inputs, and the various connectives are represented by shading the areas for which the output is true, Fig. 11.2 illustrates A OR B and Fig. 11.3 illustrates A NAND B. If we think of each of the four outputs as binary digits, there are altogether sixteen different possible combinations. Some of these, like AND and NOR have already been defined and these are the important ones.

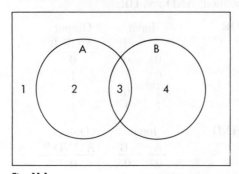

Fig. 11.1

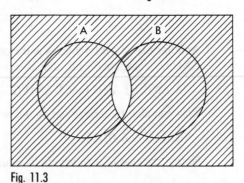

Fig. 11.2

Fig. 11.3

Looking again at Fig. 11.1 we see that the four areas correspond to various combinations of NOT, AND and OR as set out below:

Area	Representation
1	NOT (A OR B)
2	A AND (NOT B)
3	A AND B
4	(NOT A) AND B

thus for example NAND, which corresponds to regions 1,2 and 4, can be defined as:
    A NAND B ≡ {NOT (A OR B)} OR {A AND (NOT B)} OR {(NOT A) AND B}

Similarly we can define all of the sixteen operators in terms of just these three, which are said to form an adequate set of connectives. Obviously hardware designers prefer to work with a small number of distinct components so this set of three is important, furthermore, there are two important relations known as De Morgan's Laws:

    A OR B   ≡ NOT {(NOT A) AND (NOT B)}
    A AND B ≡ NOT {(NOT A) OR (NOT B)}

Therefore (NOT and OR) and (NOT and AND) both form adequate sets of connectives.

The question poses itself as to whether we can reduce the set from two to one operator, and it can be shown that this is only possible with NAND and NOR and each of these can be used alone to define NOT, AND and OR:

    NOT A ≡ A NAND A
    A OR B ≡ {(A NAND A) NAND (B NAND B)}
    A AND B ≡ {(A NAND B) NAND (A NAND B)}
    NOT A ≡ A NOR A
    A OR B ≡ {(A NOR B) NOR (A NOR B)}
    A AND B ≡ {(A NOR A) NOR (B NOR B)}

The representation of half adder

The addition of two binary digits, x and y, can be represented in a table as shown below, bearing in mind that there are two outputs, the sum and the carry:

Representation of half adder

x	y	sum	carry
0	0	0	0
0	1	1	0
1	0	1	0
1	1	0	1

The carry corresponds to the logical operator x AND y whereas the sum corresponds to a new operator x XOR y, also written x + y which is the **exclusive or** and can be interpreted as 'x or y but not both'. These can be expressed simply in a logic diagram as in Fig. 11.4 but Fig. 11.5 shows a diagram implementing the half adder using just NOT, AND and OR, while Fig. 11.6 shows the implementation with NOR alone.

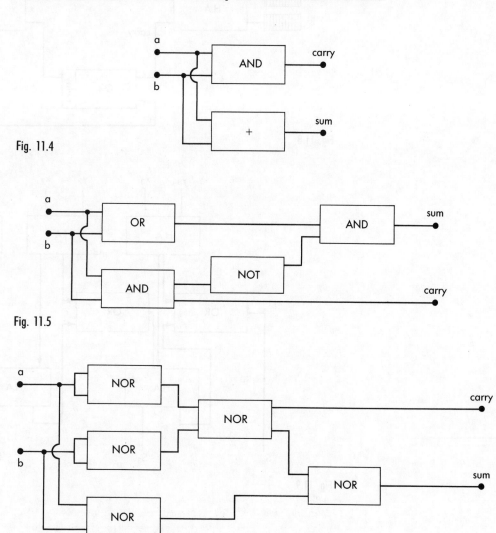

Fig. 11.4

Fig. 11.5

Fig. 11.6

The representation of adders

Representation of adders

The circuits in the previous section refer to a device known as the **half adder** because it performs the addition on a single pair of binary digits: in practice we need to be able to add binary numbers of several digits in length and take account of the carry forward from the previous digit. The simplest form of full adder is shown in Fig. 11.7 and is constructed from two half adders and an additional OR gate. There are two ways in which these elements can be incorporated into a **full adder** for longer binary numbers: the first is by serial addition where a single binary adder is used and the binary digits are fed in a pair at a time as shown in Fig. 11.8. The second method is to use parallel addition where several full adders are connected together and each receives the output from the previous as shown by the 3-bit adder in Fig. 11.9.

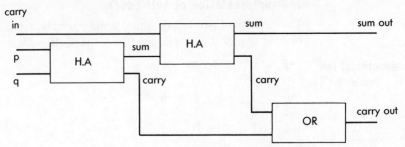

Fig. 11.7

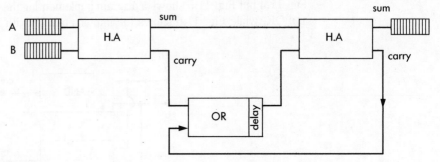

Fig. 11.8

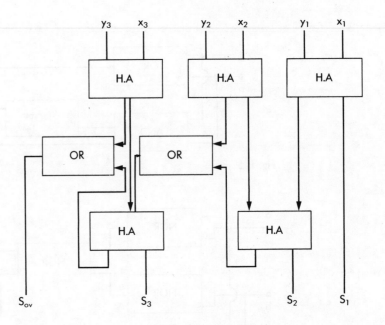

Fig. 11.9

EXAMINATION QUESTIONS

SHORT QUESTIONS

Question 1

A particular computer which uses two's complement arithmetic has 16-bit words, and uses two adjacent words to store floating-point numbers.

Floating-point numbers are held with a sign-bit, a 23-bit normalised fraction and an 8-bit exponent stored in excess-128 format.

Explain briefly the underlined terms. (Northern Ireland 1989)

Question 2
a) Express the NOT operation on a Boolean variable using only NAND logic.
b) Express the NOR operation on two Boolean variables using only NAND logic.
(AEB 1988)

Question 3
Show that each of the logic gates AND, OR and NOT may be replaced by NAND gates.
(Northern Ireland 1989)

Question 4
The following short section of pseudo-code has been written by a programmer who intends to implement it in some suitable programming language:

```
set avalue = 0
repeat
        . . . . .

        . . . . .
        add 0.1 to avalue
until avalue = 10
```

How many times do you think the programmer intends the loop to be executed?
What would be the effect of executing the above algorithm, and why?
(Northern Ireland 1989)

Question 5
When a, b and c are declared in a program as real variables, when might the evaluation of (a/b)*c give a different result from (a*c)/b?
(NEAB 1988)

Question 6
Express each of the folowing Boolean expressions in its simplest form:
a) $\overline{A} . \overline{B} + \overline{A} . B + A . \overline{B}$

b) $\overline{A + \overline{B.C} + \overline{C}.B}$
(AEB 1989)

Question 7
Write down the binary digit patterns that would result for a 12-bit word computer from the storage in fixed-point format of +17 and −17 in each of the following cases:
a) one's complement of negative numbers   (4)
b) two's complement storage
c) sign and magnitude storage
(London 1984)

LONGER QUESTIONS

Question 8
The contents of a storage location may be interpreted in a number of different ways depending on the circumstances in which it is used. For a particular computer with a 12-bit word length, a certain word holds the binary pattern
100101100100

a) What value is represented in the above word if it is interpreted as each of the following? Show your working.
   i) An unsigned integer, e.g. an address
   ii) A signed integer in two's complement form
   iii) An unsigned three-digit integer in binary coded decimal
   iv) A signed floating point number. The left-most eight bits are used for the mantissa, and represent a two's complement binary fraction with the binary point immediately after the left-most (sign) bit. The binary exponent is in the right-most four bits and is an integer in two's complement form. Numbers are stored in normalised form.
      State the range of values which may be stored in each of the above representations. (Where appropriate, you may express your answers in powers of two.)
b) Explain what is meant by 'storing floating point numbers in normalised form'. Why is it done?
c) The decimal number 0.4 corresponds to the recurring binary fraction 0.011001100110011 . . . . Show how this number would be stored as accurately as possible using the representation described in a) iv).

d) The computer has seventy-two machine code operations, eight registers and four addressing modes. Draw a diagram to show a suitable format for a machine code instruction.

e) An algorithm for multiplying two positive floating point numbers together may be expressed as follows.

1 Multiply the mantissas and add the exponents

2 Normalise the result

When the above algorithm is used to multiply 13¼ by 1¼ on this computer the result is 16½ instead of 16 9/16. Account for the error which has been introduced.

(Cambridge 1984)

Question 9

Integers may be represented in **sign-and-magnitude** form or in **two's complement** form. Using an 8-bit wordlength for the examples:

a) Explain how negative integers are represented in each form.

b) Show how each form would represent the denary integers −29 and −99.

c) For both forms, show how the following arithmetic would be conducted and explain the working:
   i) $(+54) - (+29)$
   ii) $(-54) + (-29)$

d) Similarly, show how each form would be used to attempt the sum $(-29) + (-99)$, and comment on the result.

e) Suggest an advantage of the complement form over sign-and-magnitude form.

(AEB 1983)

Question 10

a) Explain why AND and NOT form a complete set of logical operations but AND and OR do not.

b) Simplify the logical expression

   [NOT (A OR C)] AND [B AND (NOT A)] AND [NOT (C OR (NOT B))].

c) Two binary digits are to be added together, and the result is to be added to the carry from a previous addition of the same type. Give and explain logical expressions from:
   i) the sum, and
   ii) the carry, which result.

(Oxford 1986)

Question 11

Summarise the major concepts of Boolean algebra and explain how they may be applied in the design of logical devices. Write down truth tables to describe the properties of AND, OR, NAND and NOR gates, using two inputs in each case. Using Boolean algebra expression or otherwise, show how the AND and OR gates can be expressed in terms of NOR gates alone.

(WJEC 1982)

Question 12

a) Write down the truth table for a NON-EQUIVALENCE (EXCLUSIVE OR) gate for two inputs A and B. Show that it can be replaced by an equivalent logical circuit consisting of AND, OR and NOT gates. Name *one* use of a NON-EQUIVALENCE gate in a computer.

b) Four binary input signals are denoted by J,K,L and M where JKLM represents a hexadecimal integer. The output signal, Y, is 1 if JKLM represents a prime number in hexadecimal notation, viz. 2,3,5, B or D, and is 0, otherwise.

   Write down a truth table to represent the above system and sketch a minimal equivalent logic diagram using AND, OR and NOT gates.

(WJEC 1984)

OUTLINE ANSWERS

SHORT QUESTIONS

Question 1

Floating-point can be explained by analogy with the representation of denary numbers on electronic calculators and in the output from programs written in Basic in an exponent form where the numbers are expressed in two parts, first a decimal number, usually between 0.1 and one called the fraction and second a power of ten, called the **exponent**.

Normalisation or **normalised form** represents the mantissa as a number with zero before the point and, except in the representation of zero, a non-zero digit immediately following the point.

Excess-128 format is a representation of signed numbers by storing them as their value plus 128, it is often used for exponents as it has a simple implementation of addition and subtraction. Multiplication and division are difficult in this mode.

Question 2

a)   NOT A ≡ A NAND A
b)   A NOR B ≡ NOT (A OR B)
        NOT X ≡ X NAND X
        A OR B ≡ {(A NAND A) NAND (B NAND B)}
A NOR B ≡ {(A NAND A) NAND (B NAND B)} NAND {(A NAND A) NAND (B NAND B)}

Question 3

A AND B ≡ {(A NAND B) NAND (A NAND B)}
A OR B   ≡ {(A NAND A) NAND (B NAND B)}
NOT A   ≡ A NAND A

Question 4

The programmer appears to intend the loop to be executed 100 times but on running it there are likely to be rounding errors in evaluating

    add 0.1 to avalue

and so avalue will never reach exactly ten and will become an infinite loop, probably terminating on an overflow condition.

Question 5

If a and b are nearly the same, a/b may evaluate to 1 and in working to a fixed precision be accurate only to 1 significant figure so the evaluation of (a/b)∗c will give a different result from (a ∗ c)/b.

Question 6

Express each of the following Boolean expressions in its simplest form:

a)   if X = $\overline{A} . \overline{B} + \overline{A} . B + A . \overline{B}$

Setting out as a truth table

A	B	$\overline{A}$	$\overline{B}$	$\overline{A}.\overline{B}$	$\overline{A}.B$	$A.\overline{B}$	X
0	0	1	1	1	0	0	1
0	1	1	0	0	1	0	1
1	0	0	1	0	0	1	1
1	1	0	0	0	0	0	0

$$\overline{A} . \overline{B} + \overline{A} . B + A . \overline{B} = \overline{A.B}$$

b)   if   Y = $\overline{A} + \overline{B.C} + \overline{C}.B$

A	B	C	$\overline{C}$	$\overline{A}$	$\overline{B.C}$	$\overline{C}.B$	$\overline{Y}$	Y
0	0	0	1	1	1	0	1	0
0	0	1	0	1	1	0	1	0
0	1	0	1	1	1	1	1	0
0	1	1	0	1	0	0	1	0
1	0	0	1	0	1	0	1	0
1	0	1	0	0	1	0	1	0
1	1	0	1	0	1	1	1	0
1	1	1	0	0	0	0	0	1

so Y = $\overline{A} + \overline{B.C} + \overline{C}.B$ = A.B.C

Question 7

The number $+17$ in denary is 11 in hexadecimal which is 00010001 in binary, which, in a 12-bit word computer would be stored as 000000010001. This positive number will be represented in the same form whether in one's complement, two's complement or sign-and-magnitude storage. It is the representation of -17 which differs in each case:

a) one's complement of -17 is
   111111101110
b) two's complement
   111111101111
c) sign-and-magnitude will be
   100000010001

This was set as a 4-mark question and so no further explanations need to be given.

LONGER QUESTIONS

Question 8

We are given the binary pattern 100101100100:

a) i) As an unsigned integer, we first convert to hexadecimal so that 100101100100 is first grouped
    as   1001 0110 0100   and then represented
    as   9   6   4   which is
        $9 \times 256 + 6 \times 16 + 4 = 2404$
    The range is zero to $2^{12} - 1$
    or   0 to 4095
    ii) Interpreted as a signed integer in two's complement form this will be a negative number since the most significant digit is 1. Thus it must be complemented as below:
                   1001 0110 0100
    one's complement   0110 1001 1011
    two's complement   0110 1001 1100
    in hexadeximal   6   9   C
        $6 \times 256 + 9 \times 16 + 12 = 1692$
    So the representation is of -1692, which is, of course, $-(4096 - 2404)$. The range is -2^{11} to $+2^{11} - 1$ or -2048 to 2047.
    iii) Binary coded decimal treats each group of four bits as a single decimal digit coded in binary. The characters are the same as the hexadecimal interpretation but correspond to a different numerical value so that
            1001 0110 0100
    is 9   6   4   in BCD
    The range is 0 to 999
    iv) Taking 100101100100 as a signed floating point number. If the left-most eight bits are used for the mantissa as a two's complement binary fraction then the value is 10010110 which is the complement of 01101010 and so represents -0.1101010. The binary exponent is 0100 which as an integer in two's complement form represents $+4$ so the point is to be moved four places so the number is
        -1101.010 as a binary number or
        -13.25 in denary

    The largest value of the exponent is 0111 in binary or 7, the largest mantissa in binary is 0.1111111 so the largest number will be:
        $+1111111$ in binary or $+127$
    the negative mantissas range, in binary, from
        11111111 to 10000000 which complement as
        00000001 to 10000000 which are interpreted as
        -0.0000001 to -1.0000000 so the largest negative number will be
        $-1 \times 2^7 = -128$

b) Storing floating point numbers in normalised form means that the first digit of the mantissa is non-zero (except where the number itself is zero). This is done so that the numbers are stored to the greatest possible precision.

c)   The recurring binary fraction 0.011001100110011 .... will be stored as a mantissa 0.1100110 and exponent −1 which will be stored as 1111 so the number will be represented in the machine as 011001101111.

d)   There is a wide diversity in the storage of machine code instructions in different computer systems. Some require a number of bits to refer to the required register, others incorporate the register reference in the instruction code. The same could apply to the addressing mode, but a possible answer here would use seven bits to specify the machine code operation, three bits to select the register and two bits to select the addressing mode. Thus we use one 12-bit word to store the instruction and a second word (or perhaps two words) to store the operand. The diagram is shown in Fig. 12.10.

e)   13¼ in binary is 1101.01 which in floating point will have a binary mantissa 0.110101 and an exponent which can be represented in denary as 4.

1¼ in binary is 1.01 which in floating point will have a binary mantissa 0.101 and an exponent which can be represented in denary as 1. Multiplying 0.110101 × 0.101 is 0.100001001 which will be normalised and rounded to 7 bits as 0.1000010, and adding the exponents gives denary 5. The answer then becomes in binary 10000.10 which is 16½ instead of 16 ⁹⁄₁₆; the error is introduced when the product of the mantissas is rounded to 7 bits.

Question 9

a)   Negative integers are represented in an 8-bit sign-and-magnitude form by using only the least significant seven bits to represent the numeric value and setting the most significant bit to one for negative numbers and one for positive numbers. In two's complement form, negative numbers are represented as their two's complement.

b)   29 in binary is 11101 and 99 is 1100011, in 8-bit sign-and-magnitude −29 and −99 will be represented as
      10011101   and   11100011
for two's complement we represent each as their magnitudes:
      00011101   and   01100011
then reverse the 0s and 1s
      11100010   and   10011100
and add 1 to give:
      11100011 for −29   and   10011101 for −99

c)   +54 is in 8-bit binary   00110110
      −54 will be   10110110 in sign-and-magnitude
      and   11001010 in two's-complement
For sign-and-magnitude:
   i) (+54) − (+29) will be carried out by subtracting the magnitudes to give 25 and then taking the sign from the first operand to give +25
   ii) (−54) + (−29) will be carried out by adding 29 to 54 to give 83 and then take the sign from the first operand to give −83
For two's complement we proceed as follows;
   i) (+54) − (+29) is done by taking the complement of 29 and adding

```
   00110110
   11100011
   00011001
11 11
```

The rule is that the final carry bit is ginored since the two operands have opposite signs. The answer converts to +25.
   ii) (−54) + (−29) is done by complementing both and adding:

```
   11001010
   11100011
   10101001
11  1
```

The final carry is ignored again and the answer is a negative number and being the two's complement of 01010111, represents −83.

d) For sign-and-magnitude $(-29) + (-99)$ will be carried out by adding the magnitudes and then giving a negative sign to the result:

$$
\begin{array}{lll}
-29 & 1 & 0011101 \\
-99 & 1 & \underline{1100011}
\end{array}
$$

adding magnitudes $\underline{10000000}$ which indicates an overflow since the magnitude of the sum requires 8 bits.

For two's complement $(-99) + (-29)$ is done by adding the complements

$$
\begin{array}{ll}
-29 & 11100011 \\
-99 & \underline{10011101} \\
& 00000000 \\
& 11111111
\end{array}
$$

The two operands have a different sign to the result which indicates overflow.

e) Ease of machine implementation of arithmetic is an advantage of the complement form over sign-and-magnitude form. There is no need to deal with signs and magnitudes separately.

LONGER QUESTIONS

Question 10

a) We showed in the chapter, by means of a Venn diagram, that all the logical operators can be expressed in terms of OR, AND and NOT. Since we can also represent OR in terms of AND and NOT by using one of De Morgan's laws:

A OR B $\equiv$ NOT{(NOT A) AND (NOT B)}

AND and NOT form a complete set of logical operations. AND and OR do not form a complete set because it is not possible to express NOT in terms of AND and OR alone.

b) In simplification of the logical expression

[NOT (A OR C] AND [B AND (NOT A)] AND [NOT (C OR (NOT B))]

it is best re-expressed using the alternative notation of + for OR, . for AND and ' for NOT to give:

(A + C)'.(B.A').(C + B')'

and using De Morgan's laws on the first and last expressions we have

(A'.C').(B.A').(C'.B)

from which brackets may be removed

A'.C'.B.A'.C'.B

and removing duplication

A'.C'.B

which gives (NOT A) AND B AND (NOT C).

c) When two binary digits are added together, and the result is to be added to the carry from a previous addition, there are three inputs and two outputs as shown in the truth table:

x	y	Carry in	Sum	Carry out
0	0	0	0	0
0	0	1	1	0

x	y	Carry in	Sum	Carry out
0	1	0	1	0
0	1	1	0	1
1	0	0	1	0
1	0	1	0	1
1	1	0	0	1
1	1	1	1	1

i) using x an y for the digits and for the carry in, the sum can be expressed as
$$x'.y'.c + x'.y.c' + x.y'.c' + x.y.c$$
or
$$(x'.y' + x.y).c + (x'.y + x.y').c'$$
which can be expressed as
{NOT(x XOR y) AND c} OR {(x XOR y) AND (NOT c)}

ii) the carry can be expressed as
$$x'.y.c + x.y'.c + x.y.c' + x.y.c$$
or
$$(x'.y+x.y').c + x.y.(c'+c)$$
or
$$(x'.y+x.y').c + x.y$$
which can be expressed as
{(x XOR y) AND c} OR (x AND y)

Question 11

The major concepts of Boolean algebra are described in the chapter and the definition of the logical operators may assist in the design of logical devices. The chapter also includes truth tables for AND, OR, NAND and NOR which define the operation of the corresponding logic gates. The following expressions demonstrate how the AND and OR gates can be expressed in terms of NOR alone:
A AND B ≡ {(A NOR A) NOR (B NOR B)}
A OR B ≡ {(A NOR B) NOR (A NOR B)}

Question 12

a) The truth table for a NON-EQUIVALENCE (EXCLUSIVE OR) gate shows that the output is true if either A or B is true but not both:

A	B	XOR
0	0	0
0	1	1
1	0	1
1	1	0

The table shows that A XOR B can be represented by either:
{(NOT A) AND B} AND {A AND (NOT B)}
or
(A OR B) AND {NOT (A AND B)}
One use of a NON-EQUIVALENCE gate in a computer is the sum bit in a half-adder.

b) The truth table to representing the system for determining whether a hexadecimal digit is prime is shown below:

Hex	J	K	L	M	Prime
0	0	0	0	0	0
1	0	0	0	1	0
2	0	0	1	0	1
3	0	0	1	1	1
4	0	1	0	0	0
5	0	1	0	1	1
6	0	1	1	0	0
7	0	1	1	1	1
8	1	0	0	0	0
9	1	0	0	1	0
A	1	0	1	0	0
B	1	0	1	1	1
C	1	1	0	0	0
D	1	1	0	1	1
E	1	1	1	0	0
F	1	1	1	1	0

One possible simplification is

$$\overline{J}.\overline{K}.L \; + \; \overline{J}.K.M \; + \; \overline{K}.L.M \; + \; K.\overline{L}.M$$

or

from 2,3   5,7   3,11   5,13

$$\equiv \overline{J}.\overline{K}.L \; + \; \overline{K}.L.M \; + \; \overline{J}.K.M \; + \; K.\overline{L}.M$$
$$\equiv \overline{K}.L \, (\overline{J} + \overline{M}) \; + \; K.M \, (\overline{J} + \overline{L})$$

STUDENT ANSWERS WITH EXAMINER COMMENTS

Question 1

A particular computer which uses 2's complement arithmetic has 16-bit words, and uses two adjacent words to store floating-point numbers.

Floating-point numbers are held with a sign-bit, a 23-bit <u>normalised</u> fraction and an 8-bit <u>exponent</u> stored in <u>excess-128</u> format.

Explain briefly the underlined terms.

> **This is vague, the precise format must be given.**

> **This confuses the exponent with the base or power.**

> **It should be 'subtracting' 128; it is called excess-128 as it is stored after adding 128.**

```
Normalised floating-point means the number is represented in a
standardised form expected by the computer.

Floating-point numbers are expressed in two parts, first a number,
usually between 0.1 and 1 called the fraction and second a power of
some number called the exponent for example if the number is
0.11011010 × 2¹¹ then the exponent is 2.

Excess-128 format is a representation of signed numbers where they
are interpreted by adding 128 to their stored form.
```

Question 4

The following short section of pseudocode has been written by a programmer who intends to implement it is some suitable programming language;

```
    set avalue = 0
    repeat
            . . . . .
            . . . . .
            add 0.1 to avalue
    until avalue = 10
```

How many times do you think the programmer intends the loop to be executed? What would be the effect of executing the above algorithm, and why?

> **This misses the point of the question which is really concerned with the rounding errors in decimal arithmetic.**

```
The programmer appears to intend the loop to be executed 101 times
with avalue taking the values 0 to 10 in steps of 0.1 but it will only
execute 100 times as the loop will terminate when avalue takes the
value 10 and the last pass will be for the value 9.9.
```

LOW-LEVEL LANGUAGES

GETTING STARTED

The elements of low-level languages were introduced in Chapter 3 and a simple one-address language was used to illustrate the fetch–execute cycle and to explain the concepts of operator and operand together with the role of the various registers used within the control unit. In Chapter 7 there was a classification of the various types of programming language both in terms of **level** and **generation** and the range of popular high-level languages was studied. In Chapter 11 whilst looking at binary number systems we saw that some past examination questions made reference to the format of machine language instructions, a theme which will be further explored.

In this chapter we shall look at some of the features common to first generation or low-level languages. However it is important to realise, as for high-level languages, that it is not possible to learn to program in a language from just one chapter in a book. The theory will be related to the structure of the assembly languages used in the microcomputers found in schools and colleges, with particular reference to the memory addressing modes available in such systems.

ESSENTIAL PRINCIPLES

The distinction between high-level languages, assembly code, and machine code is illustrated in the following short program, written for the BBC microcomputer. It uses a unique feature on the BBC computer, namely that assembly code may be embedded within Basic and when enclosed in square brackets will be assembled as the program is run:

```
100 PRINT '"Demonstration of Single Byte Addition"
110 LET P% = &2000
120 [
130 .addup
140 LDA£&35\Load &35 into accumulator
150 CLC\Clear carry
160 ADC£&22\Add &22
170 STA &70\Store result in &70
180 RTS
190 ]
200 REM calling routine
210 CALL addup
220 PRINT "&70 contains"; ?&70
>RUN
2000
2000          .addup
2000 A9 35   LDA£&35\ Load &35 into accumulator
2002 18       CLC \ Clear carry
2003 69 22   ADC£&22 \ Add &22
2005 85 70   STA &70 \ Store result in &770
2007 60       RTS
```

Demonstration of Single Byte Addition
&70 contains 87

The statements PRINT '"Demonstration of Single Byte Addition" and

LET P% = &2000

are high-level language statements written in Basic, whereas:

ADC£&22

and

STA &70

are assembly language statements. The machine language program is shown, one or two bytes at a time in the output from the program and is:

A9 35 18 69 22 85 70 35

The interpretation of the high-level language statements is fairly obvious; a LET instruction is used for assigning values and PRINT is used for the tabulation of results. The statements in assembly code are, at first sight, obscure and need the annotation which is added to each line to describe the operation. The machine code

A9 35 18 69 22 85 70 35

appears simply as a sequence of hexadecimal digits but, when displayed by the assembler program, is as shown below:

```
2000 A9 35    LDA £&35    \Load &35 into accumulator
2002 18       CLC          \Clear carry
2003 69 22    ADC £&22     \Add &22
2005 85 70    STA  &70     \Store result in &70
2007 60       RTS
```

We can see that A9 corresponds to the operator LDA and thirty-five is the hexadecimal value of the operand. The 2000 specifies the location where the operator code is to be stored. This shows the fundamental characteristic of an assembly language, i.e. the one–one relationship with machine code.

CHARACTERISTICS OF MACHINE CODE

❝ Characteristics common to most assembly languages ❞

We can identify the following characteristics *common* to most assembly languages:

- The format and instructions are dependent on the processor, or in some cases, on the make and model of computer.
- The instructions are hardware orientated and so the programmer needs a knowledge of the machine architecture.
- The instructions are binary digit patterns usually represented in hexadecimal.
- Unlike high-level languages there is no division between program and data within the memory, both are stored as binary numbers.

There are a number of *disadvantages* in writing programs in machine code:

❝ Disadvantages of writing programs in machine code ❞

- There is a need to memorise instruction codes, such as 69 for ADC for add with carry.
- Each instruction refers to a specific 'absolute address' in memory thus the programmer must maintain a map of memory usage.
- The use of absolute addresses means that if a new instruction is to be inserted between two others, there may be a need for a great deal of revision of operands in other instructions.
- It is difficult to understand the operation of a machine code program without a great deal of annotation.
- As a consequence, it is often most difficult for a programmer to modify another programmer's machine code program.

ASSEMBLY LANGUAGES

The conventional means of programming in a low-level language is to use an **assembly language** where the instructions codes, or operators, are mnemonics or abbreviations of the instructions. For example, CLC for clear carry, BNE for branch if not equal to zero, AND for a logical and of memory with the accumulator. The operands are also given names. As assembly language is thus a machine-dependent language derived from its corresponding machine code. In its simplest form, it is a symbolic representation of the machine code with meaningful instruction names and symbolic addresses.

Assembly languages are usually augmented by the following additional instruction types:

Data definition

Special instructions which simply reserve areas of memory for the storage of data in specified formats. These correspond to the dimension statements and type declarations in high-level languages.

❝ Instruction types used to augment assembly languages ❞

Assembler directives

Commands to the assembler, for example, to specify where in memory the object program is to be located. This type of control is not normally accessible in high-level languages.

Macro instructions

A macro is a **pseudo instruction** which has the look or format of an assembly language instruction but, when assembled or translated, this instruction may be replaced by a subroutine. The term macro is derived from this idea of replacing a single assembler instruction by many machine language instructions. This idea of a macro is also used in operating systems and in some application programs. A good example is the word processor VIEW on the BBC microcomputer where standard paragraphs or sections of text may be defined as macros and incorporated in the document by a single macro command. Macros definitions may also incorporate parameters in the same way as high-level language procedures.

THE ASSEMBLY PROCESS

There is a direct analogy between assembly and compilation. An **assembler** is a program which translates a source program written in a low-level language, called an assembly language, into an object program in machine code. As with compilers, at the same time as

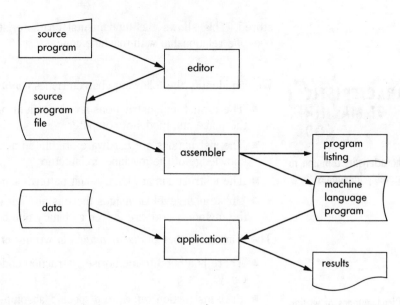

Fig. 12.1 Function of the compiler

the translation takes place, the assembler detects and reports syntax errors in the source code. The function of a compiler is illustrated in Fig. 12.1.

Once again, the language written by the programmer is called the **source program**, and the output from the assembler is called the **object program** and, as with compilation, it will be unusual if, in examination questions on assemblers or the assembly process, answers can be given without defining what is meant by a low-level language and contrasting it with high-level languages. **Assembly language** is a programming language which expresses its corresponding machine language in a symbolic form. It is therefore machine-dependent, being orientated around the machine structure and architecture.

The assembly process has as *input* a source program in a low-level language and appropriate assembler directives. It provides as *output*:

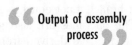
Output of assembly process

- A tabulation or **listing** of the source program
- A list of syntax errors
- A storage allocation map
- A printed version of the object program including the machine addresses of the variables used
- A machine code version of the object program, either in memory, on backing store, or both

There is an important distinction between compilation and assembly, in that although the *assembly* process needs lexical analysis, it does not require the same level of syntactical analysis. The structure of the language is essentially simple with its operator–operand format: each assembly language instruction is translated to a single machine code instruction, the exception being **macro** instructions, where the macro call is replaced by a set of instructions which have been previously defined and stored on the disc. This is in stark contrast to the *compilation* process, where the possible variations from an IF statement, for example, are almost infinite, and a single source program statement may generate a large number of machine code instructions.

Assembly can almost be reduced to references to translation tables. There will be a table containing a list of valid assembly language operators and the corresponding binary machine codes. The assembler will also create and maintain tables of data names and also procedure references, since the data names will be required in the translation of data movement and also in arithmetic instructions, whilst the latter will be required for translating branch instructions. Since the translation is carried out by reading and translating one statement at a time, there can be a problem in the direct translation of 'forward' jumps because the location referred to will not yet have been reached in the translation and so will not be contained within the table. This problem resolves generally into one of forward and backward references.

The simplest form of translation is to scan the program twice, this is called a **two pass assembler**; on the *first pass* there is a syntax check. Here the operators are checked for validity and translated from the symbol table. The operands are used as labels and in data definition, are used to construct the relevant symbol tables. Within the source program the operands are replaced by the symbol table reference. In the *second pass* the tables are accessed to determine the actual machine location. This is then substituted for the table reference and used to generate the actual machine code. Many modern assemblers use techniques which allow the translation in a single scan of the source code. These are distinguished by the names one and two pass assemblers.

DISASSEMBLERS AND MONITORS

There is a range of software which is invaluable in the development of programs in low-level languages and these come under the general heading of **monitors**. A monitor is a program which provides assistance in the testing and development of programs at machine code level. It will have some or all of the features given below:

Features of monitors

- To display areas of memory, possibly as characters or as hexadecimal digits
- To modify the contents of memory locations by keeping in new value
- To move or compare blocks of memory
- To trace the test run of a program by slowing the execution and displaying the contents of various registers after each statement
- To enable the programmer to set 'break points' in a program, that is to specify a particular address and when the program counter points to that address, execution will be suspended to allow the programmer to examine and modify memory and registers
- There may also be facilities to allow individual disc sectors to be examined

The process of using a monitor to examine and modify memory or disc sectors is often referred to as **zapping** and spoken of as disc zapping or memory zapping. Examples of monitors include the front page mode on the RML 380Z computers and the ROM-based programs Exmon and Disc Doctor on the BBC microcomputer.

THE 6502 MACHINE CODE

The 6502 processor provides a good example of a low-level language. It is the processor used on, amongst others, the BBC microcomputer, the Apple II and the Commodore PET. It is also not dissimilar to the Z80 used on the RML 380Z and 480Z and CP/M systems. In order to study the assembly language, as explained several times earlier in this text, it is necessary to understand the machine architecture, in particular the registers of the control unit which are illustrated in Fig. 12.2. The six registers used by the processor are:

Registers used by the processor

A   the Accumulator
X   the X-register
Y   the Y-register
PC the program counter
SP the stack pointer
P   the processor status register

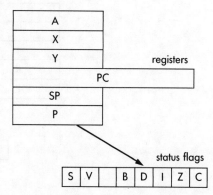

Fig. 12.2

All these are 8-bit registers, with the exception of the program counter which is sixteen bits, which allows programs to be stored in memory cells with addresses 0–65,535 whereas all the arithmetic is carried out on 8-bit words or bytes, hence the description 8-bit processor.

All arithmetic and logic operations are carried in the accumulator which is a general purpose register also used for transfers of data between memory locations. The X-register and Y-register can also be used to transfer data between memory locations but cannot be used for arithmetic operations other than counting, for example in loops. Their main use is as index registers, to act as pointers to data held in lists or arrays. The program counter as described in Chapter 4 holds the memory location of the next instruction to be executed, the stack pointer refers to a set of 256 temporary storage locations reserved in memory addresses 100 to 1FF (in hexadecimal) which are used store the return address locations when subroutines are entered or interrupts are processed. The processor status register can be considered as eight independent binary digits, each of which can indicate a particular status of the processor. These are:

S *Subtract*, set to 1 if last operation gave a negative result
V o*Verflow* on last operation
B *Break*, set when BRK instruction encountered
D *Decimal* mode, set when arithmetic to be carried out in decimal rather than binary
I *Interrupt* disable
C *Carry* set from arithmetic operation
Z *Zero*, set if last operation had result zero

The machine code is a one-address language with instructions which can be one byte, two bytes or three bytes in length. The operator is a single byte in all cases. For a 1-byte instruction there is no operand, the instruction may refer to a register, for example the assembly instruction INX which increments the X register. The 2-byte instructions may refer to a location in the first 256 locations, the so-called zero page 0000 to 00FF, or to an actual hexadecimal digit to be loaded or added to a register or the accumulator. The 3-byte instructions have a 2-byte memory address as the operand.

THE Z80 MICRO-PROCESSOR

The registers of the Z80 processor are illustrated in Fig. 12.3. This processor has an 8-bit accumulator similar to the 6502 but has, in addition six other registers called B,C,D,E,H and L which are grouped in pairs and can, in some cases, be used, in effect, as 16-bit registers. The program counter, as for the 6502 has sixteen bits as do the index registers X and Y and the stack pointer, so that these can point to any of the 64K memory locations. The status registers refer to sign of last operation, zero, auxiliary carry, parity/overflow subtract (negative) and carry. There is also a duplicate set of registers which may be used at any time to store a copy of the main registers and to swap from one set of values to another.

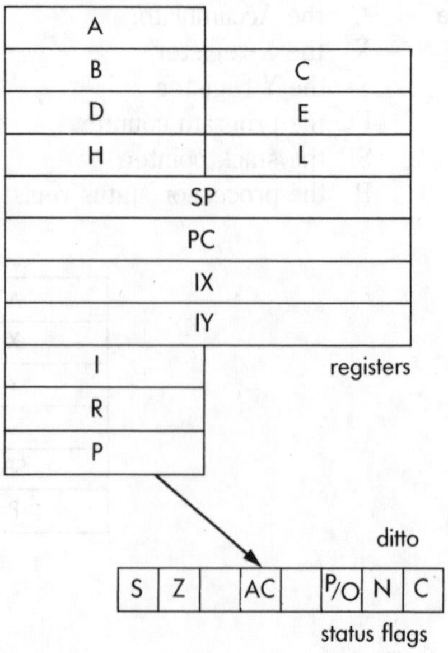

Fig. 12.3

MODES OF ADDRESSING

Both the 6502 and Z80 allow a number of different modes of addressing memory, the most important are described below with examples from the 6502 assembly language:

- **Direct addressing** is where the 2-byte operand is used to address directly a memory cell, for example.
  LDA MEM1
  which loads the accumulator with the contents of the memory location MEM1

■ **Indexed addressing** uses an index register, the contents of which is added to the operand, for example, in the instruction
  LDA MEM1,X
the operand MEM1 refers to the address of the start of a list of items in memory and the register X will have been loaded with a number containing the position of the required element in the list

Modes of addressing

■ **Indirect addressing** is where the operand refers to an address which contains the address where the value of the operand is stored, for example
  STA (POINTER)
The contents of the accumulator are stored in the memory location which has its address stored in the location with address POINTER, this is not dissimilar to the use of an index register except that the indirect address stores the complete operand and not just a displacement within a table. In general indirect addressing instructions are shorter than direct address instructions but take longer to execute because the 'fetch' part of the cycle will have to be executed twice, however, the indirect address can be longer than direct addresses and so can be used to address a greater range of store.

■ **Relative addressing** is used particularly with branch instructions and uses a single byte operand representing a two's complement number specifying the target address as a displacement from the curent instruction, for example
  BNE £−24
will branch back 24 bytes if the zero flag is set.

■ **Immediate addressing** in the 6502 uses a single byte operand to specify the data to be used by the instruction.
  AND £&C0
carries out an AND operation with the accumulator and the hexadecimal mask & C0 which is the binary pattern 11000000 so this instruction replaces the contents of the accumulator with a new byte which has the same two high order bits as the original, with the rest replaced by zero.

■ **Implied addressing** are 1-byte instructions which use operands which are normally registers and are implied by the operator, for example
  TAX
which transfers the contents of the accumulator to register x.

16-BIT MICRO-COMPUTERS

It is worth taking a brief look at a typical 16-bit processor, the INTEL 8086. This uses registers of sixteen bits in length. There are four general purpose 16-bit registers labelled AX, BX, CX and DX which can, alternatively, be treated as eight 8-bit registers, there are four pointer and index registers; the stack pointer, the base pointer, a source index and destination index and four segment registers called code, data stack and extra, and finally an instruction pointer and a register containing binary flags corresponding to the status register on 8-bit machines.

The processor has a 16-bit data bus and a 20-bit address bus thus the data can be transferred in and out of the registers in units of sixteen bits, the memory itself is organised in bytes but can be transferred in pairs. The 20-byte address bus means that the memory limit is 2^{20}, or 1,024K, or one megabyte (1 Mb). Memory itself is subdivided into segments of 64K, the direct address instructions use 16-bit operands which are added to the 20-bit value formed by adding four zeros to the right of the 16-bit value contained in the relevant segment register thus giving a 20-bit address.

Machine code on mainframe computers

Most of this chapter has been orientated around low-level languages specifically for microcomputers. This is for two reasons: firstly, that these are the machines likely to be available to most students reading this text, and secondly, because as we move upwards through the various categories of computer, so the machine language becomes more and more remote from the programmers. Indeed it is not uncommon for the machine language not to be released by the manufacturer, and so a company buying such a computer will not even have an assembler. Therefore, from the point of view of the student, low-level languages are important mainly in the context of microcomputer systems.

EXAMINATION QUESTIONS

SHORT QUESTIONS

Question 1
The contents of the 16-bit accumulator represent the status of sixteen switches. A process can only begin if bits 0,3,5,10,12 and 15 are set to 1. The status of the other switches has no effect on the process. Write the three key assembly language instructions to check whether the process can take place.   (AEB 1989)

Question 2
Identify a problem in assembling a program containing forward reference and describe one solution to the problem.   (Northern Ireland 1987)

Question 3
What is a *forward reference* in an assembly language program?
Describe how a forward reference can be dealt with in a **two** pass assembler.
                                        (AEB 1987)

Question 4
In a particular assembly language program the following sequence of instructions is encountered:

    ADD +42   ;immediate addressing
    ADD 42   ;direct addressing
    ADD (42)   ;indirect addressing

where ADD means 'add to the accumulator' and the address part of the instruction to be used as an immediate operand, a direct address and an indirect address respectively.

What will the contents of the accumulator be after executing *each* of these instructions if location 42 holds the value 21 and location 21 holds the value 33? You may assume that the accumulator initially contains zero.   (Northern Ireland 1989)

Question 5
a)   The contents of an 8-bit register is to be interpreted as a two's complement integer. The register contains 11110101.
     Write down:
     i) The effect of carrying out an arithmetic right shift of one place 1110101
     ii) The effect of carrying out a logical right shift of one place 1110101
     iii) The decimal value of the original contents and of the two new bit patterns created by the above shift operations
b)   Explain how you would transform the byte 10001111 into 11111000 using shift operations.   (London 1989)

Question 6
Briefly describe the mechanism by which a processor executes a subroutine (procedure).
                                        (Northern Ireland 1988)

LONGER QUESTIONS

Question 7
a)   What is the difference between one-address and two-address instructions? Which is the more popular and why?
b)   Explain why the direct method of addressing is not adequate in a modern computer system. What are the other methods of addressing? Give an example of each of these modes of addressing.
c)   By considering two distinct instructions, describe the effect that the various modes of addressing have on the size of the instructions and on the decoding algorithms.
                                        (Welsh 1986)

Question 8
Reverse Polish notation is frequently used as an intermediate form between the source code of an expression and the object code produced for it by a compiler.

a) i) Write down the Reverse Polish form of the following expression:
       (a −b) *(c− d * e)
    ii) Use your answer to illustrate the features of Reverse Polish notation which make it
        useful as an intermediate form.

b) A computer for which object code is to be produced has a single address instruction
    format. Some of its instructions, written in assembly language form, are as follows:

    ld   x   load contents of address x into accumulator
    st   x   store contents of accumulator in address x
    ad   x   add contents of address x into accumulator
    sb   x   subtract contents of address x from accumulator
    rsb x   subtract contents of accumulator from contents of address x and place
              result in accumulator
    my   x   multiply accumulator by contents of address x

    Write down, in assembly language form, the object code that could be produced from
    the Reverse Polish form of the expression in part a).   (Cambridge 1983)

Question 9

A simple computer has four 8-bit general purpose registers, and its assembly language
includes the following instructions:

    ld   r,x   load register r with contents of address x
    st   r,x   store contents of register r in address x
    ldn   r,n   load register r with the value n
    adn   r,n   add to register r the value n
    sbn   r,n   subtract from register r the value n
    sll   r,n   logical shift left register r by n places
    src   r,n   cyclic shift right register r by n places
    bnz   r,l   if register r is not zero, branch to label l
    bnn   r,l   if register r is not negative, branch to label l

The following is a fragment of program:

```
        ldn     0,8
        ldn     1,0
        ldn     2,0
        ld      3,p
a:      sll     1,1
        src     3,1
        bnn     3,z
        adn     2,1
        adn     1,1
z:      sbn     0,1
        bnz     0,a
        st      1,p
        st      2, q
```

a) i) Explain what the fragment of program does, by showing the contents of the
       registers at various stages and the contents of addresses p and q at the end.
       Assume the contents of address p to be 10101110 at the start.
    ii) What would be the contents of address p if the fragment of program was repeated
        twice? Five times? Eighteen times?

b) Describe in outline how the same task could be carried out by a fragment of program
    written in a typical high-level language. Point out in particular the different types of
    operation necessary.   (Cambridge 1985)

Question 10

a) Describe how the recent rapid developments in computer technology have led to a situation in which a large range of mainframe computers and a variety of microcomputers are currently in use.

b) Distinguish between *direct* and *indirect addressing* and show how these modes affect the range of accessible storage.

     Give one example of each of:

 i) one-address

 ii) two-address

instructions and indicate the consequences of each type of instruction. How can each of these modes be used to best effect?   (WJEC 1983)

Question 11

a) In an assembly language, what is a *macro*? Why are programs split into *segments*? Outline the main fuctions of an assembler, explaining how macros and assembly language segments are handled.

b) In an assembly language program explain how a *test* and a *loop* are used. Write down annotated assembly language fragments demonstrating the use of a test and a loop.

c) Describe the transformations that occur as an integer is read, processed and displayed by a computer assembly language program.   (WJEC 1983)

OUTLINE ANSWERS

SHORT QUESTIONS

Question 1

If the contents of the 16-bit accumulator have bits 0,3,5,10,12 and 15 which are set to 1 the bit pattern will be 1001010000101001 or hexadecimal 9429.

    The three assembly language instructions required would be; clear status flags, a subtract of hexadecimal 9429 from the accumulator and a branch if zero.

Question 2

When a program contains forward references it means that a branch, for example, is referring to a symbolic address not yet processed. The solution is to use a token instead of the address and replace the token on a second read or pass of the program.

Question 3

This is effectively the same question as the previous but set out differently.

Question 4

Initially the accumulator contains zero, after ADD+42 it will contain 42;

after   ADD42   it will contain the contents of 42 or 21;

after   ADD(42)   it will contain the contents of the location whose address is stored in 42, i.e. the contents of location 21 or 33.

Question 5

a) If an 8-bit register contains an integer in two's complement form 11110101:

    i) An arithmetic right shift of one place will give 10111010

    ii) A logical right shift of one place will give 11111010

    iii) The hexadecimal value of the original contents is F9 or decimal 249. After the arithmetic shift it contains hexadecimal BA or decimal 186 and after the logical shift it contains hexadecimal FA or decimal 250

b) The byte 10001111 can be transformed into 11111000 using four logical right shift operations.   (London 1989)

Question 6

A processor executes a subroutine at machine language level by storing the contents of the sequence control register (normally in a stack) and executing a branch to the subroutine. Return from the subroutine retrieves the stored sequence register contents and the calling routine will then be resumed.

LONGER QUESTIONS

Question 7

a) A one-address instruction uses a single operand whereas a two-address instruction has two operands and can carry out an operation involving two different memory locations. In simple terms a two-address language would carry out a program in less instructions than a one-address language is likely to require less memory. Thus the one-address language is more popular in modern computer systems and the intelligent use of registers allows the one-address instruction set to imitate many of the more powerful two-address instructions.

b) The direct method of addressing is not adequate in a modern computer system because it can restrict the extent of addressable memory and would make table access difficult to implement. The other methods of addressing which need to be described are indexed addressing, indirect addressing, relative addressing, immediate addressing and implied addressing for which examples are given in the chapter.

c) A direct address instruction to load a byte into the accumulator inan 8-bit microcomputer might be of the form:

LDA mem

this will be a 3-byte instruction with a 2-byte address, the indirect address equivalent might be

LDA (imem)

which would be a 2-byte instruction with the operand giving the 1-byte address of the location in memory which stores the 2-byte indirect address. In decoding this instruction there will be an extra fetch cycle, one to get the indirect address and a second to get the byte to be stored in the accumulator.

Question 8

a) i) The Reverse Polish form of the expression

$(a - b) * (c - d * e)$

can be verified from the program in Chapter 10 as

$ab - cde * - *$

ii) The features of Reverse Polish notation which make it useful as an intermediate form were covered in Chapter 10 and the ease of code generation is shown in the answer to part b).

b) The assembly code for implementing $ab - cde * - *$ is shown below and uses a memory cell given the label temp.

```
ld      a
sb      d
st      temp
ld      d
my      e
rsb     c
my      temp
```

this leaves the result in the accumulator.

Question 9

a) We can annotate the program:

```
 1        ldn 0,8    load 8 into register 0
 2        ldn 1,0    load 0 into register 1
 3        ldn 2,0    load 0 into register 2
 4        ld 3,p     load currents of p into register 3
 5     a: sll 1,1    logic shift register 1 place
 6        src 3,1    cyclic shift register 3 1 place
 7        bnn 3,z    branch to z if register 3 has 0 in msb
 8        adn 2,1    add 1 to register 2
 9        adn 1,1    add 1 to register 1
10     z: sbn 0,1    subtract 1 from register 0
11        bnz 0,a    loop back to a if register 0 is positive
                     (this loops 8 times)
```

```
12      st 1,p
13      st 2,q
```

i) The operation of the program can be studied using a device called a trace table which shows the changes in register contents. In an exam it is sufficient to show just enough to illustrate the program execution as below:

Inst	Operand		Reg 0	Reg 1	Reg 2	Reg 3	State
1	ldn	0,8	00001000				
2	ldn	1,0		00000000			
3	ldn	2,0			00000000		
4	ld	3,p				10101110	
a	sll	1,1		00000000			
6	src	3,1				01010111	
7	bnn	3,z				01010111	pos.
z	sbn	0,1	00000111				
11	bnz	0,a	00000111				pos.
a	sll	1,1		00000000			
6	src	3,1				10101011	
7	bnn	3,z				10101011	neg.
8	adn	2,1			00000001		
9	adn	1,1		00000001			
z	sbn	0,1	00000110				
11	bnz	0,1	00000110				pos.
a	sll	1,1		00000010			
6	src	3,1				11010101	

We will see that q gives a count of one 1-bits and p is altered from its original value by having the sequence of its bits reversed.

ii) If the fragment of program was repeated twice then p would be returned to its original value. Further repetitions would alternate between the two values so that after five times it will contain 01110101 and after eighteen times 10101110.

b)   This task does not translate directly into a high-level language because individual bits are not readily accessible. However, the logical shift left is equivalent to multiplication by 2. The cyclic shift and testing the most significant bit can be achieved in two steps: use of the operator MOD to identify the least significant bit and integer division to implement the right shift. In BBC BASIC this becomes:

```
100   R1% = 0
110   R2% = 0
120   R3% = p
130   FOR I = 1 TO 8
140   R1% = R1% * 2
150   Bit% = R3% MOD 2
160   R3% = R3%/2
170   IF Bit% = 1 THEN R2% = R2% +1:R1% = R1% + 1
180   NEXT I
190   p = R1%
200   q = R2%
```

Question 10

a)   The recent rapid developments in computer technology have given rise to smaller, faster and cheaper hardware. This has led to the proliferation of microcomputers, with the prices falling to such an extent that computer power costing millions of pounds in the 1950s can be purchased for less than £500. The same microprocesor technology and growing sales volumes have had a similar snowball effect on the growth of the range of mainframe computers.

b)   The distinction between direct and indirect addressing is described with examples in the previous question. The use of indirect addresses allows operands of greater length than would be available within the machine language format of a direct address instruction and so a greater range of memory can be accessed.

i) An example of one-address instruction could be

    JMP partb

which is an unconditional branch to the location with address part b.

ii) A two-address instruction could be

JNEG partc

which implements a branch to the location partc if the content of the accumulator is negative.

Question 11

a) A *macro* in an assembly language is a pseudo-statement which the assembler replaces with a sequence of instructions rather than a single machine code instruction.

The term *segment* is used in a number of different contexts in computing; one use in 16-bit mcirocomputers is as a 64K division of memory. The most common meaning is as an independent program unit which is loaded into the memory. When programs are run the segments are loaded and executed one at a time.

The major functions of an assembler are described in the chapter. They are the translation of a source program written in an assembly language into a machine code object program. Macros can be translated from definitions which can either be within the program or from an external library on the backing store. Segments are assembled independently and segment calls are normally programmed as macro calls.

b) Taking 6502 assembly code as an example, each test normally involves two steps; firstly, the value to be tested is loaded into the accumulator and secondly, a conditional branch is used. For example:

LDA value   \Load byte into accumulator

BNE done   \Branch if not zero to the location done

A loop can be implemented by a branch backward until a condition is reached

.start   \beginning of loop

. . . .   \statements of loop

BNE start   \loop back to start if zero not found

One of the index registers can be used to count the repetitions of a loop with the instruction DEX, for example, which decrements the X-register, being used to subtract 1 from the count until zero is detected.

c) An integer will be read a character at a time and will be subject to a lexical scan and parsing similar to that within a compiler. The first step will be to identify the sign and then the integers will be translated one at a time by a nested multiplication to form a binary integer. All the arithmetic processes will be carried out in binary with arithmetic likely to be carried out a byte at a time. Screen display will require a transformation back to a denary form.

THE STRUCTURE OF DATA

GETTING STARTED

We have already established, in Chapter 3, the distinction between a computer's memory and its file storage within computer systems. In Chapter 6 we made a more detailed study of file storage peripherals and the common techniques of organising the data in files within the system. Although there is a fundamental distinction between *memory*, which is within the processor, giving almost immediate access to a finite number of cells of equal size, and *files*, which are peripherals with slower access but a much greater potential capacity, a number of structures are common to both forms of storage.

It is worth recalling from Chapter 5 the basic definitions of **file**, **record, field** and **character** and the answers in examinations will normally need examples to be given to supplement the definitions. It is also worth recalling the definition of **key field** which, in a serial file, is the field, or group of fields, which specify the sequence into which the file is to be sorted and is also known as the **sort key**. In a direct access file it is the field or fields used by the addressing algorithm to locate a record.

Some high-level languages have constraints which restrict programs to the use of only three different structures or variable types, namely arithmetic variables, string variables and arrays. Arrays and records are implemented in Cobol, Pascal and Fortran 77. In Chapter 6 we studied in some detail the structure of records including variable length records and in Chapter 12 it was mentioned that modern microprocessor machine codes implement an additional structure called a stack. Stacks are found in many assembly languages but stacks and the companion structure called a queue usually have to be implemented by the programmer and will be explained at length in this chapter.

THE STRUCTURE OF DATA IN MEMORY

ESSENTIAL PRINCIPLES

This chapter is concerned with data structures within memory, but most strategies are easily extended to file organisation if the volumes of data are large, as will be pointed out from time to time.

Arrays

The most common extension of the simple variable is the **array**, which is used to represent matrices. In most high-level languages it is implemented by using subscripts, so that X_i is represented as X(i) and elements in a table element $A_{i,j}$ are represented by A(i,j). There is a fundamental difference between *arrays* and *records*; in an array, all the elements are identical in structure but in **records**, all the fields can be diffferent in type and size. There is, however, one type of structure, called a **ragged array**, shown diagrammatically in Fig. 13.1 in which the elements are of the same type but may be of different length and will be described in detail later in the chapter.

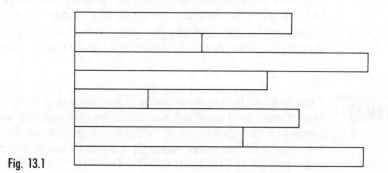

Fig. 13.1

Binary search

In many computer applications there is a need to hold a list of data and search through the list to find the position of a specific element. Perhaps the most obvious approach is to search the list from beginning to end until the item is located, this is called a **linear search**; but if the list contains say, 1,000 elements there will be an average of 500 comparisons until the required item is found. A common alternative, known as **binary search** is to store the elements in sequence, and then to examine the element at the mid-point of the list. The list is then divided into two halves, one of which will contain the target element. This can be repeated until the list only contains one element. In this strategy, starting with 1,000 elements the first step will reduce it to 500, the second to 250, the third to 125, then sixty-three then thirty-two then sixteen, eight, four, two, one in ten tests, against the 500 comparisons in a linear search.

A binary search algorithm to search a list stored in an array L containing N elements to find a value X can be represented as:

```
 1   set begin to 1
 2   set end to N
 3   WHILE end > begin
 4       set pointer to (begin + end)/2
 5       IF X < L(pointer)
 6           THEN
 7               end = pointer − 1
 8           ELSE
 9               begin = pointer
10       END IF
11   END WHILE
12   IF pointer = 0 THEN pointer = 1
13   IF L(pointer) = X
14       THEN
15           Found
16       ELSE
17           Not found
18   END IF
```

❝ Binary search algorithm ❞

Step 12 is needed because, in some circumstances, if X is less than the first element then step 7 could have set the pointer to zero.

VARIABLE LENGTH FIELDS AND RAGGED ARRAYS

In Chapter 6 we introduced the idea of variable length data structures covering both fields and records. Variable length records, for both normal processing and in particular sorting, need to be divided into a fixed length part and a variable length portion. The fixed length part must contain the sort key as one or more fields, and in the same position, relative to the start of the record, on every record in the file as well as a field containing the length or some parameter from which may be deduced the length of the record.

The diagram in Fig. 13.1 could refer to a set of names which could be names of employees in a company or, to relate this to a particular aspect of computer software, a symbol table in a compiler or assembler. Symbol tables were mentioned in Chapter 9 relating to compilers and again in Chapter 12 where it was seen that during the translation of an assembly language program, the assembler will maintain symbol tables of both variables and program references. These table entries, particularly in the case of lists of high-level language data names may be variable; some languages allow names of variables to be as short as one character or as long as thirty-two characters. Typical names are about four or five characters long, and so a conventional array with each element a string of thirty-two characters would take far more space than is necessary, hence the development of structures to handle data, in particular alphanumeric lists.

ACCESS VECTORS

Variable length list elements can be stored consecutively in a one-dimensional array with a second array used as an index. Such an array is called an **access vector**. There are two pieces of information required for access of an element, the start position of the element within the array and either its length or its end position. For example, if a list contained the characters CATSCHESSPHANTOM OF THE OPERASTARLIGHT EXPRESS, then an access vector or index could be:

First	Length
1	4
5	5
10	20
30	17
@	0

with the entry @ used to indicate 'end of list', a convention which will be continued throughout the chapter.

An alternative would be

First	Last
1	4
5	9
10	29
30	46
@	0

In this example there is no need for the second entry because there are no gaps between the entries, but in a dynamic table where items can be deleted from the list and new items added in the gaps then the two parameters are essential. There will be reference to this type of structure under operating systems in the next chapter, because it will be seen that the directory within a disc operating system can work on the same principle.

One other alternative is to use a special terminator at the end of each entry to mark the end of information, so that the previous example might look like:

CATS@CHESS@PHANTOM OF THE OPERA@STARLIGHT EXPRESS@

USE OF A POINTER

A very different approach to the storage of data in a ragged array is to incorporate the access vector entries within the list itself, so that the items contain three sub-fields:

either   POINTER   DATA   Terminator
or   POINTER   LENGTH   DATA

where the **pointer** gives the address in the list of the next element in sequence; **data** refers to the actual data within the entry and the limit of the item is specified either by explicitly storing the **length** or using a **terminator character**. These two techniques are illustrated in Fig. 13.2 which stores the list of items: Swanage, Poole, Bournemouth, Weymouth. The maintenance of such a structure – that is the deletion, insertion and amendment of entries – demands special program procedures as well as the periodic use of a further routine to remove the gaps left by the deleted entries. These structures are called **linked lists**, specifically they are called one-way lists because it is only possible to move forward through the list; to retrace steps would need a second pointer so that we store successor and predecessor which would give a two-way linked list.

0	1	2	3	4	5	6	7	8	9	10	11	12	13	14	15	16	17	18	19
9	S	W	A	N	A	G	E	@	16	P	O	O	L	E	@	29	B	O	U

20	21	22	23	24	25	26	27	28	29	30	31	32	33	34	35	36	37	38	39
R	N	E	M	O	U	T	H	@	39	W	E	Y	M	O	U	T	H	@	

Fig. 13.2

PROCESSING A LINKED LIST

❝ Operations for linked lists ❞

There are three operations which need to be defined for linked lists. They are:

i) Location of an element
ii) Deletion of an element
iii) Insertion of an element

Insertion and deletion will not be covered here but the location of an element is shown in Fig. 13.3 which defines a procedure for searching the list, which is assumed to be in ascending sequence, determined by the values of DATA(P). The output from the subroutine is either "FOUND" or "NOT FOUND", but could easily be changed to retrieve the pointer or to set a logical variable to indicate if the element can be found. There is always a need to adopt a consistent notation to describe the different types of element in the list, in this example:

START indicates the postion of the initial element in logical sequence; the list (after subsequent deletions this may not be the first).
DATA(P) to be the identifier or key contained within the list element starting at P;
NEXT(P) is the pointer to the next element;
@ end of list
A the Data value to be located

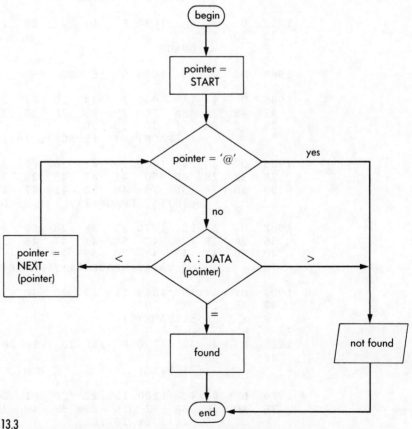

Fig. 13.3

This algorithm can, however, be expressed more elegantly in the following top-down design:

```
1   Set pointer to Start of List
2   WHILE Pointer not ="@"and A<Data(Pointer)
3        Set Pointer = Next(Pointer)
4   END WHILE
5   IF A = Data(Pointer)
6        THEN PRINT "Found"
7        ELSE PRINT "Not Found"
8   END IF
```

THE STORAGE IN MEMORY OF BASIC LANGUAGE STATEMENTS

A good practical example of the use of linked lists is provided in the storage of Basic program text within a computer's memory. The format used for each instruction is as follows:

byte 1	Hexadecimal 0D the code for 'Return'
bytes 2 & 3	Statement number in binary
byte 4	Statement length in bytes
bytes 5–	Basic statement with the keywords replaced by a single byte

The program below tabulates the bytes stored in the memory of a program in BBC Basic with the output tabulated in Fig. 13.4. The first statement is, in the run shown, stored from the memory location with hexadecimal representation of the statement number 1000,

```
>RUN
Add   Ret    Stmt  No    length          statement
1900  D    3  E8   1000  15   21   20   F4   20   4D   65   6D   6F   72
      79   20  44   69    73   70   6C   61   79
                   Memory Display

1915  D    3  F2   1010  8    8    20   EB   20   33

191D  D    3  FC   1020  35   53   20   F1   20   22   41   64   64   20
      20   52  65   74    20   20   5F   53   74   6D   74   20   20   4E   6F
      5F   5F  20   6C    65   6E   67   74   68   20   20   20   20   20
      20   73  74   61    74   65   6D   65   6E   74   22
                   "Add    Ret    Stmt   No    length          statement"

1952  D    4  6    1030  E    14   20   E9   20   4C   50   41   47   45
      3D   90
                   LPAGE=

1960  D    4  10   1040  6    6    20   F5

1966  D    4  1A   1050  22   34   20   F1   20   3B   7E   4C   50   41
      47   45  3B   8A    36   29   3B   7E   28   3F   4C   50   41   47   45
      29   3B  8A   31    30   29   3B
                   ; LPAGE; 6);  (LPAGE); 10);

1988  D    4  24   1060  29   41   20   F1   20   8A   31   30   29   3B
      7E   3F  28   4C    50   41   47   45   2B   31   29   3B   8A   31   33
      29   3B  7E   3F    28   4C   50   41   47   45   2B   32   29   3B
                   10); ?(LPAGE+1); 13); ?(LPAGE+2);

19B1  D    4  2E   1070  23   35   20   E9   20   4E   4F   3D   32   35
      36   2A  3F   28    4C   50   41   47   45   2B   31   29   2B   3F   28
      4C   50  41   47    45   2B   32   29
                   NO=256*?(LPAGE+1)+?(LPAGE+2)

19D4  D    4  38   1080  11   17   20   4C   3D   3F   28   4C   50   41
      47   45  2B   33    29
                   L=?(LPAGE+3)

19E5  D    4  42   1090  F    15   20   F1   20   8A   31   37   29   3B
      4E   4F  3B
                   17);NO;

19F4  D    4  4C   1100  16   22   20   F1   20   8A   32   32   29   3B
      7E   4C  3B   8A    32   36   29   3B   4C   3B
                   22); L; 26);L;
```

```
1AOA   D   4   56   1110 A   10   20   53   24   3D   22   22
             S$=""

1A14   D   4   60   1120 20   32   20   E3   20   49   20   3D   20   4C
       50  41   47   45   20   2B   20   34   20   B8   20   4C   50   41   47
       45  20   2B   20   4C
             I = LPAGE + 4      LPAGE + L

1A34   D   4   6A   1130 B   11   20   E9   20   58   3D   3F   49
             X+?I

1A3F   D   4   74   1140 F   15   20   F1   20   22   20   20   22   3B
       7E  58   3B
             "   "; X;

1A4E   D   4   7E   1150 2C   44   20   E7   20   58   3C   33   32   20
       84  20   58   3E   31   32   36   20   8C   20   53   24   3D   53   24
       2B  22   5F   22   20   8B   20   53   24   3D   53   24   2B   BD   28
       58  29
             X<32    X>126    S$=S$+"  "   S$=S$+ (X)

1A7A   D   4   88   1160 8   8   20   ED   20   49
             I

1A82   D   4   92   1170 10   16   20   F1   20   27   8A   31   30   29
       3B  53   24   27
             ' 10);S$'

1A92   D   4   9C   1180 16   22   20   4C   50   41   47   45   20   3D
       20  4C   50   41   47   45   20   2B   20   4C
             LPAGE = LPAGE + L

1AA8   D   4   A6   1190 14   20   20   FD   20   4C   50   41   47   45
       20  2B   20   32   20   3D   20   92
             LPAGE + 2 =
```

Fig. 13.4

the next cell stores fifteen which is twenty-one in hexadecimal, followed by the statement which is followed by F4 which is the token for REM and the text of the remark 'Memory Display'.

The rest of the output is to a similar format and gives a full dump of the program:

```
1000 REM Memory Display
1010 MODE 3
1020 PRINT "Add Ret __ Stmt No__ length        statement"
1030 LET LPAGE=PAGE
1040 REPEAT
1050 PRINT ;~LPAGE;TAB(6) ;~(?LPAGE) ;TAB(10) ;
1060 PRINT TAB (10) ;~?(LPAGE+1) ;TAB (13) ;~?(LPAGE +2) ;
1070 LET NO=256*?(LPAGE+1) +?(LPAGE+2) ;
1080 L=? (LPAGE+3)
1090 PRINT TAB (17) ;NO;
1100 PRINT TAB (22) ;~L;TAB (26) ;L;
1110 S$=""
1120 FOR I = LPAGE + 4 TO LPAGE + L − 1
1130 LET X=?I
1140 PRINT " ";~X;
1150 IF X<32 OR X>126 THEN S$=S$+"__" ELSE S$=S$+CHR$(X)
1160 NEXT I
1170 PRINT 'TAB(10) ;S$'
1180 LPAGE = LPAGE + L
1190 UNTIL LPAGE + 2 = LOMEM
```

This program exhibits several features peculiar to BBC Basic:

PAGE stores the address of the start of the program
?I means the contents of the memory cell with address I
PRINT ~L prints L as a hexadecimal number
LOMEM is the first available address beyond the end of the program

STACKS

A **stack** may be described as a data structure where the retrieval is implemented as **last in first out** or LIFO. It is commonly used for the storage of the "return addresses" from subroutine calls. "CALL" to a subroutine adds a return address to the list and "RETURN" retrieves the last entry to be re-loaded into the program counter or sequence register. A stack can be implemented in a high-level language using a one-dimensional array with a pointer as a subscript for the array and a parameter storing the stack limit, or maximum length of the list.

Insertion in a stack stored in the array A may be described by the algorithm:

" Insertion "

```
1   IF Pointer less than Limit
2        THEN
3            Add 1 to Pointer
4            Insert element in position A(Pointer)
5        ELSE
6            Print "Stack Full"
7   END IF
```

Removal may be implemented by:

" Removal "

```
1   IF Pointer is greater than zero
2        THEN
3            Retrieve A(Pointer)
4            Subtract 1 from Pointer
5        ELSE
6            Print "Stack Empty"
7   END IF
```

If the requirement were to process variable length records then the algorithm can be adapted simply to replace the assignment of A(Pointer) by a loop for the characters of the element, which will be terminated by a 'separator' character. It is worth recognising that, within the program, the elements are stored in reverse order, that is A(1) is 'lower' in the stack than A(2). The pointer will be zero when the stack is empty.

QUEUES

A **queue** is a linear data structure where, like patrons queueing in a shop, items are added one at a time and also served one at a time with a discipline of **first in first out** referred to as FIFO. Just as for the stack, we may implement a queue as a one-dimensional array. It could be processed in the same way as a physical queue, treating insertion as adding elements to the end of the list and implementing removal by actually moving all the elements up one place in the list. Fig. 13.5 shows an alternative treatment as a 'cyclic list' with the queue illustrated at different points of time by the shaded elements in the array. The insertion and removal are carried out at opposite ends of the list and the 'active' part of the list varies as items are added and removed so that we maintain two pointers, head and tail corresponding to the head and tail of the list. The algorithm for insertion could be:

" Algorithm for insertion "

```
1   Increment tail
2   If tail> limit then set tail to 1
3   If tail = head and A(head) not equal to "@"
4        THEN
5            Print "Full"
6        ELSE
7            Insert element in A(tail)
8   END IF
```

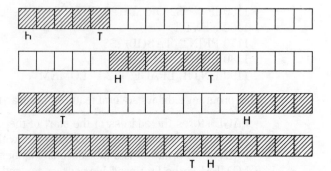

Fig. 13.5

The tail pointer is incremented and then tested, first against the queue array limit, (which, if exceeded, re-sets the pointer to 1) and then against the value of head which would indicate that the queue is full. If the queue is empty then head will hold the value"@". The initial setting of the queue values for an empty queue will be

tail = 0   head = 1   A(1) = "@"

The following algorithm implements the removal of an element from the queue. The first test is to see if the queue is empty which is indicated by A(1) taking the value"@" the element is removed from the head of the queue by copying it into the memory location X. The change in the pointer to the head of the queue has three possible conditions:

head = tail which indicates queue full
head at the limit which needs to set the head to 1
normal condition simply to increment head

```
1    IF A(1) = "@"
2         THEN
3                   Print "Empty"
4         ELSE
5                   Set X to A(head)
6                   IF head = tail
7                        THEN
8                                  Set tail to 0
9                                  Set head to 1
10                                 Set A(1) to"@"
11                       ELSE
12                                 Increment head
13                                 IF head > limit set head to 1
14                       END IF
15   END IF
```

A good illustration of the use of a queue is to quote the buffers used in many computer systems, for example the keyboard buffer where key depressions are stored in a queue in memory and displayed as the processor is free. This can be illustrated very easily on the BBC microcomputer which allows the programmer to 'type ahead' instructions whilst the machine is, for example, carrying out a disc back-up or compact and will process the keystrokes from the buffer as soon as the processor is free.

TREE STRUCTURES

Perhaps the most useful of the structures to be studied in this chapter is the tree which, when used in programming has the characteristic, as compared to the list structures, of having a single predecessor but, potentially, more than one succesor. The first type of tree encountered by most people is the family tree used to illustrate the relationships between various generations within a family, another simple type is the structure chart introduced in an earlier chapter which illustrates the logical connection between the various modules in a program. Used as a data structure within a program, the most common and simplest implementation is the **binary tree** which is illustrated in Fig. 13.6 and restricts each element to be directly related to just two successors which are called **descendants**. The

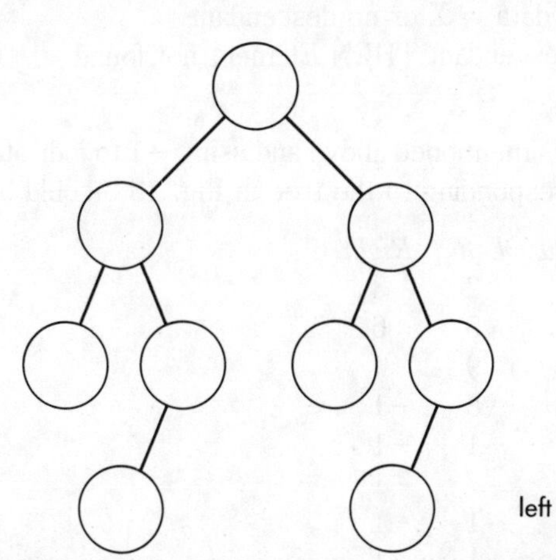

Fig. 13.6 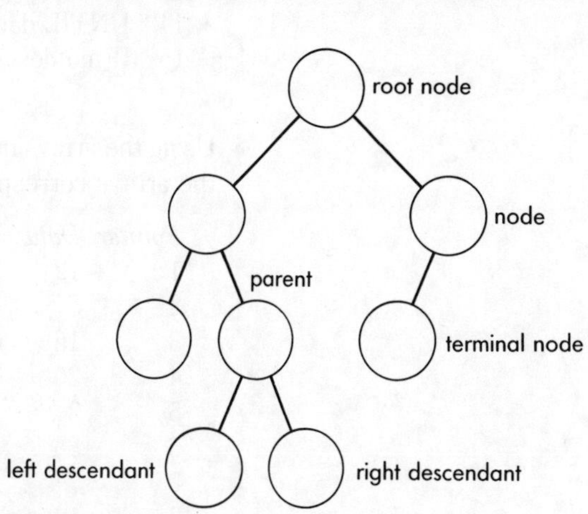   Fig. 13.7

terminology associated with trees is defined in Fig. 13.7 where it is seen that the foundation of the tree is a **root node**, normally shown at the top of any diagram and, in a binary tree, the two successors are called the right and left descendants, a node with no descendants is called a terminal node.

A typical application of the binary tree structure is to arrange data on nodes so that the 'value' of the record, i.e. the sort key, is such that each parent is greater than or equal to the left descendant and less than or equal to the right descendant, as shown in Fig. 13.8. Such a tree may be accessed sequentially to locate any required record, but programming this algorithm will require at least three arrays which can be called "DATA", "LEFT", and "RIGHT". This last pair correspond to the array "NEXT" in the linked list structure but one gives a link to the left descendant and the other to the right descendant. The algorithm shown below searches the structure using Pointer as a subscript to search arrays for the data element X as below:

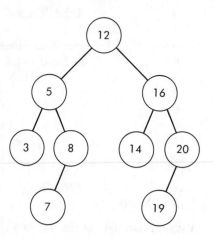

Fig. 13.8

```
 1   Go to root node
 2   REPEAT
 3           IF data at node is equal to X
 4                   THEN
 5                           Element found
 6                   ELSE
 7                           IF X less than node value
 8                                   THEN
 9                                           Set pointer to left descendant
10                                   ELSE
11                                           Set pointer to right descendant
12                           END IF
13                   END IF
14   UNTIL data = X or no descendant
15   IF no descendant THEN Element not found
```

Using the arrays mentioned above and using −1 to indicate no descendant, the contents of the arrays corresponding to the tree in Fig. 13.8 could be:

Pointer	Data	Left	Right
1	12	2	3
2	5	5	6
3	16	9	4
4	20	8	−1
5	3	−1	−1
6	8	7	−1
7	7	−1	−1
8	19	−1	−1
9	14	−1	−1

So the algorithm can be restated:

```
1   Pointer = 1
2   REPEAT
3        IF DATA(pointer) = X
4            THEN
5                     PRINT "Element found"
6            ELSE
7                 IF X < DATA(pointer)
8                     THEN
9                            pointer = LEFT(pointer)
10                    ELSE
11                           pointer = RIGHT(pointer)
12                END IF
13       END IF
14  UNTIL DATA(pointer) = X or pointer = −1
15  IF pointer = −1 THEN PRINT "Element not found"
```

A well-known implementation of trees is the **viewdata** structure used in Prestel and local viewdata systems. Each record or **page** in the system can have up to ten descendants and these links can be to any other page in the database so that any page may be the descendant of any other and thus might have several parents.

Another example of a tree which we shall see in the next chapter is the implementation of directories in operating systems which is found in virtually all operating systems used in mainframe computers and most microcomputers which support hard discs. There are also many examples which can be observed in computer applications where the user selects an option from a menu and then may be offered a further set of 'sub-options' within the original selection. A good example of this is the Lotus-1-2-3 package where the user selects a command from an initial menu, and after selecting *file,* for example, at this level, a further menu with options including *retrieve* and *save* is displayed. On selecting retrieve, the system will display a list of spreadsheets files which may be 'retrieved' and loaded from the disc.

Choice of data structure

The data structures described in this chapter are the most common examples found in computer applications but should not be regarded as the only examples which may be applied to data within the computer. In designing a computer program it is essential to select a data structure which suits the application rather than fitting the data to a conventional structure.

The structures have been defined in terms of memory organisation but all of them can be applied to disc file organisation, particularly the linked list and the tree. One extension of the linked list is the **multi-list** where a file can contain several link addresses so that, for example, a file containing the order received by a company could be processed as a linked list by product or alternatively as a linked list by customer.

Database systems

The term database is often used misleadingly to refer to a package which is really only a simple information retrieval program from a list held in memory. Nearly every school and home microcomputer has available for purchase a program called **Database** or with database in the title or in the product description. To be strictly accurate, the term database should be reserved to refer to a file-orientated system designed around a major file supplying the information needs of a number of different applications. In early computers a manufacturing company might process orders using the same data entered separately in several independent applications, perhaps once for a stock control system, once for production control to manufacture or replace stock, once for the accounting system and again for sales analysis, etc. etc. In a database system the order data is entered once and then accessed by all the different applications, this not only ensures greater accuracy but makes the data available to all the systems at the same time instead of being passed from one to the other and causing one or more to run with out-of-date information. Thus a database may be considered as an integrated collection of files used in one or more related applications.

EXAMINATION QUESTIONS

SHORT QUESTIONS

Question 1
By describing their main features, distinguish between a *stack* and a *queue*. Give an example of how **each** data structure is used within a computer system.

(Welsh AS 1989)

Question 2
What is a stack?
Show how a stack may be used to carry parameters in and out of a closed subroutine.

(AEB 1987)

Question 3
Describe the data structure known as a queue. Name a situation in which a queue might be used.

(AEB 1987)

Question 4
Describe **two** applications where a tree structure would be a good method of data representation.

(NEAB 1988)

Question 5
A computer has a stack with data items entering the stack via the input stream.
The only operations available are
    PUSH –   push the next item in the input stream onto the stack
    POP –   pop the top item off the stack and put it in the output stream
Given the input stream ABCDE which of the following are possible output streams?
  i) ACEDB   ii) BCEAD
  iii) CBAED   iv) EACBD
For the possible output streams show, using the instructions PUSH and POP, how they can be obtained.

(London 1989)

LONGER QUESTIONS

Question 6

a)   Describe, with the aid of diagrams, how names may be stored in alphabetical order using a linked list structure by using arrays. Use the names Rachel, Majid, Sian, Mary, Jonathan as example data.

b)   Show how the free space can be managed so that items can be easily added to or deleted from the linked list. Use as examples:
    i) Adding the name Henry to the list
    ii) Deleting the name Majid from the list

(Cambridge 1989)

Question 7
In the context of data structures, explain what is meant by a stack.
Give algorithms to
i) Add an item to a stack
ii) Remove an item from the stack
You should check for underflow and overflow.

(London 1988)

Question 8
A low-level language routine uses stack operations to process an input sequence consisting of English words. The stack is made up of storage elements, each of which can hold an English word of any length.

a)   Assuming that the input sequence consists of the first seven words of this question and that 'low-level' may be treated as one word, which of the following word sequences could be generated using a single stack.?

i) A language low-level routine operations stack uses
ii) language A low-level uses routine stack operations
iii) A routine language low-level operations stack uses
In *each* case the stack operations should be indicated.

b)   How would the presence of a second stack affect the generation of each of the sequences?   (Welsh 1985)

Question 9

A queue is to be held in main memory during the execution of a program. Items will be added to and removed from the queue. Draw diagrams to illustrate the situation when,

a)   there are several items still in the queue
b)   the queue is empty
c)   the queue contains one item   (6)

Explain what is meant by the terms *underflow* and *overflow* in relation to a queue.   (2)

Give algorithms for the addition of a new item to the queue and for the removal of an item from the queue, where the queue is held in a vector that is large enough to hold all the items at one time.   (4)

Explain how the size of this vector may be reduced to the maximum length of the queue by forming a circular representation of the queue. What changes may be needed to your algorithms for the addition of items to and removal of items from the queue?   (3)
(London 1984)

Question 10

A certain type of data structure allows a variable number of items to be held. Items may be added to the data structure, or removed from it, one at a time. The characteristic feature of the data structure is that when an item is removed, it is the item that has been longest in the data structure that goes.

a)   What is this type of data structure usually called?

b)   A data structure of the type described is to be set up in a program, to hold items which are integers. Several thousand integers will enter and leave the data structure during the execution of the program, but there should never be more than 100 held in it at any one time.
   Describe how this data structure can be organised and used efficiently in the program. Your description should include diagrams to show the organisation of the data structure, together with details of the algorithms:
   i) for initialising it
   ii) for adding an item to it
   iii) for removing an item from it
The algorithms should include recognition of the error conditions of attempting to add an item to an already full data structure and attempting to remove an item from an empty data structure.   (Cambridge 1985)

Question 11

a)   Explain the term *tree* as applied to a data structure.

b)   A set of items can be sorted into sequence of increasing key values by placing each key on a tree so that smaller keys always lie to the left of larger ones.
   i) Construct a flow diagram to show how the keys would be inserted into the tree.
   ii) Construct a flow diagram to show how the keys would be read from the tree in sequence.
   iii) Would this method be fast? Would it be economical of storage? Explain.   (Oxford 1985)

Question 12

A shop stocks a large quantity of different cartridges for computer games. It holds the information regarding the stock in the form of a binary tree. The information held for each item consists of
1   The part number

2 The quantity in stock

3 The shelf number

a) To provide efficient access, the shop wishes to store the information in part number order. Explain how the binary tree could be organised.

b) Using algorithms wherever appropriate show how
   i) The tree could be represented as an array
   ii) The tree could be updated, to include new items
   iii) The tree could be updated, when a customer has bought a known quantity of a particular cartridge, including the purchase of the last one of that cartridge.

(WJEC 1986)

OUTLINE ANSWERS

SHORT QUESTIONS

Question 1

A stack is a last-in-first-out structure, a queue is a first-in-first-out structure. A stack is used within a computer system to store subroutine return addresses; a queue is used to store the list of jobs waiting to use a shared peripheral such as a printer.

Question 2

A stack is a data structure where the retrieval is implemented as Last In First Out or LIFO. It is commonly used for the storage of the "return addresses" from subroutine calls where a "CALL" to a subroutine adds a return address to the list and "RETURN" retrieves the last entry to be reloaded into the program counter or sequence register. A stack can be implemented in a high-level language using a one-dimensional array with a pointer as a subscript for the array and a parameter storing the stack limit, or maximum length of the list.

Question 3

A queue is a linear data structure where, like cars queuing at a road junction, items are added one at a time and also removed one at a time with a discipline of First In First Out referred to as FIFO. Just as for the stack, we may implement a queue as a one-dimensional array. A good illustration of the use of a queue is the keyboard buffer on a microcomputer where key depressions are stored in a queue in memory and displayed as the processor is free.

Question 4

Applications where a tree structure would be a good method of data representation include the directories on a disc directory and the parsing of an arithmetic expression in a high-level language.

Question 5

i) ACEDB   can be generated using
     PUSH POP PUSH PUSH POP PUSH PUSH POP POP POP

ii) BCEAD   cannot be produced

iii) CBAED   can be generated using
     PUSH PUSH PUSH POP POP POP PUSH PUSH POP POP

iv) EACBD   cannot be produced

LONGER QUESTIONS

Question 6

a) The names Rachel, Majid, Sian, Mary, Jonathan may be stored in alphabetical order using a linked list structure by using a starting value a 'free' pointer and arrays as set out below:

    free 6
    start 5

Data	Next	
Rachel	3	
Majid	4	
Sian	@	end of list
Mary	1	
Jonathan	2	

b)   i) Adding the name Henry to the list will first involve adding Henry to the next free position, 6, then searching for the element to follow it in the list, so we examine **start** which points to 5 which is Jonathan which will follow Henry, the start pointer is changed to point to Henry and Henry points to Jonathan

free 7
start 6

Data	Next	
Rachel	3	
Majid	4	
Sian	@	end of list
Mary	1	
Jonathan	2	
Henry	5	

ii) Deleting the name Majid from the list first involves searching for Majid who is pointed to by Jonathan, Majid points to Mary so Jonathan's pointer now points to Mary. Majid is now made the first free element and points to 7, the previous first free

free 2
start 6

Data	Next	
Rachel	3	
Majid	7	
Sian	@	end of list
Mary	1	
Jonathan	4	
Henry	5	

(Cambridge 1989)

Question 7

Stack has been described in earlier answers as a data structure where the retrieval is implemented as Last In First Out or LIFO.

Adding to a stack stored in the array A may be described by the algorithm:

```
1   IF Pointer less than Limit
2        THEN
3             Add 1 to Pointer
4             Insert element in position A(Pointer)
5        ELSE
6             Print "Overflow"
7   END IF
```

Removal may be implemented by:

```
1   IF Pointer is greater than zero
2        THEN
3             Retrieve A(Pointer)
4             Subtract 1 from Pointer
5        ELSE
6             Print "Underflow"
7   END IF
```

Question 8

a)   The language can be assumed to have the following instructions:

GET   receive next input word into the work space
PUT   write word from the work space
PUSH add word from the work space to stack
POP   copy word from stack to the work space

The list of words is

A   low-level   language   routine
uses stack   operations

The three programs can be illustrated by the following trace tables:

i) A language low-level routine operations stack uses

Inst	Work space	Output	Stack
GET	A		
PUT		A	
GET	low-level		
PUSH			low-level
GET	language		low-level
PUT		language	low-level
POP	low-level		
PUT		low-level	
GET	routine		
PUT		routine	
GET	uses		
PUSH			uses
GET	stack		uses
PUSH			stack uses
GET	operations		stack uses
PUT		operations	stack uses
POP	stack		uses
PUT		stack	uses
POP	uses		
PUT		uses	

ii) language A low-level uses routine stack operations

Inst	Work space	Output	Stack
GET	A		
PUSH			A
GET	low-level		
PUSH			low-level A
GET	language		low-level A
PUT		language	low-level A

The program breaks down as the next word "A" required for output is not available for access.

iii) A routine language low-level operations stack uses *Inst Work space Output Stack*

Inst	Work space	Output	Stack
GET	A		
PUT		A	
GET	low-level		
PUSH			low-level
GET	language		low-level
PUSH			language low-level
GET	routine		language low-level
PUT		routine	language low-level
POP	language		low-level
PUT		language	low-level
POP	low-level		
PUT		low-level	

Inst	Work space	Output	Stack
GET	uses		
PUSH			uses
GET	stack		uses
PUSH			stack uses
GET	operations		stack uses
PUT		operations	stack uses
POP	stack		uses
PUT		stack	uses
POP	uses		
PUT		uses	

b) For this part, a second stack with instructions PUSH2 POP2 would allow part ii) to proceed:

language A low-level uses routine stack operations

Inst	Work space	Output	Stack
GET	A		
PUSH			A
GET	low-level		
PUSH2			A/low-level
GET	language		A/low-level
PUT		language	A/low-level
POP	A		low-level
PUT		A	low-level
POP2	low-level		
PUT		low-level	
GET	routine		
PUSH2			routine
GET	uses		routine
PUT		uses	routine
POP	routine		
PUT		routine	
GET	stack		
PUT		stack	
GET	operations		
PUT		operations	

Question 9

This question seems to assume in the first part that the queue will be stored in the same way as a physical queue, with the items joining at the back and moving along to the front as one is removed. In the second part it assumes that a long vector is available and that the queue will simply move along the array. The final part of the question refers to the implementation described in the chapter and is the one normally adopted in practice.

The diagrams for the first part are shown in Fig. 13.9.

Underflow is where it is attempted to remove an item from the queue and the queue is empty; *overflow* is where an attempt is made to add an additional item to a queue when there is no more space available.

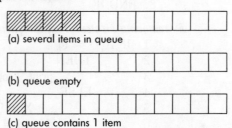

(a) several items in queue

(b) queue empty

Fig. 13.9 (c) queue contains 1 item

If the queue is held in a vector that is large enough to hold all the items at one time, an algorithm for the addition of a new item to the queue may be represented as:

1 Increment tail pointer
2 Insert element at end

The tail pointer is initialised at zero when the queue is empty and incremented each time an element is added. The other pointer, the head pointer, will be initialised to 1.

The following algorithm implements the removal of an item from the queue. The first item is to see if the queue is empty, which is indicated by tail being less than head. If the queue is not empty, the item is removed from the head of the queue by copying it into the memory location X and incrementing the head pointer.

```
1   IF head > tail
2        THEN
3                print "Empty"
4        ELSE
5                set X to A(head)
6                increment head
7   END IF
```

If the queue is to be implemented as a circular list then the initial setting for an empty queue will be

tail = 0   head = 1   A(1) = "@"

The insertion in this case, after the tail pointer has been incremented, has to be tested first against the queue array limit. If it is exceeded, then the pointer has to be reset to 1 before testing against the value of head which, if it contains "@", indicates that the queue is full. The full algorithm is given in the chapter.

The algorithm for removal of an element from a circular queue tests to see if the queue is empty by examining A(1) to see if it takes the value "@". After removing the element from the head of the queue, the incrementing of the pointer must take account of two extra conditions: firstly head = tail, which indicates queue full, and secondly head at the limit, which needs to set the head to 1. The full algorithm is shown in the chapter.

Question 10

a) A queue is a data structure which allows a variable number of items to be held with the characteristic feature that when an item is removed, it is the item that has been longest in the data structure that goes.

b) We would use a queue held in a circular list of length 100 with algorithms as below, using head and tail to represent the pointers and List to represent the array. The organisation of the queues is shown in Fig. 13.5:

i) *queue initialisation*:

```
1   set head = 1
2   set tail = 0
3   set List(1) = "@"
```

ii) *adding an item to the queue of the list*:

```
1   increment tail
2   IF tail > 100 then set tail to 1
3   IF tail = head and List(head) not equal to "@"
4        THEN
5                print "Full"
6        ELSE
7                insert element in List(tail)
8   END IF
```

iii) *removing an item from the queue*.

```
1    IF A(1) = "@"
2         THEN
3                 print "Empty"
4         ELSE
5                 set X to List(head)
6                 if head = tail
7                     THEN
8                         set tail to 0
9                         set head to 1
10                        set List(1) to "@"
11                    ELSE
```

12   increment head
13   IF head>100 set head to 1
14   END IF
15   END IF

Question 11

a)   A tree data structure is a linked list where each item, except the root node, has one or more predecessors and each element, apart from terminal nodes, has one or more successors. The simplest example is a binary tree where each node is limited to a single parent and there are not more than two descendants, termed the right descendant and the left descendant.

b)   Given a binary tree where a set of items can be sorted into sequence of increasing key values by placing each key on a tree so that smaller keys always lie to the left of larger ones.

   i) A flow diagram showing how the keys would be inserted into the tree is given in Fig. 13.10. This algorithm requires that a further data structure be created to maintain a record of the free storage available for later insertions.

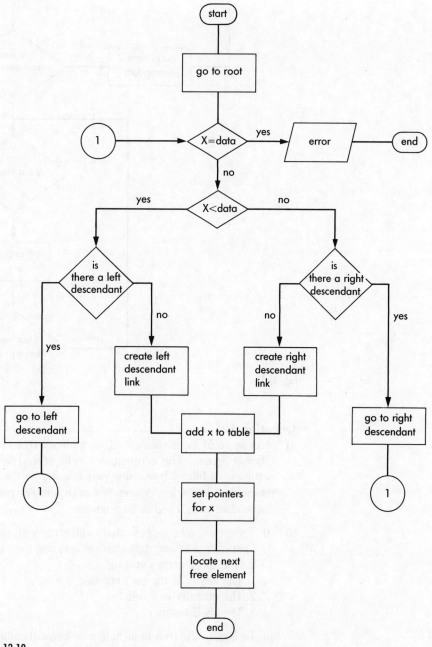

Fig. 13.10

ii) A flow diagram showing how the keys would be read from the tree in sequence is given in Fig. 13.11.

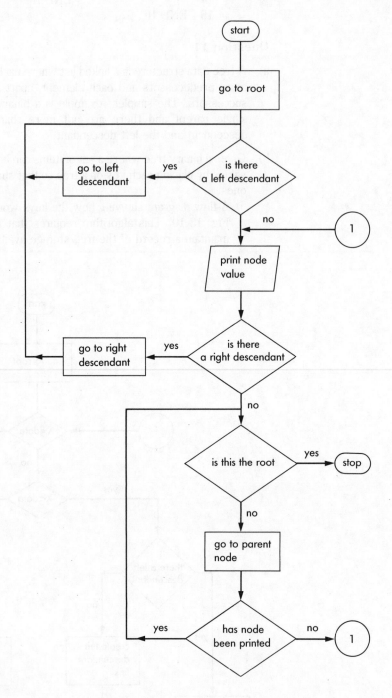

Fig. 13.11

Question 12

a) Access could be implemented by a binary tree, and could be organised to provide efficient access. The information can be stored on the tree in part number order by setting up a binary tree using part number as the key so that each node with a left descendant has a left descendant with a lower part number and, if present, a right descendant with a higher part number.

b) i) The tree can be represented as an array with two subscripts, the first being 1 or 2 to specify a left or right descendant, and the second indicating the position of the data in three arrays storing:

1 The key, i.e. the part number
2 The quantity in stock
3 The shelf number

ii) To update the tree to include new items the algorithm would be similar to the one shown in the flowchart of Fig. 13.10.

This can be represented as:

```
 1   go to root node
 2   REPEAT
 3          IF key at node is equal to part number
 4                 THEN
 5                         PRINT "error-part number exists"
 6                 ELSE
 7                     IF part number is less than node value
 8                             THEN
 9                                     set pointer to left descendant
10                             ELSE
11                                     set pointer to right descendant
12                     END IF
13          END IF
14   UNTIL part number = key or no descendant
15   IF no descendant
16          THEN
17                  print "Element not found"
18          ELSE
19                  create link to new descendant at next free element
20                  set pointer to new descendant
21                  add part number, quantity and shelf number to array
22                  update free element pointer
23   END IF
```

iii) To update the tree when a customer has bought a known quantity of a particular cartridge the record must first be located and then amended:

```
 1   Go to root node
 2   REPEAT
 3          IF key at node is equal to part number
 4                 THEN
 5                         update data
 6                 ELSE
 7                         IF part number is less than node value
 8                                 THEN
 9                                         set pointer to left descendant
10                                 ELSE
11                                         set pointer to right descendant
12                         END IF
13          END IF
14   UNTIL part number = key or no descendant
15   IF no descendant THEN PRINT "Element not found"
```

14

COMPUTER OPERATING SYSTEMS

THE PURPOSE OF AN OPERATING SYSTEM

JOB CONTROL LANGUAGES

SYSTEMS UTILITIES

PROGRAMMER UTILITIES

THE BBC MICROCOMPUTER DISC FILING SYSTEM

THE CP/M OPERATING SYSTEM

THE MS DOS OPERATING SYSTEM ON 16-BIT MICROCOMPUTERS

MULTI-USER SYSTEMS

MULTI-PROGRAMMING SYSTEMS

GETTING STARTED

We have already studied high-level programming languages in Chapter 8 and introduced low-level languages in Chapter 12. The next two chapters are concerned with other forms of software. Software consists of all the programs available to the computer and can be considered in two major categories:

i) Systems software
ii) Applications software

Chapter 15 will be concerned with **applications software** which includes all of the programs available for use within the installation, both the one-off programs written to carry out specific tasks, and major applications written in the organisation as well as all the applications packages purchased for use either for mainframe computers or for microcomputers.

This chapter is concerned with systems software, dealing in the main with the routines associated with the operating system designed for the management of the hardware resources and the organisation of the data contained in file storage. The two main roles of this software can be defined as support for the operators and support for the programmers.

ESSENTIAL PRINCIPLES

THE PURPOSE OF
AN OPERATING
SYSTEM

It would be virtually impossible to use any computer for more than the most basic of tasks without some form of operating system. The functions of an operating system can be considered by analogy with a business or, perhaps a school. If we take the school as an example, the teachers are equivalent to the applications programs and the pupils would be the data, and the operating system corresponds to the support staff, both the administrative staff in the school office, the laboratory technicians, the cleaners, caretakers, school meals service, etc. and all those staff whose job it is to make sure that the teachers are able to get down to their main function of teaching in the school and to create an environment where they can do the best of their ability. The operating system similarly supplies the 'administrative support' to the applications programs and, in particular, will carry out the following functions:

- **Job scheduling:** By which the various programs or jobs to be carried out by the computer are selected from the relevant device, loaded into the memory and executed.

- **Multi-programming:** Which is the organisation of the processor to load more than one program at a time within the memory and, by switching from one to the other, to allow more than one program to be executed simultaneously.

- **Command interpreter:** Functions which take instructions from the operator, the programmer or from within the program, interprets the commands and executes the same. The commands may be formed from statements in a special language called the Job Control Language or **JCL**.

- **Input/output:** Routines which comprise the actual machine code routines to carry out the reading and writing from peripherals. These are written in the most efficient manner possible and made available as subroutines which can be called direct from the assembly language programs and are incorporated in object code by high-level language compilers.

Functions of the operating system

- **File handling:** Routines which go a little further than the input and output routines and organise the files on the backing store thus allowing the programmer to refer to a file by name and delegate to the operating system the task of opening, closing, reading and writing.

- **Error detection** and recording during all the operations of input, output and file control.

- **Job recording:** With the logging of each job on the system in a special journal file which can record the time the job is on the system, i.e. elapsed time, the processor time used, the number of peripheral transfers, the number of input characters, the number of lines of output and the number of errors. This file can be used as a basis for statistical analysis and for the costing and charging out of resources used.

- **Language support:** To provide the facilities necesary to support the development and testing of programs in the various languages. This may well be considered to include the assemblers and compilers themselves as well as the link and loader programs to assist the development and testing of programs.

- **Systems utilities** are a group of systems software products designed to carry out specific tasks, typically file manipulation, to assist programmers and operators.

JOB CONTROL
LANGUAGES

We need to have some means of communicating commands to the operating system to enable us to run any program on a computer and to specify the requirements of any processing task. In the early, punched card-orientated systems, this was implemented by preparing special control cards which preceded and separated the various batch processing jobs. These control statements were written in a very simple language which, with the more complex operating systems in use today, has truly developed into a language in its own right, known as the job control language. As the complexity of operating systems increases so the languages have increased in their sophistication and have all the three constructs of sequence, selection and iteration as well as implementing 'subroutines' by the use of **macros**.

Before looking in detail at some examples of operating systems it will be rewarding to study some of the operations which fall under the heading of **utilities** to identify some of the tasks which can be carried out by the operating system.

SYSTEMS UTILITIES

This is a collection of software tools designed to carry out certain functions for which, otherwise, programs would have to be written. They may be divided into two classes.

1) Utilities principally for the operator
2) Utilities for the programmer

The actual utilities will vary from machine to machine, or more exactly from operating system to operating system, but the examples quoted here are common to a number of operating systems.

OPERATIONS UTILITIES

Operations utilities, though being programs or routines provided to undertake tasks required by the operators, are often used by the programmer as well. In fact, when using microcomputers, most of these utilities will be used direct by the programmer since the programmer is operator as well. Examples:

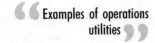
Examples of operations utilities

- **File dumps** are programs which tabulate the contents of files to give the programmer the chance to examine the contents of input and output files whilst a program is being tested.

- **System back-ups** or archiving, which are more comprehensive file dumps where the files are 'dumped' to another medium for security so that the system can be 'restored' subsequently after a failure.

- **File reorganisation**, for example when an indexed file is detected (by the operating system) as making excessive use of overflow areas there is the possibility of using a utility to re-organise the file with new indexes created.

- **System maps** to tabulate the sectors on the disc files, for example, where files and programs are stored.

- **Disc formatting** where each disc or disc cartridge, before it is used for storing data, must be initialised by labelling the disc sectors and initialising the directory.

- **Disc maintenance** which may be required when a disc has been in use for a while, particularly if a great deal of file creation and deletion has taken place, or if many files have been extended. This utility will re-organise the files to 'tidy up' the disc and make access more efficient.

- **Spooling** software which allows input and output to be carried out simultaneously with processing.

PROGRAMMER UTILITIES

Programmer Utilities are provided to assist the programmer in the writing, development and testing of source programs. Typical examples:

- **Dynamic file dumps** are similar to the file dumps mentioned as one of the operating utilities but when used in program development they can be used in the testing of a program by specifying that at certain points during the execution of a program a chosen file is to be 'dumped', i.e. tabulated in a particular format, on the screen or to a printer.

- **Memory dumps** (or snapshot dumps) give a tabulation of a required section of memory which may be presented in alphabetic format, in octal, hexadecimal or in some cases as disassembled assembly code. A common form of dump is the **post-mortem** dump, automatically produced at an abnormal end of the program.

- **Trace prints** are a little more specific than dumps since they display the values stored by the variables within the program similar to the 'debug' prints which might be inserted by the programmer. Some systems have the ability to switch a trace on and off at will to print a reference to the line number of the program and, in some cases, the result of the arithmetic operation carried out on that line.

Examples of programmer utilities

■ **Test data generators** can be used when testing a program, to provide input and files containing data to test the logic. This utility is particularly useful in testing subroutines or modules since it allows small sections of programs to be tested independently. In some systems, the term *test bed* is used to describe a combined facility of test generator, trace and dump.

■ **Sort and merge programs** meet the common requirement to sort a file in a prescribed sequence or to merge together two sorted files. The techniques of coding such programs have been refined to such an extent that the utilites are far more efficient than any program which could be produced by an applications programmer.

■ **Disc catalogue commands** are available to the programmer to tabulate the names of the files stored on a disc and normally have options which will show the size of each file and which sectors they occupy on the disc.

■ **Editors** are programs which allow source programs to be entered and amended by the programmer. Many editors have additional facilities which provide many of the features of word processors.

■ **Help files** provide a most useful feature on many computers, particularly the large mainframes to allow the programmer to type the command"HELP"or press a special key to obtain a display on the terminal of sections of the manual. Further facilities allow requests for help on specified topics, e.g. HELP SORT would result in the display of text describing the use of the sort utility.

THE BBC MICROCOMPUTER DISC FILING SYSTEM

The *Disc Filing System* (DFS) implemented on the BBC Microcomputer has among its commands:

*CAT	to obtain a catalogue of files
*RENAME	to change the name of a file
*DELETE	to delete a file
*COPY	to copy files from one disc to another
*BACKUP	to copy a complete disc to another
*INFO	to give characteristics of the files

This operating system is worth study not only because of its popularity in schools and colleges, but also because of its simplicity. This operating system uses the first two sectors of track zero of each disc to store the index of files, each of these sectors contains 256 bytes divided into thirty-two groups of eight bytes. The first eight bytes on each of these sectors store the displayed title of the disc and other data including the number of write operations, the number of files and also the number of sectors on the disc, the remaining thirty-one pairs of eight bytes refer to the maximum of thirty-one files which can be stored on a disc using this operating system. For each file, the eight bytes on the first sector store the seven character file name and the directory reference letter, the eight bytes on the second sector store four numbers which can be displayed in hexadecimal by the *INFO command. These four numbers are:

the sector number where the file starts
the length of the file in bytes
    and where relevant, i.e. for object programs
the address in memory to which the program is loaded
the address in memory where execution would start

This operating system may group the files in coherent sets by using the command *DIR to assign a file to a 'directory' identified by a single letter. This allows programs to be identified as distinct from documents and source programs.

This operating system is peculiar in that it is only used on the BBC microcomputer, and in some versions of the Acorn Electron, and its file index and storage is very simple. Files are stored in consecutive sectors, whereas most other operating systems allow files to be split and use any available sectors, thus the 'disc full' error message may occur when there is sufficient space for the file but not in consecutive sectors. In this case it is familiar to users that a *COMPACT operation on the disc will cause the files to be re-arranged on the disc so that all the unused space is in one section at the 'top end' of the disc.

THE CP/M OPERATING SYSTEM

CP/M was developed very early on in the evolution of computers and dates from 1975, two years after the development of the Intel 8080 microprocessor. It became the standard operating system used on 8-bit microcomputers based on the Intel 8080, Intel 8085 and Zilog Z80 microprocessors. Apart from its simplicity of use, one of the main reasons for its universal adoption, and this is a justification for the ideas of structured programming design introduced in Chapter 7, is that the machine dependent features are collected together in a single module, called the BIOS which is well and comprehensively defined so that it is quite straightforward to implement the operating system on a variety of computer systems. It was the operating system used on the RML 380Z and 480Z microcomputers.

Examples of commands in this system are:

ERA to erase files
DIR to give a directory or catalogue of the files
REN to rename files
TYPE to type the text contained in a file

The system also supplies a number of utility programs, including:

STAT to give the status of the files on the disc
PIP to transfer files from one disc to another
ED a simple text editor
ASM an assembler

This became so much of a standard operating system that it was adopted on some of the early 16-bit microcomputers.

THE MS DOS OPERATING SYSTEM ON 16-BIT MICROCOMPUTERS

This is the operating system used on the so-called IBM-compatible 16-bit microcomputers and is, to all intents and purposes, compatible with the operating system PCDOS used by IBM on their microcomputers. Many of its commands are similar to those in CP/M but it introduces one most vital extension, there is a command MKDIR, abbreviated to MD which allows a sub-directory to be created from a current directory. This allows the files to be catalogued in structured subsets of a manageable size, thus each directory when catalogued may contain named files and named sub-directories. The tree structure is illustrated in Fig. 14.1 from which the following path may be extracted. Starting from the top directory, called the **root directory**, there is a sub-directory called PROGS which in turn has a sub-directory called BASIC with a further sub-directory called MATHS which contains the file GEOM.BAS which illustrates the format of program names as a name followed by a three character extension. This program is identified on the system as:

\PROGS\BASIC\MATHS\GEOM.BAS

This type of tree structure is essential for any computer which can store more than a couple of dozen files on a single device, and with the advent of the Winchester hard disc on microcomputers costing under £1,000 means, effectively, every future disc-based microcomputer and every minicomputer and mainframe system.

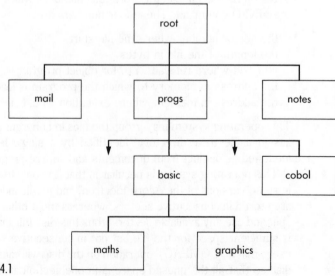

Fig. 14.1

MULTI-USER SYSTEMS

It is a characteristic of almost every mainframe computer, most minicomputers and a number of microcomputers that hardware resources are to be shared by a number of users simultaneously. The shared resource may be one or more of the following:

- A high capacity file store
- An expensive peripheral, such as a laser printer or a digital plotter
- Files, this is where it is the access to a database or a library of files which is essential and even if the cost of duplicating the hardware is not prohibitive it may not be feasible or efficient to duplicate the files
- Where remote access from a small terminal, possibly a portable computer is desired

There are three main methods of implementing such multi-access systems:

" Methods of implementing multi-access systems "

1 By the use of a so-called **dumb-terminal** such as a VDU which simply allows input from its keyboard and output from the computer to be displayed on the screen. All processing is done by using the processor of the computer to which the terminal is connected.
2 By use of a **network** of individual computers, usually microcomputers connected by a line to a special computer called the network controller which may have peripherals, almost certainly a large disc file store, which may be accessed by any computer on the network (see Fig. 14.2). All processing is done using the processor of the microcomputers.
3 The use of **intelligent terminals**, usually microcomputers, as terminals to a mainframe system where the major part of the processing will be carried out on the mainframe computer, but there is the potential on the terminal for additional processing and local printing and storage of files.

All these are heavily dependent on powerful operating systems, all require users to identify themselves by logging codes and passwords so that files can be maintained in security from other users and access can be restricted to authorised users. This is particularly important when access is from remote locations using, for example, the public telephone network.

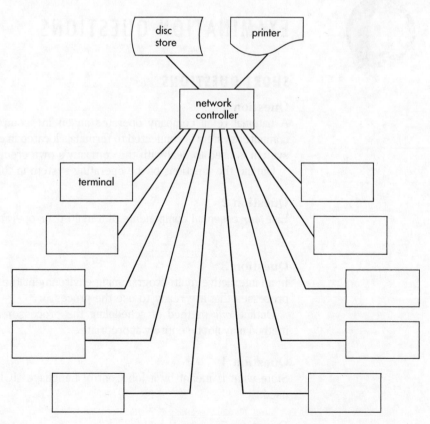

Fig.14.2

MULTI-PROGRAMMING SYSTEMS

A number of applications, including multi-access, require that more than one program can be resident within the memory of the computer at the same time. This requires a special type of operating system called a multi-programming operating system or **multi-programming executive**, which carries out the following functions:

- Control of access to the system.
- Division of the memory into compartments of relevant size for the various programs.
- The scheduling of job starts.
- The loading and swapping of the various jobs to be executed.
- The sharing of the processor resource, either by a time-slice system where each program in turn is given a small time unit of the central processor on a round-robin basis or on some priority system to determine which program is to be executing at a given instant of time.
- The handling of interrupts so that the operating system can respond to remote enquiries and determine priorities based on available peripherals.
- The allocation of memory space, file space, and output volumes either for accounting or for budgeting resources between user.
- The transmission of messages to operators and processing of commands entered by the operators.
- The maintenance of records of access and resource usage, both for security and for accounting.

> ❝ Functions of multi-programming executive ❞

Multiprocessor systems

It is worthwhile considering a further aspect of resource sharing in sharing processors where two or more central processors are linked together to share the processing tasks. A common and simple example is the use of a computer as an interface between the users and the mainframe computer to handle all the communications. Such a computer is called a **front-end processor**. Another implementation is for processors to provide backup for one another when continuous processing is required.

EXAMINATION QUESTIONS

SHORT QUESTIONS

Question 1
A national retail company operates an on-line computer system in which a mainframe computer system is connected to terminals located in each of the company's branches. The system is used to deal with the company's own credit cards.

Outline the functions of the operating system in this application. (London AS 1989)

Question 2
List *four* essential components of a multi-user operating system.

(Northern Ireland 1989)

Question 3
In an interactive multi-programming environment the operating system maintains a list of processes that are ready to use the processor.

Outline *one* method of scheduling the processor and describe a situation when this method may not be entirely appropriate. (London 1989)

Question 4
State what is meant by a Job Control Language (JCL) and two purposes for which it is used. (AEB 1989)

Question 5
Many implementations of BASIC on microcomputer systems allow the use of PEEK and POKE statements to examine or replace the contents of absolute addresses in memory.

Why should such statements not be provided for users of multi-access time sharing systems on mainframe computers? (Northern Ireland 1988)

Question 6
Disc directories record information about files that are stored on disc. Name *five* items of information that could be stored in the disc directory of a file. **(NEAB 1988)**

Question 7
Why is it necessary for the manufacturers of computers to supply a disc operating system such as DFS or MSDOS along with the hardware? (Northern Ireland 1988)

Question 8

a) Distinguish between a *batch processing system* and a *multi-user on-line system*. Identify those additional features required in a multi-user on-line system that are not needed in a batch processing system. Give *one* example of a realistic use of *each* system.

b) What is meant by a *distributed computer system*? Why might an educational establishment consider purchasing a distributed system in preference to other types of computer system? (Welsh AS 1989)

LONGER QUESTIONS

Question 9

a) A floppy disc unit connected to a single user microcomputer system is used for the permanent storage of programs and data. What facilities would you expect the operating system of the computer to provide to enable the users to maintain their disc files?

b) A large multi-access computer system provides on-line disc storage for programs and data. What precautions should be taken to protect users' files in the event of either hardware and software malfunction which results in the accidental destruction of some or all the disc files? Describe how the filing system could be reconstructed if such a malfunction did occur. (Cambridge 1983)

Question 10
Multi-programming operating systems permit tasks to be run concurrently.

a) Explain what is meant by this statement.
b) Describe *three* different functions performed by an operating system.
c) With the aid of an example, explain why it may be advantageous to have priorities associated with tasks in order to improve utilisation of the hardware. (AEB 1984)

Question 11
A mainframe computer with magnetic disc and tape backing storage, one printer, and a number of interactive terminals, runs a multi-access operating system. A microcomputer for one user has a floppy disc drive and a printer.

a) Describe what problems the operating system of the mainframe computer has that do not occur in the operating system of the microcomputer. Your answer should make specific reference to running programs, printing files, storing and retrieving files, and accepting commands from a user terminal.

b) Suggest some tasks that, in spite of these difficulties, the mainframe computer can do better than the microcomputer. Give reasons for your answer. (Cambridge 1985)

Question 12

a) Give *two* different reasons why a large computing system could need to check the identity of a user before allowing access to its facilities. Explain how the user could identify himself and how the system could check his identity.

b) Why is it usual to allocate resource limits to users of a large computing system? How can a system keep records of the use of resources controlled by such limits? What should be done if limits are exceeded? (Oxford 1984)

OUTLINE ANSWERS

SHORT QUESTIONS

Question 1

A national retail company operating an on-line computer system with terminals located in each of its branches will need a multiprogramming operating system to carry functions which include:

   i) control of access to the system by branch code and password;
   ii) shared access to applications programs;
   iii) the allocation of memory space, file space, and output volumes between users;
   iv) the maintenance of records of access and resource usage, both for security and for accounting.

Question 2

Among the essential components of a multi-user operating system are:

- control of access to the system;
- division of the memory into compartments of relevant size for the various programs;
- the scheduling of job starts;
- the loading and swapping of the various jobs to be executed;
- the sharing of the processor resource;
- the allocation of memory space, file space, and output volumes;
- the maintenance of records of access and resource usage.

Question 3

One method of scheduling the processor in an interactive multiprogramming environment is on a FIFO (first in first out) basis using a queue. This method may not be entirely appropriate when a large job may monopolise the machine and hold up every other, it is for this reason that a 'time-slice' round robin system is often employed. Queues have to be used for peripherals such as printers where users will be familiar with the situation of a long print job delaying every other document.

Question 4

Job Control Languages provide a means of communicating commands to the operating system to enable the user to run any program on a computer and to specify the requirements of any processing task. Two examples are the commands given by a programmer, for example to compile, link and run a Pascal program, and the commands given by an operator with system manager status to set up a new user with an access code and password.

Question 5

Implementations of BASIC on microcomputer systems can use PEEK and POKE statements to examine and replace the contents of absolute addresses in memory, this will not be provided for users of multi-access time sharing systems on mainframe computers since PEEK could be used to search memory for data intended to be secure to another user, such as the password or data being processed by the program, and POKE could corrupt the workspace of another user, or even the operating system.

Question 6

Information about a file that is stored on disc directory includes:

- file name;
- file size;
- location on the disc;
- protection, i.e. is writing to the file disabled;
- date created;
- date last amended;

and in a multi-access system

- owner;
- access allowed by other users;
- date last dumped.

Question 7

It is necessary for the manufacturers of computers to supply, in addition to the hardware, a disc operating system such as DFS or MSDOS, because otherwise every program would have to be allocated and maintain, informally, its own area of disc and the programmer would have to remember where on disc each program was stored and write a small 'loader' to run even a simple program.

It is worth noting that two of the best known operating systems CP/M for 8-bit micros and UNIX for multi-access systems were originally written by programmers given experimental or development hardware who wrote the original versions of the operating systems simply to allow program development to proceed.

Question 8

a) In a *batch processing system* input data is accumulated in a transaction file and then run through the system simultaneously as a single batch. In a *multi-user on-line system* the transactions are processed individually as they arise; this is often referred to as *demand processing*. Batch processing uses serial access to files whilst demand processing with a multi-user on-line system uses direct access and so requires some form of disc store and a multi-user operating system.

Payroll is a typical batch processing application and a cash-point terminal is a typical multi-user on-line system.

b) In a *distributed computer system*, some of the hardware resources available to the users are shared by all the users and is linked to the users by some form of network. The shared resource may be one or more of the following:
i)   a high capacity file store
ii) an expensive peripheral, such as a laser printer or a digital plotter
iii) a powerful processor.

An educational establishment consider purchasing a distributed system to allow students to work from terminals or microcomputer workstations and share a single printer or to load programs or data from a shared file store. In a University, the students will use on-line terminals connected to a powerful mainframe processor.

LONGER QUESTIONS

Question 9

a) The principal facilities expected of an operating system of a single user microcomputer with a floppy disc unit for the permanent storage of programs and data that would enable users to maintain their disc files are:
1 There must be, within the programming languages, statements or functions to implement:
a) Opening of files
b) Closing of files
c) Reading from a file
d) Writing to a file
2 A CATalogue command to list the files on a disc. This is implemented at CAT on the BBC microcomputer and DIR on CP/M computers.
3 A COPY command to copy files from disc to disc, PIP in CP/M.
4 A BACKUP facility for copying a complete disc.
5 A DELETE command for deleting files, ERA in CP/M.
6 A command to log into different discs or sides of discs.
7 The ability to "type" or display the contents of a file.
8 Command to "run" machine code programs.
9 The facility to execute a batch of commands from a disc file.

b) The principal precaution to take to protect users' files in the event of either hardware or software malfunction resulting in the accidental destruction of some or all of the disc files in a large multi-access computer system with on-line disc storage for programs and data, is to back-up or archive the complete disc store at regular intervals. Therefore if such a malfunction did occur, the back-up copy could be used to re-create the file in its form at the time of the archive. There is one other requirement in reconstructing the filing system after such a malfunction has occurred, namely that *changes* must not be lost. In the case of an on-line booking system these might be transactions, or in the case of electronic mail might be important messages. Therefore, a further dump, or *journal* of all transactions must be maintained. This can be run against an archived master to reconstitute the file in its exact form at the time of the malfunction.

Question 10

a) The concurrent running of tasks by a multi-programming operating system refers to the ability to hold two or more programs in memory in independent *partitions*, while appearing to run the tasks simultaneously by switching control rapidly between the various jobs. Typically, a job will be run for a fixed unit of time, called a time-slice, or until a peripheral transfer is required, then the operating system moves on to another. The users will, in many cases, as with the TTNS system, have the impression that they are the sole users of the system. In cases where there are a large number of users all making heavy uses of the resource, or where one user is running a memory-intensive task, like CAD, response to all users becomes slower and slower.

b) Three of the functions performed by an operating system are:
   1 Job handling; the transition from one job to another
   2 Peripheral transfers
   3 Usage recording and error detection

c) It may be advantageous to have priorities associated with tasks in a multi-programming operating system to speed up the overall resource usage and response time. For example, it might be pertinent to give a higher priority to tasks using the slowest peripherals. The latter because the time required between peripheral transfers may be long in relation to the actual processing required.

Question 11

a) In running programs, the operating system of the mainframe computer will load programs from the main backing store into a partition of memory assigned to that task. It will then run the program simultaneously with the other tasks in memory.

   In printing files, and to make use of a shared lineprinter, the output will be directed to a disc file called a *spool file*. When complete, the output will be inserted in a queue for printing as one of the multi-programming tasks.

   As regards storing and retrieving files, the files will be stored in the users' private file area or in some global access area. The operating system will have to determine whether the user has sufficient privilege to read or write to the particular file.

   Accepting commands from a user at a terminal has rather different problems that do not occur in the operating system of the microcomputer. This is because there may be a large number of different users typing commands simultaneously and the operating system will have to accept one key at a time from each keyboard and process the command when a "return key" is detected.

b) In spite of these difficulties, the mainframe computer is better than the microcomputer for the following tasks, among others:
   - Queries to a large database by a large number of users, since the use of microcomputers would require duplication of the file for each computer
   - Any application which needs some expensive shared resource, such as microfilm output or graph plotting.

Question 12

a)   The two reasons why a large computing system needs to check the identity of a user before allowing access to its facilities are:

1 To maintain a log of access to the system for the purpose of charging for the resources used

2 To ensure that the user is entitled to access the system or the required programs and files

The user will normally provide two codes for identity; firstly, a *logging code* to provide a basis for the charging, and secondly, a *password* to validate the entitlement to access. Normally the logging codes may conform to a pattern and be widely known by users, perhaps even publicised and used as mailbox addresses. However, the password will be known only to the user, kept with security and changed regularly.

The system can check the identity of a user by checking the password against a table of users' passwords assigned to logging codes contained on the backing store of the computer.

b)   It is usual to allocate resource limits to users of a large computing system, i.e. to impose some budget on the individual users to make sure that, in a remote access situation, one group of users is not able to take an unfair share of the computer time or disc store. In many systems each user has a rigid limit on the amount of disc file store available, and in a number of colleges, for example, students are given an allocation of terminal access time to make sure that one group do not overuse the system to the detriment of others.

The system will maintain records of resources used by recording usage on a journal file against the validated access code provided when logging into the system.

If an attempt is made to exceed the disc storage limit, the user will be prevented from saving the current data to disc, similar to the refusal to save when a floppy disc is full, but will have the opportunity to delete files from the disc before proceeding. If there is a limit on access time, there will be a warning when the limit is close to being exceeded. The operating system may either terminate the session when the limit is reached or, more sensibly, allow the session to continue but simply refuse any subsequent access until the system controller allocates an additional allocation of time.

COMPUTER APPLICATIONS AND PACKAGED SOFTWARE

APPLICATIONS PACKAGES

STANDARD MICROCOMPUTER APPLICATIONS

PURCHASE OF PACKAGED SOFTWARE

PRIVACY AND SECURITY

GETTING STARTED

Chapter 14 introduced the idea of applications software which, during the 1980s was a major growth area in computing. There was a long time when it was felt that companies needed to develop their own packages, even if using standard applications, with a belief that each company had unique problems. Modern thinking is that application packages should be used wherever possible and "in-house" programming carried out only as a last resort. This has coincided with great improvements in the standards of programming, documentation and adaptability of programs.

The advantages of implementing an application package compared with the development of a set of programs within the user's own data processing department were outlined in Chapter 3 as:

- No need to employ a programmer or use a programmer's time
- The program is ready immediately
- The programmers of the package may possess more expertise
- It may be possible to get help from other users

Among the disadvantages of application packages are:

- The programs may be too general and not exactly what is required by the business
- It is difficult to evaluate a program package without extended trials
- The programs may not be able to adapt to the growth of the company

These points will be expanded in this chapter and, in addition, students should be familiar with one program in each of the following categories or with a package which combines all three:

- Word processing
- Information retrieval
- Spreadsheets
- Graphical display of data
- Communications

These have become the standard packages used on all business microcomputers.

ESSENTIAL PRINCIPLES

An application package is a complete working system with programs, documentation and systems design to implement an application, usually a business application, or to provide the means for a user to create programs or models. It has the advantage of immediate availability for use and in many cases has been tested by use in other companies. It is convenient to consider applications under a number of headings:

Types of applications

- **Standard applications**, such as a payroll or accounting which have been generalised to become usable by a large number of different organisations
- **General programs**, such as a database package, which allow a user to develop special applications without needing to write programs
- Programs written within an organisation to meet their special requirements

In practice the last category is not considered to be an application package, the term being restricted to programs purchased from outside of the organisation rather than written within. It is normally expected that, in addition to the programs, the package will contain full documentation, a training guide and sample documents.

Program packages

Packages were often unpopular for mini- and mainframe computers, with companies preferring to develop their own systems, but the proliferation of microcomputers has made a much wider market available for these products. The price of such software may vary from £10 for a simple business program for a micro to £3,000 or more for a complex mainframe system. Some important points to note in considering application packages are:

- Quality is not always proportional to price
- If the source code itself is purchased, a company can make its own local amendments starting from a working system
- It is important for prospective purchasers to demand a demonstration of the package before purchase.

Turnkey systems

A **turnkey system** is an extension of the software package where the vendor provides the user with a complete package including hardware and software. The name is derived from the idea that all the user has to do is to 'turn the key' to start, the system will then be automatically loaded with a series of menu programs or programs giving instructions to the user who need not know anything about the operating system of the computer. This idea can be imitated on the BBC microcomputer by the use of the 'shift-break' technique of loading programs when a disc can be configured so that when a user puts it into a disc drive, holds down the shift key and then presses and releases the break key then the computer will execute a sequence of commands held in a file saved with the name !BOOT, one of these commands could be an instruction to load and run a menu program. The MSDOS operating system, and the IBM PCDOS systems use a similar technique, where simply switching on the computer causes the operating system to execute the sequence of commands stored in a file called AUTOEXEC.BAT.

There are five application packages which are becoming accepted as a set which are often provided as standard with a business microcomputer:

- Word processing
- Information retrieval
- Spreadsheets
- Graphical display of data
- Communications software

Word processing

Word processing is the use of computer technology for the entry, editing, storage, formatting and display of text. In its simplest form it imitates the role of a typewriter with text being entered from a keyboard, held in the memory of the computer or on the backing store before being printed.

The common word processing systems found in schools and colleges are, for the BBC microcomhuter, View, Wordwise and Edword, with View being provided as a standard feature in the BBC Master range of computers. On the RML 380Z computers, the most popular example is Wordstar, which is probably the most widely used microcomputer-based word processor in the world. Another popular example is the Amstrad PCW256 and PCW512 computers which are delivered with an excellent word processor, Locoscript, as part of the software included in the price of the computer. On 16-bit micros typical packages are Microsoft Word, Word Perfect and Displaywrite.

There is another type of word processor provided with many of the editing facilities known as a **text editor**. A text editor is normally provided as part of the operating system of a mainframe computer or minicomputer to allow, in particular, the entry and editing of the source programs for high-level languages, in the absence of a word processor it may be used to prepare documents. In microcomputer systems the compilers normally have a 'built in' text editor, the screen editor on the BBC microcomputer used for programming in Basic is a good example, as is the editor built into the Acorn Pascal system, though programs in both languages can be prepared using one of the word processing packages. Some editors, like TXED on the RML computers have additional features normally associated with word processors, which are mainly concerned with the formatting and presentation of text; for example, allowing a fixed line length and implementation of features such as centred text, underlining of sections of the text and putting standard headers and footers, including the numbering of pages.

At the other end of the spectrum are **desktop publishing** systems which not only provide additional word processing facilities in columnar output and multiple print fonts but also have graphics handling features for cutting and pasting pictures, graphs and charts. These are often used with laser printers or with high quality dot matrix or ink-jet printers. Examples of these packages are AMX Page Maker, Fleet Street Editor, Ventura and Pagemaker.

Information retrieval

There are many applications which involve the creation of a number of records to a fixed format for storage in a simple serial file. The file is then used for the retrieval of records and the processing of requests to tabulate sets of records. A common example used in many schools and colleges is to set up a file with a record for each student in one year of a course. Each record will contain a field or fields which give details of the subjects studied and the file can then be interrogated to provide class lists which can be sorted into alphabetical sequence.

The packages commonly used in schools and colleges include Inter-base, Quest and Betabase on the BBC microcomputer and Cardbox, DBaseIII and DBaseIV on 16-bit microcomputers. One application in a business environment could be the setup and maintenance of a file of all items of equipment and all vehicles, together with serial numbers, location and maintenance dates. A second, very common, example is the maintenance of a file of customers and potential customers giving names, addresses and interests and using an information retrieval package to identify those likely to be interested in a new product. For a specific example, the clients of an estate agent to be notified when a new property comes on the market; these names and addresses can, with many application packages be merged into a standard letter or used to print adhesive address labels.

Many of the examples on small microcomputers, though often described as disc versions, simply read the complete file into memory and process all the records in memory, thus limiting the file size though giving fast access to the records and when the processing is complete the file is then saved back to the disc. Many such programs have the name **database** in the title or in the program description but this ought to be considered a misuse of the word because, as stated earlier, the word database ought to be reserved for a large file-orientated system often with many linked subfiles referred to from other files.

Spreadsheets

A spreadsheet program is an application developed for microcomputers, with the first popular example being Visicalc which ran on the Apple II, the Tandy TRS80 and Commodore PET computers. It gives the user a large array, called the sheet, of cells in

File Edit Formula Format Data Options Macro Window

F11 | =SUM(F6:F9)

Worksheet1

	A	B	C	D	E	F
1			Sample Spreadsheet			
2						
3	Item	Price	Opening	Closing	Sales	Value
4			Balance	Balance	Units	
5						
6	Pens	1.15	154	73	81	93.15
7	Pencils	0.17	295	126	169	28.73
8	Rulers	0.36	56	31	25	9.00
9	Notepads	1.75	367	191	176	308.00
10						
11	Total					438.88
12						
13						
14						
15						
16						
17						
18						
19						

rows, usually labelled with numbers, and columns, labelled with letters. The best-selling package Lotus 1-2-3 allows 8,192 rows and 256 columns with each cell able to contain either text in the form of labels, numbers, or a formula.

Fig. 15.1 shows a simple sheet of the form created on the program Viewsheet. Column A contains labels, the figures in columns B, C and D are simply entered as numbers, but the cell E6, for example, contains a formula which computes the units sold from the stock balance, F6 has a formula for the value of sales whilst F11 has a formula to add all the value in the column. Typing in a new value in cell D6 will result in the contents of these last three cells being recalculated automatically.

Examples of spreadsheet programs used in schools and colleges are, for the BBC microcomputer, Viewsheet, which is a standard package on the Master series, Ultracalc and Beebcalc; on the RML 380Z and 480Z and many other machines, Multiplan is used. Multiplan is also used on the 16-bit micros and other popular packages are Supercalc, Excel, Symphony and Lotus.

Spreadsheets are used in business for all manner of financial models as well as for standard accounting procedures and can also be applied readily to any type of statistical calculation. The index of this book was prepared with Supercalc, using its 'Arrange' facility.

Business graphics packages

Business graphics programs are often included as part of one of the other packages, with data extracted either from a spreadsheet or a database by a program which can produce bar charts, pie charts, graphs and other displays. The charts can be displayed in colour or black and white and can also be reproduced on an appropriate printer.

Spreadsheet programs on 16-bit microcomputers, such as Excel and Lotus 1-2-3, contain the graphs as standard features. One program popular in education is 'Mini-office' which contains all four of the programs, i.e. a word processor, a database, a spreadsheet and a graphics program, whilst another example for the BBC microcomputer is the program Beebplot. One of the most popular packages on 16-bit microcomputers is the Harvard Graphics package.

Communications software

The last of the software is communications software which allows a microcomputer to become an 'intelligent terminal', to enable it to be used to communicate with a remote computer, often to national electronic mail systems such as Telecom Gold or TTNS or to Viewdata systems like Prestel. This software will not only implement the access to the computer but is likely to have options to make copies of the transmitted data to a disc file for later off-line editing. Conversely data can be prepared off-line and then transmitted to the computer from disc. This is particularly appropriate where the computer access is expensive, either because of the telephone charges, or the system connect charge is high, as is often the case with commercial on-line database systems.

Implications of the use of the standard packages

Without doubt the flexibility of the standard program packages has enabled new or non-specialist users to use spreadsheet programs to create programs or models with a level of complexity which would take many years experience of programming to imitate. The same is true of the flexibility of 'database' programs which allow users to devise information retrieval systems to suit almost any requirement. Furthermore, the data created in both these packages can be fed into the graphics package or module to display a variety of graphs and charts. Having generated the required results it is often possible to 'spool' the output to a file which can then be processed, annotated and edited by the word processor for incorporation in reports and/or letters.

Commercial applications

In contrast to the program packages described in detail above, there are many applications which, though in many cases available for purchase as a package, are designed to implement one specific application. Examples are:

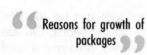
Packages implementing
one specific commercial
application

- A company payroll
- Inventory and stock control
- Order processing and invoice preparation
- Public utility billing: gas, water or electricity
- On-line medical records processing
- Seat reservation for theatres and sports events

Finally, there are other packages, such as computer aided design which, although aimed at a specific application area, can be applied to a broad range of problems.

Reasons for growth of use of packages

There are a number of reasons for the rapid expansion in the use and greater acceptance of the packages described in this chapter:

1 A gradual realisation that programming and program design is expensive and often unnecessary

Reasons for growth of packages

2 Improved standards and programming techniques used by software houses in the design of packaged programs
3 The increased sales of computers has greatly increased the number of users who are potential customers for program packages
4 The increased use of computers has created a new type of user in a small organisation who could not afford or would not consider employing programming staff
5 The increased potential sales has reduced the cost of packages
6 The bulk sales have made the production of quality documentation worthwhile
7 The specialised features of many microcomputer systems have made it difficult for users to reach the standards achieved by the software houses, with a growing number of applications being programmed in low-level languages

PURCHASE OF PACKAGED SOFTWARE

The following list of points should be closely considered in the purchase or selection of packaged software:

- **Don't believe the salesman**. Never trust the brochures which claim the package will run on *any* computer in a range, e.g. all CP/M machines or all IBM compatibles. See it demonstrated.

- **What is the program intended for?** For example, is it a home accounts package or a business application?

Points to bear in mind in selection of package

- **What are file capacities?** For example, how many accounts can be held, how many products can be held on the master file?

- **Can you understand the documentation?** If not, it is the fault of the package not the user.

- **Is is menu driven?** (In the case of interactive programs).

- **How well is the data validated?** Are mis-keyings readily detected?

- **Who else is using the program?** Is it popular and can the supplier offer assistance in the case of problems?

- **Will it be brought up to date?** (If there are subsequent changes in tax rates or legal requirements).

- **Is it compatible with other applications?** For example, can the data output from the program be accepted as input to other programs, e.g. in a word processor?

- **Read reviews.** Get an expert opinion of the package.

- **See a working version**, on a computer of identical configuration.

- **Consider other products** of the same company as to reputation, reliability and style.

- **Is it compatible with your printer?** Or are many features lost if not using the one specific model?

- **Are there on-line help screens?** Most high quality 16-bit microcomputer packages present the relevant parts of the manual on the screen for a single keystroke.

PRIVACY AND SECURITY

It is important, particularly since the passing, in 1984, of the Data Protection Act, to be aware of the distinction between privacy and security in relation to data and information.

Privacy is concerned with what information should be kept secret, and from whom.

Security is about how information can be kept secret.

It is a current social and business problem that whilst privacy is independent of computers, the evolution of computer systems has made the possible abuse of privacy a greater threat and though computers may reduce the risk of inaccuracy and may increase the potential control of data. The Data Protection Act seeks to give protection to individuals in respect of three specific danger areas identified in a Government White Paper as long ago as 1975 in response to a report known as the 'Younger Report' which had been published in 1972:

- The use of information which is inaccurate, incomplete or irrelevant

- The access to personal information by people who should not or need not have it

- The use of personal information in a context or for a purpose other than that for which it was collected, and in conjunction with other such data

In 1977, the Council of Europe made recommendations including the following:

- No personal data should be processed unless approved by local legislation or a data controller with legal backing

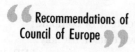
Recommendations of Council of Europe

- Individuals should have the right to access and correct records about themselves through data controllers. No exception could be made on the grounds of secrecy or confidentiality

- Data controllers should co-operate across international borders

- A standing committee should be set up, of members from each signatory nation to overcome the operation of proposals

There are many areas where individuals can have their privacy threatened, for example:

- Credit ratings
- Medical records
- School reports
- Bank statements
- Mailing lists

All of these are examples of computer systems which contain personal data designed for use in a particular context, information which may be damaging or misleading if used in a completely different application.

The Act deals specifically with computer-based information systems and many provisions do not apply if the information is stored, for example, on microfiche, where a $6'' \times 4''$ microfiche card can store 80,000,000 characters and the speed of access from a set of 150 is five seconds, so the speeds and volumes are comparable.

Although the Data Protection Act does not appear explicitly in the syllabus for all examinations, its social implications are so great that it is worth quoting in answers and may well be expected by examiners. An example of its effect, which is close to many students, is the maintenance of student records by teachers and lecturers which, though normal and worthwhile if carried out on a computer, needs to be registered with the Data Protection Registrar. Teachers taking such discs home to work on their own computers are breaking the terms of the Act. Furthermore, in colleges and schools where internally-marked exams have the results stored and processed on a computer – even if simply using a spreadsheet to ensure or help accuracy in the calculations – the figures must be available for inspection by the students who have, under the Act, a right to examine the data relating to themselves.

EXAMINATION QUESTIONS

SHORT QUESTIONS

Question 1
State an appropriate application for a database package in an Estate Agent's Office.
State *three* measures of performance on which to base this selection.

(London AS 1989)

Question 2
'Information stored in a typical computer system is more secure than information stored in a typical manual filing system'
Give *two* points in support of this statement and *two* points against. (AEB 1989)

Question 3
A micro-computer system is to be installed for use in a small office. The application to be run will include customer mailing, storage and processing of customer accounts and look-up of details for individual customers or customer groups.
List *three* hardware and *three* software components which you would expect the system to contain. (Northern Ireland 1989)

Question 4
Give *two* different applications where a spreadsheet package may prove useful.

(AEB 1989)

Question 5
What do you understand by the term 'user friendly' in the context of computer software? Give *three* examples of features which make software user friendly.

(AEB 1989)

Question 6
Word processors and desktop publishing systems are becoming widely used. List *three* drawbacks which have emerged with the use of these systems.

(Northern Ireland 1989)

LONGER QUESTIONS

Question 7
For *two* of the following applications discuss why and describe how a computer system would be used and describe the hardware and software that would be required:
   Computer aided design,
   Public utility billing,
   On-line medical records processing. (AEB 1984)

Question 8
Briefly describe *one* example of a computer application package to handle invoicing procedures. What are the principal benefits of such a package?
Name *three* possible categories of users of the above package. (Welsh 1983)

Question 9

Computer aided design, viewdata, (e.g. Prestel) and computer based type-setting are all examples of applications which involve the use of computer graphics.

a) For *two* of these applications describe:
   i) reasons why computers are used,
   ii) hardware which is a specific feature,
   iii) details of the function of the software,
   iv) the effects of using computers on the people who work in the applications described and on society in general.

b) Describe *two* differences in the graphics technology used in the two applications you have selected.
(AEB 1987)

Question 10

A newsagent has purchased a package of programs for his microcomputer system to assist him with the organisation of his daily newspaper deliveries. There are three files that have been set up on floppy discs to contain the following data:

Newsboy File containing the newsboy's and newsgirl's names and codes for their delivery rounds.

Customer File containing the customers' names, their street names and the newspapers they wish to receive.

Delivery Round File containing the numeric codes for the delivery rounds and the street names that make up each round. (No street appears in more than one round.)

File maintenance programs are provided to enable changes to be made including:

The addition, deletion or change of newsboy's or newsgirl's name and delivery round code in the Newsboy File.

The addition or deletion of the whole of a customer's details from the Customer File.

The change of newspapers delivered to a customer in the Customer File.

The addition or deletion of a street name from the Delivery Round File.

These maintenance programs and the main programs producing delivery lists are controlled from a master program through a menu.

a) Draw a system chart to represent the system.

b) Explain how you would carry out the testing of the whole of the newsagent's package to cover the following aspects:
   i) the robustness of the system;
   ii) the user friendliness of the system;
   iii) the correctness of the delivery lists produced.
(London 1985)

Question 11

a) Discuss briefly the developments in computing that have led to the widespread use of computers in homes, offices and factories.

   What developments are likely to occur in computer technology in the forseeable future? How will such developments change the way computers are used?

b) It has been suggested that people need protecting from computers. Why may this be so, and what safeguards could be introduced to bring it about?
(Cambridge 1985)

OUTLINE ANSWERS

SHORT QUESTIONS

Question 1

An Estate Agent would find it useful to maintain files of clients and properties for matching requirements either when a new client registers or when a property becomes available.

   Measures of performance which could be used to base this selection could be:

   file capacity

   speed of retrieval

   ease of use .

   applicability to non-expert users, i.e. office staff.

Question 2

Information stored in a typical computer system needs to be more secure than information stored in a typical manual filing system:

a) because of the legal requirements of the Data Protection Act 1984;
b) because unlike a burglar, a *hacker* might access files from a remote location, undetected.

As regards points against this statement it is difficult to know what was in the mind of the examiner. It could be argued that both should be equally secure since both could contain valuable data or sensitive personal data and no relaxation of security below the maximum possible can be tolerated.

Question 3

Hardware components expected in the system would be a processor, a number of VDU's, a disc store, a printer and communications equipment.

Software components would be a multi-access operating system, an accounting package, and a word processor with mailmerge facilities.

Question 4

A spreadsheet package may prove useful in preparing accounts and financial models, also in the analysis of statistical data, particularly if, like most packages on 16-bit computers there are extensive graphics facilities.

Question 5

User friendly is a common term in the context of computer software to indicate that it is designed to make the input and the dialogue sympathetic to the user, particularly the novice user. Many modern computer packages have developed this to such an extent that they can be run without reference to manuals.

Examples of features which make software user friendly are meaningful prompts for input, operation selections by menus and the implementation of help facilities.

Question 6

Drawbacks in the wide use of word processors and desktop publishing systems include:

i) ease of correction can lead to endless redrafting in the search of the perfect document and thus take much longer than traditional methods;
ii) ease of use has taken the document preparation away from those trained in this area, i.e. secretaries and printers, and so frequently there are lower standards of document presentation, spelling and grammar. This became apparent when the daily newspapers switched to new technology;
iii) when the same person creates, enters and transmits a document there are fewer built-in checks as to accuracy, style and interpretation.

LONGER QUESTIONS

Question 7

In dealing with a question such as this it is best to look at both the hardware and the software requirements under four subheadings:

Output   Input   Files   Procedures

For the purposes of this outline answer these four headings will be taken in turn but all three applications taken together. There are many other examples of applications which could be used in examination questions and so it is better to look at the general approach to such questions rather than concentrating on one or two specific examples.

Output

The output from a computer aided design program would be drawings and designs and so the hardware would be a plotter for the final drawings and a high resolution video display for development.

The public utility billing application will require a printer for the customer accounts and for the tabulations required by the company, and, because of the volumes of output, this will need to be a fast printer.

On-line medical records processing will need a VDU to display the response from an enquiry with a printer to give hardcopy as required.

Input

Computer aided design will need a lightpen or mouse for input as well as a keyboard for the entry of text and system commands.

Public utility billing will require some form of keyboard input, probably with a VDU attached and might well use a mark reader or optical character reader to speed the input of customer meter readings.

On-line medical records processing would require some form of on-line terminal to key in the input, perhaps in the future this might be supplemented by input from instruments recording patient details.

Files

Computer aided design will maintain files of drawings which, because of their high resolution, will require a high capacity storage direct access file storage device such as a hard disc.

Public utility billing will also need high capacity file storage because of the number of customers, but the file will almost certainly be maintained by serial access so that magnetic tape could be used. The file will contain records for each account storing the name, address, account details and possibly details of a number of past readings to assist in the computation of estimated readings if access to the meter is not obtained for a quarter.

On-line medical records processing will need some fast access direct access device, almost certainly magnetic disc, and will contain the name, reference number and address of the patient together with such details as the doctor may wish to record, this may well be in a free, variable length, format.

Procedures

Computer aided design is likely to use a purchased package because the generality of the requirements and the complexity of the program make it worthwhile for packages to be developed in this area.

Public utility billing is likely to be developed by the organisation and will need to receive customer meter readings, details of new customers and not only print the (quarterly) demands but maintain an accounting system to process payments, send reminders, final demands and eventually court summonses and lists of customers to be disconnected.

On-line medical records processing involves, essentially, a file maintenance and interrogation program.

Question 8

This is another example of the type of question described above on the description of computer applications. The output from an invoicing system will be printed accounts to be sent to customers demanding payments. This is often carried out with multiple sets, separated by carbon paper, providing the invoice, a delivery note to go with the goods, a packing note for the warehouse, an advice note to tell the customer that the goods are about to be despatched and various copies for filing within the company.

The input will be a customer reference number and details of the goods ordered, product number and quantity, which will be used in conjunction with at least three files, a stock file containing product details, one containing customers' names and addresses and one containing accounting information.

The procedures, in outline, will be that the input customer reference will be used to access the customer file to extract the name, address and possibly to check for credit, the product numbers will be used to access the stock file for the product description, price and availability. This data will be merged to provide the information for the invoice set and also to update the accounting files.

The principal benefits of such a package are likely to be

- a saving in clerical effort
- more accurate information
- invoices sent out more rapidly
- automatic provision for reminders for payment
- integration with other applications such as order processing, stock control and the general accounting system

The system could be used by a wide variety of businesses, for example, builders merchants, clothing manufacturers and book retailers.

Question 9

a) For the purposes of this answer we will look at all three systems.

Computers are used in computer aided design to assist in the creation of designs, both in the actual drawing and in the storage and retrieval of part drawings, also to store and plot finished designs. The drawings for an aircraft, for example, might require a vast storage area but could be stored on a disc.

i) Computers are used in viewdata systems such as Prestel to provide on-line interactive access for untrained users needing access to a large database.

Computers are used in computer based type-setting to allow easy conversion from the source text to printed document with a wide variety of fonts and styles.

ii) Hardware which is a specific feature for computer aided design is a mouse, a high resolution VDU and a plotter or laser printer.

Hardware which is a specific feature for viewdata systems is a viewdata terminal, a modem and a host database system.

Hardware which is a specific feature in computer based type-setting is a keyboard, a display screen and a high quality printer as well as an interface to the type-setting equipment.

iii) The software for computer aided design will support graphics handling, storage and retrieval.

The software for viewdata systems will support communications, handle teletext graphics as well as the storage and retrieval of frames.

The software in computer based type-setting will handle all aspects of text manipulation and display.

iv) The effects of using computers on the people who work in computer aided design and computer based type-setting will be to provide improved facilities and services. Society in general benefits from access to the databases maintained in viewdata systems.

b) The graphics technology used in computer aided design may be colour or monochrome but with extremely high resolution and with sophisticated graphics. For computer based type-setting it will require high quality text display in many different fonts and styles but is likely to be monochrome. For viewdata systems it will process eight colours, use block graphics and very basic text.

Question 10

a) One possible system chart representing the system is shown in Fig. 15.2.

b) Testing the robustness of the system needs to involve the shop staff operating the system in an extended trial without direct supervision to see if there is a good validation of data; protection against the input of wildly inaccurate data or a catastrophic failure caused by pressing a wrong key, such as the accidental pressing of the escape or break key.

The user friendliness of the system is again a test to be carried out by the shop staff who should be completely satisfied that the instructions displayed on the screen are adequate and intelligible.

The correctness of the delivery lists produced can be tested by a pilot run on one or two rounds with a check against the previous, manual preparation of the lists.

Question 11

a) Over the past few years the size of computer processors has halved each year and as they have become smaller and smaller and the number of chips required in a computer has become fewer and fewer, prices have reduced and then been further reduced by the volumes of sales in a rapidly increasing trend which shows no signs of losing pace. For example, in 1976 a minicomputer with less than 100K bytes of memory and 15mB of disc storage cost about £100,000, in 1979 the first microcomputers with about 16K memory and cassette storage cost about £800, but in 1986 it became possible to buy an Amstrad computer with 1mB memory, 20M disc storage plus a floppy disc drive for under £1,000. This advance speaks for itself.

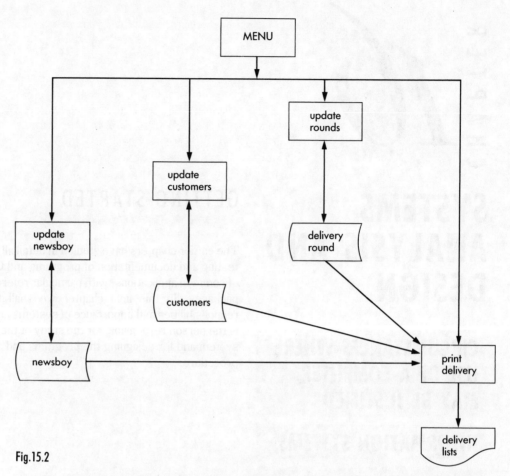

Fig.15.2

Developments likely to occur in computer technology in the forseeable future are hard to predict but laser technology as applied to videodiscs and compact discs when extended to media such as the credit card could mean that a vast amount of personal information could be carried around by individuals. The reduction in size is likely to replace the pocket calculator by a pocket computer and it is likely that college if not school students may purchase a computer along with other stationery and materials. At the same time the advent of home banking and information services like Prestel may change the way in which people handle their personal finances and use reference material in the full range from travel timetables to encyclopaedias.

b) The suggestion that people need protecting from computers has been taken up, in 1984, by the passing of the U.K. Data Protection Act. The dangers of the storage and processing of information on computers, which were identified before its implementation, included:

■ the use of information which is inaccurate, incomplete or irrelevant;
■ the access to personal information by people who should not or need not have it;
■ the use of personal information in a context or for a purpose other than that for which it was collected, and in conjunction with other such data.

16

SYSTEMS ANALYSIS AND DESIGN

CIRCUMSTANCES WHERE USE OF A COMPUTER MAY BE JUSTIFIED

INFORMATION SYSTEMS

SYSTEMS ANALYSIS AND ORGANISATION AND METHODS

THE STAGES OF SYSTEMS ANALYSIS

METHODS OF FACT-FINDING

REASONS FOR THE FAILURE OF COMPUTER SYSTEMS

GETTING STARTED

The earlier chapters have studied in detail all aspects of the development, testing and documentation of programs and Chapter 15 looked at a range of common applications, with particular reference to the use of application packages. In this final chapter we shall take a look at the duties, responsibilities and importance of systems analysts. The systems analyst is the person responsible for the study of the requirements of a computer system and for designing the programs and associated forms and clerical procedures.

ESSENTIAL PRINCIPLES

Before studying the job responsibilities of a systems analyst it is important to list the circumstances when it is likely to be fruitful to use a computer:

- When there are large volumes of data requiring repetitive processing
- For problems with logical or mathematical complexity
- In an area of work where a large clerical workforce is employed in repetitive tasks
- Where a job is not done because clerical costs exceed the savings
- Where large data files are maintained
- Where there is a need for improvement in the overall planning, direction and control of a specific area of activity in an organisation

CRITERIA FOR THE JUSTIFICATION OF COMPUTER SYSTEMS

Arising from the points listed above, we may list some criteria which may be used to justify the use of a computer:

Improvement of information

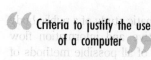

Criteria to justify the use of a computer

There may be an improvement in both the quantity and detail of the information provided, which may be more up-to-date, more accurate and allow cross-referencing between applications. For example, in a school, the data used in class lists may also be used in examination entries. In most cases, the improved services can be the greatest justification rather than direct cost savings.

Cost savings

The cost savings may be brought about by reductions in staff, by labour saving, by reduction of stock held if the re-order strategy is carried out more intelligently (a company spending £10,000 on a computer which results in £20,000 less stock being held in store has an extra £10,000 in the bank). Greater efficiency in project planning may save wages by a reduction in overtime working and also avoid failing to meet schedules and, in general improve operating efficiency.

New techniques

New technology may increase the potential for the use of specialised procedures and equipment, for example real-time reservation systems for theatres and sports events. It may also encourage the use of mathematical techniques in planning. These are known as operational research techniques. It may also lead to an integration of information systems so all the departments in an organisation have access to the same data which is more likely to be up-to-date.

Changing environment

It is often the stimulus of other changes within an organisation or its environment which provide a justification for the use of computers. Specific reasons may be the obsolescence of existing equipment, a rapid expansion of the company or its activities, the need for more information either because of poor performance or because of changes in legislation such as tax or the retirement law or loss of key staff who may be difficult or impossible to replace.

An information system may be defined as an organised set of people, procedures and equipment, designed to allow all levels of management of an organisation to gain better control of the business. The function of an information system is to collect data, store it, convert it, and present it as the information required to manage the business so that **data processing** is an integral part of any information system.

Systems may be classified under the following headings:

Deterministic or mechanistic

Whatever the input, the output from the system is uniquely determined, as in the case of evaluating a formula.

Probabilistic or stochastic

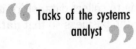

A degree of uncertainty exists so that the output is specified in terms of averages or distributions, as with the use of random number simulations.

Adaptive or cybernetic

Where a system adapts itself to changes in environment, for example a stock control problem where the re-order strategy is adapting to changes in demand.

In real life few systems are truly deterministic but we often create deterministic models for systems which are stochastic or even adaptive. A common use of **modelling** is the technique of designing a computer system to represent a live business system so that it may be studied for one of the following reasons:

- Analysis – e.g. most accounting functions
- Control – e.g. process control and monitoring
- Forecasting – e.g. prediction of future sales

These correspond to past, present and future:

- Analysis of past performance
- Control of current activities
- Forecasting future requirements

SYSTEMS ANALYSIS AND ORGANISATION AND METHODS

Organisation and methods (O and M) is be defined as the systematic study of a public body or a private firm with a view to improving the administrative and information flow procedures. An O and M investigation will embrace the study of all possible methods of solution, including manual, mechanical and the use of microcomputers and computers.

Systems analysis is often defined as the detailed analysis and design of a computer implementation of an O and M problem and thus may appear to be just a branch of O and M. However the speed, power and independent operation of a computer demands a far deeper analysis and more complete specification than that associated with clerical systems and so **systems analysis** exists as a separate discipline although many of its skills are shared with other branches of O and M.

A systems analyst in a computer department will be responsible for liaison with users and potential users to design a set of procedures to fit their justified requirements and part of this design will include specifications of the programs to be written. These specifications will be passed to the programmers for implementation.

THE STAGES OF SYSTEMS ANALYSIS

The job of a systems analyst can be summarised by the following list of tasks:

- Identification
- Feasibility study
- Investigation
- Analysis
- Design
- Implementation
- Review
- Maintenance

- **Identification** is deciding on an appropriate application area which may merit further study.

- **Feasibility study** is the carrying out of a preliminary investigation into the system to evaluate the possibility of a computer system with an estimation of costs and benefits. It might also try to select which method of solution might be most effective.

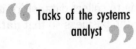

- **Investigation** is the fact-finding exercise where the systems analyst determines the requirements of the system and studies the current methods and procedures.

- **Analysis** is the review of the results of the investigation to document and bring together the findings of the investigation.

- **Design** is the creation of the specifications for the computer programs and also the clerical or manual procedures to be carried out in conjunction with the computer system. This will involve the design of flowcharts or top-down designs.

- **Implementation** is in two parts; firstly supervising the programmers in the coding and testing of the programs and secondly the supervision of the introduction of the system, which means instructing the users and the operators in their various duties.

- **Review** means an evaluation of the system after it has been implemented to ensure that it is being applied in the manner specified by the analyst and that it meets the original objectives.

- **Maintenance** may be required at some time in the future if it is found that the system has flaws, fails to meet its requirements or simply if, for some reason, the requirements change.

METHODS OF FACT-FINDING

It is worth considering the investigation stage in some detail. There are four common methods of fact-finding available to the systems analyst which may be used in the feasibility study, the main investigation and the systems review:

- Interview
- Observation
- Record inspection
- Questionnaires

All systems investigations need to be carried out to a plan as in the following pattern:

- Establish a plan
- Decide exactly what is to be found out
- Discover who can provide the information
- Arrange appointments and communication and state:
  - Terms of reference
  - Name of analysts/investigators
  - Anticipated duration

The *terms of reference* must be provided before any investigation takes place and should specify:

- Who has authorised the study;
- What is the scope of the investigation;
- What are the objectives of the study;
- What resources are to be used – who and for how long;
- Any constraints, that is, practices to be left unchanged and individuals not to be involved;
- Who is to receive the final report;
- The time limit.

Interviewing is probably the most common technique in fact-finding. It is a face to face chat between the analyst and individuals concerned with the present system and will be used to achieve two objectives; firstly to establish and verify facts and secondly to ascertain, and possibly overcome, any resistance to change.

The conduct of the interview should be carried out in a manner where the analyst will listen but guide the course without inhibiting the interviewee's answers. Planning the interview should allow for ample time. It is vital to gain the cooperation and respect of the individuals concerned, and this involves maintaining privacy and respecting confidences, and to take care over the use of words, to avoid misunderstanding.

There are a number of techniques for recording facts during the interview, including:

- Taking written notes, which, if used, should be done in such a way as to try not to cause delays

- The filling in of questionnaires or check lists

- Tape recording (which should not be done without asking permission and may inhibit the interviewee)

- Drawing rough charts

- Collecting documents

Fact-finding by observation

This means getting permission first (or don't get found out) and should avoid long periods of observation, mainly because anything or anybody being observed will change. Workers may work faster or more efficiently to impress the observer or may deliberately mislead, so it is important to ensure that staff are aware of the activity and its purpose.

Recording techniques include:

- Taking notes
- Drawing charts
- Photography or videotape
- Special record keeping or logging

Fact recording by record inspection

There are two sources of formal records which might include:

- Procedure manuals
- Results of past investigations
- Examination of existing records, and informal records, which might be notes recorded from a colleague or information from a predecessor when handing over a job.

Fact-finding by questionnaire

In general the use of questionnaires should be a last resort and so it is important to take care in the design. Most people think they can design forms but do not appreciate the great skills required in this task. Questionnaires are often unpopular with the recipient, particularly if they are time-consuming to complete, so give full instructions and make the form both brief and easy to fill in. Other tips are to maintain anonymity if possible, to be aware of exaggeration in responses and to avoid leading questions which may bias the responses.

Situations where questionnaires are suitable include where the analyst is remote from staff; where answers can be yes/no or numerical in content, where a sample return is sufficient; also where there is a large population of respondents, or where verification of data obtained by other methods is needed.

REASONS FOR THE FAILURE OF COMPUTER SYSTEMS

As a final topic it is important to study the major causes of the failure of a computer system because, unfortunately, despite all the techniques and practices, many systems are considered failures by the organisations in which they are used. Some of the reasons for this are:

- A badly managed feasibility study causing a poor design to be adopted
- An inefficient costing of the hardware, media, staffing or development
- A lack of user acceptance
- A poor standard of documentation
- Inflexibility to match existing procedures and practices within the organisation
- Unrealistic estimates of the timescale for development
- Overall lack of project control

EXAMINATION QUESTIONS

SHORT QUESTIONS

Question 1
Describe briefly *three* different methods of fact finding available to a systems analyst.

(AEB 1987)

Question 2
A software house has decided to develop a general software package for theatre bookings. It will consist of a number of interrelated modules. Outline the separate stages that have to be performed before a working package is ready for demonstration or marketing.

(Cambridge 1989)

Question 3
A computer application follows a systems life cycle which takes it from its birth as an initial idea, through its development into a working system and through its life until it is finally discarded.

Identify and briefly describe *five* distinct stages of this systems design life cycle.

(NEAB 1989)

Question 4
List *five* steps in the systems design life cycle, in the order in which they occur, when developing a computer information system.

(Northern Ireland 1988)

Question 5
Name *two* classes of data user which have exemptions from the Data Protection Act.

(NEAB 1988)

Question 6
State *three* duties which the Data Protection Act imposes on data users.

(NEAB 1987)

LONGER QUESTIONS

Question 7
In the context of a data processing system write brief notes on the following:
a) feasibility study,
b) validation procedures
c) security
d) application system maintenance.

(AEB 1984)

Question 8
A data processing department employing both systems analysts and programmers is required to develop and implement a new computer-based information system. Describe in an *essay:*
i) the tasks that need to be carried out;
ii) the ordering of the tasks;
iii) the responsibilities of *all* the people involved.

(AEB 1983)

Question 9
The parent teacher association in a school has organised many successful 'bring-and-buy' sessions to raise money for the school. The school has surplus stock after each of these sessions. It has also acquired a new microcomputer for the school. It consults a systems analyst on the viability of producing a computerised system to keep track of all the surplus items and to answer enquires from whatever source. If you were the systems analyst, outline the steps involved before such a system could be implemented. Indicate how additional resources might be used to minimise the running costs of the system.

(Welsh 1986)

Question 10
a) Write down in logical order *five* of the major steps in systems analysis.

b) A car rental firm is considering a computer system to improve the running of the business. The firm owns a variety of cars, no more than three years old. Some of the cars are damaged and others are being serviced. Cars can be hired from many points within Britain but need not be returned to the pick-up point.

Suppose you were a systems analyst consulted by the firm, suggest possible computer systems, mentioning data handling facilities, terminal requirements and staffing implications. Outline the factors which should be considered by the firm before selecting a particular computer system.

Indicate the benefits likely to be gained by the firm if a computer system were to be installed.

(Welsh 1983)

OUTLINE ANSWERS

SHORT QUESTIONS

Question 1

The principal methods of fact finding available to a systems analyst are:

- **Interview** or speaking to users face to face;
- **Inspection** of records which may be any formal or informal descriptions of the system prepared during earlier investigations;
- **Questionnaires** which may not always get a good response or even an accurate response but reach a wider group of individuals;
- **Observation** to examine what actually happens rather than what is supposed to happen.

Question 2

The development of a general software package ready for demonstration or marketing for theatre bookings will require the stages undertaken in any systems design:

Identification of the scope of the package
Investigation of the requirements
Analysis of the requirements
Design of the system
Detailed program design
Program implementation
Test data design
Program testing
System testing
Evaluation against the original requirements.

Question 3

A computer application follows a systems life cycle which, taking a project from its birth as an initial idea, through development into a working system and through its life, would be taken from the standard systems design life cycle. The question asks for *five* stages and so some of the tasks shown in the list on p.251 need to be combined:

Identification and specification to establish the requirements
Feasibility study
Systems design including investigation and analysis
Implementation
On-going review and maintenance during the lifetime of the system

Question 4

Unlike the previous two questions where one concentrated on the programming and one on the complete lifespan of the system, this question is only concerned with the design and so a slightly different grouping would appear to be relevant:

Identification (possibly including a feasibility study);
Investigation of the current or proposed system;
Analysis of the requirements;
Design of the new system;
Testing and implementation.

Question 5

Data users having exemptions from the Data Protection Act 1984 are:

A data user holding personal data only for payroll and accounts
Personal data held by an individual on his or her own family for personal and domestic use
Data held for unincorporated members' clubs with the consent of the members

Question 6

Duties which the Data Protection Act 1984 imposes on data users are:

- registration
- compliance with the principles of the Act
- operation within the terms of the register entry.

LONGER QUESTIONS

Question 7

a) A feasibility study is the carrying out of a preliminary investigation into the system to evaluate the possibility of using a computer system with an estimation of its costs and benefits. It might also try to select which method of solution would be most effective. The exercise is likely to be carried out by a systems analyst but, in large companies, may be carried out by a team which would include users and top management.

b) Validation procedures were covered in detail in Chapter 6 where it was stressed that it is the responsibility of the systems analyst to ensure that there are adequate validation procedures incorporated within the systems design. This answer should concentrate on two particular themes: validation of individual records and validation, typically by control total, of the complete file.

c) One of the implications of the Data Protection Act is that the systems design must pay due regard to the security of data within the system. However, even without the legal requirements, any organisation is likely to have their own demands for the non-disclosure of information which may have value to competitors or which they may not wish to have widely distributed within the organisation.

d) Application system maintenance is the final stage of systems analysis and design and allows for changes to be incorporated at some time after implementation if it is found that the system has flaws, fails to meet its requirements or simply if, for some reason, the requirements change.

Question 8

This question refers to both systems analysts and programmers and so it is a good plan to start with a brief statement about the responsibilities of each and then incorporate all the three requirements into a single essay which will cover the tasks that need to be carried out in their sequence with an account of the responsibilities of the various people involved, including other members of staff inside and outside the computer department.

The *systems analyst* is responsible for liaison with users and potential users to design a set of procedures to fit their justified requirements and part of the design will include specifications of the programs to be written.

The *programmers* are responsible for the coding of the various programs to meet the specifications of the design produced by the systems analyst.

The stages in the design of a computer system are as follows:

- **Systems identification** is the selection of an appropriate application area for a computer system this may be carried out by the systems analyst but might be initiated by a user department, the computer manager or the managing director.

- **A feasibility study** is the carrying out of a preliminary investigation to assess the possibility of a computer system with an estimation of costs and benefits. It might be carried out by the systems analyst alone or might involve senior management and users as well.

- **Fact finding** is carried out by the systems analyst to determine the requirements of the system and the current methods and procedures.

- **Analysis** is the review of the results of the investigation and the full documentation of the findings; it will be carried out by the systems analyst.

- **Systems design** will be carried out by the systems analyst who will prepare a comprehensive report to specify the computer programs and the clerical or manual procedures to be followed in conjunction with the computer system. This will involve the design of flowcharts or top-down designs and also the forms to be used for input and output as well as instructions for the users.

- **Implementation** will firstly involve the programmer in translating the design into computer programs which must be coded, tested and further documented and secondly the systems analyst will supervise the introduction of the system which means instructing the users and the operators in their various duties and gradually phasing the new procedures into every day use.

- **Review** of the system, sometimes called 'systems audit' means an evaluation of the system after it has been implemented to ensure that it is being applied in the manner specified by the analyst and that it meets the original objectives. This is best carried out by another systems analyst or by someone in the user department.

- **Systems maintenance** may be required at some time in the future if it is found that the system has flaws or needs modification. It will involve the same stages and same staff as the original design.

Question 9

In answering a question of this type, as with any project in systems analysis, it is important to identify the important facts in the problem. We have a parent teacher association with money available which one presumes could be used for a computer, and an information retrieval problem to keep track of all the surplus items and to answer enquiries from whatever source. A systems analyst should approach this problem in the same systematic manner as any other (larger) systems project. The steps involved would therefore be:

A systems analyst will liaise with the users, who would be the PTA, to design a set of procedures to meet their requirements and prepare specifications of the programs to be written. These specifications should be passed to a programmer for implementation. The question does not mention the programming, one may presume it could be carried out by a teacher, a pupil or a parent.

We should study the stages of systems analysis in logical sequence:
Identification; feasibility study; investigation; analysis; design; implementation; review and maintenance.

The identification stage in selecting an appropriate application area has already been carried out with the stock enquiry system chosen.

It will be important to carry out a study to investigate the possibility of a computer system; to evaluate the feasibility of the application with respect to both the technical feasibility of a program meeting the requirements and the practical problems of finding a suitable programmer so making the machine available for the system to run as and when required.

The main fact-finding exercise will expand on the feasibility study to obtain a precise determination of the requirements of the system with volumes, frequency of use and the nature of the enquiries. It may be that the exercise would stop at this point since it is not at all clear from the wording of the question that there is any real worth in proceeding with a computer system, and this would be a valid response from a feasibility study. To use the system on-line for queries might mean assigning a computer exclusively to this task, but if there was no requirement for immediate response then a card file might be a better solution.

After the investigation, the analyst will review the results and provide the documentation for the programs and procedures.

Design is the creation of the specifications for the computer programs and also the clerical or manual procedures to be carried out in conjunction with the computer system. This will involve the design of flowcharts or top-down designs.

Implementation will involve the writing of the programs and briefing the PTA members in the way programs should be run.

The review stage will involve getting the systems analyst to look at the operation of the system after it has been used for a while to ensure that the programs run as was intended and that the PTA members make the best use of the system.

It is not obvious what additional hardware resources might be used in this question but the most likely answer would be to purchase an appropriate applications package rather than specifying and writing the programs. The role of the systems analyst would be just as important in analysing the requirements, selecting a package and supervising the implementation.

Question 10

a) Five of the major steps in systems analysis are:
   Feasibility study to establish overall requirements
   Investigation of the existing system
   Analysis of the results of fact finding
   Design of the computer system
   Implementation of the design

b) Again it is important to extract the main points from the specification; the car rental firm operates from many points within Britain and cars can be hired from one point and returned to another.

   The factors which should be considered by the firm before selecting a particular computer system are listed in the chapter under 'circumstances where the use of a computer may be justified' and the systems analyst might consider the following possibilities:

   - Are there large volumes of data requiring repetitive processing?
   - Is there logical or mathematical complexity?
   - Is a large clerical workforce employed in repetitive tasks?
   - Is there a task not done because clerical costs exceed the savings?
   - Are there large data files to be maintained?
   - Is there a need for improvement in the overall planning and control of a particular activity?

   In this problem:

   - there are large volumes of transactions of rentals for processing;
   - there is logical complexity in locating the vehicles;
   - there are clerical tasks common to each pick-up point;
   - there may be tasks tabulating management information because costs exceed the benefits;
   - there is a large data file of cars to be maintained;
   - there is an identified need for improvement in the control of the hire business.

   The benefits likely to be gained by the firm if a computer system were to be installed are taken under the usual headings:

   - **Improvement of information**: the information provided on the cars should be more up-to-date, more accurate and allow cross-referencing between regular clients and problems with particular vehicles.

   - **Cost savings**: the cost savings may be little or nothing here, there may be labour saved but probably no reduction in numbers of staff employed, however staff may do their work more effectively. There may be a reduction in the number of vehicles required if the resource scheduling is more effective. This will be balanced against money paid out for equipment.

   - **New techniques**: the use of the on-line terminals may increase the communication and exchange of information between pick-up points so all the staff have access to the same data which is more likely to be up-to-date.

   - **Changing environment**: it may be that business is expanding so as to strain the current resources.

STUDENT ANSWERS WITH EXAMINER COMMENTS

Question 8

A data processing department employing both systems analysts and programmers is required to develop and implement a new computer-based information system. Describe in your essay:

   i) the tasks that need to be carried out;
   ii) the ordering of the tasks;
   iii) the responsibilities of all the people involved.

> **No mention of identification of the application or of a feasibility study.**

> **Too general; the analyst may need to identify which staff can be of help and then concentrate on those alone.**

> **Mention the systems procedures carried out off the computer, i.e. data capture procedures, distribution of output, responsibilities of staff.**

> **Try to avoid being sexist; use job titles rather than pronouns.**

The tasks which need to be carried out in the Systems Life Cycle are:
Investigate
Analyse
Design
Implement
Review and Maintain

> **No. The Systems Analyst will be directed by management to investigate a particular system.**

The Systems Analysts will first find out what is wanted on the new computer system by an exercise of fact finding which means:

   i) interviewing all the staff
  ii) sending out questionnaires
 iii) inspecting records
 iv) watching people doing their jobs

> **The systems analyst may recommend but management will decide.**

He will record all this information on special forms and charts so he can later analyse the results and decide what is best for the company. Next he will design the programs for the new computer system, drawing the flowcharts and designing the files, the forms and the screen displays for the programmers. The programmers will write and test the computer programs which can then be brought into use.

> **The systems analyst is responsible for final testing and systems testing, particularly the overall systems test before live running; mention the introduction by pilot or parallel running here.**

The job of the systems analyst will not stop with implementation, he will also be required to review the system continually and make changes and improvements so that he keeps the system up to date.

> **Although review and maintenance is vital, so is the development of new applications; the analyst should not tinker with the system unless instructed by management.**

INDEX